THE COMMANDERS

OF

CHANCELLORSVILLE

Edward G. Longacre

Rutledge Hill Press®
Nashville, Tennessee
A Division of Thomas Nelson Publishers
www.ThomasNelson.com

Published by Rutledge Hill Press, a Division of Thomas Nelson, Inc., P.O. Box 141000, Nashville, Tennessee, 37214.

Rutledge Hill Press books may be purchased in bulk for educational, business, fundraising, or sales promotional use. For information, please email SpecialMarkets@ThomasNelson.com.

Library of Congress Cataloging-in-Publication Data
Longacre, Edward G., 1946–
    The commanders of Chancellorsville : the gentleman vs. the rogue / Ed Longacre.
       p. cm.
    Includes bibliographical references and index.
    ISBN 1-4016-0142-1 (hardcover)
    1. Chancellorsville, Battle of, Chancellorsville, Va., 1863. 2. Lee, Robert E. (Robert Edward), 1807–1870. 3. Generals—Confederate States of America—Biography. 4. Hooker, Joseph, 1814–1879. 5. Generals—United States—Biography. 6. Strategy—Case studies. 7. Command of troops—Case studies. I. Title.
E475.35.L66 2005
973.7'33—dc22   2005015172

Printed in the United States of America

05 06 07 08 09—5 4 3 2 1

In Memory of My Uncle,
PFC Albert G. Weisser, U.S.A.,
351ˢᵗ Infantry Regiment, 88ᵗʰ Division,
KIA, Italy, 25 September 1944

Table of Contents

Acknowledgments

My first debt is to Rod Gragg of Conway, South Carolina, for suggesting a need for this book and urging me to write it. I also thank my publisher, Larry Stone, of Rutledge Hill Press, and my editor, Geoff Stone.

For providing source materials on Robert E. Lee I thank Toni Carter and Greg Stoner of the Virginia Historical Society, John and Ruth Ann Coski of the Museum of the Confederacy, and the reference staffs of the University of Virginia's Alderman Library and the College of William and Mary's Earl Gregg Swem Library. For making available the unpublished papers of General Hooker, I am indebted to John Rhodehamel of the Henry E. Huntington Library, Jon Stayer of the Pennsylvania State Archives, and Lauren Eisenberg and Sandra Trenholm of the Gilder Lehrman Collection. Cheryl Nabati at the interlibrary loan desk of the Bateman Library, Langley Air Force Base, provided me with numerous hard-to-find sources.

For perceptive observations about Lee, the soldier and the man, and for developing an in-depth personality assessment of Joseph Hooker, I thank Professor Gary Leak of the Department of Psychology, Creighton University. Debbie Pogue of the United States Military Academy Special Collections provided valuable information about the academic careers of both Lee and Hooker. Robert Oliver of Newport News, Virginia, helped shape my theory of the military applications of chess and poker. And Ted Zeman of Philadelphia, Pennsylvania, supplied me with Hooker's post-battle congressional testimony, which constitutes the general's only published report of Chancellorsville.

The illustrations for this book were prepared for publication by Bill Godfrey of Hampton, Virginia, and the maps were drawn by my long-time cartographer, Paul Dangel of Berwyn, Pennsylvania. For research assistance and moral support throughout the project, I am indebted, as always, to my wife, Melody Ann Longacre.

Introduction

Military historians are fond of describing battles in terms of a chess match in which kings, queens, bishops, knights, rooks, and pawns—i.e., combat units—are moved strategically across a precisely patterned board of play—i.e., the battlefield—toward an ultimate goal of conquest, the capture and killing of the opponent's most critical piece. To some extent, the chess analogy has much relevance. Chess, like warfare, emphasizes the need for planning ahead and plotting contingencies. Chess strategy rests on the ability to preserve a player's strength while tricking his or her opponent into expending strength via complex maneuvers. Misdirection and deception are key elements in the game. Pure skill determines the victor and the vanquished. Chess nomenclature even mirrors the vocabulary of combat. Players are known as "friend" and "foe," the rows on the chessboard are "ranks" and "files," and the basic maneuvers of chess are described as "attacking" and "defending."

Yet there are limitations to viewing warfare through the prism of chess strategy. At the start of every game, the opposing forces are evenly matched. With few exceptions, chess pieces have strictly defined ranges and capabilities. Chess moves often conform to venerable patterns recognizable to one's opponent. Most significantly, at any point in a match a player can view the full range of an opponent's resources and gauge the power those resources represent. These advantages and others available to chess players are hardly characteristic of actual warfare.

If the chess analogy falls short, one might more profitably describe military operations in terms of poker. In contrast to chess pieces, the cards dealt to a poker player are not fixed properties. The value of a card changes in relation to the other cards in a player's hand. So, too, can the power and capability of military resources shift in relation to time, terrain, the commitment of friendly forces, the intervention of enemy units, and a host of other variables. As in warfare, the stakes of a poker game escalate as the game progresses and the bidding mounts. And while a resourceful poker player can estimate the value of an opponent's hand, that value cannot be determined precisely until the cards are laid on the table. Although often portrayed as high-stakes risk taking, poker is essentially a game of risk management via various stratagems such as deception and bluff. These characteristics likewise define the art and science of warfare.

The gaming analogy has been applied to many wars in many eras, but perhaps no more frequently than to the American Civil War. A battle that lies at the midpoint of that long and bloody conflict—Chancellorsville, fought in eastern Virginia during the first four days of May 1863—offers a near-perfect example of the interplay of chess and poker strategies. The ranking antagonists in that complex and sometimes confused clash of arms—Gen. Robert Edward Lee, commander of the Confederate Army of Northern Virginia, and Maj. Gen. Joseph Hooker, leader of the Union Army of the Potomac—were defined by sharply contrasting combat philosophies. These philosophies can be viewed as embodying the fundamental differences between chess and poker play.

The fifty-six-year-old Lee, one of the most distinguished soldiers of the prewar United States Army and by mid-1863 the Confederacy's most successful field commander, practiced war in the manner of a chess master. He fought according to carefully patterned modes of warfare, especially those propounded by Baron Antoine Henri Jomini (1779–1869). The Swiss historian, whose tactical analyses of the campaigns of Napoleon and Frederick the Great made him one of the most influential military theorists of the early nineteenth century, bequeathed to Lee and other disciples a set of tactical and strategic "maxims" which, if adhered to with precision and thoroughness, virtually guarantee success on the field of battle. In sharp contrast, the forty-eight-year-old Hooker, like Lee a West Point graduate but no student of Jomini, was an inveterate poker player whose gambler's mentality—a unique combination of nerve, braggadocio, and bluff—forever colored his approach to warfare.

The opposing commanders posed a striking contrast not only in their strategic and tactical philosophies but also in their personal characteristics.

Scion of one of Virginia's oldest families—son of "Light-Horse Harry" Lee, George Washington's cavalry commander—Robert E. Lee was a gentleman born and bred. He exuded rectitude, respectability, and erudition (he was graduated from the Military Academy in 1829 second in his class, with not one demerit on his conduct record), and he carried the mantle of authority with the ease and grace of the genuine aristocrat.

His adversary enjoyed no such advantages. Of respectable birth but lacking a celebrated pedigree, Joe Hooker ranked below the middle of the West Point class of 1837. Although he made an honorable record in the prewar army, his professional standing did not match that of Light-Horse Harry's son. Moreover, while Lee remained in the army throughout the years leading to the Civil War, Hooker resigned his commission in 1853 in order to farm in northern California. Victimized by unwise business decisions and gambling debts, he sank almost to the level of ne'er-do-well. Rescued by the outbreak of war in 1861, after a slow start he rose steadily though the ranks, in the process gaining the sobriquet "Fighting Joe." Flaws and vices accompanied his elevation. Even after gaining command of the great Union army in the East, he indulged a fondness not only for games of chance but for strong drink and women of questionable virtue (although *hooker*, denoting a prostitute, does not appear to have derived from his hedonistic lifestyle).

The gentleman and the rogue squared off only once, at Chancellorsville. The course of that engagement reflected—and to a large extent was influenced by—the salient characteristics of each man. As the battle evolved, however, it also marked a change in the tactical predilections of one of them. At its outset, Robert E. Lee remained the chess master, but by battle's end, the consummate Virginian had abandoned the elegant strategy of the chessboard for the less refined atmosphere of the poker table. In so doing, despite facing long odds and desperate prospects, he beat Fighting Joe at his own game.

This book attempts to portray the battle, as well as the larger campaign of which it formed the centerpiece, through the eyes of Lee and Hooker. When necessary in order to make the strategic situation understandable to the reader, the author shifts to lower levels of command, but the upper-echelon viewpoint remains paramount. It is hoped that this perspective will illuminate the personal and professional qualities of the men who decided the outcome of one of the most pivotal engagements in our nation's most important war.

The Antagonists

Note: *Unless otherwise designated, all references are to infantry units.*

Army of the Potomac
MG Joseph Hooker

Provost Marshal General
BG Marsena R. Patrick
93rd New York
6th Pennsylvania Cavalry (2 cos.)
8th United States (6 cos.)
United States Cavalry (detach.)

Provost Marshal Brigade
COL William F. Rogers
Maryland Light Artillery (Baty. B)
21st New York
23rd New York
35th New York
80th New York (20th Militia)
Ohio Light Artillery (12th Baty.)

Engineer Brigade
BG Henry W. Benham
15th New York Engineers
50th New York Engineers
United States Engineer Battalion

Signal Corps
CPT Samuel T. Cushing

Ordnance Detachment
LT John R. Edie

Guards and Orderlies
Oneida (N. Y.) Cavalry

Artillery
BG Henry J. Hunt

Artillery Reserve
BG Robert O. Tyler
1st Connecticut Heavy (Baty. B)
1st Connecticut Heavy (Baty. M)
New York Light (5th Baty.)
New York Light (15th Baty.)
New York Light (29th Baty.)
New York Light (30th Baty.)
New York Light (32nd Baty.)
1st United States (Baty. K)
3rd United States (Baty. C)
4th United States (Baty. G)
5th United States (Baty. K)

Train Guard
 4th New Jersey (7 cos.)

First Army Corps
 MG John F. Reynolds

Escort
 1st Maine Cavalry (1 co.)

First Division
 BG James S. Wadsworth

First Brigade
 COL Walter Phelps, Jr.
 22nd New York
 24th New York
 30th New York
 84th New York (14th Militia)

Second Brigade
 BG Lysander Cutler
 7th Indiana
 76th NewYork
 95th New York
 147th New York
 56th Pennsylvania

Third Brigade
 BG Gabriel R. Paul
 22nd New Jersey
 29th New Jersey
 30th New Jersey
 31st New Jersey
 137th Pennsylvania

Fourth Brigade
 BG Solomon Meredith
 19th Indiana
 24th Michigan
 2nd Wisconsin

6th Wisconsin
7th Wisconsin

Artillery
 CPT John A. Reynolds
 New Hampshire Light (1st Baty.)
 1st New York Light (Baty. L)
 4th United States (Baty. B)

Second Division
 BG John C. Robinson

First Brigade
 COL Adrian R. Root
 16th Maine
 94th New York
 104th New York
 107th Pennsylvania

Second Brigade
 BG Henry Baxter
 12th Massachusetts
 26th New York
 90th Pennsylvania
 136th Pennsylvania

Third Brigade
 COL Samuel H. Leonard
 13th Massachusetts
 83rd New York (9th Militia)
 97th New York
 11th Pennsylvania
 88th Pennsylvania

Artillery
 CPT Dunbar R. Ransom
 Maine Light (Baty. B)
 Maine Light (Baty. E)
 Pennsylvania Light (Baty. C)
 5th United States (Baty. C)

Third Division
MG Abner Doubleday

First Brigade
BG Thomas A. Rowley
121st Pennsylvania
135th Pennsylvania
142nd Pennsylvania
151st Pennsylvania

Second Brigade
COL Roy Stone
143rd Pennsylvania
149th Pennsylvania
150th Pennsylvania

Artillery
MAJ Ezra W. Matthews
1st Pennsylvania Light (Baty. B)
1st Pennsylvania Light (Baty. F)
1st Pennsylvania Light (Baty. G)

Second Army Corps
MG Darius N. Couch

Escort
6th New York Cavalry (2 cos.)

First Division
MG Winfield S. Hancock

First Brigade
BG John C. Caldwell
5th New Hampshire
61st New York
81st Pennsylvania
148th Pennsylvania

Second Brigade
BG Thomas F. Meagher
28th Massachusetts

63rd New York
69th New York
88th New York
116th Pennsylvania (1 batt.)

Third Brigade
BG Samuel K. Zook
52nd New York
57rd New York
66th New York
140th Pennsylvania

Fourth Brigade
COL John R. Brooke
27th Connecticut
2nd Delaware
64th New York
53rd Pennsylvania
145th Pennsylvania

Artillery
CPT Rufus D. Pettit
1st New York Light (Baty. B)
4th United States (Baty. C)

Second Division
BG John Gibbon

First Brigade
BG Gen. Alfred Sully
COL Henry W. Hudson
COL Bryon Laflin
19th Maine
15th Massachusetts
1st Minnesota
34th New York
82nd New York (2nd Militia)

Second Brigade
BG Joshua T. Owen
69th Pennsylvania

71st Pennsylvania
72nd Pennsylvania
106th Pennsylvania

Third Brigade
COL Norman J. Hall
19th Massachusetts
20th Massachusetts
7th Michigan
42nd New York
59th New York
127th Pennsylvania

Artillery
1st Rhode Island Light (Baty. A)
1st Rhode Island Light (Baty. B)

Sharpshooters
1st Co. Massachusetts

Third Division
MG William H. French

First Brigade
COL Samuel S. Carroll
14th Indiana
24th New Jersey
28th New Jersey
4th Ohio
8th Ohio
7th West Virginia

Second Brigade
BG William Hays
COL Charles J. Powers
14th Connecticut
12th New Jersey
108th New York
130th Pennsylvania

Third Brigade
COL John D. MacGregor
COL Charles Albright
1st Delaware
4th New York
132nd Pennsylvania

Artillery
1st New York Light (Baty. G)
1st Rhode Island Light (Baty. G)

Reserve Artillery
1st United States (Baty. I)
4th United States (Baty. A)

Third Army Corps
MG Daniel E. Sickles

First Division
BG David B. Birney

First Brigade
BG Charles K. Graham
COL Thomas W. Egan
57th Pennsylvania
63rd Pennsylvania
68th Pennsylvania
105th Pennsylvania
114th Pennsylvania
141st Pennsylvania

Second Brigade
BG J. H. Hobart Ward
20th Indiana
3rd Maine
4th Maine
38th New York
40th New York
99th Pennsylvania

Third Brigade
COL Samuel B. Hayman
17th Maine
3rd Michigan
5th Michigan
1st New York
37th New York

Artillery
CPT A. Judson Clark
New Jersey Light (Baty. B)
1st Rhode Island Light (Baty. E)
3rd United States (Baty. F/K)

Second Division
MG Hiram G. Berry
BG Joseph B. Carr

First Brigade
BG Joseph B. Carr
COL William Blaisdell
1st Massachusetts
11th Massachusetts
16th Massachusetts
11th New Jersey
26th Pennsylvania

Second Brigade
BG Joseph W. Revere
COL J. Egbert Farnum
70th New York
71st New York
72nd New York
73rd New York
74th New York
120th New York

Third Brigade
BG Gershom Mott
COL William J. Sewell
5th New Jersey

6th New Jersey
7th New Jersey
8th New Jersey
2nd New York
115th Pennsylvania

Artillery
CPT Thomas W. Osborn
1st New York Light (Baty. D)
New York Light (4th Baty.)
1st United States (Baty. H)
4th United States (Baty. K)

Third Division
BG Amiel W. Whipple
BG Charles K. Graham

First Brigade
COL Emlen Franklin
86th New York
124th New York
122nd Pennsylvania

Second Brigade
COL Samuel M. Bowman
12th New Hampshire
84th Pennsylvania
110th Pennsylvania

Third Brigade
COL Hiram Berdan
1st United States Sharpshooters
2nd United States Sharpshooters

Artillery
CAPT Albert A. von Puttkammer
CAPT James F. Huntington
New York Light (10th Baty.)
New York Light (11th Baty.)
1st Ohio Light (Baty. H)

Fifth Army Corps
MG George G. Meade

First Division
BG Charles Griffin

First Brigade
BG James Barnes
2nd Maine
18th Massachusetts
22nd Massachusetts
2nd Co. Massachusetts
  Sharpshooters
1st Michigan
13th New York (1 batt.)
25th New York
118th Pennsylvania

Second Brigade
COL James McQuade
COL Jacob B. Sweitzer
9th Massachusetts
32nd Massachusetts
4th Michigan
14th New York
62nd Pennsylvania

Third Brigade
COL Thomas B. W. Stockton
20th Maine
Michigan Sharpshooters (1 co.)
16th Michigan
12th New York
17th New York
44th New York
83rd Pennsylvania

Artillery
CPT Augustus P. Martin
Massachusetts Light (3rd Baty.)

Massachusetts Light (Baty. E)
1st Rhode Island Light (Baty. C)
5th United States (Baty. D)

Second Division
MG George Sykes

First Brigade
BG Romeyn B. Ayres
3rd United States (6 cos.)
4th United States (4 cos.)
12th United States (8 cos.)
14th United States (8 cos.)

Second Brigade
COL Sidney Burbank
2nd United States (5 cos.)
6th United States (5 cos.)
7th United States (4 cos.)
10th United States (3 cos.)
11th United States (8 cos.)
17th United States (7 cos.)

Third Brigade
COL Patrick H. O'Rorke
5th New York
140th New York
146th New York

Artillery
CPT Stephen H. Weed
1st Ohio Light (Baty. L)
5th United States (Baty. I)

Third Division
BG Andrew A. Humphreys

First Brigade
BG Erastus B. Tyler
91st Pennsylvania

10

126th Pennsylvania
129th Pennsylvania
134th Pennsylvania

Second Brigade
COL Peter H. Allabach
123rd Pennsylvania
131st Pennsylvania
133rd Pennsylvania
155th Pennsylvania

Artillery
CPT Alanson M. Randol
1st New York Light (Baty. C)
1st United States (Baty. E/G)

Sixth Army Corps
MG John Sedgwick

Escort
MAJ Hugh H. Janeway
1st New Jersey Cavalry (1 co.)
1st Pennsylvania Cavalry (1 co.)

First Division
BG William T. H. Brooks

Provost Guard
4th New Jersey (3 cos.)

First Brigade
COL Henry W. Brown
COL William H. Penrose
COL Samuel L. Buck
COL William H. Penrose
1st New Jersey
2nd New Jersey
3rd New Jersey
15th New Jersey
23rd New Jersey

Second Brigade
BG Joseph J. Bartlett
5th Maine
16th New York
27th New York
121st New York
96th Pennsylvania

Third Brigade
BG David A. Russell
18th New York
32nd New York
49th Pennsylvania
95th Pennsylvania
119th Pennsylvania

Artillery
MAJ John A. Tompkins
Massachusetts Light (Baty. A)
New Jersey Light (Baty. A)
Maryland Light (Baty. A)
2nd United States (Baty. D)

Second Division
BG Albion P. Howe

Second Brigade
COL Lewis A. Grant
26th New Jersey
2nd Vermont
3rd Vermont
4th Vermont
5th Vermont
6th Vermont

Third Brigade
BG Thomas H. Neill
7th Maine
21st New Jersey
20th New York

33rd New York
49th New York
77th New York

Artillery
MAJ J. Watts De Peyster
New York Light (1st Baty.)
5th United States (Baty. F)

Third Division
MG John Newton

First Brigade
COL Alexander Shaler
65th New York
67th New York
122nd New York
23rd Pennsylvania
82nd Pennsylvania

Second Brigade
COL William H. Browne
COL Henry L. Eustis
7th Massachusetts
10th Massachusetts
37th Massachusetts
36th New York
2nd Rhode Island

Third Brigade
BG Frank Wheaton
62nd New York
93rd Pennsylvania
98th Pennsylvania
102nd Pennsylvania
139th Pennsylvania

Artillery
CPT Jeremiah McCarthy
1st Pennsylvania Light (Baty. C/D)
2nd United States (Baty. G)

Light Division
COL Hiram Burnham
6th Maine
31st New York
43rd New York
61st Pennsylvania
5th Wisconsin
New York Light Artillery (3rd Baty.)

Eleventh Army Corps
MG Oliver O. Howard

Escort
1st Indiana Cavalry (2 cos.)

First Division
BG Charles Devens, Jr.
BG Nathaniel C. McLean

First Brigade
COL Leopold von Gilsa
41st New York
45th New York
54th New York
153rd Pennsylvania

Second Brigade
BG Nathaniel C. McLean
COL John C. Lee
17th Connecticut
25th Ohio
55th Ohio
75th Ohio
107th Ohio

Unattached
8th New York (1 co.)

Artillery
New York Light (13th Baty.)

Second Division
BG Adolph von Steinwehr

First Brigade
COL Adolphus Buschbeck
29th New York
154th New York
27th Pennsylvania
73rd Pennsylvania

Second Brigade
BG Francis C. Barlow
33rd Massachusetts
134th New York
136th New York
73rd Ohio

Artillery
1st New York Light (Baty. I)

Third Division
MG Carl Schurz

First Brigade
BG Alexander Schimmelfenning
82nd Illinois
68th New York
157th New York
61st Ohio
74th Pennsylvania

Second Brigade
COL Wladimir Krzyzanowski
58th New York
119th New York
75th Pennsylvania
26th Wisconsin

Unattached
82nd Ohio

Artillery
1st Ohio Light (Baty. I)

Reserve Artillery
LTC Louis Schirmer
New York Light (2nd Baty.)
1st Ohio Light (Baty. K)
1st West Virginia Light (Baty. C)

Twelfth Army Corps
MG Henry W. Slocum

Provost Guard
10th Maine (1 batt.)

First Division
BG Alpheus S. Williams

First Brigade
BG Joseph F. Knipe
5th Connecticut
28th New York
46th Pennsylvania
128th Pennsylvania

Second Brigade
COL Samuel Ross
20th Connecticut
3rd Maryland
123rd New York
145th New York

Third Brigade
BG Thomas H. Ruger
27th Indiana
2nd Massachusetts
13th New Jersey
107th New York
3rd Wisconsin

Artillery
CPT Robert H. Fitzhugh
1st New York Light (Baty. K)
1st New York Light (Baty. M)
4th United States (Baty. F)

Second Division
BG John W. Geary

First Brigade
COL Charles Candy
5th Ohio
7th Ohio
29th Ohio
66th Ohio
28th Pennsylvania
147th Pennsylvania

Second Brigade
BG Thomas L. Kane
29th Pennsylvania
109th Pennsylvania
111th Pennsylvania
124th Pennsylvania
125th Pennsylvania

Third Brigade
BG George S. Greene
60th New York
78th New York
102nd New York
137th New York
149th New York

Artillery
CPT Joseph M. Knap
Pennsylvania Light (Baty. E)
Pennsylvania Light (Baty. F)

Cavalry Corps
MG George Stoneman

First Division
BG Alfred Pleasonton

First Brigade
COL Benjamin F. Davis
8th Illinois
3rd Indiana (6 cos.)
8th New York
9th New York

Second Brigade
COL Thomas C. Devin
1st Michigan (1 co.)
6th New York
8th Pennsylvania
17th Pennsylvania

Horse Artillery
New York Light (6th Baty.)

Second Division
BG William W. Averell

First Brigade
COL Horace B. Sargent
1st Massachusetts
4th New York
6th Ohio
1st Rhode Island

Second Brigade
COL John B. McIntosh
3rd Pennsylvania
4th Pennsylvania
16th Pennsylvania

Horse Artillery
2nd United States (Baty. A)

Third Division
BG David M. Gregg

First Brigade
COL H. Judson Kilpatrick
1st Maine
2nd New York
10th New York

Second Brigade
COL Percy Wyndham
12th Illinois
1st Maryland

1st New Jersey
1st Pennsylvania

Reserve Brigade
BG John Buford
6th Pennsylvania
1st United States
2nd United States
5th United States
6th United States

Horse Artillery
CPT James M. Robertson
2nd United States (Baty. B/L)
2nd United States (Baty. M)
4th United States (Baty. E)

Army of Northern Virginia
Gen. Robert E. Lee

First Corps
McLaws's Division
MG Lafayette McLaws

Wofford's Brigade
BG William T. Wofford
16th Georgia
18th Georgia
24th Georgia
Cobb's (Ga.) Legion
Phillips (Ga.) Legion

Kershaw's Brigade
BG Joseph B. Kershaw
2nd South Carolina
3rd South Carolina
7th South Carolina

8th South Carolina
15th South Carolina
3rd South Carolina Battalion

Semmes's Brigade
BG Paul J. Semmes
10th Georgia
50th Georgia
51st Georgia
53rd Georgia

Barksdale's Brigade
BG William Barksdale
13th Mississippi
17h Mississippi
18h Mississippi
21st Mississippi

Artillery
COL Henry C. Cabell
Carlton's (Ga.) Baty.
Fraser's (Ga.) Baty.
McCarthy's (Va.) Baty.
Manly's (N. C.) Baty.

Anderson's Division
MG Richard H. Anderson

Wilcox's Brigade
BG Cadmus M. Wilcox
8th Alabama
9th Alabama
10th Alabama
11th Alabama
14th Alabama

Mahone's Brigade
BG William Mahone
6th Virginia
12th Virginia
16th Virginia
41st Virginia
61st Virginia

Wright's Brigade
BG Ambrose R. Wright
3rd Georgia
22nd Georgia
48th Georgia
2nd Georgia Battalion

Posey's Brigade
BG Carnot Posey
12th Mississippi
16th Mississippi
19th Mississippi
48th Mississippi

Perry's Brigade
BG Edward A. Perry
2nd Florida
5th Florida
8th Florida

Artillery
LTC John J. Garnett
Grandy's (Va.) Baty.
Lewis's (Va.) Baty.
Maurin's (La.) Baty.
Moore's (Va.) Baty.

Artillery Reserve
Alexander's Battalion
COL E. Porter Alexander
Eubank's (Va.) Baty.
Jordan's (Va.) Baty.
Moody's (La.) Baty.
Parker's (Va.) Baty.
Rhett's (S. C.) Baty.
Woolfolk's (Va.) Baty.

Washington Artillery
COL J. B. Walton
Eshleman's 4th Co.
Miller's 3rd Co.
Richardson's 2nd Co.
Squires's 1st Co.

Second Corps
LTG Thomas J. Jackson
MG Ambrose P. Hill
BG Robert E. Rodes
MG James E. B. Stuart

A. P. Hill's Division
MG Ambrose P. Hill
BG Henry Heth
BG William D. Pender
BG James J. Archer

Heth's Brigade
BG Henry Heth
COL J. M. Brockenbrough
40th Virginia
47th Virginia
55th Virginia
22nd Virginia Battalion

McGowan's Brigade
BG Samuel McGowan
COL O. E. Edwards
COL Abner Perrin
COL D. H. Hamilton
1st South Carolina (Provisional Army)
1st South Carolina Rifles
12th South Carolina
13th South Carolina
14th South Carolina

Thomas's Brigade
BG Edward L. Thomas
14th Georgia
35th Georgia
45th Georgia
49th Georgia

Lane's Brigade
BG James H. Lane
7th North Carolina
18th North Carolina
28th North Carolina
33rd North Carolina
37th North Carolina

Archer's Brigade
BG James J. Archer
COL B. D. Fry
13th Alabama
5th Alabama Battalion
1st Tennessee (Provisional Army)

7th Tennessee
14th Tennessee

Pender's Brigade
BG William D. Pender
13th North Carolina
16th North Carolina
22nd North Carolina
34th North Carolina
38th North Carolina

Artillery
COL R. Lindsay Walker
Brunson's (S. C.) Baty.
Crenshaw's (Va.) Baty.
Davidson's (Va.) Baty.
Marye's (Va.) Baty.
McGraw's (Va.) Baty.

D. H. Hill's Division
BG Robert E. Rodes
BG Stephen D. Ramseur

Rodes's Brigade
BG Robert E. Rodes
COL Edward A. O'Neal
COL J. M. Hall
3rd Alabama
5th Alabama
6th Alabama
12th Alabama
26th Alabama

Doles's Brigade
BG George Doles
4th Georgia
12th Georgia
21st Georgia
44th Georgia

Colquitt's Brigade
BG Alfred H. Colquitt
6th Georgia
19th Georgia
23rd Georgia
27th Georgia
28th Georgia

Iverson's Brigade
BG Alfred Iverson
5th North Carolina
12th North Carolina
20th North Carolina
23rd North Carolina

Ramseur's Brigade
BG Stephen D. Ramseur
COL F. M. Parker
2nd North Carolina
4th North Carolina
14th North Carolina
30th North Carolina

Artillery
LTC Thomas H. Carter
Reese's (Ala.) Baty.
Carter's (Va.) Baty.
Fry's (Va.) Baty.
Page's (Va.) Baty.

Early's Division
MG Jubal A. Early

Gordon's Brigade
BG John B. Gordon
13th Georgia
26th Georgia
31st Georgia
38th Georgia
60th Georgia
61st Georgia

Smith's Brigade
BG William Smith
13th Virginia
49th Virginia
52nd Virginia
58th Virginia

Hays's Brigade
BG Harry T. Hays
5th Louisiana
6th Louisiana
7th Louisiana
8th Louisiana
9th Louisiana

Hoke's Brigade
BG Robert F. Hoke
6th North Carolina
21st North Carolina
54th North Carolina
57th North Carolina
1st North Carolina Batt.

Artillery
LTC R. Snowden Andrews
Brown's (Md.) Baty.
Carpenter's (Va.) Baty.
Dement's (Md.) Baty.
Raine's (Va.) Baty.

Trimble's Division
BG Raleigh E. Colston

Paxton's Brigade
BG Elisha F. Paxton
COL J. H. S. Funk
2nd Virginia
4th Virginia
5th Virginia
27th Virginia
33rd Virginia

Jones's Brigade
  BG John R. Jones
  COL T. S. Garnett
  COL A. S. Vandeventer
  21st Virginia
  42nd Virginia
  44th Virginia
  48th Virginia
  50th Virginia

Colston's Brigade
  COL E. T. H. Warren
  COL T. V. Williams
  LTC S. T. Walker
  LTC S. D. Thruston
  LTC H. A. Brown
  1st North Carolina
  3rd North Carolina
  10th Virginia
  23rd Virginia
  37th Virginia

Nicholls's Brigade
  BG Francis R. Nicholls
  COL J. M. Williams
  1st Louisiana
  2nd Louisiana
  10th Louisiana
  14th Louisiana
  15th Louisiana

Artillery
  LTC Hilary P. Jones
  Carrington's (Va.) Baty.
  Garber's (Va.) Baty.
  Latimer's (Va.) Baty.
  Thompson's (La.) Baty.

Artillery Reserve
  COL Stapleton Crutchfield

Brown's Battalion
  COL J. Thompson Brown
  Brooke's (Va.) Baty.
  Dance's (Va.) Baty.
  Graham's (Va.) Baty.
  Hupp's (Va.) Baty.
  Smith's (Va.) Baty.
  Watson's (Va.) Baty.

McIntosh's Battalion
  Maj. David G. McIntosh
  Hurt's (Ala.) Baty.
  Johnson's (Va.) Baty.
  Lusk's (Va.) Baty.
  Wooding's (Va.) Baty.

Reserve Artillery
  BG William N. Pendleton

Sumter Battalion
  LTC Allan S. Cutts
  Patterson's Baty. (B)
  Ross's Baty. (A)
  Wingfield's Baty. (C)

Nelson's Battalion
  LTC William Nelson
  Kirkpatrick's (Va.) Baty.
  Massie's (Va.) Baty.
  Milledge's (Ga.) Baty.

Cavalry
  MG James E. B. Stuart

Second Brigade
  BG Fitzhugh Lee
  1st Virginia
  2nd Virginia
  3rd Virginia
  4th Virginia

Third Brigade
    BG W. H. F. Lee
    2nd North Carolina
    5th Virginia
    9th Virginia
    10th Virginia
    13th Virginia
    15th Virginia

Horse Artillery
    MAJ Robert F. Beckham
    Hart's (S.C.) Baty.
    McGregor's (Va.) Baty.
    Moorman's (Va.) Baty.
    Stuart Horse Artillery

A Man of Honor,
a Soldier of Genius

Early on the frigid afternoon of December 13, 1862, Robert E. Lee, from a hilltop along the right-center of his army's lines southwest of Fredericksburg, Virginia, became a spectator to mass murder. Shortly before noon, thousands of armed men in blue caps, pants, and overcoats—members of Maj. Gen. Ambrose E. Burnside's Army of the Potomac—had poured out of the streets of Fredericksburg and onto a vast, open plain that fronted an

Gen. Robert E. Lee, CSA

array of hills, ridges, and lower elevations occupied by their gray- and butternut-clad enemy. In common with many of those sixty thousand waiting Confederates, General Lee had stared in disbelief at the sight of so many soldiers moving in well-aligned ranks and with apparent nonchalance across ground that provided little protection against the thousands of rifles and the dozens of cannons pointing in their direction. Lee's senior subordinate, Lt. Gen. James Longstreet, who for much of the day shared the army commander's vantage point, noted that "the flags of the Federals fluttered gayly, the polished

21

arms shone brightly in the sunlight, and the beautiful uniforms of the buoyant troops gave to the scene the air of a holiday occasion rather than the spectacle of a great army about to be thrown into the tumult of battle."[1]

That tumult commenced as soon as the leading ranks came within range of the nearest guns, those along the Confederate right, the sector supervised by Lee's Second Corps commander, Lt. Gen. Thomas Jonathan "Stonewall" Jackson. With Jackson's guns, followed by Longstreet's, "tearing through their ranks, the Federals pressed forward with almost invincible determination, maintaining their steady step and closing up their broken ranks." Although men fell at every step, comrades pressed ahead toward a stone wall along a sunken road at the foot of Marye's Heights, a position held by one of Longstreet's brigades. "As they came within reach of this brigade," Longstreet recalled, "a storm of lead was poured into their advancing ranks and they were swept from the field like chaff before the wind. A cloud of smoke shut out the scene for a moment, and, rising, revealed the shattered fragments recoiling from their gallant but hopeless charge."[2]

For a time, Longstreet's superior feared the attack was far from hopeless. As soon as one charging column was reduced to human debris, another double-quicked forward to take its place. Burnside's great advantage in manpower—attackers outnumbered defenders nearly two-to-one—appeared to give him the unlimited ability to close the gaps torn in his lines. When a third wave swept forward as if determined to succeed where its predecessors had failed, Lee turned toward the subordinate he called his "Old War Horse," and said in a tone of deep concern: "General, they are massing very heavily and will break your line, I am afraid." He appeared unreassured by Longstreet's sweeping reply: "If you put every man now on the other side of the Potomac on that field . . . and give me plenty of ammunition, I will kill them all before they reach my line."[3]

Longstreet's boast was no exaggeration. Although Burnside's troops achieved a temporary breakthrough along Jackson's line, they could make no headway against the Confederate left and center. For the better part of the day Lee and his First Corps commander watched in horrified fascination as column after column of bluecoats appeared about to seize Marye's Heights and other equally well fortified sectors of Lee's six-mile-long line, only to be blown apart short of their objectives. The unrelieved carnage imparted such a macabre rhythm to the spectacle that at one point Lee—at last assured that Burnside could gain no advantage over him no matter how many troops he sacrificed to the effort—exclaimed to Longstreet and everyone else within earshot:

"It is well that war is so terrible—we should grow too fond of it!"[4]

DESPITE THE CAUTIONARY note thus expressed and the morality lesson it conveyed, Robert E. Lee was fond of warfare. A devout Christian, his natural inclination was to regard war as a detestable blot on the human character. But although he professed to abhor its violence and destruction, combat exerted an exhilarating effect on him that appears to have satisfied a basic need. When away from the field of conflict he could be moody, depressed, even morose, but invariably his spirits rose when battle beckoned.

Expressions of his enthusiasm for combat predated Fredericksburg by almost fifteen years. During the war with Mexico, in which he had served as an engineer officer on the staff of the commanding general, Winfield Scott, he had won plaudits not only for his technical acumen but for his coolheadedness and soldierly bearing under fire. The battlefield held no terrors for him; as he confided to a fellow participant in the Mexican campaign, "a little lead, properly taken, is good for a man." To this colleague Captain Lee confessed to the excitement he derived from battling the army of that "miserable populace" below the Rio Grande. Short weeks after he had distinguished himself and won promotion during the storming of Mexico City, he expressed his desire for another go at the enemy: "Should they give us another opportunity, they will be taught a lesson. . . . They will oblige us in spite of ourselves to overrun the country and drive them into the sea."[5]

At least one historian has suggested that Lee's enthusiasm for battle was the symptom of a repressed personality overcompensating for habitual passivity. While a psychologist may reject this diagnosis as simplistic, it is true that in early youth Robert Edward Lee developed an affinity for self-control and self-denial, qualities that would characterize him throughout his life. These traits were, in large part, products of his upbringing in a family that was both a bastion of Virginia aristocracy and a source of notoriety and scandal. His parents were the primary motivators in his life. His pious and long-suffering mother taught him the virtues of self-denial, while his obsessive, prolifigate father showed him the depths to which one devoid of self-control could sink.

He came into the world on January 19, 1807, the next-to-last of six children born to Henry "Light-Horse Harry" Lee and his second wife, Ann Hill Carter Lee. Four other Lee children—brothers Charles and Sidney Smith, and sisters Ann and Catharine—lived to maturity (the firstborn, a son, had died at sixteen months). For the first six years of his life Robert lived with his parents and siblings—including a half brother twenty years his senior, the product of his father's first marriage—at Stratford, one of the most imposing estates in Westmoreland County, Virginia.[6]

The first two years of this period were relatively happy and tranquil for the Lee family, whose prominence in Virginia society appeared inviolate. In addition to having won military fame in the Revolution, Robert's father had served several terms in Virginia's General Assembly and three in the governor's mansion in Williamsburg. During the presidential administration of his commander and friend, George Washington, Henry had led the army that had suppressed the Whiskey Rebellion. He had even gained support in some quarters as a presidential successor to the man from Mount Vernon.[7]

Robert's mother was the daughter of Charles Carter, one of the wealthiest residents of the Old Dominion. Although public office and private interests kept Henry away from Stratford for long intervals, he and Ann gave every indication of enjoying a happy home life. Mrs. Lee doted on her children, although Robert was clearly her favorite. The two became almost inseparable when, as Robert entered his teens, his brothers departed the home and his sister contracted a chronic illness, transforming the youngest son into his mother's principal companion. When at eighteen he, too, left the nest, to attend the U.S. Military Academy, their estrangement was keenly felt by both. "How can I live without Robert?" Ann asked dolefully. "He is both son and daughter to me."[8]

The stability of the Lee household was painfully brief. Before Robert turned three his father had twice been jailed for failure to pay debts. Obsessed with his family's financial health and enamored of money-making schemes, Henry Lee had lost thousands of dollars in a series of speculative enterprises that a level-headed investor would have avoided like the cholera. By 1810, when at last released from prison, he had descended into poverty, but creditors continued to hound him. The Lee children never forgot the chains their father placed across the doors of Stratford to prevent sheriff's deputies from serving him with court papers.

By 1811, having bequeathed Stratford to his eldest child (also named Henry), Light-Horse Harry moved his wife and children to Alexandria, where they settled into a modest brick house, one more in keeping with the family's reduced circumstances. Briefly, peace returned and Ann gave birth to her last child, Catharine. But in the summer of 1812 the family fell apart, never to be reassembled. Upon the outbreak of America's second conflict with England, Henry Lee, a committed Federalist, became a vocal opponent of the Madison administration's military and diplomatic policies. That summer his desire to champion antiwar activists lured him to Baltimore, where a young editor named Hanson whose newspaper had condemned the war in print had come under attack by angry neighbors who considered him unpatriotic and even treasonous.[9]

Along with other supporters, Henry Lee was in the editor's home when a vengeful mob, whipped into a frenzy by Hanson's latest editorial, lay siege to the place and threatened to kill everyone inside. Militia broke up the assemblage before it became a riot. But after Lee, Hanson, and the other targets of the crowd's ire were remanded to jail—ostensibly for their own protection—attackers gained entrance and savagely beat the inmates, one of whom died as a result. Ignorant of, or unmoved by, Henry Lee's celebrated service to the nation, the mob not only pummeled him into unconsciousness but maimed his apparently lifeless body, nearly blinding him.

By some miracle, Henry survived the ordeal, but his health had been permanently impaired. After a long and uncertain convalescence, he staggered back to Alexandria, where he remained for less than a year. In the summer of 1813, seeking both restoration of health and escape from his most persistent creditors, he took ship for Barbados, leaving his sorrowing family behind. The money-making ventures he pursued in the West Indies failed to materialize, but he never again saw his wife, sons, and daughters. Long before his death in March 1818, Ann Lee began to refer to herself as a widow.[10]

Irrespective of the grief it caused, Henry Lee's abandonment of his family had a profound effect on his youngest son, who was mortified by this blot on the Lee name. His shame was only intensified when in later years his half brother (known forever afterward as "Black-Horse Harry Lee") further sullied the family's reputation through financial mismanagement, which eventually forced the sale of Stratford, and sexual scandal, the result of dalliance with a minor—his wife's sister—whom he impregnated and whose estate he looted.

As if in reaction to these much publicized sins, young Robert Lee resolved to make himself into a model of rectitude and integrity. In this effort he received unwavering support from Ann Lee, who, as biographer and historian Douglas Southall Freeman observes, had been shaken to the depths of her being by her husband's fall from grace: "She was determined that his grim cycle of promise, overconfidence, recklessness, disaster, and ruin should not be rounded in the lives of her children. Self-denial, self-control, and the strictest economy in all financial matters were part of the code of honor she taught them from infancy."[11]

Robert proved particularly responsive to his mother's patient, kindly, but unyielding efforts at character-molding. He saw in her instruction evidence of an abiding love, which he reciprocated measure for measure. To the day of her death in 1829, he showered Ann Lee with affection and care. He rarely strayed from her side while she enjoyed fair health and after she fell victim to sickness he constantly attended her, reading to her, joining her in singing hymns from the Episcopal Book of Common Prayer, squiring her about when she felt well enough to leave home, and nursing her day and night.

He resented having to leave her side even to attend to his own education. Returns on a small trust her father had established gave Ann enough money to support her children's schooling. For Robert this included a term of unknown duration at a school in Fauquier County established by his Carter relations, where his classmates included many of his cousins.

He did well enough at his early studies, but he was always happy to leave school on holiday to return to his family, which at some point after 1815 had moved to a larger house on Washington Street. The family's financial situation had improved somewhat following the death of Henry Lee during a failed attempt to return by ship to the home and family he had deserted five years before. A year or two afterward, Robert quit the school in Fauquier County and matriculated at the Alexandria Academy, which offered a classical education free of tuition to the sons of local families. Freeman notes that under the tutelage of the headmaster, for the next three years the boy "read Homer and Longinus in Greek. From Tacitus and Cicero he became so well grounded in Latin that he never quite forgot the language. . . . In mathematics he shone, for his mind was already the type that delighted in the precise reasoning of algebra and geometry." Presumably at this time, if not earlier, he was introduced to chess, with its mathematical underpinnings and highly structured strategy.[12]

The family's marginal prosperity did not last. While Light-Horse Harry's passing stayed the hand of his creditors, by the time Robert reached college age his mother lacked the funds to send him to a four-year institution such as Harvard, from which his oldest brother, Charles, had graduated, second in his class, in 1819. Ann's second son—known in the family by his middle name— had not required higher education, for in 1820 Smith had received a commission as a midshipman in the U.S. Navy. A formal education was neither contemplated nor considered necessary for Robert's sisters. But in Robert's case—given the special hopes his mother entertained for him—it was considered both a requirement and a problem that by 1823 could not be put off much longer.

To a great extent, the question of where the sixteen-year-old should be educated depended on the profession he chose to enter. His apparent preference was to become a gentleman farmer. Since early youth he had entertained a fondness for the soil, one he might have indulged had the family remained in the Westmoreland County countryside. But he had no land on which to begin his husbandry, nor the prospect of acquiring any. Although a devout Episcopalian like his mother, he had no desire to enter the ministry. Nor, it seems, did he give serious thought to other professions deemed worthy of his pedigree.

In the end, it was decided that the family should apply to their political representative in hope of securing a military academy appointment for Robert. This course was thought proper because, although the youth had no discernible interest in the profession of arms, he had been thoroughly indoctrinated in the family's military history. This history naturally centered around his father's campaigns in the southern colonies, on the subject of which Henry Lee had published a lengthy memoir. The overriding issue, however, was securing an affordable education for the boy—that academy nestled in the Hudson River Valley charged neither tuition nor board.

More to fit his family's circumstances than to gratify a personal ambition, in February 1824 Robert agreed to hand-carry his application to the secretary of war, John C. Calhoun, who allocated Academy appointments among the nation's congressional districts. The teenager was accompanied to Washington by a letter of introduction from the family's lawyer, William H. Fitzhugh, which emphasized the critical services the boy's father had rendered to the country while minimizing "the misfortune of his later years." The counselor testified to the physical, mental, and educational qualifications of Light-Horse Harry's son, while adding that his age—erroneously stated as eighteen—"and the situation of his mother require that he should lose no time in selecting the employment to which his future life is to be devoted."[13]

Fitzhugh's promotional efforts were probably unnecessary—no son of a Revolutionary War hero, an intimate of Washington's, was going to be denied entrance to West Point. Even so, Virginia had a backlog of appointments, requiring Robert to wait a full year to enter upon his studies. He spent the period brushing up on his mathematics at a local boys' school. His term there appears to have fully prepared him for the Academy. His instructor testified that "he was a most exemplary pupil in every respect. He was never behind time at his studies; never failed in a single recitation; was perfectly observant of the rules and regulations of the institution; was gentlemanly, unobtrusive, and respectful in all his deportment to teacher and his fellow students." The rules of right living Robert had learned from his mother, and the lessons he had gleaned from his father's flouting of them, had taken hold.[14]

ROBERT E. LEE ENTERED West Point on July 1, 1825, and left it four years later with an exemplary record both in classroom performance and personal deportment. The significance of his total avoidance of demerits throughout that period is sometimes overemphasized—five other members of the class of 1829 achieved the same distinction. Even so, it ranks as a remarkable achievement, suggesting that even in his teens he had perfected the difficult art of self-control. Cadets who lacked this faculty suffered for it. Of his class, which began with eighty-seven students, fewer than fifty graduated, and more than a dozen of these failed due to defective conduct. The dropouts included two of Lee's fellow Virginians, leaving him and future Confederate Gen. Joseph Eggleston Johnston as the only remaining representatives of their state. The frequency with which demerits were handed out and the great variety of punishable offensives—many of them quite trivial and some without apparent application to military conduct—serve to emphasize Lee's accomplishment.[15]

Gen. Joseph E. Johnston, CSA

Another twenty-six of his fellows failed to graduate due to academic deficiencies. In contrast, Lee excelled in the classroom although not without effort—he had to study long and hard to maintain his high standing on the roll of general merit. From his first semiannual examination, in January 1826, he achieved grades high enough to assure him—if he kept them up—of graduating with honors and gaining admission into one of the army's elite branches, the topographical or construction engineers. On occasion his place-standing in the various disciplines showed a slight decline, principally due to the demands made on his study time by additional duties such as those imposed by his selection, during his third and second-class (i.e., sophomore and junior) years as a tutor in mathematics to his fellow cadets. Through a strong-willed determination to excel, however, he recovered from every downturn in his class standing and upon graduation ranked second in his depleted class of forty-six. The grades he achieved on his final examinations, added to his lofty position on the conduct roll, enabled him to amass 286 credits in mathematics out of a maximum of 300, 295 out of a possible 300 in the general physics course known as natural philosophy, and 192 out of 300 in engineering. Out of a maximum of 2,000 points in overall merit, he had been awarded 1,966½.

As remarkable as were his academic achievements, they were exceeded by those of Charles Mason of New York, a peerless scholar. Mason, the ranking graduate of the class of 1829, would go on to an undistinguished military career, one cut short by his resignation after fewer than three years of active duty. Lee, however, stood higher than his principal rival in soldierly deportment as well as in the estimation of instructors and fellow students.

His studious bent and unflagging quest for soldierly perfection did not prevent Cadet Lee from forging close personal associations. Years later his fellow Virginian, Johnston, recalled that "we had the same intimate associates, who thought as I did, that no other youth or man so united the qualities that win warm friendship and command high respect. For he was full of sympathy and kindness, genial and fond of gay conversation, and even of fun, while his correctness of demeanor and attention to all duties, personal and official, and a dignity as much a part of himself as the elegance of his person, gave him a superiority that every one acknowledged in his heart. He was the only one of all the men I have known that could laugh at the faults and follies of his friends in such a manner as to make them ashamed without touching their affection for him."[16]

Testimony to the high regard in which he was held was his appointment to the sought-after post of corps adjutant. This distinction, awarded in September 1828 at the start of his first-class year, recognized his exemplary soldiership and his mastery of drill. The honor solidified his standing as a "distinguished cadet" and testified to popularity among his classmates. Presumably, it also served to quiet the pangs of self-doubt that continued to nag him, causing him to question the career path he had marked out.

Another indication of Lee's military aptitude was the perfect score of 200 he amassed in the tactical courses offered during his final year of study. The principal instructional manual available to members of his class was a two-volume textbook on the science of war and fortifications written by Col. Guy De Vernon, professor of engineering at the Polytechnic School of France. Approved for use at French military institutions by a review board empanelled by Napoleon himself and translated into English by Capt. J. M. O'Connor of the U.S. Army, the work offered a general survey of grand tactics based on the operations of European armies. De Vernon's observations did not rest on the teachings of any particular theorist, but the version taught at West Point during Lee's term of study contained a 106-page appendix supplied by the translator that professed to include "the best principles and maxims of such writers as Guibert, Lloyd, Tempelhoff, and Jomini, particularly of the latter, whose work is considered a masterpiece and as the highest authority." In Captain O'Connor's estimation, "no man should pretend to be capable of commanding any considerable body of troops unless he has studied and meditated on the principles laid down by Jomini." Elsewhere in his appendix the translator claimed that "General

Jomini has transcended all writers on war and has exhibited the most extraordinary powers of analyzing and combining military operations."[17]

Jomini's precepts, as interpreted by O'Connor, would influence a generation of West Pointers, many of whom fought in, and had a major influence on, the Civil War. As historian David Donald points out, "every serious military student" of Lee's era "made Jomini's works his Bible." Another historian of the twentieth century contends that "many a Civil War general went into battle with a sword in one hand and Jomini's *Summary of the Art of War* [first published in France in 1838] in the other." Donald adds: "In fact, the military history of the first two years of the war reads like little more than exegesis of Jomini's theories."[18]

One reason for Jomini's popularity was the air of confidence with which the Swiss bank clerk-turned-soldier asserted his theories. His observations on strategy and tactics are reducible to a few basic principles ("maxims," as he called them), which a commander violated at his peril but which, if followed to the letter, virtually guaranteed victory. The simplicity of his approach and the easily discernible patterns of the maneuvers he described were comforting to would-be officers who felt overwhelmed by the convoluted formations called for in the standard tactics manuals of the nineteenth century. Too often, neophyte warriors overlooked Jomini's caveat that only on the lower operational level could success be guaranteed by adherence to so few rules. On the higher levels of warfare—the realm of strategy and grand tactics—Jomini made it clear that war, "far from being an exact science, is a terrible and impassioned drama." He attempted to reconcile these conflicting dimensions by insisting that his maxims could be successfully executed only by a commander imbued with "high moral courage, capable of great resolutions" as well as "physical courage which takes no account of danger . . . A man who is gallant, just, firm, upright, capable of esteeming merit in others instead of being jealous of it, and skillful in making this merit conduce to his own glory." Clearly, this genus was not to be found on every battlefield.[19]

Central to Jomini's teachings was the employment of forces in battle. The success of this activity—which Jomini described in terms that appear to mirror chess strategy—depended upon the application of two critical principles, "the first being, to obtain by free and rapid movements the advantage of bringing the mass of the troops against fractions of the enemy; the second, to strike in the most decisive direction, that is to say, in that direction where the consequences of his defeat may be most disastrous to the enemy, while at the same time his success would yield him no great advantages. The whole science of great military combinations is comprised in these two fundamental truths."[20]

Other Jominian maxims stressed the desirability of gaining and maintaining the offensive and thus the undesirability of static operations reliant on earthworks and fortifications ("a general who waits for the enemy like an automaton, without taking any other part than that of fighting valiantly, will always succumb when he shall be well attacked"). Still other axioms concerned the importance of determining "objective points of maneuvers" whose seizure would help a commander dislodge and destroy his enemy; the necessity of taking risks when seeking to control an enemy's center of gravity; the "deplorable" effects of war councils, which were liable to produce divergence of thought rather than consensus; and the role in strategic planning of centers of government, territorial capitals, and other objectives that combined military and political value.[21]

Jomini's focus was always on the conduct of battle, which he envisioned as proceeding with geometrical precision. Combat began with armies drawn up in long ranks on opposite sides of the battlefield. Once artillery had softened up the enemy, the commander who had seized the offensive committed his infantry—supported in the rear and on both flanks by cavalry—in waves of close-order assault. After drawing the enemy's fire at less than optimum range and before it could complete the cumbersome and time-consuming process of reloading, the attacker delivered a bayonet charge—preferably one aimed at the enemy's flank rather than his center—that carried the day through a combination of tactical and psychological effectiveness.

The attackers could advance in a variety of formations. Jomini described at least a dozen in terms such as "simple parallel order," "the parallel order with a defensive or offensive crotchet [i.e., option]," and "the order by echelon on the center." As Donald points out, "all of this sounds theoretical," but by 1861 "commanders were actually drawing up their troops in accordance with Jomini's idealized schemes."[22]

By the time of the American Civil War many of Jomini's eighteenth- and early nineteenth-century tactics had become impractical and downright dangerous. Within thirty years of Lee's graduation from West Point, they were overtaken by advances in weapons technology. "Optimum range" for drawing the fire of the typical musket-wielding soldier of the 1820s and 1830s was barely more than one hundred yards. After the introduction into the armies of the United States and Europe of the conical-shaped Minié ball, whose soft, hollow base caused the projectile to expand upon discharge, enabling it to grip the rifling inside the barrel of the shoulder-arms of the late 1850s, the effective distance of infantry fire increased fourfold. Attackers could be decimated long before they reached the enemy's line, not only because of the increased effective range of the rifle but also due to its relatively quick loading process.

The problem was that many of Jomini's students, including Robert E. Lee, never forgot the theorist's emphasis on offensive warfare and direct attack. And while his disciples may have realized that times had changed, they did not always factor change into their interpretation of the master's teachings. For this reason, among others, the Civil War would prove to be the bloodiest, most costly exercise in violence in our nation's history.[23]

CADET LEE'S LOFTY STANDING on the roll of general merit earned him a commission in the prestigious Corps of Engineers. His gratification at obtaining a desired posting was outweighed, however, by his mother's death only weeks after he returned to Alexandria from the Hudson highlands. He was at her bedside, ministering to her, when she breathed her last. "He turned from her bed," Freeman writes, "in a grief that he never forgot."[24]

After burying Ann Carter Lee and settling her insubstantial estate, he sadly prepared to embark on his first tour of active duty, the repair and strengthening of coastal fortifications at Savannah, Georgia. Before he left Virginia, however, he said his farewells to relatives, friends, and acquaintances in a series of visits that under the circumstances might have proved somber but which he enlivened with determined efforts at conviviality.

One of his stops was at Arlington, the baronial-style mansion that overlooked Washington City from the heights of Alexandria. There he spent time with a childhood playmate, now-twenty-year-old Mary Anne Randolph Custis. She was the only child of the master of Arlington, who was the grandson of Martha Custis Washington and the adopted son of her husband

George. Neither on this occasion nor ever afterward did Second Lieutenant Lee fall madly in love with his host's elegant and accomplished daughter, but he found himself happy and content in her company. He experienced the same feelings during return visits over the next two years when on leave from the army.

By slowly arousing his romantic interest, Mary gave the young, dashing, but poor junior officer an appreciation of the advantages of marrying well—something the men of the Lee family did as a matter of course. Robert realized that a union with Martha Washington's great-granddaughter would gain him entry into America's most prestigious family while making him heir to an elegant and historic home that was a veritable shrine to the Father of His Country. Since youth he had regarded Washington as a model of accomplishment, refinement, and stature on which to pattern his own life. Whether or not, as historian Thomas Connelly suggests, Lee was "as much enamored of Arlington as he was of Mary," his growing interest in her was readily reciprocated. Through those first two years of Lee's military career, the couple drew ever closer via his frequent visitations and the many letters they exchanged while apart. In June of 1831 Lee returned to Arlington from the site of his latest posting, Fort Monroe, to wed his sweetheart.[25]

If he was bedazzled by the majesty of the Custis estate, Mary was almost pathologically attached to it. Although she consented to accompany her husband to Fort Monroe as well as to a few subsequent duty stations, she could never reconcile herself to an estrangement from home and family. She returned to Arlington at every opportunity—often for periods so lengthy that Lee began to feel like a bachelor. Bereft of romantic attachment, he took solace in the company of other women including the wives of fellow officers. His relations with these females were without exception innocent and aboveboard, but the pleasure he derived from his many harmless flirtations suggests a deeply felt need for romance that Mary could not fulfill.

With increasing frequency, Mrs. Lee retreated to Arlington for health reasons. There she could receive close attention and, when needed, round-the-clock nursing for a series of ailments including pelvic infections that took a steady toll on her constitution. By her fifties she was confined to bed or wheelchair, forcing her husband, when at home, to resume his former role as attendant to an invalid.

Despite her frailty, Mary bore her husband three sons and four daughters—
George Washington Custis, born in 1832; Mary, in 1835; William Henry
Fitzhugh (whom his father called "Rooney"), in 1837; Annie Carter, in 1839;
Eleanor Agnes, in 1840; Robert Edward Jr., in 1843; and Mildred Childe, in
1846. Lee was a caring, affectionate father, but as his children advanced
toward maturity he lectured them as his mother had lectured him. From a
series of far-off duty stations he wrote long letters, some containing gentle,
fatherly advice; others, however, were stern admonitions to tread the right-
eous path and avoid the pitfalls of immorality. In these same letters he
exhorted his wife to exert the utmost care and energy in shaping their char-
acters and guiding their conduct.[26]

Thomas Connelly suggests that Lee's fixation on instructing his children to
strive for perfection sprang from two sources. His constant postings to installations far from home rendered him an absentee father, causing him to fear he
was failing his family when it needed him the most. Then, too, he desired that
his sons and daughters lead such exemplary lives that they would cleanse, by
their example, the family's reputation. Many years after their indiscretions, he
still shuddered at the disgrace heaped on the Lee name by Light-Horse Harry
and his Black Horse son.

He continued to be nagged, as well, by the suspicion that he was unequal
to the demands of the profession he had embarked upon. Misplaced fears of
inaptitude occasionally combined with regret over his unhappy family situation to leave him moody, depressed, and sharp of temper, emotions that would
recur throughout his life. His pangs of inadequacy, however, flew in the face
of the consistent satisfaction he gave his superiors, all of whom were impressed
by his soldierly bearing, technical expertise, and leadership.[27]

BEFORE THE WAR with Mexico Lee had been known as an officer of great
promise. His service below the Rio Grande, 1846–47, solidified his reputation
as one of the army's most accomplished officers. Ordered to San Antonio in
August 1846 from the forts of New York harbor, now-Captain Lee crossed the
Rio Grande in a column commanded by Brig. Gen. John E. Wool. Wool was a
competent general, but his engineer officer set his sights on serving an officer of
larger reputation and higher rank. After reconnoitering enemy positions near

Saltillo, he abruptly joined the expedition under Winfield Scott that was bound for the port city of Vera Cruz. For the rest of the conflict, Lee occupied a high position on Scott's staff, where he served alongside his West Point comrade Joseph Johnston and soon-to-be famous soldiers such as P. G. T. Beauregard and George B. McClellan.[28]

During the siege of Vera Cruz, Lee won favorable notice for leading scouting missions, laying out fieldworks, and repairing batteries damaged during exchanges with Mexican guns. Following the city's surrender on March 29, 1847, he accompanied Scott into the enemy interior. Approaching the fortified eminence known as Cerro Gordo, where the Mexican commander, Santa Anna, lay in wait at the head of twelve thousand troops, Lee's commander asked

Bvt. Lt. Gen. Winfield Scott, USA

him to locate an avenue of approach to the apparently impregnable position. Displaying skill and courage, Lee, accompanied by a single colleague, gained the enemy's left rear by a winding route that he later brought to Scott's attention, but only after a hairbreadth escape from near-capture. On April 15 Lee guided along this same path an infantry division that attacked and broke through, forcing Santa Anna to flee minus a third of his force lost to casualties.

Lee's critical contribution to the victory brought him praise from many quarters. Additional plaudits came as Scott's forces closed in on the Mexican capital. Four months after Cerro Gordo, Lee duplicated his earlier performance by locating a passable route along the edge of a *pedregal* (lava field) by which Scott assaulted strategic outposts south of Mexico City. In his after-action report of the fighting at Churubusco and Contreras, Scott called his favorite staff officer "as distinguished for felicitous execution as for science and daring."[29]

Lee's heroics at Cerro Gordo had earned him the brevet rank of major; those outside Mexico City—which included a reconnaissance under fire that

36

enabled his army to storm the fortified castle of Chapultepec and seize the San Cosme Gate into the capital—made him a lieutenant colonel and colonel by brevet. For his part, the modest, self-critical officer insisted that "I did nothing more than what others in my place would have done much better." General Scott believed he knew better. The ability and grace under pressure Lee had displayed throughout the Mexican campaigns prompted Scott to declare in official correspondence that his aide was "the very best soldier that I ever saw in the field." Over the years numerous comrades—peers, superiors, and subordinates—would express a similar opinion.[30]

By June 1848 Bvt. Col. Lee was back in the States, where he resumed the seemingly unending succession of service tours at coastal installations that he had interrupted to go to war. Not even Commanding General Scott's "almost idolatrous fancy" for his stalwart engineer saved him from menial tasks and arduous labor. In addition to loading him down with operational and administrative burdens, his duty assignments kept him far from home, feeding his suspicion that he was a failed husband and an insignificant influence in the lives of his children.[31]

A break with monotonous routine finally came his way in September 1852, when he was appointed superintendent—chief administrative officer—of his alma mater. In some ways the assignment was a godsend. It reunited him with his family, for Mary managed to tear herself from Arlington and, along with the younger children, share his quarters. The post enabled him to develop close associations with other faculty and staff members who as officers in the Civil War he would either fight alongside (Richard S. Garnett, Gustavus W. Smith) or against (George H. Thomas, Seth Williams, Fitz John Porter). And it enabled him to monitor the schooling of his eldest son—Custis had matriculated at the Academy in 1850—and that of a favorite nephew, Fitzhugh Lee, Smith's son, whose thirst for amusement and habitual truancy almost resulted in his expulsion.

The appointment also saddled Lee with a raft of problems, chiefly of a budgetary nature, with many being caused by the physical improvements he believed critical to the Academy's educational mission. Then, too, he was distressed to perceive that during the twenty-three years since his graduation, the institution's once-rigid code of conduct had been weakened. One result was his having to adjudicate a greater number of disciplinary problems than he had anticipated. The task of punishing delinquent cadets took a toll. On one of his regular visits to the Academy, Secretary of War Jefferson Davis was surprised to see so many gray hairs on the head of the forty-seven-year-old administrator. When Lee admitted with a wan smile that "the cadets did exceedingly worry him," Davis saw "that his sympathy with young people was rather an impediment than a qualification for the superintendency."[32]

Freeman observes that "the years as head of the academy added to Lee's professional equipment, though to an undetermined extent." Although his official duties left him little time for private study, he borrowed almost fifty books from the West Point library, including several on military history, biography, and strategy. Those he checked out most frequently dealt with the late eighteenth-century campaigns of Napoleon; they included the Corsican's own notes on Jomini's *Traite des Grands Operations Militaires*. Meanwhile, Lee's personal library, which he built up substantially during this period, included Jomini's seminal *Precis de l'Art de la Guerre*. Although surviving copies of these works contain no marginal notes or comments in Lee's hand, Freeman believes that his reading of them "probably was critical and detailed."[33]

Although his return to West Point gave him much satisfaction and provided happy memories, Lee must have felt relief when he was returned to field duty in April 1855. His new assignment marked a significant departure from his earlier career path, as it separated him from the Corps of Engineers. Secretary of War Davis had named him lieutenant colonel of the newly created Second U.S. Cavalry, which was to be posted to Texas. Concerned about growing unrest on the Indian frontier, Congress had authorized the formation of four additional Regular regiments—two of foot soldiers and two of horsemen—to be commanded by promising officers of both staff and line. The army had few more promising officers than Robert E. Lee. At first Lee, who had not sought the position, hesitated to accept the transfer to line duty. At length he decided that "promotion, if offered an officer, ought . . . to be accepted, but it need not be sought unless deserved."[34]

After escorting his family back to Arlington, he traveled to Louisville, Kentucky, to assume command of the Second Cavalry in the temporary absence of Col. Albert Sidney Johnston, a Mexican War hero and former secretary of war of the Texas Republic. There, later at Jefferson Barracks, Missouri, and later still on the Texas frontier, he forged personal and professional ties with numerous subordinates who were to become household names, including Lee's West Point colleague, George Thomas, as well as Maj. William J. Hardee; Capts. Earl Van Dorn, Innis Palmer, Kenner Garrard, William H. Emory, George Stoneman, and Richard W. Johnson; and Lts. John Bell Hood, George B. Cosby, and Fitzhugh Lee—the latter having survived his many indiscretions to graduate from West Point following his uncle's departure.[35]

Despite the possibility of imminent combat with Comanches and Kiowas, Lieutenant Colonel Lee found frontier duty almost as monotonous and enervating as his postings to forts in need of repair. As Freeman writes, "the months stretched on ahead, with no promotion and little opportunity—the familiar story of Lee's military career, differing only in setting." With plenty of time for reflection, he probably considered leaving the army, especially now that Mary was confined to bed at Arlington, which had passed into her hands upon the recent death of her father.[36]

Increasingly, Lee's mind turned on the political issues of the day, especially the ever-widening sectional divide that, if unchecked, might swallow up the nation. The seemingly inexorable march toward disunion worried and saddened him terribly. Meditating upon the November 1856 election of James Buchanan, a northern-born Democrat, he wrote to Mary, "I hope he will be able to extinguish fanaticism North and South, cultivate love for the country and Union, and restore harmony between the different sections." He was convinced that the American form of government was, and ought to be regarded as, a model for the world; its disruption by fiery rhetoric and precipitate action would be a dire tragedy.[37]

On the slavery question, Lee was a lifelong moderate. As one reared in a slaveholding home who had inherited other slaves through marriage, he believed in the economic necessity of the practice. Even so, he saw slavery as a baleful influence on both races and hoped a way might be found to end it without imperiling southern prosperity. On the other hand, he distrusted the motives of abolitionists and resented their sometimes blatant, sometimes underhanded attempts "to interfere with & change the domestic institutions of the South."[38]

Lee's hope that national amity would prevail was not realized. Long before his tour of duty in the Southwest ended, he perceived that cataclysmic events were in the offing. One of the first of these demanded his personal involvement. On October 17, 1859, during an extended leave for the purpose of executing his father-in-law's complicated will (which, among other things, provided for the manumission at a specified future date of Arlington's entire slave force), he was summoned to Washington. At the War Department he received sealed orders to report without delay at Harpers Ferry, Virginia, where federal property had been attacked by insurrectionists.

Upon reaching that river town in the lower Shenandoah Valley he assumed command of a contingent of U.S. Marines sent to oppose insurgents who had raided the local armory and arsenal. Led by the militant abolitionist John Brown, the raiders intended to liberate and arm enough slaves to support a statewide uprising. Chance and circumstance had foiled their plans, compelling them to take refuge in the arsenal's firehouse along with more than a dozen hostages. During the two-day standoff that ensued, Lee had effective control not only of the regular troops but of local militia and various officers who, like him, had been available for special duty. The latter included Lt. James Ewell Brown Stuart of the First U.S. Cavalry, a cadet favorite of Lee's during his West Point superintendency who served as his principal emissary to the besieged raiders.

By the time the crisis ended with the storming of the firehouse, the freeing of the hostages, the killing or mortal wounding of five abolitionists, and the capture of three others including Brown (who would be tried and hanged at nearby Charles Town), the passions of Americans North and South had been dreadfully aroused. The effects of the raid on Lee were no less significant for the calm, detached behavior he had displayed throughout the crisis. Above all else, Brown's precipitate action served to confirm Lee's suspicions about the motives of antislaveryites and to worsen his fears for the continued health of the body politic.[39]

With the praise of state officials ringing in his ears, Lee returned to Arlington, finished his legal dealings, bade farewell to his family, and returned to his regiment, now in the role of commander of the Department of Texas. For another four months he and his regiment warred against hostile Indians and Mexican bandits. When not actively campaigning, he suffered from bouts of depression brought on by homesickness, monotonous routine, and career woes, especially the unlikelihood of promotion to regimental command, much less to star rank. Although desirous of rejoining the engineers, he was deeply disappointed when, early in 1860, he was passed over for the position of quartermaster general in favor of his fellow West Pointer and Mexican War associate Joseph Johnston.[40]

When Abraham Lincoln, the representative of the minority Republican Party, won the White House in November 1860 despite polling almost two million fewer votes than his combined Democratic and Whig opponents, Lee realized that advancement in the U.S. Army would soon cease to concern him. Southern politicians had long warned that a "black Republican" president would trigger secession, and late in December South Carolina made good on that threat by declaring itself out of the Union. Six other Deep South states followed during the next six weeks and by early February 1861 representatives of each had gathered in Montgomery, Alabama, to lay the hull of the Confederate States of America. Former War Secretary and U.S. Senator Jefferson Davis was elected provisional president of the Confederacy, and Alexander H. Stephens of Georgia, vice president. Given the prevailing assumption that the Lincoln administration would not permit secession to go unopposed, the infant Southern nation took steps to defend itself by raising both a provisional and a regular military establishment.[41]

During the first weeks of the secession crisis, Virginia, one of the northernmost of the states below the Mason-Dixon Line and home to a strong Whig influence, was viewed as a bastion of moderation. But as 1861 progressed, more states left the fold and both sections adopted a war footing. Lee suspected correctly that his state would cast its lot with its departed brethren, and in that event he would go with it. He had no choice, for like many another Southerner born and bred on the states' rights doctrine, he could not bear the thought of taking up arms against his family, neighbors, and friends.

Early in February 1861 General in Chief Scott relieved his former aide from duty in Texas and ordered him to Washington. Lee remained ignorant of the reason until the first week in March, when he reached the War Department after a long, roundabout journey from San Antonio and a brief reunion with Mary and the children. The substance of the discussion between Lee and his old commander went unrecorded but one may suppose it had to do with Lee's availability for a future assignment.

Lee was again summoned to the capital on April 18, six days after South

Carolina forces began to bombard the U.S. Army garrison inside Fort Sumter, in Charleston Harbor; three days after Lincoln called for seventy-five thousand volunteers to put down the growing rebellion; and one day after Virginia passed an ordinance of secession. He met first with Francis P. Blair Sr., a confidant of Lincoln, Scott, and Secretary of War Simon Cameron. On behalf of all three, Blair made Lee an offer so powerful that even a loyal son of the Old Dominion would give it serious consideration: command of all United States forces in the conflict then beginning.

The prospect of commanding so vast a force might have staggered a man of lesser conviction or greater ambition, but for all the emotional turmoil it had caused him, Lee had made up his mind. Without hesitation, he rejected the offer. Later in the day he repeated his decision in Scott's office. The old general shook his head sadly: "Lee, you have made the greatest mistake of your life; but I feared it would be so."[42]

A somber Lee soon left the War Department, rode across the Potomac, and went home to Arlington. There he would have ample time to gauge the accuracy of Scott's prediction.

On the Brink of Greatness

From Arlington on April 20 erstwhile Bvt. Col. Robert E. Lee of the U.S. Army wrote his brother Smith about his recent actions and the motivations behind them: "After the most anxious inquiry as to the correct course for me to pursue, I concluded to resign, and sent in my resignation this morning. I wished to wait till the Ordinance of Secession should be acted on by the people of Virginia [a public referendum would be held in late May]; but war seems to have commenced, and I am liable at any time to be ordered on duty, which I could not conscientiously perform" until severing his ties with what was now a foreign power, the United States of America.[1]

Lee's simple and straightforward statement of fact contained a single major contradiction. His reference to imminent orders clashed with his closing sentence: "I have no desire ever again to draw my sword." Yet he must have realized that, once word of his resignation became public, Virginia would clamor for the services of her most celebrated soldier. (The only other claimant to that distinction had shown himself to be a traitor. Winfield Scott, a Virginian by birth, was already being reviled in the Southern press for his disloyalty to the region from which he had sprung.) Lee's professed desire never to soldier again would not withstand an appeal from the officials of the commonwealth.[2]

That appeal was not long in coming. Gov. John Letcher wasted no time following the recommendation of an advisory council—an adjunct to the secession convention still sitting in the capital—by offering Lee command of Virginia's military and naval forces with the rank of major general. In response to the governor's summons, on April 22 Lee left Arlington for what would prove to be the last time. Once in Letcher's office, he accepted the proffered position in the same unhesitating manner he had displayed before Blair and Scott. Approval by the convention was a mere formality. Lee entered upon his new duties at once from a downtown office within easy reach of the capital.

Although Lee claimed that his decision to leave the U.S. Army had been a wrenching experience, he had rushed to the defense of his state and region with remarkable promptitude. It may have been an inevitable course, but it was also a precipitate one. Some historians suggest that Lee was in negotiation with Letcher and other state officials before he formally tendered his resignation.[3]

For the next seven weeks, Lee, enjoying a level of rank and authority he had never expected to attain in his lifetime, tried to create a state army and navy from whole cloth. He also developed plans for erecting defenses of various kinds while determining which objectives should be held at all costs and which could be relinquished under pressure. Initial results were mixed. His efforts to defend the Norfolk Navy Yard—where Smith Lee, who recently had accepted rank in the fledgling naval forces of the Commonwealth, had been assigned—were successful. So were his attempts to build up a force at Harpers Ferry, where Joseph Johnston, now a Confederate brigadier, was about to assume command. He had also managed to fortify other strategic points on the Virginia coast and in the state's interior. At the same time, Lee supervised the recruitment of state troops (and subsequently oversaw their transition to the field forces of the Confederacy). He managed the formation of various units—companies, battalions, regiments, batteries—and he advised Letcher on the merits of men aspiring to commissioned rank and those seeking resources—mainly arms and ammunition—for organizations they were raising.

As large as it appeared on paper, the influx of recruits was insufficient to prevent a body of Northern troops from crossing the Potomac on the evening of May 23, hours after Virginia's secession ordnance was ratified at the polls, and seizing Alexandria, including the Custis-Lee property. The invasion forced Mary and the girls to take sanctuary in the homes of relations and friends. Custis and Rooney, now twenty-eight and twenty-four, respectively, had followed their father's lead by offering their services to the Confederacy; in time each would wear the wreathed stars of a general. The youngest son, Rob, now a student at the state university at Charlottesville, would join them in the ranks at a later date though his youth would prevent him from rising above the rank of company officer.[4]

The invaders of Alexandria took possession of Arlington, which would never return to the Lee family. Mainly, it would appear, in retaliation for Lee's siding against his country and its army, the venerable estate would be transformed into a burial ground for Union soldiers who gave their lives during the four years of fighting that lay ahead.

Confederate President Jefferson Davis

By late May, Lee was no longer serving solely on the staff of Governor Letcher. The seat of government of the Southern nation had moved to Richmond, and Lee's office had been placed under Jefferson Davis. This event brought the two men into close contact for the first time since Lee left his administrative post at West Point. They resumed their former cordial working relationship, one built on mutual respect and admiration and now strengthened by their shared determination to make a success of this regrettable but necessary experiment in rebellion. Under Davis, Lee's responsibilities expanded to the point that he frequently felt exhausted. Still, he regarded his situation with biblical stoicism: "When I reflect upon the calamity impending over the country, my own sorrows sink into insignificance."[5]

By early June, when Virginia's land and sea forces were taken into the Confederate ranks and Lee's commission was transferred to the Regular army of the Confederate States, the state's mobilization was essentially complete. Now Lee could step back and take a broader view of the South's military situation, which dovetailed with Virginia's. Everything considered, he was forced to admit, the picture was bleak. In addition to the Alexandria region, Union forces had invaded the western reaches of the state and were making inroads beyond the Alleghenies. In the first days of June a small army under George B. McClellan—a celebrated engineer officer who had been a member of Scott's staff in Mexico and was now a major general in command of Ohio volunteers—routed fifteen hundred pea-green Confederates at Philippi and occupied neighboring Grafton, within easy reach of strategic Staunton. A few days later, troops out of Fort Monroe at the southeastern tip of the Virginia Peninsula (one of only two Southern garrisons that remained in U. S. hands) advanced against a Confederate outpost on the road to Hampton, precipitating the battle of Big Bethel, the first fairly substantial land engagement of the conflict. The Federals had been defeated largely through their own inexperience and ineptitude; even so, the larger command of which they were a part appeared capable of, as well as intent on, advancing against strategic Yorktown.[6]

The most serious threat to Virginia and the Confederacy was posed by a simultaneous invasion of the Shenandoah Valley and the defenses along Bull Run Creek, near Manassas Junction on the Orange & Alexandria Railroad, less than thirty miles southwest of Washington. The operations made parallel progress, but the Valley situation was the first to grab headlines. In mid-June, an army largely composed of Pennsylvania troops occupied Harpers Ferry after evicting Johnston's command from the town. A battle near Falling Waters on the Potomac on July 2 furnished Johnston's ranking subordinate, Brig. Gen. Thomas J. Jackson, with his first sustained combat experience since Mexico.[7]

Johnston's evacuation and fallback was troubling, especially to Davis, who considered every foot of southern soil sacred ground. The threat to the Bull Run line, however, seemed more immediate and therefore more grave. Union officials had publicized their determination to preempt the opening session of the Confederate Congress in Richmond, scheduled for July 22. Fear swept Richmond when, on the sixteenth, thirty-five thousand raw but eager recruits left Washington and trudged south under Brig. Gen. Irvin McDowell, Winfield Scott's fallback choice to lead the forces of the Union to quick victory. Over the next four days the invaders clashed with forward elements of a smaller but equally untutored army under P. G. T. Beauregard, yet another member of Scott's Mexican War staff, now a Confederate brigadier as a result of his successful reduction of Fort Sumter.[8]

Jefferson Davis, who realized that the impending battle might decide the fate of his newborn nation, could not bear the suspense. Early on Sunday, the twenty-first, he departed Richmond for the battlefield, leaving Lee at his post to hope and pray for a successful outcome. It was evening before Richmond heard reliable reports of McDowell's retreat and victory for Beauregard, both largely due to the eleventh-hour arrival at Manassas of thousands of Johnston's troops from the Valley—a railroad-borne transfer operation ordered by Davis after consultation with Lee. Beauregard and Johnston were the heroes of the day, but there was glory enough to go around. Lee could take pride in the knowledge that he had chosen Beauregard's position along Bull Run and had forwarded to him more than one-fourth of the troops who had held it.[9]

Although sobered by the carnage of the twenty-first—some twenty-six hundred Federal and two thousand Confederates had become casualties—Lee, in common with virtually every Richmonder, sighed with relief. In his case, however, release from anxiety was brief. Within a week he was packing for a journey to western Virginia, where another crisis was at hand.

Maj. Gen. George B. McClellan, USA

IN RECENT FIGHTING among the Allegheny foothills, Confederate forces had suffered two stinging reverses. During the second of these, at Corrick's Ford, the theater commander, Brig. Gen. Robert S. Garnett, had been killed. Credit for the Federal victory had gone to George McClellan, who had since been summoned to Washington to revive the fortunes of the army defeated at Manassas. In fact, McClellan was heading east in answer to Lincoln's call even as Lee traveled in the other direction at the behest of Jefferson Davis.[10]

Lee was Davis's choice to succeed Garnett. The president was banking that his most esteemed military advisor would regain the lost section of the state east of the Kanawha River and southeast of the Baltimore & Ohio Railroad. Lee's task was a Herculean one, given the inadequate resources, uncertain weather, and uncooperative and quarreling subordinates he would encounter in his new sphere of authority.

As might be expected, he did his best with the men and arms at his disposal. On September 12, six weeks after arriving at Staunton to take command of the Army of the Northwest with the rank of full general in the Confederate service, he was leading a two-column offensive against an enemy force ensconced atop Cheat Mountain, southeast of Huttonsville. In a special order issued at the outset of the march, he reminded his troops—which included his cavalry officer son Rooney—that "the eyes of the country are upon you. The safety of your homes and the lives of all you hold dear depend upon your courage and exertions."[11]

His admonition went unheeded, and as a result the first large-scale military operation he ever supervised ended in ignominious failure. En route to his objective he lost the critical element of surprise when the leader of the second column failed to attack a weakly manned outpost in advance of Lee's assault. The officer's faintheartedness doomed the operation, especially after he mistakenly alerted the enemy to his approach. The operation was further compromised by the low morale of the troops, which made Lee doubt that a secondary attack would succeed even had secrecy been maintained. Attributing his defeat not to human error or weakness but to the will of God, the frustrated Lee ordered a full withdrawal.[12]

The debacle at Cheat Mountain was closely followed by the defeat of another Confederate force, this not under Lee's direct command, at Carnifex Ferry on the Gauley River. In the wake of the two failures, Lee tried to lure a Yankee force dug in on top of another Kanawha Valley eminence into attacking his recently enlarged command. The strategy almost worked, which would have enabled him to recoup lost prestige. In the end, however, it failed: the enemy commander sniffed out the trap and withdrew to safety under cover of darkness.[13]

Convinced that nothing further could be accomplished in this quarter until spring, Lee returned to Richmond early in November. En route, he missed an opportunity to see Mary, who was visiting relatives at Shirley Plantation on the James River, but, as always, he accepted the outcome philosophically. As he wrote one of his daughters, "among the calamities of war the hardest to bear, perhaps, is the separation of families and friends. Yet all must be endured to accomplish our independence and maintain our self-government." Instead, he repaired to the Confederate War Department, where he was promptly given a new assignment.

His new orders sent him to South Carolina to supervise the strengthening of coastal fortifications against an imminent army-navy invasion. Lee traveled to

Port Royal Sound in the capacity of a departmental commander whose authority extended to coastal Georgia and a part of Florida. He arrived too late, however, to prevent a Yankee flotilla from overwhelming the forts guarding the sound, whose garrison Lee had authorized to withdraw before it could be captured. The next several weeks were devoted to building up less vulnerable defenses along the coast including those at Charleston and Savannah. He despaired, however, of defending every important island and waterway in his domain. The enemy, Lee observed, "can be thrown with great celerity against any point, and far outnumbers any force we can bring against it in the field." The situation gave him a heightened appreciation of his country's plight. He concluded that given its limited resources, no mere defensive strategy could save the Confederacy. The South would have to concentrate her forces and use them in attacks in the hope of wearing down the foe physically and morally.[14]

Lee's coastal operations—the static, defensive nature of which gained him a local reputation as "the King of Spades"—continued into the first months of 1862. In February, as the result of three well-publicized surrenders of Confederate forces—at Forts Henry and Donelson, in Tennessee, to Maj. Gen. Ulysses S. Grant, and at Roanoke Island, North Carolina, to Maj. Gen. Ambrose E. Burnside—the War Office ordered the withdrawal of forces from the various fortified islands to points inland and their transfer to the western theater.

This drastic effort accomplished little, for Grant followed Henry and Donelson with an even more celebrated triumph near Shiloh Church and Pittsburg Landing, just above the Tennessee-Mississippi border. There he successfully counterattacked a formidable army under Albert Sidney Johnston, Lee's immediate superior in the Second Cavalry, who fell mortally wounded in the melee. The withdrawal of forces from Lee's department did, however, produce a lessening of his duties. As a result, on March 2 he was recalled to Richmond.[15]

Upon his return, he found the capital abuzz with rumors of a new Yankee offensive, probably to be made via overland march from Washington by the rejuvenated and greatly augmented army under McClellan. To avoid being overwhelmed, the force that remained on the Manassas line, now under Joe Johnston, began to evacuate on March 8. It fell back to the banks of the Rappahannock River, midway between Washington and Richmond. Resuming his role as military advisor to President Davis, Lee spent weeks thoroughly acquainting himself with the threat posed by "Little Mac," which looked even more formidable than that of McDowell the previous July.[16]

The situation appeared to worsen with amazing swiftness. Before March was out, McClellan, who had disdained to pursue Johnston, was placing his Army of the Potomac aboard transports off Alexandria. Days later the first wave was landing at Fort Monroe and marching toward Yorktown. In Richmond it was feared that the ultimate destination of "Little Mac" was the Confederate capital itself.

That was in fact McClellan's ultimate objective, but in order to secure it, he believed he had to confront the defensive line that Maj. Gen. John B. Magruder had built across the Peninsula west of Yorktown. That line was thin in many places, but Magruder's flair for deception and his opponent's native caution dictated a siege rather than an attack. In the first days of April, Joe Johnston joined his army to Magruder's, took command on the Peninsula, and held McClellan at bay for a month. During that period the besiegers ringed Yorktown with batteries but on May 3, just before the guns opened, spoilsport Johnston evacuated and withdrew to Richmond. Reaching the capital with minimal difficulty, he stocked its works with his sixty thousand troops and awaited McClellan's arrival.[17]

Like Johnston, Lee and Davis feared that the Army of the Potomac, more than one hundred thousand strong, would either storm the capital's defenses or slowly strangle the city via investment. To prevent expected reinforcements from reaching McClellan by overland march from the north, Lee in late April ordered General Jackson, who had earned the sobriquet "Stonewall" at Manassas, to create a strategic diversion in the Shenandoah Valley. Jackson responded with a remarkable performance. For two months he rampaged hither and yon, overwhelming outposts, waylaying supply trains, outdistancing pursuers, and frightening the Lincoln administration into recalling the additions earmarked for the siege of Richmond.[18]

Late in May Lee joined Davis in conferring with Johnston on the subject of how best to oppose the Army of the Potomac, which had dug in a few miles east of the capital. In the end they approved Johnston's plan to attack the lower end of McClellan's elongated line—the Third and Fourth Army Corps—which held an isolated position south of the rain-swollen Chickahominy River. A sortie such as this was a risky proposition, but there seemed no alternative. Lee contented himself with the thought that an offensive carefully aimed at a critical center of enemy power was properly Jominian.

But it was not Jominian in its conduct. Launched on the morning of May 31, the multipronged attack was a belated, mismanaged effort, characterized by blunders on the part of subordinates including Longstreet. Desperate fighting broke out around Seven Pines and Fair Oaks Station, but the attackers had made relatively little headway when the action halted at sundown with the shored-up Union flank still intact. By now, however, Johnston was no longer in command, having been incapacitated by two wounds. His senior subordinate, Gustavus Smith, Lee's West Point faculty colleague, assumed command but appeared confused and uncertain of his course. That evening Jefferson Davis took the fateful step of assigning Lee to head the command now formally known as the Army of Northern Virginia. Johnston would never regain his position.[19]

ON JUNE 1, Lee permitted General Smith to exercise control—such as it was—over the renewed fighting east of Richmond. When it ended inconclusively late in the day, Lee ordered the troops newly entrusted to him to return to their prebattle positions. The weary, combat-scarred enemy did not pursue, giving Lee the time to inspect his new command and acquaint himself with its leaders.

Maj. Gen. James E. B. Stuart, CSA

Some Johnston loyalists expressed resentment that a desk officer had replaced their fighting general. But Johnston himself, who had long been at odds with Jefferson Davis, while convalescing from his wounds expressed his gratification that "they have in my place one who does possess it [Davis's confidence], and who can accomplish what I never could have—the concentration of our armies for the defence of the capital of the Confederacy."[20]

And defend it Lee did. In the hope of finding weak points in the position held by his powerful but lethargic enemy, he sent the dashing and resourceful J. E. B. Stuart, his aide during the Harpers Ferry crisis and now the brigadier general commanding the cavalry, to probe yet another isolated portion of McClellan's command, its right flank, north of the Chickahominy. Following an unauthorized circuit of the entire enemy position, Stuart brought word that the flank in question was "in the air," unanchored by a natural barrier such as a watercourse or a ridge. Lee intended to attack that sector. By now, based not only on the strategic thinking he had engaged in while Davis's chief military advisor but also on his experiences in western Virginia and South Carolina, Lee had decided that in order to survive the armies of the South had to adopt an offensive-defensive posture. This entailed concentrating and attacking at key points, forcing the enemy to devote his resources and attention to the defense of these positions and thus preventing him from attacking simultaneously across the board. McClellan's right flank, in the vicinity of Mechanicsville and Beaver Dam Creek, was the first of these chosen points of attack.

Despite the thought that went into it, when launched on June 26 against the position held by Maj. Gen. Fitz John Porter's Fifth Corps, Lee's offensive went awry. Coordination with Jackson, whose command had been recalled from the Valley, proved lacking. Forced to act unilaterally, Lee's troops rushed head-on against Porter's well-defended works astride Beaver Dam Creek, in the process absorbing between thirteen hundred and fourteen hundred casualties compared to fewer than four hundred Union losses. But in defeat Lee learned a lesson that would yield ultimate success. Unstrung by his opponent's aggressiveness, late in the day McClellan ordered Porter to withdraw toward the Chickahominy. While Porter complied, the balance of the Army of the Potomac abandoned its siege lines exactly as Lee had hoped and commenced a long retreat to the James River.

Lee pursued and on the twenty-seventh attacked Porter's new position along Boatswain's Swamp, south and east of Gaines's Mill. Unaware that McClellan had decided to transfer his base of supply from the York River to the James, Lee ordered a series of assaults toward the York. Thanks again to a lack of energy and aggressiveness on Jackson's part, not until near dark did Lee achieve a coordinated offensive that broke Porter's line and forced his retreat below the Chickahominy.[21]

Over the next four days, Lee, finally aware of his enemy's intentions, strove to bring McClellan to bay short of the James, where the Federals would be in supporting range of a gunboat fleet. Virtually every encounter en route ended in McClellan's favor, in large measure the result of mistakes by subordinates who did not yet know what Lee expected of them. For his part, Lee gave his generals too many opportunities to err. He believed that his job was to maneuver the army into an advantageous position, then allow its field leaders to shape the tactical situation.

In later months Lee's lieutenants would prove capable of handling the leeway given them, but not during the pursuit to the James. During the balance of the so-called Seven Days' battles—Garnett's and Golding's Farms (June 28), Savage's Station and Allen's Farm (June 29), White Oak Swamp or Glendale (June 30)—his generals could not gain a decisive advantage over the enemy or injure him critically. Even so, McClellan refused to halt his headlong rush to the river.[22]

Having successfully staked all on the kind of offensive Jomini would have applauded, Lee suddenly fell victim to overconfidence and disdain for his weak-willed foe. On July 1, as the main body of the Army of the Potomac neared the river within hailing distance of Shirley Plantation, Lee found his path blocked by McClellan's rear guard, which commanded the approaches to a steeply inclined plateau, Malvern Hill. Refusing to fall back or approach indirectly, Lee made plans to attack this formidable position. But when his army moved up, confusion reigned. Some elements were slow to get into their proper positions and some never did. Despite the chaos, Lee ordered a general assault. Those troops that responded—chiefly the divisions of Magruder, Daniel Harvey Hill, and Lafayette McLaws—were halted by banks of artillery and waves of sharpshooters.

Throughout the fight, the carnage was tremendous, but rather than cut his losses Lee continued to throw troops into the cauldron, until by sunset he had suffered more than fifty-three hundred casualties—40 percent more than his enemy. When the violence finally ceased, a Union officer on the summit looked down upon "an appalling spectacle. . . . Over five thousand dead and wounded men were on the ground, in every attitude of distress. A third of them were dead or dying, but enough were alive and moving to give the field a singular crawling effect."[23]

In later days it became evident that McClellan was no longer a threat to Richmond. By early August, in fact, the Union commander was transferring his army from the Peninsula to the environs of Washington. The newly appointed general in chief of the U.S. armies, Maj. Gen. Henry Wager Halleck, intended that at least some of these troops should reinforce a second, newly created command in Virginia, led by John Pope, a general who had gained some success in the West and had bragged that he would enjoy more at Lee's expense. The latter had other ideas. Flush from his success against one presumptuous opponent, Lee was determined to neutralize this second braggart, who was also something of a bully, having waged war against defenseless civilians as well as soldiers. Lee considered the commander of the sixty-thousand-man Army of Virginia a "miscreant" who had to be "suppressed." Given the forbearance he habitually displayed toward his fellow men, even those in Yankee blue, this was an unusually harsh characterization. It indicated how much Lee had been affected by the invasion of his state, and how much he despised those Federals, like Pope, who targeted the entire Southern nation for violence and bloodshed.[24]

Lee did suppress his opponent—not through head-on attack but by a dazzling combination of feint, maneuver, fancy footwork, and offensive audacity in the Jominian tradition. Some historians believe Lee's adoption of a maneuver strategy on this occasion was a reaction to the sobering losses he had suffered on the Peninsula, which induced caution. Yet what followed was hardly a model of restraint, as a thoroughly lost and befuddled Pope would testify.

In advance of forcing a showdown with the Army of Virginia in its entirety, Lee sent Jackson—who appeared to have recovered from his Peninsula lethargy—to challenge Pope's advance echelon. A meeting-engagement took place on August 9 at Cedar Mountain, ten miles north of one of Pope's major objectives, the rail junction at Gordonsville. For most of the day the Yankees held a tactical advantage and Jackson was hard pressed, his line close to collapse. But a late counterattack by Maj. Gen. Ambrose P. Hill negated Union gains and enabled Jackson to salvage a draw.[25]

Jackson's battered command fell back south, where Lee, at the head of Longstreet's command, joined it. Hoping to strike a blow before McClellan could reinforce Pope, Lee—his confidence restored after his misstep at Malvern Hill—planned an assault against the east flank of his opponent's reunited command, now seventy thousand strong, along the Rapidan River. Circumstances beyond Lee's control, however, enabled Pope to flee to high ground along the Rappahannock, forcing cancellation of the assault. Lee then struck at the Union rear with Stuart's cavalry, which raided Pope's headquarters at Catlett's Station on the Orange & Alexandria. Then Lee planned boldly in a way that Jomini would not have approved. Taking a calculated risk, on the twenty-fifth he divided his fifty-five-thousand-man force, sending Jackson on a wide sweep around Pope's right and into his rear. The following day Jackson looted and burned the supply depot at Manassas before tangling on the twenty-seventh with Pope's much larger force at Groveton, along the southwestern edge of the old Bull Run battlefield.[26]

Lt. Gen. James Longstreet, CSA

Jackson's superb handling of his limited resources kept Pope occupied while Lee, with Longstreet, completed his double envelopment. Pope again clashed with Jackson on the twenty-ninth, this time above Groveton, but, as before, failed to overwhelm his adversary. Next day fighting resumed north of the Warrenton Turnpike and west of Bull Run. By now Longstreet had moved into position on Stonewall's right, but Pope, intent on crushing Jackson, ignored his presence—to his everlasting regret. By the afternoon of the thirtieth Pope had resumed his attacks on Jackson, who held his complete attention. Suddenly Longstreet made his presence felt via an attack that collapsed the Union left and eventually caused Pope's retreat to the Washington defenses. In besting his second enemy army in less than two months, Lee had suffered fewer than ten thousand casualties as against Pope's sixteen thousand. By now, if not before, the general affectionately known as "Marse Robert" and "the Tycoon" had overcome the stigma of that earlier nickname, "King of Spades."[27]

WITH THE ARMY OF VIRGINIA content to remain inside its capital, Lee again took the strategic initiative. In furtherance of a long-considered plan, he moved his victorious forces across the Potomac and into southern Maryland. He hoped to winter his army in that lush region, sparing his native state of some of war's baleful effects while recruiting his ranks and replenishing its supply coffers. McClellan, who eventually regained overall command

and integrated Pope's survivors into his Army of the Potomac, staged a typically cautious pursuit, one that lagged even after September 13, when his soldiers discovered a copy of an order from Lee to his several subordinates, disclosing his dispositions and suggesting his intentions.[28]

Four days later, following savage but inconclusive fighting along the rim of South Mountain, McClellan brought Lee to bay east of Antietam Creek and not far from the village of Sharpsburg. Although at a critical disadvantage—much of Jackson's command, which had been sent to capture strategic Harpers Ferry, was not on the ground when the fighting began—Lee repulsed a succession of attacks by McClellan. The first of these, spearheaded by Maj. Gen. Joseph Hooker's First Corps, struck Lee's north (left) flank. Then the assaults moved progressively south, until, late in the day, the Ninth Corps of Maj. Gen. Ambrose E. Burnside slowly forced its way across the Antietam to imperil the Confederate right. As if on cue, A. P. Hill's hard-marching division arrived from Harpers Ferry to throw back Burnside and end the fight, although on an uncertain note.[29]

McClellan's ineptitude and Hill's last-minute heroics appeared to have saved the Army of Northern Virginia from the consequences of its commander's faulty planning. Lee had given battle with a high river to his back, and he had chosen to fight on ground that offered too little maneuvering room, especially on the northern edge of the field where he tried but failed to turn the Union right.

Lee's misreading of the local topography was a troubling lapse, but the source of the error was more troubling still. Having so easily cowed and beaten McClellan on the Peninsula and Pope on the Rappahannock, he had grown defiant of the odds against him and contemptuous of the talents of his adversaries. He had begun to believe his troops invincible, capable of overcoming handicaps that would reduce an army of Yankees to quaking immobility.

The butcher's bill on this, the bloodiest day in American history, ran to almost 23,000 casualties. The preponderance—approximately 12,400 men killed, wounded, or captured—had occurred in the Union ranks. This statistic represented, however, only 25 percent of the troops engaged, while Lee's 10,300 casualties amounted to 31 percent of the number committed to the fight. Added to the losses suffered on the Peninsula and in the campaign to "suppress" Pope, these were near-catastrophic figures. They strongly suggested that Lee's style of warfare was inappropriate to his situation. Because the North's manpower pool was so much deeper, Lee's enemies could afford the losses they were sustaining. Lee's resources, however, were finite—they could not be replaced. If he continued to take the offensive, feeding his appetite for audacious maneuvering and his hunger to defeat his adversaries psychologically as well as physically, attrition would do to his army what Yankee generalship could not.[30]

At battle's end, Lee found new ways to show his contempt for McClellan and his command. He realized that he could not tarry in his constricted position— given time even George McClellan would comprehend his advantages of position and numbers. When he was not attacked on the eighteenth, Lee began to recross the Potomac by night. He did not stray far from where he landed. Certain that he had learned all there was to know about George McClellan, he rested his battered and weary troops in the Shenandoah Valley, daring Little Mac to pursue. This did not happen for more than a month, an error fatal to McClellan's ambitions. Finally reaching Virginia in the last days of October, he lackadaisically followed Lee and Longstreet to the line of the Rappahannock while failing to drive Jackson from his blocking position in the lower Valley. By early November Abraham Lincoln had had enough, and McClellan was sent home to New Jersey to await orders that would never come.[31]

For his own reasons, Lee was sorry to see McClellan go. As he remarked to Longstreet, with only a hint of sarcasm: "We always understood each other so well. I fear they may continue to make these changes till they find some one whom I don't understand."[32]

That someone was not Little Mac's successor, the unimaginative, stubborn, vacuous Ambrose Burnside. The balding, bewhiskered Indianan inspired neither fear nor respect in his opponent. Lee's only unanswered question was why the man had been elevated so far above his limited abilities. Thus he was surprised, not to say shocked, when in mid-November Burnside outraced him to Falmouth, opposite Fredericksburg, where he might cross the river for an advance on Richmond while also covering Washington, a strategic concern never far from Lincoln's mind.

But although he moved quickly enough at first, Burnside permitted himself to be delayed at Falmouth by a lack of bridging materials. Unwisely, perhaps, he jettisoned his original plan, to cross the river farther upstream and occupy the heights that commanded Fredericksburg. Instead, his dawdling allowed Lee to get there first. By early December, when Lee reunited his army by recalling Jackson from the Valley, Burnside's once-golden opportunity had turned to dross.

Initially Lee had not intended to fight at Fredericksburg; he planned to withdraw to more defensible terrain along the North Anna River, which also afforded greater opportunities for offensive maneuvering. He changed his mind in the face of Burnside's almost criminal slowness and for once decided to assume the defensive. In violation of Jomini's warnings against static warfare, Lee had his men dig in to repel an attack that Burnside would have neither the sense nor the courage to withhold.

When it came, on December 13, Lee was prepared to meet it, having strengthened his elongated position almost to impregnability. Burnside further obliged his opponent by directing his assaults against the most formidable sector of the Rebel line, Marye's Heights and the high ground on either side of it. The result was a bloodbath so mesmerizing in its horrific effects that it drew forth an expression of awe from the man who had engineered it.[33]

The disparity of the casualties suffered this day suggested a Confederate victory of sublime proportions. It was that, but only in the tactical sense. In the days before Burnside's attack, Stonewall Jackson had attempted to persuade his superior that while the army's position was conducive to defense, it lacked the depth to permit a counterattack. The same open ground that made Burnside's attack so unconscionable would defeat any attempt to follow up Lee's success. Along the north bank of the river Burnside had loaded the crest of Stafford Heights with dozens of artillery batteries; an advance against them would produce the same bloodbath as Burnside had brought upon himself.

Jackson urged Lee, instead, to return to his plan of withdrawing to the North Anna, but the army commander refused. The result was an incomplete victory. When the fighting ceased the Army of the Potomac withdrew safely to the north bank under the cover of the guns on the high ground. It would take time, but eventually the Yankees would salve their wounds, make good their losses, and renew the fight, probably under a more level-headed commander. Forced to remain on the defensive, Lee had been unable to strike the kind of blow that might have destroyed his enemy. Having fallen short of that goal, he had gained nothing of strategic consequence at Fredericksburg.[34]

LEE BELIEVED HE KNEW Burnside from the inside out, but the man was capable of surprises. Two months later he gave Lee another jolt by refusing to consider the Fredericksburg campaign at an end. The disaster in front of Marye's Heights had savaged his army's morale as well as its manpower, but Burnside thought he could gain ultimate victory by a second attempt to cross the Rappahannock. In mid-January 1863 he began shifting upriver toward Banks's Ford. From there, three miles west of Falmouth, he hoped to move into his enemy's rear before anyone could stop him.

Although scouts detected Burnside's buildup and suspected a crossing, the move caught the main army off-guard. Lee was in Richmond, conferring with President Davis on the general military situation, when preliminary operations began. Rushing back to Fredericksburg, he quickly decided that Burnside intended to force a crossing somewhere on the river above Fredericksburg, but he could not say where. The uncertainty was troubling, but in the end his concern was allayed, not by anything that he or his opponent did, but by the weather. It had been extremely cold for the past several weeks, but just as Burnside's movement got underway the skies opened with a wicked combination of snow, sleet, and freezing rain. The result was a Federal army bogged down on roads awash in ice, slush, and, after a sudden thaw set in, mud—seas of mud. By month's end Burnside's weather-beaten troops had returned to their camps at Falmouth, ending what would become known throughout the Army of the Potomac as the "Mud March."[35]

So, too, ended Burnside's tenure in command. As Lee later learned, the Union leader suffered greatly for having lost the confidence of his senior subordinates. A few of them had taken the drastic step of going behind their superior's back to lobby Lincoln for his relief. One of the most disgruntled was Joseph Hooker, who told anyone who would listen that Burnside was a rank incompetent undeserving of high command. Hooker was too shrewd to risk his own neck by making an unofficial visit to the White House. He did, however, encourage those who eventually did so. His Machiavellian efforts served him well, for in late January the War Department announced Burnside's relief and his replacement by the general whom the public knew as "Fighting Joe."[36]

At the time the change was made, Lee knew little about his new opponent beyond some basic facts of military service and the nickname he had acquired, supposedly in recognition of his combative proclivities. Soon enough, however, Hooker—in the manner of Pope and, to a somewhat lesser extent, McClellan and Burnside—began to boast loudly of what he would do to the Army of

Library of Congress

Drawing of Burnside's "Mud March"

Northern Virginia once he had it where he wanted it. Hooker's pronouncements soon found their way into print—the general was colorful and quotable enough to be a favorite of reporters—and Lee began to take note of the man's behavior.

For their intelligence value Lee regularly scanned the Northern newspapers, which, being largely uncensored, often disclosed military secrets. He was not impressed by the coverage given Hooker's bellicose and egotistical statements, but he was amused enough by the general's sobriquet that he began to refer to him as "Mr. F. J. Hooker." What did not amuse Lee was his inability to determine Hooker's plans for the oncoming spring. In the first weeks of his tenure, the Union leader made frequent display of the power of his army, which remained intact even as its morale sagged under the weight of Fredericksburg and the Mud March. On February 6 Lee wrote to his daughter Agnes: "General Hooker is obliged to do something. I do not know what it will be. He is playing the Chinese game, trying [to see] what frightening will do. He runs out his guns, starts wagons and troops up and down the river, and creates an excitement generally. Our men look on in wonder, give a cheer, and all again subsides in statu quo ante bellum."[37]

Whatever Hooker decided to do, it surely would be different from what his predecessor had attempted. Lee could only guess at its nature but he understood that, given the losses the Federals had suffered on December 13, Hooker would need several weeks to return his army to fighting shape. Then, too, with the Mud March in mind, Hooker was not likely to launch an offensive until spring crept closer and the roads along the river began to congeal.

WITH A DRAMATIC SERIES of combat successes under his belt Lee, and by extension his army, appeared poised on the brink of greatness. Yet commander and command had much to do before it could rightfully claim that title. Thus the months following the victory at Fredericksburg constituted a period of preparation looking carefully to the future. There was much to be done before Lee and his troops were ready to counter whatever moves Gen. Joseph Hooker saw fit to make. Since the battle Lee had been strengthening his army's twenty-five-mile-long defensive line, which extended from Banks's Ford downriver as far as Port Royal. Put on hold when the Mud March began, the work resumed with new intensity as soon as Burnside bogged down and retreated. One who helped strengthen the position commented that "no time, labor, or skill was spared in its construction and when completed an almost impregnable barrier was presented to the progress of the Federal army throughout this whole distance." At the same time, Lee lengthened Stuart's picket lines, including those below Fredericksburg maintained by the mounted brigade of newly promoted Brig. Gen. W. H. F. Lee and those patrolling the river above the town, under Rooney's cousin Fitz.[38]

In the weeks following the Mud March, Lee tended to some long-standing administrative issues. He worked closely with Longstreet and Jackson to reorganize the army's staff and reduce the friction that sometimes arose between the corps headquarters staffs. Working closely with his chief artillerist, Brig. Gen. William N. Pendleton, Lee also revamped the artillery. From the meeting of their minds came the creation of a single artillery corps, composed of battalions, each of which comprised four batteries. The battalions would be attached to the army's corps, not to lower-level organizations as heretofore, thus providing for more centralized control of the army's 264 cannons while giving the arm more compactness and uniformity. At about this same time Lee also oversaw the formation of the army's first full-size regiment of engineers.[39]

That winter the army faced a critical shortage of horses. Lee did all in his power to persuade officers, troopers, teamsters, and others who rode or drove horses to conserve the animals' health. A major contributor to the problem was a general scarcity of forage in the Fredericksburg area. The situation had forced Stuart to send his three brigades, one after the other, to areas far from the front where fodder was more abundant.

The dispersal process compromised the readiness of Lee's mounted arm. In late February he sent Fitz Lee and four hundred riders from his brigade to cross the river and attack the enemy's picket lines in the vicinity of Hartwood Church, eight miles northwest of Fredericksburg. With commendable stealth Fitz slipped inside the lines manned by a West Point comrade, Brig. Gen. William Woods Averell. He attacked the picket posts of Averell's division, surprised and routed their inhabitants, and returned home with dozens of captives in tow.

Angry and embarrassed that Fitz had exposed his lax security, three weeks later Averell assaulted his old friend's pickets south of Kelly's Ford. The resulting battle, a several-hour succession of charge and countercharge, ended badly for Fitz, even after Stuart lent a hand. Each of Fitz's five regiments was forced into retreat at some point, and the army's leading horse artillerist, Maj. John Pelham, was mortally wounded in the affair. Averell's force outnumbered Fitz Lee's, perhaps preventing a fair fight. Fitz had to bear the brunt of the lopsided fight because Stuart's other brigades, Rooney Lee's and Brig. Gen. Wade Hampton's, were foraging too far from the scene of the battle to prevent the first signal defeat of Stuart's command.[40]

Lee's army suffered from a shortage of rations as well as forage. By late in January, the army had been down to a single week's worth of provisions before the situation improved—marginally. Lee was able to address the problem as the unforeseen result of the mid-February movement of the Union Ninth Corps down the Potomac to Fort Monroe. The operation was supervised by Burnside, who upon his relief from army leadership had returned to command of the corps he had led before and at Antietam. The movement might have been viewed as the outcome of Hooker's wish that his predecessor be transferred to a new duty station.

Although not originally bound for the western theater, most of the Ninth Corps was eventually ordered to Kentucky. Initially, however, Lee feared it was going to strike at Richmond or the railroads that linked the Confederate capital with the Deep South. To cover all bases, Lee ordered half of Longstreet's corps—the divisions of George E. Pickett and John Bell Hood—to Southside Virginia, the fertile region below the James where Hampton's cavalry brigade was wintering.[41]

In early April, when Burnside's ultimate destination became clear, Lee did not recall Longstreet. Instead, he utilized his senior subordinate to prevent further detachments from Hooker to the West, where the war was going badly for the Confederacy. Although 1862 had ended with the defeat of a two-pronged Union offensive against strategic Vicksburg, Mississippi—one column thwarted by raids on its communications, the other turned back in battle—Lee worried that the overall commander, Grant, would try again come spring. Then, early in January, Braxton Bragg's Confederates had been forced to retreat after a two-day struggle outside Murfreesboro, Tennessee, with the Army of the Cumberland, led by Maj. Gen. William S. Rosecrans, an opponent of Lee's in western Virginia. Lee was further concerned that the Yankees were about to attack Charleston, where the peripatetic P. G. T. Beauregard now commanded, or perhaps the less heavily guarded port of Wilmington, North Carolina.[42]

In his new position on the Southside, Longstreet was assigned several objectives, including countering any attack on Richmond; standing ready to reinforce Lee should Hooker finally advance; containing the strategic outpost of Suffolk, which Burnside had augmented; and gathering subsistence in the fertile region between the James and the Blackwater River. Secretary of War James Seddon considered a thoroughly undertaken foraging operation the key to solving Lee's commissary problems. Lee could find no flaw in this premise with the exception that the indefinite absence of Pickett and Hood had reduced the forces holding Fredericksburg and vicinity to sixty-two thousand, less than half the number Hooker could put in the field.[43]

Even with this pared-down force, Lee considered himself capable of offensive operations if given an opening. Early in the winter his thoughts turned toward the Shenandoah Valley, where the local commander, Maj. Gen. Robert H. Milroy, was outdoing John Pope in making miserable the lives of local civilians. The Yankee was extorting tribute from Southern sympathizers upon penalty of having their homes and farms burned to the ground.

Lee's efforts to suppress this bullying opponent already had been curtailed by Burnside's movement down the Potomac. Now they were sidetracked indefinitely by a severe throat infection that struck Lee sometime in late March and which Douglas Southall Freeman claims brought on an attack of pericarditis. For more than three weeks the army leader was confined to a sickroom and, for days after he regained his feet, to light activity. According to modern-day medical authorities, the ailment represented the early symptoms of the cardio-vascular disease from which Lee would suffer for the rest of his life and which would kill him seven years hence.[44]

When Lee finally recovered sufficiently to plan yet another offensive, his attention had shifted from Milroy. To Secretary Seddon he suggested that should Hooker remain on the defensive by early May, "the readiest method of relieving the pressure upon General Johnston [now in overall command of Confederate forces in the West] and General Beauregard would be for this army to cross into Maryland." The only obstacles to implementation were the deplorable condition of the roads leading to the Potomac crossings and the general want of provisions and transportation. If these problems could be resolved, Lee was confident that a second sojourn in the Old Line State would prove more advantageous, as well as lengthier, than the first.[45]

But he was given no opportunity to prove it. In mid- and late April, with spring in the air and the roads becoming more dusty than muddy, his enemy made the opening movements of what would come to be known as the Chancellorsville campaign. On the thirteenth a sizable grouping of horsemen was seen along the upper Rappahannock. Initially, Lee was led to believe them bound for the Shenandoah. The Yankees attempted to cross at Kelly's Ford but were driven back by a sudden blast of rain and hail, which quickly raised the stream above flood stage.

Ten days later, and more than thirty miles downstream, a small fleet was observed crossing the Rappahannock at Port Royal. The light craft carried no more than three hundred soldiers, but heavy columns of infantry clogged the riverbank as if ready to cross in the wake of the little flotilla. They failed to advance, however, and the troops who paddled to the south bank tarried only long enough to scour the vicinity for horses, mules, and other resources worth appropriating from the citizenry. Then, as suddenly as they had come, they returned to the starting point of their raid.

Even in combination, these activities appeared innocuous enough, at least to the unpracticed eye. But to Robert E. Lee they heralded an end to the respite that had prevailed since the Mud March. "Taken in connection with the reports of scouts," he would later recall, the unexpected occurrences "indicated that the Federal Army, now commanded by Major General Hooker, was about to resume active operations."[46]

Officer and Gambler

On the morning of April 4, 1863, in the midst of a freak spring snow-storm, Abraham Lincoln and a small party that included his wife, Mary, and the ten-year-old son they called Tad, boarded a steamer at the Alexandria wharf and sailed down the Potomac to visit the army named for that river. The president was traveling in response to an invitation from the army's commander, Joseph Hooker, to review the troops and confer with the man who would lead them into the spring campaign. Lincoln enjoyed any excuse to roam free of the political pressure cooker that was the nation's capital. Although he traveled infrequently he never failed to appear rejuvenated by the experience. It enabled him to elude the cloud of melancholy that appeared to follow wherever he went in official Washington.

President Abraham Lincoln

The present excursion offered a several-days respite during which Lincoln planned to inspect every corps and nearly every division and brigade of the army. He was in an animated mood throughout the first day of the trip and well into the evening. Long after most of his fellow travelers had retired for the night, Lincoln sat up past midnight chatting with an old friend, newspaperman Noah Brooks. At first lighthearted, the conversation suddenly turned to the impending naval attack on Charleston, which the president seemed to sense would prove a failure, as indeed it would. Before repairing to his cabin Lincoln, who, as Brooks recalled, "had been jocular and cheerful during the evening, began despondingly to discuss the probabilities of defeat." Yet by the next morning, Easter Sunday, when the steamer hove to at Aquia Landing, the main Union supply base on the Potomac, the president had regained his earlier demeanor. He moved with a sprightly step while treating everyone within range of his voice to his trademark humor—simple and rustic to the point of cornball but which, delivered wittily and with adroit timing, never failed to coax a grin from his audience.[1]

At Aquia Landing the presidential party—which also included Attorney General Edward Bates and Dr. A. G. Henry of the Washington Territory, another long-time friend of the Lincolns—trudged through the still-falling snow to a waiting train that would convey it to General Hooker's headquarters. The accommodations were far from fancy, consisting as they did of an ordinary freight car "fitted up," Brooks wrote, "with rough plank benches, and profusely decorated with flags and bunting. A great crowd of army people saluted the President with cheers when he landed from the steamer and with 'three times three' when his unpretentious railway carriage rolled away."[2]

Rocking and jouncing down the tracks toward Falmouth, the train traversed a countryside blighted by war, passing "half-destroyed fences, and the ruins of dwellings and outhouses without any inhabitants." Arriving at Falmouth Station the visitors were greeted by Hooker's chief of staff, the portly, urbane Maj. Gen. Daniel Butterfield of New York, founder of a transportation company that would become known as American Express. After an exchange of official greetings, the visitors boarded two ambulances in which they traveled, flanked by a cavalry escort two hundred strong, to the spacious private dwelling the army leader had appropriated for his quarters.

Much of Lincoln's visit would be taken up in elaborately staged reviews of various units of Hooker's command. The first day was to be devoted to Maj. Gen. George Stoneman's cavalry corps. The weather, however, was so raw and the ground so mushy that the event was postponed until the sixth. In the interim, the president dined with Hooker, who introduced to the president

68

and his entourage not only General Stoneman but also the commanders of the army's seven infantry corps.

The following morning, the snow having ceased, Lincoln and Hooker, trailed by subordinates and staff officers in profusion, traveled on horseback to a vast open plain outside Falmouth, in the midst of which a rough-hewn reviewing stand had been erected. The figures at the head of the elongated procession could not have presented a more marked contrast: the gaunt, sallow-skinned president, looking taller than usual in his black suit and stovepipe hat, his legs dangling in the stirrups of a horse two or three hands too small for his lanky frame; and, riding at his side, the pink-cheeked, clean-shaven general, cloaked in military finery, erect in the saddle astride his white charger. Whether inspired by the sight of two powerful men or tickled by the incongruity of their pairing, the soldiers who lined the road to the parade ground cheered and waved their caps in unfeigned delight.[3]

For fully half an hour the commander in chief, escorted now by General Stoneman, rode along the lines of horsemen. The next hour and a half was consumed by the mounted units, accompanied by four horse artillery batteries, marching past the reviewing stand. The splendidly mounted columns presented a spectacle so grand as to call forth expressions of admiration not only from the onlookers at Falmouth but possibly also from the Rebel pickets on the Fredericksburg side of the river. Spectacle, however, could be deceptive. As army officer and historian John Bigelow points out, "Lincoln was not a soldier. He could not critically inspect or test the great machine that he had come to see. Nor was it exhibited to him in a way to show its essential excellencies or deficiencies."[4]

Rather, these reviews were primarily intended to give the president a sense of how thoroughly this army—which had been decimated under Ambrose Burnside—had been revived and reconstructed under that luckless general's successor. The symptoms of this transformation could not have escaped even a neophyte warrior like Lincoln. In fact, everywhere he went on this trip it was obvious that the unruly, wrathful mob that had seethed with resentment over its sacrifice at Fredericksburg even as it mourned the loss of so many comrades had evolved into a well-conditioned, well-armed, well-equipped fighting force, its morale high, its confidence restored. This was an army anxious to prove itself to an enemy that had humiliated it while bleeding it dry on the frozen earth before Marye's Heights. It was obvious, as well, that virtually to a man

National Archives

Maj. Gen. Joseph Hooker, USA

the army considered Joe Hooker its savior—an attitude Hooker wished conveyed to his civilian superior as forcefully as possible.

The elaborate, carefully crafted way in which Hooker had set out to influence Lincoln's perception of him was characteristic of the man. He was driven to promote himself relentlessly, especially to those who, like the president, not only wielded power but had the ability to confer it upon others. As Lincoln's host saw it, no one was more deserving of power and authority than Joseph Hooker. For this reason he stands as a near-classic example of what twenty-first-century psychologists classify as someone with chronically high levels of self-esteem. Such people tend to believe they possess desirable qualities—intelligence, attractiveness, wit, taste, popularity. They see themselves in a positive light regardless of whether this image is consistent with reality. And they take a jaundiced view of those who fail to agree with them.[5]

High self-esteem people are poor at self-assessment and high on self-deception. While a majority of his soldiers credited Hooker for positive acts such as those that had enabled them to regain poise and confidence, Hooker had more than his share of critics in uniform. These not only faulted him on purely military grounds but also for character flaws that Hooker could not have, or would not have, acknowledged.

Two of the most frequently noted characteristics of those high in self-esteem, especially those with narcissistic tendencies such as Hooker displayed, are optimism about their ability to achieve and succeed, and boastfulness in proclaiming that ability. High-esteem people also tend to criticize and blame others who pose threats to their self-image. At every level of army command Hooker had criticized his superior officers and faulted their abilities, decisions, and performances. He had not been averse to condemning trivial mistakes or blaming others for undesirable outcomes beyond their ability to control. Such behavior had been quite effective in promoting Hooker's career. He had risen to the top of the Army of the Potomac—the greatest prize of his long and varied military career—largely because he so deftly undermined his former superior, Burnside, and so persuasively urged his colleagues to do the same, that Lincoln concluded the army leader had lost the confidence of his subordinates, a situation that militated against the army's success.

As for optimism and boastfulness, these were as much a part of Hooker's character as his unflagging quest for advancement. Throughout the president's visit, Hooker barraged his guest with grandiose pronouncements of future operations. He several times repeated, with minor variations, his central theme, that the spirited veterans under Lincoln's eye were members of "the finest army on the planet." As soon as the spring campaign opened, no one could prevent these men from overwhelming Robert E. Lee's weather-beaten, ragged, half-starved troops and ending the war in the East virtually in a single stroke.[6]

The highlight of the president's visit was a dinner party that Hooker threw for his visitors, at which each of his corps commanders was present. It was a festive night of good food, choice wine, and animated conversation, but Noah Brooks, for one, noted with disapproval the words that Hooker kept feeding his most influential guest: "One of his most frequent expressions when talking with the President was 'When I get to Richmond,' or 'After we have taken Richmond,' etc." This repeated reference bothered Lincoln. Perhaps during the party but more likely on a later occasion he quietly but firmly corrected his general: Lee's army should be his primary objective. As a politician, Lincoln understood better than any soldier that by this point in the conflict the life's blood of the Confederate nation was in its military forces. If Lee's army were crushed—even if Rebel forces in the West remained intact and menacing—the war would end in a matter of weeks.[7]

This was not the extent of the advice Lincoln imparted during his visit. Even when not engaged in battle, Hooker should "fret" his opponent and "continuously harass and menace him." Lee had already detached from his army to gather provisions on the Southside; Hooker should strike before these troops returned to Fredericksburg. Still another piece of advice the president withheld until the eve of his departure. When alone with Hooker and his senior subordinate, Maj. Gen. Darius N. Couch, commander of the Second Corps, Lincoln spoke of the failure of McClellan at Antietam and Burnside at Fredericksburg to commit fully their abundant resources. "I want to impress on you two gentlemen," he said slowly and distinctly, "in your next fight put in all of your men."[8]

The president could not judge whether his words had been taken to heart. Up to the moment he entrained for the return to Aquia Landing, Hooker continued to bend his ear about the ease with which he would overpower the opposition and the early date at which the president could expect to hear of the army's success. Lincoln said nothing but he could not help thinking that other commanders had spoken just as confidently of their prospects. He had put his trust, successively, in McDowell, McClellan, Pope, and Burnside. He had accepted their assessments of their army's power and readiness, had believed their predictions of victory—perhaps only because he had wanted to believe them. In the end, however, each man let him, and the country, down. And here was another making the same promises but in a louder voice, one that fairly swaggered. When alone for a moment with Noah Brooks, Lincoln said with a sigh: "That is the most depressing thing about Hooker. It seems to me that he is overconfident."[9]

JOSEPH HOOKER, the fifth of his line to bear that name, was born in the sprawling agricultural town of Hadley, Massachusetts, on November 13, 1814. He was the fourth child and first son of Joseph Hooker IV, a native of Cambridge, and his second wife, Mary Seymour Hooker, of Hadley. At the time of the boy's birth, the Hooker family enjoyed moderate prosperity arising from a dry goods store of which the elder Joseph was proprietor. But economic stability did not endure. The War of 1812, then still in progress, had a profound effect on the Hookers much as it had, albeit for different reasons, on the family of Robert E. Lee. By depriving American merchants of hitherto fertile sources of raw material and foreign markets for their exports, the war with Great Britain brought on a business depression that struck New England especially hard. The dry goods business foundered, and the Hooker family went down with it. Joseph IV tried to make a living at another occupation, but, as his son's biographer, Walter H. Hebert, notes, "he never got back on his feet financially. He seemed whipped by his business reverses, and only the resolution and courage of Mary Hooker kept the family going." By 1817, the downturn in the family's finances forced it to move out of a spacious, comfortable home and into smaller, rented quarters along the banks of the Connecticut River.[10]

The demands of his new career as a cattle buyer forced Joseph IV to be frequently away from home. His youngest child grew up in a feminine household presided over by his strong-willed mother. Mary Hooker loved her daughters but she doted on her blond-haired son, in whom, at an early age, she believed she saw greatness. She taught him the virtues of hard work although she undoubtedly spoiled him to some degree. Joseph took her words to heart and labored unstintingly at any number of odd jobs to provide additional income for his family—gathering wood for fuel, driving neighbors' cows to pasture, and harvesting the broom corn that, until the advent of tobacco growing, was the area's principal cash crop.

The family's economic distress notwithstanding, Mary was determined that her children should receive a solid education, at least part of it financed by their own labors. For his part, Joseph paid his tuition at the local academy by toiling in Hadley's broom and brush industry. Because the demands of his job prevented him from devoting optimum time to his studies, he did not excel in the classroom except in a few favorite subjects. His impressive performance in one of these, public speaking, suggests that at an early age he enjoyed presenting himself, his words, and his ideas before an audience.

As was true of the Lee family, the choice of a profession for the youngest son was left to his mother. In later life, Joseph recalled that Ann Hooker originally intended that he should enter the ministry, a preference that, in light of his later, irreligious lifestyle, he considered "an infinite joke." Apparently the family had no clerical tradition and when her son showed no interest in starting one, Ann turned her attention, as well as his, toward the military. Here, at least, there was a family link. The boy's grandfather had served with distinction in the French and Indian War and the Revolution, attaining a captaincy in the latter conflict. Two of Joseph's uncles had also marched and fought in the Continental army, while a third, older, uncle had furthered British interests in North America by participating in the Louisburg Expedition of 1744.[11]

While Mary Hooker's son had an interest in military history, he seems to have given no serious thought, either in youth or adolescence, to entering the profession of arms. Nevertheless, his mother's unshaken intention that he should receive a finished education made her consider the tuition-free U.S. Military Academy.

She appears to have shared her thoughts with one of Joseph's instructors at the Hadley Academy, who had been impressed by the maturity and aplomb the youth displayed in the classroom even when unable to translate a Latin passage or solve a mathematical problem. The teacher contacted a politician friend, an associate of U.S. Rep. George Grinnell. In the fall of 1832 the congressman was prevailed upon to nominate the seventeen-year-old for an Academy appointment. It came through in time for Joseph to enter the class of 1837, which he did with some of the same misgivings that had troubled Robert Edward Lee.[12]

Thanks to the tutelage of his instructor, Joseph passed the entrance examination (which he probably discovered to be less difficult and exacting than he had been led to believe) and matriculated at West Point. The young plebe may not have thought of himself as soldier material, but he cut an impressive figure in his cadet uniform. His physical appearance at this stage of his life did not alter appreciably until he was well into his forties, when he added a lot of weight. The description of one who observed him years later would have been apt in the summer of 1833: " . . . fully six feet high, finely proportioned, with a soldierly, erect carriage, handsome and noble features . . . a rosy complexion, abundant blond hair, a fine and expressive mouth, and—most striking of all—great, sparkling gray-blue eyes."[13]

To those meeting him for the first time, Hooker's most imposing feature was not his eyes but his skin tone, or "roseate hue," as one contemporary put it. "His complexion is red and white most beautifully blended," this man noted, "and he looks as rosy as the most healthy woman alive. His skin never tans nor bleaches, but peels off from exposure, leaving the same rosy complexion always visible." The tone was capable, however, of variation. Those who observed him when he drank claimed that even moderate alcoholic consumption caused him to flush deeply. At other times, his face would redden due to excitement and stress, causing some who considered him an alcoholic to accuse him of imbibing even when he had not.[14]

Details of Cadet Hooker's West Point experience are lost to history, the result of a fire that gutted the Academy's archives during the year following his graduation. Those documents that survive, however, cast light on his academic achievements, while calling into question some published statements about them. Hooker's biographer contends that he "ranked well above the average in final grades, but in his four years of training he had acquired enough demerit marks to bring his standing down to twenty-ninth in a class of fifty." While correct about Hooker's final ranking, Hebert overstates the impact on his class standing of the demerits the future general amassed at the Academy. During his fourth-class (freshman) year, 1833–34, Hooker picked up only nine demerits, enabling him to rank twenty-seventh out of 242 in the student body on the roll of general conduct. By the end of his third-class year, he had accumulated twenty-eight black marks, followed by twenty-one and sixty-three, respectively, during his junior and senior years. Although the sixty-three represents a threefold increase over the previous total, upon graduation he stood relatively high in general merit—sixty-fifth of 211 students, a ranking better than he had achieved two years earlier.[15]

Rather than the demerits he gained for violating the Academy's numerous, picky, and often arbitrarily enforced rules of conduct, Hooker's academic performance exerted a much greater influence on his overall standing. During his plebe year, he did well in only one of the two core subjects on which his ninety-three-man class was graded, placing thirty-fourth in mathematics, but seventy-eighth in French. He ended his third-class year—by which time the class of 1837 had been reduced by dropouts and dismissals to seventy-six cadets—ranked forty-sixth in military drawing and sixty-second in French, while improving to twenty-eighth in math.

During his second-class year he placed twenty-third out of fifty-nine cadets in chemistry and thirty-first in drawing. And in his graduating year, which encompassed a greatly expanded course load, he performed moderately well in chemistry and drawing but ranked toward the foot of his class in natural philosophy. That year, Hooker's class finally received instruction in various tactical and engineering courses. He scored fairly high in military and civil engineering, and rather low in infantry tactics, while ranking nineteenth in his class in the tactics of the branch in which he would be commissioned, the artillery. It is not surprising, therefore, that on graduation day, July 1, 1837, Hooker ranked below the median of his class. While not a dismal student, he had not impressed his instructors in any discipline—thus his failure to rise higher on the academic roll.[16]

During Hooker's term of study, the late eighteenth-century tactical theories of Jomini continued to dominate classroom instruction at the Academy especially as interpreted by Dennis Hart Mahan (USMA 1824), the recently appointed professor of military and civil engineering and of the science of war. There is no evidence, however, that Jominian thought appealed to the Massachusetts cadet or became a part of his intellectual repertoire. During the Civil War, no one thought to identify Hooker as a student of Jomini or of Jomini's heroes, Napoleon and Frederick the Great. When David Donald asserted that "every serious military student made Jomini's works his Bible," he was not speaking specifically of Joseph Hooker.

His failure to achieve distinction either in the classroom or on the parade ground ensured that he would gain only minor honors at the Academy. In his second-class year he attained the rank of cadet sergeant, but he not only failed to rise higher, he lost his stripes, the cause of which remains unknown. Four of his classmates, however, became cadet captains and eight others gained the rank of lieutenant. The captains included three future general officers, two of whom would fight for the Confederacy: Braxton Bragg of North Carolina and William W. Mackall, a native of the District of Columbia whose academic appointment was from Maryland; the future Union general was Alexander B. Dyer—ironically, a Virginian by birth. The lieutenants in the class included a future colleague and subordinate of Hooker, Connecticut-born John Sedgwick. The position of cadet adjutant—the preeminent honor Robert E. Lee had been awarded eight years earlier—went to Israel Vogdes of Pennsylvania, another future Union general and a gifted mathematician who for twelve years before the Civil War would teach his specialty as a member of the West Point faculty.

All told, the Class of '37 produced thirteen Civil War commanders besides Hooker. In addition to those already mentioned, the list includes Union Gens. Henry W. Benham (the class's number one graduate), Eliakim P. Scammon, Lewis G. Arnold, and William H. French. Among the other Confederates were a future nemesis of Hooker's, Jubal A. Early; John C. Pemberton; William H. T. Walker; and Robert H. Chilton, the lowest-ranking graduate (forty-eighth of fifty cadets) to attain flag rank.[17]

Hooker was one of the more outgoing and popular members of his class although at times he came across as conceited and argumentative. He could be outspoken on issues important to him. Two of these, according to Hooker's biographer, were sectionalism and slavery. Hebert implies that the cadet's anti-slavery proclivities involved him in frequent confrontations with southern-born cadets. This characterization, however, appears overstated.[18]

Although a native of New England—a hotbed of liberalism then as now—Hooker was the offspring of political conservatives with Federalist roots and, as far as can be determined, no strong antislavery principles. In later life he considered himself a Democrat, at least until he found it desirable to curry favor with the Lincoln administration. Fellow officers considered him basically apolitical, a moderate on the slavery question. At the Academy he may have argued—perhaps even fought—with southerners over some aspects of sectionalism, although the geopolitical divisions in the cadet corps during the 1830s were few compared to those of a decade or more later. Still, it seems unlikely that he forged an identity as "one of the more outspoken Yankee cadets" on the subject of the Peculiar Institution.

HOOKER'S APTITUDE for the artillerist's art gained him, upon graduation, a second lieutenant's berth in the most historic unit of that branch of the army, the First U.S. Artillery. His initial duty station was Florida, where the Second Seminole War was in progress. That October several companies of his regiment took station north of Lake Okeechobee, where Fort Pierce was later erected. Over the next nine months, Hooker's unit was mainly involved in noncombat operations of a logistical nature. This was frustrating to the ambitious young officer, who found no opportunity to distinguish himself or gain the recognition of his senior officers.[19]

By the early summer of 1838, the low-intensity conflict being waged by U.S. troops and those Native Americans who resisted resettlement west of the Mississippi appeared to have reached a stalemate. Although the war would stagger on for another four years, robbing the government of blood (fifteen hundred dead) and treasure (more than thirty million dollars in support costs), during the lull in fighting the First Artillery experienced a radical change of station, being assigned peacekeeping duties along the U.S.–Canadian border. Other infantry and artillery outfits served in upper New York amid the "Patriot War" that pitted Canadian regulars against insurgents seeking to unseat the government of Upper Canada. The majority of the companies in Hooker's regiment, however, were dispatched to northwestern Vermont. There they sought to prevent blood from being shed by residents of Maine and New Brunswick vying for possession of the timberlands that skirted that poorly defined border.[20]

Peacekeeping was always arduous and risky, but by mid-1841 cross-border tensions had cooled to the point that Hooker's company was relocated to a quieter spot on the border with Canada. The dimunition of activity meant that now-First Lieutenant Hooker could be spared for a brief tour of staff duty at West Point. The assignment—adjutant of the Academy—was considered a stepping stone to career advancement, as it proved to be in Hooker's case. Within months of returning to his alma mater he was also appointed to the prestigious post of adjutant of the First Artillery.[21]

Returning to his regiment in October, he spent the next four years shuttling from one New England coastal installation to another, followed in September 1845 by a return to the Florida coast, this time at Pensacola. He continued to shoulder his adjutant's duties until May 11, 1846, the day President James K. Polk sent a message to Congress asking that it declare war on Mexico. The two countries had been at odds since March of the previous year when the United States offered annexation to the Republic of Texas over the strident protests of Mexico City. Both countries had rushed military forces to the Texas border, where

Brig. Gen. Persifor Smith, USA

a series of escalating confrontations had prompted Polk's war request, which the Congress granted within forty-eight hours.[22]

Two months after relinquishing his adjutant's duties, the ambitious Hooker, who had applied for a leave from his regiment in order to seek more active duty on the Rio Grande, received notice of his transfer to the staff of Col. of Regulars (and Brig. Gen. of Louisiana Volunteers) Persifor F. Smith, commander of an infantry brigade attached to the army of Maj. Gen. Zachary Taylor. The transfer would grant the young subaltern all the active duty he could have wished for.

Hooker saw extensive action in his first battle under Taylor, Smith, and Brig. Gen. T. L. Hamer, to whose staff he had been transferred. On September

20, 1846, with Hamer's approval, he led a portion of the latter's brigade against the center of the Mexican stronghold at Monterey. The day's action, which featured desperate street-to-street fighting, ended inconclusively, but for the nerve and skill he had displayed throughout, Hooker won favorable notice from General Taylor himself. Though he would seem to have been out of his element leading foot soldiers, the young artillerist's performance would gain him the brevet rank of captain.

Eventually Monterey fell to flank attacks by the troops of Brig. Gen. William Jenkins Worth, who would lend his name to a fort and a city in Texas. After the surrender, Taylor's troops occupied the Monterey area for two months. Hebert suggests that during this period of "leisure and social pleasure," Hooker made amorous inroads among the girls of Monterey, who "did not hold themselves too much aloof from the sunburned *americanos.*" Before long, however, the youngster was trading love for war by wangling a transfer to the army of commanding general Winfield Scott, whose mission was the capture and occupation of the Mexican capital. In April 1847 Hooker joined that part of Scott's command led by Brig. Gen. George Cadwalader. The latter concentrated at Vera Cruz, then moved inland to join Scott's main body on the road to Mexico City.[23]

En route, Brevet Captain Hooker escorted a paymaster's train laden with American dollars. Forty miles out of Vera Cruz, Mexican guerrillas ambushed the train at National Bridge over the Antigua River. Pinned down for a time by musketry, the impetuous officer broke the impasse by leading two companies of infantry across the span and toward a small fort from which most of the fire was coming. His unit carried the position, killing several irregulars, chasing others away, and opening the road for a link-up with Scott. For this gallant feat, word of which quickly made the rounds of Scott's army, Hooker became a major by brevet.[24]

Upon joining Scott in the aftermath of Cerro Gordo, Hooker found himself transferred to the staff of yet another senior commander, Brig. Gen. Gideon J. Pillow. He trudged with Pillow's infantry division from Puebla to Churubusco via the route around the local *pedregal* discovered by Captain Lee of the Engineers. Hooker served with distinction in the subsequent fighting around Churubusco, leading into battle a regiment of *voltiguers* (riflemen) and personally receiving the surrender of an enemy general.

Churubusco was followed by a month-long delay in active operations during which an armistice offer was presented to the Mexican officials. At the end of that period, diplomacy having failed, Scott moved in force against the enemy capital. On September 13, Hooker accompanied another detachment of voltiguers that stormed the western side of Chapultepec Castle. When the assault bogged down, Hooker, with the sanction of the wounded General Pillow, helped lead a second attack farther west at the head of the Sixth U.S. Infantry, whose officers included Capt. James Longstreet and Lt. George Pickett. Although only one of many efforts that finally carried the castle and gave entrance to the City of Mexico, Hooker's dash and courage won the admiration of every onlooker, favorable mention in the reports of both Scott and Pillow, and his third brevet of the conflict.[25]

Despite the escape of Santa Anna and many of his troops from Mexico City, the fall of the capital effectively ended the fighting and provided Brevet Lieutenant Colonel Hooker and his comrades with another much-appreciated period of rest and relaxation in an occupied city. When not on duty, Hooker, as one historian puts it, "soldiered with devastating effect among the senioritas of Mexico City, by whom he was known as 'El Capitan Hermoso'. In fact he was considered the best looking officer in the U.S. army . . . magnificent young Mars, ready to drink, love, or fight."[26]

As the description suggests, Hooker, who had taken a temperance pledge in his youth, was willing to backslide. He was a regular visitor to the local *cantinas*, where he drank much tequila and mescal and, whenever he could get it, good old American whiskey, some of it strong enough to set the throat afire. Card games accompanied his drinking bouts. By diligent practice he developed a reputation as one of the sharpest poker players in the army, noted for his ability to stake all on the turn of a single card. During such stressful moments he must have gone easy on the liquor, lest his flushed face betray a hot hand.

During this period he lost one gamble that would have major repercussions for his career. With the end to active operations in Mexico, a quickly escalating controversy arose involving Generals Scott, Pillow, and Worth. The commanding general charged both subordinates with planting newspaper stories that savagely criticized his generalship at Contreras and Churubusco while exalting Pillow and Worth as the true architects of victory. When both generals denied the charge in a way that bordered on insubordination, Scott placed them under arrest—only to see them released and himself removed from command by President Polk, who viewed Scott as a potential political rival.

In March 1848 a highly publicized court of inquiry sought to adjudicate the controversy between Scott and Pillow (the charges against Worth had been dropped). Hooker appeared before the tribunal in support of Pillow, whose own account of the battles at issue he forcefully substantiated. In the end, the charges against Pillow were deemed unsustained. Scott regained his post as commanding general, but he neither forgot nor forgave Hooker for testifying against him. For once, the poker sharp had dealt himself a losing hand.[27]

AT SOME POINT, Hooker returned to duty on the staff of Persifor Smith. When the army began to redeploy to the States, he returned there in company with the general and other members of Smith's staff including future Union Gen. Edward R. S. Canby. After a brief stint of duty in the Old Northwest, Smith and his aides were transferred to upper California. The officers made the long trip, via steam train, across the Isthmus of Panama and at Panama City boarded a ship for the rest of the voyage. While Smith and the others continued on to San Francisco, Hooker debarked at San Diego, having been detailed as a member of a military commission that would fix the postwar border between California and Mexico. The assignment lasted four months; when it ended, he made the ship voyage up the Pacific coast. Fellow passengers included the wife of the "Pathfinder," the celebrated explorer and army officer John C. Frémont. Hooker captivated Mrs. Frémont with the courtly charm he was capable of exuding in quantity when it served his purposes. One suspects, however, that he would have preferred impressing her influential husband.[28]

At the end of the convivial voyage Hooker joined General Smith at his headquarters amid the farming community of Sonoma. Living arrangements in that historic northern California town proved most agreeable. Hooker shared with colleagues including Capt. Philip Kearny of the U.S. Dragoons a lavish hacienda on the southwest corner of the village square. Across the plaza sat a popular watering-hole, the Blue Wing Tavern, where "whiskey and poker lured the fun-starved trapper and rancher." The establishment catered to a diverse clientele—officers and enlisted men, wealthy landowners and humble servants, law enforcement officials and those who normally avoided them, including Joaquin Murieta, "that black prince of California banditry."[29]

It was at the Blue Wing that Hooker dramatically displayed the gaming skills he had developed during clandestine card games at West Point and had honed during occupation duty on the Rio Grande. One of his poker-playing companions, Dragoon Lt. George Stoneman, made a point of studying his behavior at the card table. Stoneman was impressed by the many games that went his colleague's way strictly due to his skill at bluff and deception. But as time went on, Hooker found it increasingly difficult to face down a challenge from players with as much nerve as he. Years later, in a conversation with the editor-politician Alexander K. McClure, Stoneman, by then a major general of Union volunteers, asserted that Hooker "could play the best game of poker I ever saw until it came to the point when he should go a thousand better, and then he would flunk."[30]

At times, Hooker could summon up the poker face and the air of absolute nonchalance that had won him more than his share of big pots, but long before his duty tour at Sonoma was expected to end, his gaming losses were eating up his military pay almost as fast as he could draw it. Some years later, gambling debts would land him in court when he was sued by a man who had bought a promissory note that Hooker had presented in lieu of cash to one of his many creditors. Either because he could not afford to make settlement, or because he cared little for unfavorable publicity, Hooker refused to pay the debt, which the court ruled to be uncollectable.[31]

Hooker so enjoyed the land, weather, and lifestyle of Sonoma that before his debts could break him he purchased 550 acres of good farmland about three miles west of town. At first he expected to build on the property only after he retired from the army. But peacetime duty so far from the civilized East proved monotonous and enervating. At length he decided to get an early jump on farming. He did so, first, by securing a two-year leave of absence from his regiment. The temporary civilian built a sturdy four-room house and sowed ten acres in grapes.

Hooker's inexperience caused the wine-growing venture he had embarked upon to fail, but he vowed to succeed as a produce farmer. Deciding to commit himself fully to the soil, in February 1853 he resigned his commission. By the most unfortunate timing, a few weeks later the bottom dropped out of the local produce market, all but ruining him. Undaunted still, he proposed to recover by selling goods to local military installations. His army connections helped him land contracts to supply the Benicia Arsenal and the Presidio of San Francisco with cordwood for fuel, but troubles with subcontractors forced him to terminate this latest enterprise.[32]

Hooker, his self-confidence shaken but not broken, promptly entered yet another career field—politics. In 1853 he ran for state assemblyman on the Democratic ticket. The race ended in a tie but in the runoff election he lost by thirteen votes. That same year, however, he was elected overseer of Sonoma County roads. He continued at this job while also farming—on a smaller scale than before—until 1858, when, thanks to his intense lobbying of former colleagues and superiors, he was appointed superintendent of military roads in neighboring Oregon. Among Hooker's notable achievements in this office was the construction of a much-traveled road from Scottsbluff to Canon City that for many years bore his name.[33]

The superintendent's post provided Hooker with a living wage but it was not highly remunerative and his gambling debts continued to exert a drain on his personal finances. Perhaps for this reason, what Hebert calls Hooker's "most eligible days" went by without his taking a wife. Instead, he appeared content to buy the companionship of women of easy virtue, a habit he appears to have acquired during his service in Mexico. He would not marry until he was in his fifties, and the union would be chiefly notable for the sharply declining health of both husband and wife.[34]

Despite making only a subsistence income, Hooker never descended to the abject poverty that some historians describe. The picture they paint of Hooker, during his pre-Civil War years, as a veritable beachcomber does not square, for instance, with his 1859 appointment as a colonel in the California militia. The primary source of this exaggerated characterization appears to have been Hooker's immediate superior in the militia, Henry Wager Halleck, a San Francisco attorney who had been two years behind Hooker at West Point. At the Academy the New York native had developed an abiding interest in Jomini, which permeated the tactical treatise he published in 1846, *Elements of Military Art and Science*, and which impelled him to translate into English the Swiss theorist's monumental *Vie Politique et Militaire de Napoleon*.[35]

Halleck's attempt to denigrate Hooker appears to have been the result of a long and bitter feud between the two men. In the 1850s Halleck, who was then starting out in the legal profession, sought clients. He promoted himself especially hard to Mexican-American ranchers with claims to California lands granted by the Spanish Empire. Although the two had never been

bosom friends either at West Point or in the army, Halleck asked Hooker to advise some of these *rancheros*, with whom Hooker had become acquainted during his army days, to hire Halleck to represent their interests before a government commission seeking to determine the validity of the Spanish claims. Hooker did steer a few landowners Halleck's way. Thus he felt betrayed as well as embarrassed when the latter complained that Halleck had billed them for several thousand dollars in legal fees even before their claims were heard.

Maj. Gen. Henry W. Halleck, USA

Hooker complained to his West Point classmate in terms that he admitted were harsh enough that Halleck never forgot them. Apparently Hooker also told friends, business associates, and militia colleagues that Halleck was a shyster. Little wonder that whatever relationship the two men had forged quickly dissolved in rancor and recrimination. The results of the blow-up would prove to be long lasting, for Hooker had gained another powerful enemy who years hence would be in a position to exact a heavy retribution.[36]

HOOKER'S FAILURE-RIDDEN and trouble-plagued period in California came to an abrupt end a few weeks after the firing on Fort Sumter. Although a staunch Democrat, Hooker, as a military man, supported the hard line the Lincoln administration took against fomenters of secession. Hooker's prominence in the militia enabled him to raise a regiment of California volunteers for service in defense of the Union. In the manner of a West Point instructor, he drilled the would-be soldiers for service in the war that had broken out thousands of miles away. But when the drilling ceased and he readied his outfit for shipment East, he learned that the government—perhaps unwilling to fund the travel costs—would accept no California units for service outside their state.[37]

As a soldier of twenty years' standing, one educated at the government's expense, Hooker believed he owed it to his country as well as to himself to go to war even if his volunteers could not. He lacked the wherewithal to book passage for the east, but he did not lack friends with either the means or the willingness to support him in his time of need. Showing a remarkable degree of charity or patriotism, several of his drinking buddies and gambling partners pooled resources and funded his trip. Other friends—mainly militia colleagues—set up a banquet in his honor on May 20, 1861, the night before he embarked at San Francisco on a steamer bound for New York. Wine and alcohol promised to flow freely that evening, and the warmth of such a sendoff would have placed Hooker in a pleasant frame of mind as he began the long, tedious voyage down one coast and up another.

Uncharacteristically, he politely declined the invitation for fear it would interfere with his preparations for sailing. In a brief note to the sponsors, he expressed both gratification and regret, adding that "I go with a will and a purpose to prove my faith in, and devotion to, the Union, and to find a place however humble, among those who have take up arms to defend it."[38]

Coming from a man such as he, those last words sound arch and insincere, and yet he may have meant them. He may truly have felt humbled, standing as he did on the brink of cataclysmic events fated to work a profound and lasting change upon a nation. Great wars have a way of making a man feel small, insignificant, and introspective—even Joseph Hooker, war hero, lover, farmer, businessman, public servant, poker sharp.

Bravo for Joe Hooker

W hen the July 21 battle along Bull Run turned from a seesaw struggle into a Union rout, not only General McDowell's raw recruits were caught up in the stampede back to Washington. That morning hundreds of civilians who knew next to nothing about war but wanted to learn about it firsthand had ridden out of the capital in company with rear-guard troops going to the front. Throughout that sultry afternoon the good citizens had followed the progress of the battle from a safe distance, some while consuming a picnic lunch. When the Federals began to withdraw, however, the sightseers suddenly started for home en masse. They drove their carriages into the line of retreat, clogging roads and bridges already crowded with demoralized Federals, thus adding to the panic that swept McDowell's ranks.[1]

One who joined the stream of fugitives retreated calmly, at an unhurried pace that suggested an ability to keep his head while all about him were losing theirs. This man was Joseph Hooker, erstwhile brevet lieutenant colonel of U.S. artillery and colonel of California state militia, currently a mere civilian, an undesirable status he seemed powerless to shed. Both in New York City, where his journey from the Pacific Coast had ended seven weeks ago, and then in Washington, Hooker had sought out every military and political official whom he believed could help him land a volunteer commission, but to no avail. Not even a letter of introduction from Edward D. Baker, U.S. senator from Oregon, colonel of volunteer troops, and close friend of Abraham Lincoln, had prodded the War Department into action on behalf of the man who, Baker said, had borne a "distinguished and honorable part" in the Mexican War. Baker or some other third party had placed Hooker's credentials in Lincoln's hands, but the action produced only a note from the president to the commander of the Department of Washington stating Hooker's desire to command a volunteer regiment and asking, "Ought he to have it, and can it be done?"[2]

Evidently it could not, for nothing had come of Lincoln's rather half-hearted intercession. By now Hooker was certain he knew why: the past and present commanding general of the army, Winfield Scott, whom Hooker had testified against at Gideon Pillow's 1848 court-martial, had pigeonholed his application out of spite and a desire for revenge. Hooker seethed with resentment and frustration, but he was helpless to advance his own interests in the face of such powerful opposition.

A few days after Bull Run, with Hooker having all but decided to return to California in defeat, he accompanied another of his Mexican War superiors, George Cadwalader, now a major general of Pennsylvania troops, to the White House in hopes of securing an interview with Lincoln. His brief meeting with the president, who was still recovering from the psychological effects of McDowell's defeat, was cordial enough but apparently nonproductive. When the distracted president abruptly turned away in a gesture of dismissal, Hooker's frustration boiled over and he blurted out: "Mr. President . . . I was at the battle of Bull Run the other day, and it is neither vanity or boasting in me to declare that I am a damned sight better General than you, Sir, had on that field."[3]

The brash words boldly uttered caused Lincoln to halt, turn about, and observe the speaker as if for the first time. He later recalled that Hooker's "eye was steady and clear—his manner not half so confident as his words, and altogether he had the air of a man of sense and intelligence, who thoroughly believed in himself and who would at least try to make his words good." Extending a hand, Lincoln asked his visitor to remain: "I have use for you and a regiment for you to command."[4]

Hooker was elated at this fortuitous turn, but at the same time disappointed that he would be considered for regimental command when other, less deserving applicants for appointments were going to war in higher positions. As it turned out, however, Hooker did not have to settle for the lesser berth; ten days after Bull Run his name magically appeared on a list of eleven nominees for brigadier general sent to the Senate Military Committee. Hooker's nomination had been advanced by the Massachusetts congressional delegation, a generous gesture in light of his several-year residency in California. On August 3, his nomination was confirmed, his appointment being backdated to May 17 for purposes of seniority. Thirty-three other brigadier appointments, including that of Ulysses Grant, took effect on that same date, but Hooker was officially declared to be senior to all but fourteen of these. His turnaround of fortune had been almost unbelievably swift, but no more so, he reflected, than his past service warranted.[5]

General Hooker on his war horse

Upon being notified of his appointment, Hooker visited the tailor's, where he was fitted for the gilt-encrusted uniform of a brigadier, which, however, he did not don for some days, perhaps because he could not afford the bill until he drew his first pay. He did manage to purchase a fine war horse to carry him through the fighting that lay ahead. Aboard the steed, he repaired to the northern Virginia headquarters of George B. McClellan, commander of the Army of the Potomac. Although twelve years older than the "Young Napoleon," whom he had outranked in the prewar army, Hooker was impressed by his new superior, whom he believed he could serve with profit to the service and honor to himself. In turn, McClellan was gratified to have under him an experienced officer whose well-known talents would help him whip the demoralized fugitives of Bull Run into a command the enemy to the south would learn to respect and fear.

After leaving McClellan, and while still in mufti, Hooker joined his new brigade in camp at Bladensburg, Maryland. There, near the right-of-way of the Baltimore & Ohio, he commenced instructing its components—two regiments from Massachusetts, one each from New Hampshire and Pennsylvania. All were in dire need of training, their officers and men equally ignorant of the basics of soldiering, to say nothing of the nuances. Hooker could see that his work was cut out for him. But he was happy to have any work at all to do, any role to play in this great national drama that would make or break the reputation of many a soldier. He had entered the war late, but now that he was in he intended to make the most of his opportunity.[6]

IT WAS THE SPRING of 1862 before Little Mac could bear to commit to field campaigning the army in which he had invested so much effort, emotion, and time—eight months of almost incessant maneuvering across drill plains that stretched for miles along both sides of the lower Potomac. By now Hooker, who had done an exemplary job of persuading the recruits at Bladensburg that they could become soldiers in fact as well as in name, had been promoted to lead a division consisting of his original brigade, now commanded by Brig. Gen. Cuvier Grover (USMA class of 1850), plus the four New York regiments that composed the so-called "Excelsior Brigade."

The officer in direct command of the latter organization had also recruited and organized it: former congressman Daniel E. Sickles. A nonprofessional soldier but a quick study in the art of war, Sickles brought to the volunteer army the reputation of a *bon vivant* whose public behavior could outrage polite society. His primary claim to notoriety dated to 1859, when, within sight of the White House, he stalked and then shot to death his wife's lover, Philip Barton Key, U.S. attorney for the District of Columbia and son of the composer of the "Star-Spangled Banner." (Sickles's subsequent murder trial ended in acquittal thanks to the then-novel defense of temporary insanity as

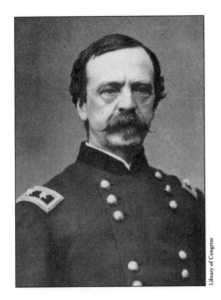

Maj. Gen. Daniel E. Sickles, USA

skillfully argued by his chief counsel, Edwin McMasters Stanton, now the imminent successor to Simon Cameron as Lincoln's secretary of war). Not surprisingly, perhaps, Hooker forged a warm friendship with his somewhat notorious subordinate as he later would with Col. Dan Butterfield, a sophisticated New Yorker with a taste for wine, women, and bugle calls (the following summer he would compose the haunting refrain known as "Taps").[7]

Hooker got to test his enlarged command in battle for the first time when McClellan, at Lincoln's demand, finally moved to the seat of war. He shipped his army, more than one hundred thousand strong, down Chesapeake Bay, bound for Richmond via the Virginia Peninsula. The promising offensive, however, bogged down outside Yorktown. After wasting a month besieging Johnston's troops, Little Mac pursued the Confederates through Williamsburg. Outside the old colonial town, Hooker, whose division formed part of Maj. Gen. Samuel P. Heintzelman's Third Army Corps, saw his first battle action since the capture and occupation of Mexico City. McClellan was not on the field; the battle was directed by his senior subordinate, Edwin Vose Sumner, an elderly and slow-moving commander whose caution in engaging the rear of Johnston's column Hooker thought excessive.

Frustrated at being forced to fight James Longstreet's division at arm's length, Hooker called for reinforcements that would enable him to assume the offensive, but Sumner demurred. Without orders, the inveterate gambler impulsively attacked Longstreet's heavier force, a decision that cost Sickles's New Yorkers dozens of casualties but kept the Rebels off-balance. When a part of his line broke, Hooker chased down the fugitives and by word and gesture persuaded most of them to return to the firing-lines.

For a time his unauthorized advance threatened to cost Sumner the battle and perhaps Hooker his new command, but the day was saved when another of Heintzelman's divisions, under Hooker's old Sonoma comrade Philip Kearny, now also a brigadier of infantry, reached the field at the head of another division just in time to shore up Hooker's lines. The battle ended with the enemy resuming their retreat up the Peninsula but much the worse for wear for having tangled with Hooker.[8]

For his dramatic seizure of the initiative as well as for the courage and leadership he had displayed throughout the fight, Hooker was the recipient of favorable newspaper coverage. Now or shortly thereafter, he received

Brig. Gen. Philip Kearny, USA

a celebrated nickname, supposedly applied to him through the error of a compositor on a New York newspaper who merged two separate phrases and headed a report of the fighting on the Peninsula "FIGHTING JOE HOOKER." Its recipient never liked the title, believing it made him sound like a battle-hungry fool. Yet it would cling to him for the rest of his life.[9]

At about this same time, Hooker added a dubious element to his reputation. When McClellan, apparently resentful that a subordinate should reap so much glory and he himself so little, failed to mention Hooker's command in his early reports of Williamsburg beyond citing its heavy losses, Hooker's relations with his superior took a downturn. Thereafter, he was so critical of Little Mac's abilities that he became known in some quarters as a malcontented army politician. Hooker's artillery commander expressed the opinion of many critics when he wrote in his diary that his superior was "bound in honour [sic] not to speak against McClellan for he owes his promotion in the volunteer service, and his commission as Brig. Gen. . . . to McClellan. I am sorry though that such considerations have but little influence with him. . . ."[10]

The hard knocks it had taken at Williamsburg for a time relegated Hooker's command to rear-guard duty. Its leader speedily patched the holes in his ranks and rejoined the army in time for the battle of Fair Oaks, Joe Johnston's last fight with the Army of Northern Virginia. Held out of action on the first day, Hooker's division was heavily engaged on the second, again being cuffed about by superior numbers until reinforced by Phil Kearny. At last able to advance, Hooker encountered a swamp that an officer of another division claimed could not be crossed. Hooker roared at the man: "Get out of the way. I have two regiments here that can go anywhere!" Pushing through the muck with remarkable speed, his command drove its opponent from the field at the point of the bayonet.[11]

During the nearly month-long lull that followed Fair Oaks, Hooker grew restless for another opportunity to show his and his division's ability. It came his way on June 25, when Hooker's command opened the Seven Days' battles with a hard-driving attack on Lee's picket lines at Oak Grove (or King's Schoolhouse), then against large columns of infantry farther to the rear. Caught up, much against his will, in McClellan's subsequent retreat to the James, Hooker saw action on two more of the Seven Days, White Oak Swamp (Glendale) on June 30 and Malvern Hill the following day. In both actions his troops gave a strong account of themselves, shielding the rear of McClellan's main body as it fled south in what Hooker considered shameful haste. Despite its denouement, however, the campaign added to Hooker's laurels. He had proven himself a stout fighter regardless of the odds against him, willing to take a risk and contemptuous of danger. Viewing him in action at this stage of the conflict, one of his officers described him as "always present on the field, alert and vigilant, conspicuously mounted on a white horse—with flashing eyes, florid face, and high shirt collar, that soon wilted down when we got engaged— but as cool and collected under fire as if directing a parade or a picnic."[12]

When McClellan's army was removed from the Peninsula, Hooker went west with the Third Corps to reinforce John Pope in his showdown against Lee, Longstreet, and Jackson. Instead of marching overland, the division moved by ship to the doorstep of Washington, then by the Orange & Alexandria Railroad to Manassas Junction and from there to Warrenton Junction. Hooker's first mission on this new front was to run to earth Jackson's troops, who had cut the O & A at Manassas just after Fighting Joe and his men passed through. Hooker promptly advanced on the enemy, which had moved to Bristoe Station, and in a several-hour fight on August 27 drove Maj. Gen. Richard S. Ewell's division from that depot.[13]

Two days later, having joined Pope, Hooker was directed to assault, with half of his command and without ready reinforcement, the left center of Jackson's line along the Groveton-Sudley Road. Hooker protested the order, which he considered suicidal, but when Pope insisted he led the attack. At first it appeared to succeed despite the odds; the men of Cuvier Grover overran a Rebel brigade in their path and caused others to waver. In the end, however, the outnumbered attackers were repulsed at a loss of one-third of the number engaged. "It was the most brutal kind of fighting," writes one historian. "—many of the dead were bayonetted or had their skulls staved in by the butts of muskets." Hooker had been beaten, but only because the obtuse Pope had failed to support him with so much as a single regiment.[14]

After being caught up in yet another humiliating retreat to the Washington defenses, the army was reorganized under McClellan. Subsequently Hooker moved up to command one of Pope's corps, which, as a result of its integration with Little Mac's forces, became the First Corps, Army of the Potomac. Early in September, Hooker led nearly fifteen thousand soldiers toward the place where Lee had crossed the Potomac into Maryland. On the fourteenth the corps fought stoutly and long to secure Turner's Gap in South Mountain, and two days later it experienced its share of the horrific carnage along the Antietam.

Hooker's men landed the opening blows of the fight on the seventeenth, shoving John Bell Hood's Confederates through cornfields and woodlots until the sluggish pace of the overall offensive enabled Lee to shift forces from quieter sectors and halt Hooker's drive. In the desperate, close-up fighting that resulted, the newly minted corps leader took a rifle ball through his foot. The disabling wound forced him to the rear. Although some critics later charged that the injury was less severe than Hooker claimed, it hobbled him for weeks. While recuperating in the capital, he was ministered to by two of his married sisters, who rushed to his side from their homes in New England.[15]

During his convalescence—which was rendered the more bearable by word that he had been appointed a brigadier in the Regular army—Hooker made the acquaintance of influential civilians including one who would become his political patron, secretary of the treasury Salmon P. Chase, the handsome, charismatic leader of the abolitionist wing of the Republican Party. The two highly ambitious men soon reached an accommodation and forged an unlikely alliance: Chase would champion Hooker for higher command and Hooker would vocally support Chase in his projected run for his party's nomination in 1864. It was at this point that long-time conservative Democrat Joseph Hooker began to think of himself as a convert to Republicanism and the antislavery cause.[16]

WHEN MCCLELLAN LOST his command early in November 1862, Chase worked hard to replace him with his new protégé. He could not, however, overcome the opposition of Hooker's opponents, which included not only General in Chief Halleck but also Secretary of War Stanton. Instead, the prize went to Ambrose Burnside, whose poor performance at Antietam told Hooker that the government had chosen most unwisely. Even after Burnside elevated him to the command of the two corps that made up the army's newly designated Center Grand Division, Hooker criticized his superior mercilessly although not to his face, faulting almost every administrative decision he rendered and every operational move he made. Burnside quickly became aware of Hooker's near-insubordinate behavior but retained him in hopes of profiting from the skill and courage the man always exhibited in battle.

Maj. Gen. Ambrose E. Burnside, USA (standing, center) with his subordinates, November 1862: Brig. Gen. Marsena R. Patrick (standing, far left); Brig. Gen. Henry J. Hunt (seated, far left); Maj. Gen. Winfield S. Hancock (seated, second from left)

Yet not even those qualities could save the army from Burnside's almost criminal stubbornness and tactical ineptitude, which at Fredericksburg on December 13 combined to produce a defeat of epic proportions. Late that day, after the battle was effectively lost—Edwin Sumner's Right Grand Division having been decimated in front of Marye's Heights and elsewhere along Lee's near-impregnable line—Burnside ordered Hooker's Fifth Corps, under Dan Butterfield, to be thrown into the cauldron. As he had at Second Manassas, Hooker tried mightily to convince his superior the folly of such an assault, to no avail.

As a grand division commander, he correctly remained on the Falmouth side of the Rappahannock while Butterfield's troops went forward into a blizzard of shot and shell. After observing their mounting losses for an hour or more, however, Hooker became so distressed that he galloped across the river and brought the futile effort to a halt. By then, as he later explained with naked sarcasm, "I had lost as many men as my orders required me to lose."[17]

If Hooker's censure of Burnside had been harsh and unremitting before Fredericksburg, it increased geometrically once the army limped back to Falmouth to salve its many wounds, and especially after it endured the Mud March. By mid-January 1863, Hooker's blows appeared to take effect, as Burnside's hold on his position began to slip. After a complaint session with Hooker, Maj. Gen. George Gordon Meade, future commander of the Fifth Corps, recorded that his colleague "spoke very freely . . . gave one or two hits at Burnside, and rather hinted it might not be very long yet before he was in command" of the army.[18]

By now Hooker had spent some time politicking in his own behalf among those Washington officials who could advance his career—not only Secretary Chase but also Sens. Ben Wade of Ohio and Zachariah Chandler of Michigan, members of the powerful Joint Committee on the Conduct of the War, a military watchdog panel with a radical Republican tinge.

Hooker's machinations provoked Burnside to try to rid himself of Hooker and other vocal critics of his generalship. The day after the Mud March ended, the army leader drew up a list of those to be decapitated and prepared to issue it publicly. The rather long-winded draft of General Order No. 8 announced that Hooker was being dismissed from the service "as a man unfit to hold an important commission during a crisis like the present." The grand division commander was charged with "having been guilty of unjust and unnecessary criticisms of the actions of his superior officers, and of the authorities [in Washington], and having, by the general tone of his conversation, endeavored to create distrust in the minds of officers who have associated with him, and having, by omissions and otherwise, made reports and statements which were calculated to create incorrect impressions, and for habitually speaking in disparaging terms of other officers . . ." In addition to the principal miscreant, three brigadiers were ordered dismissed, while six officers including Maj. Gen. William B. Franklin, commander of the army's Left Grand Division, and one of Franklin's corps commanders, Maj. Gen. William Farrar Smith, were relieved of command as being "of no further service to this army."[19]

Burnside was about to promulgate his sensational order when a staff officer reminded him that it could be done only upon the approval of the commander in chief. A suddenly prudent Burnside presented it to Lincoln at a meeting at the White House, declaring that if the order were not sanctioned he would resign his command. The president's reaction, while not totally unexpected, was a blow to Burnside's pride. Lincoln did not doubt that his general had been systematically undermined by a cabal of discontented subordinates, but he appreciated the furor the order would generate. Furthermore, he doubted that the army could afford the loss of so much senior leadership, however basely these men had acted. He therefore disapproved the order, which was never published, and regretfully accepted Burnside's resignation.[20]

Hooker did not learn of the existence of General Order No. 8 until a fortnight after it was written, and when he read it he was incensed. In a subsequent conversation with the army's chief provost marshal, Brig. Gen. Marsena Patrick, he swore that he would make Burnside eat his words or Hooker would "have his ears, as soon as the War is over." Almost twenty years later the document, which Hooker called "conceived in sin, and born in iniquity," continued to infuriate him. Given Hooker's chronically high levels of self-esteem, he could never view himself in the harsh light of Burnside's criticism, a characterization he considered monstrously incorrect. As Hooker saw it, his criticisms of his superior had been intended not to hurt anyone but to help the army in its hour of darkest distress. Why did so few people seem capable of understanding his motivations?[21]

WHATEVER HIS TRUE INTENT, Hooker's words and actions had been highly effective. Once Lincoln had determined to let Burnside go, he had almost no one to turn to besides Fighting Joe. The latter, at least, had the advantage of popularity outside the army; Lincoln believed him to be "stronger with the country today than any other man." Hooker also enjoyed the advantage of rank. Other generals worthy of promotion such as George Meade and Maj. Gen. Henry W. Slocum, commander of the Twelfth Corps, were junior to him by date of appointment. More senior commanders—Sumner and Heintzelman, for example—were too old and infirm. Other possible successors to Burnside, including crusty General Couch and John F. Reynolds, the much-admired commander of the First Corps, did not want the position due to the political problems that came with it. Lincoln had misgivings about the ability and possibly the loyalty of still other ranking officers, notably Franklin. After brief consideration, he called Hooker to the White House on January 26, 1863, and, over the continuing objections of Stanton and Halleck, appointed him to command the Army of the Potomac.

In acting as he did, the president was not rewarding intrigue and insubordination; he was merely bowing to the demands of necessity. He made his reservations clear in an extraordinary personal letter handed to the new commander on the day of his appointment. In it Lincoln admitted that there were "some things in regard to which I am not quite satisfied with you. . . . I think that during General Burnside's command of the army, you have taken counsel of your ambition, and thwarted him as much as you could, in which you did a great wrong to the country and to a most meritorious and honorable officer."[22]

Lincoln went on to mention credible rumors that disturbed him. For one thing, Hooker had declared that both the army and the nation needed a stronger hand—or, as he put it, a dictator. Hooker had indeed said as much in conversation with Henry J. Raymond, editor of the *New York Times*. "Of course," Lincoln added, "it was not for this, but in spite of it, that I have given you the command. Only those generals who gain successes can set up dictators. What I now ask of you is military success, and I will risk the dictatorship."[23]

Supposedly Hooker was chastened by Lincoln's well-intentioned admonition, which he vowed to respond to once "I have won him a great victory." Although the humility in this response sounds forced or contrived, Hooker may have intended to show his subordination to one whose goodwill would be crucial to his pursuit of self-worth through military success.[24]

Another phrase that suggests synthetic humility was Hooker's expression of his state of mind upon being elevated to command of the Union's premier fighting force: "I trembled at the task before me, in entering upon so important a Command." He repeated this sentiment in much the same language before Senator Wade's oversight committee. Upon the latter occasion, however, he also admitted to a self-serving motivation: "to vindicate myself from the aspersion that I made use of improper influences to obtain the command."[25]

Hooker also told the committee of how he had negotiated with Lincoln as to the extent of his new command. He claimed to have turned down the opportunity to expand his authority over the defense forces of Washington, now headed by General Heintzelman, and units stationed on the upper Potomac. He gave as his reason for declining so much additional power his concern "that I would not be able to save the Army of the Potomac [from demoralization] if my whole time was not devoted to its rescue."[26]

Hooker also recalled extracting a concession from Lincoln, upon which rested his acceptance of army command. It strains credulity to suppose that he would have turned down the president's offer had any condition not been met. Even so, Lincoln granted Hooker's stipulation that in his official relations with the government he be permitted to deal directly with the president, bypassing Halleck. Hooker believed the commanding general nursed a grudge against him dating to their California years, one that militated against a productive working relationship. His concerns presumably allayed, Hooker returned to Falmouth and announced his assumption of command.[27]

Not surprisingly, his succession drew mixed reviews from the officers and men he would lead in the field. The army knew of his combativeness and coolheadedness under fire—like Robert E. Lee, battle exhilarated him and brought out some of his best qualities—and the fact that he always seemed to get a lot of hard fighting out of any troops he led. These attributes won him a certain amount of approval. One admirer observed that "he always goes at everything with a dash." Another claimed that impeccable manners made Hooker "a perfect model of a gentleman."[28]

Yet a majority of the army's senior leadership did not think much of Lincoln's choice. According to General Patrick, in the army as a whole "confidence enough is felt in Hooker," but he lacked support among senior members of the officer corps. More than a few of his inherited subordinates continued to pledge allegiance to their first commander, whom Hooker had criticized and undermined as he had Burnside. As one officer put it in a letter to a politician friend, "Hooker is not very popular with our wing of the Army . . . General McClellan's men." Another officer stated flatly that "McClellan alone has the confidence of this army." The conservative clique of the army's hierarchy, including Generals Couch, Smith, and Meade (the latter having been Stanton's and Halleck's choice to succeed Burnside) feared that Hooker, while competent enough at the division and corps level, would prove a failure in army command. Meade at least had the good grace to add that were fighting spirit the only quality required in such a position, Hooker "will certainly distinguish himself."[29]

Some critics viewed Hooker's combativeness as a drawback rather than an asset. As one put it, the new commander had proven himself "too rash & anxious to fight." A comrade agreed that "as far as haste or rashness is concerned Hooker is worse than Burnside"—a low blow, considering that Burnside's primary fault was not rashness but an inability to modify, cancel, or postpone a decision he had spent long hours making but which events had proven to be impracticable. A New England soldier was fatalistic in his outlook: "We all expect Hooker will soon make his grand failure & patiently wait for it."[30]

A few of Hooker's subordinates believed his personal habits unfitted him for high station. Charles F. Adams Jr., a captain in a Massachusetts cavalry regiment, wrote his father, the American minister to the Court of St. James, about the new leader, "who in private character is well known to be—I need not say what." Maj. Gen. Oliver Otis Howard, recently appointed to head the army's Eleventh Corps—a cold-water man of long standing who had studied for the ministry before entering West Point—strongly disapproved of Hooker's reputation as a tippler, which he feared would bring both him and the army to grief.[31]

That reputation was an old and hoary one, but it appears that Hooker strove to keep it current even after ascending to army command. According to General Patrick, a stern-minded Puritan who relentlessly assailed the army's moral quotient, less than a month after taking command Hooker went on a bender and gambling spree in Washington, losing the pay he had recently drawn. A few weeks later Patrick fielded a complaint from an army surgeon who had witnessed a drunken Hooker topple from his horse while riding through one of his camps. Yet others who claimed to know him well, did not consider Hooker a frequent imbiber. One asserted that "though thrown in very close contact with him through six months, I never saw him when I thought him the worse for liquor." General Meade testified that whatever Hooker's former habits, "since I have been associated with him in the army I can bear testimony of the utter falsehood of the charge of drunkenness."[32]

Other perceived flaws and shortcomings inspired doubts among the rank-and-file. Col. Charles S. Wainwright, the well-educated commander of Hooker's First Corps artillery, found the man wanting in intellect: "Hooker may have learned a great deal since I left him, but judging from what I saw, I do not think him much of a general in the higher branches of that position. His bravery is unquestioned, but he has not so far shown himself anything of a tactician." Wainwright also faulted the army leader for his overweening pride and egotism, believing that "it is well for a commanding general to have confidence in himself and in his plans, but I fear that Hooker has too much of it. He certainly talks too much about what he can do; it sounds very much like braggadocio, and should he fail, great will be his fall." Meade agreed that Hooker "talked too much and too indiscreetly," especially among the politicos in Washington. For his part, Captain Adams of the cavalry considered his commander a fraud; any example of humbuggery that came to Adams's attention he described as "pure Joe Hookerism."[33]

WHETHER OR NOT HE ENJOYED its confidence at the outset, before he was through with it Hooker intended to make the army his own in thought, word, and deed. The best way to do this, he theorized, was to restore the morale, the self-confidence, and perhaps the will to fight that had been lost somewhere between the Maryland campaign and that humiliating slog through the January mud. He saw with clarity how the army had deteriorated, physically and mentally, under his predecessor. As he informed Secretary Stanton when attempting to defend himself against the charges leveled at him in General Order No. 8, Burnside had "no other idea of the organization and government of an army than that of arranging it in a way that the commanding general will have nothing to do. . . . In his opinion, this army had become tolerably good during his exercise of its command, and yet it was on the verge of dissolution; he did nothing and knew nothing of it." Hooker would not make the same mistake.[34]

Confident that some day the government would wake up to a realization of his genius, Hooker had prepared long and hard for the position he had finally succeeded to. For months he had made a mental list of those reforms he considered vital and which he was now in a position to institute. He believed these would bear fruit because the army was fertile soil. Although under Burnside it had become almost fatally disorganized and demoralized, Hooker considered the discipline that it was capable of displaying "superior . . . to that of our adversary." He admired the inner strength he perceived in this misused command, which he contrasted with the flawed work ethic of the enemy. Looking back years later on the army's first campaign under his command he pronounced it "a contest between sinews, and muscles hardened by labor with those who never knew what work was."[35]

Maj. Gen. Daniel Butterfield, USA

In his efforts to rectify the army's material deficiencies and revive its spirit, Hooker was ably assisted by the officer he selected as his chief of staff, Dan Butterfield. His reliance on the dapper New Yorker mystified many subordinates. Butterfield may have enjoyed administrative and organizational talent, but as a former militia commander with no real-world military experience he was looked down upon by the professionals among the officer corps. Because Butterfield did not care what others thought of him, he had no incentive to moderate his officious, condescending nature or curb his desire to play army politics. As a result, he was widely disliked, feared, and criticized. Colonel Wainwright called him "most thoroughly hated by all . . . as a meddling, over-conceited fellow." Brig. Gen. Andrew A. Humphreys, a division commander in the Fifth Corps, agreed but went further, calling the staff officer "the most detested and most despised man in the Army, false, treacherous, and cowardly." On numerous occasions General Patrick expressed himself as "much disgusted" with the man he called "Dan the Magnificent," particularly with "the view he takes of our affairs—his Ex Cathedra way of speaking, & the flippancy of the whole Head Quarter[s] establishment," which the man appeared to embody.[36]

Along with Dan Sickles, Hooker and Butterfield formed what Charles Adams, in an allusion to the generals' unsavory past, called "the drunk-murdering-arson dynasty now prevailing" at headquarters. The proper Bostonian considered the unholy three "the disgrace and bane of this army, they are our three humbugs, intriguers and demagogues," whose immoderate behavior gave the entire army a bad name. For a time after Hooker's assumption of power, Adams's unit did escort duty at army headquarters, which the captain later described as "a place where no gentleman cared to go, and no lady could. It was a combination of bar-room and brothel."[37]

Some faulted Hooker less than the other members of the triumvirate, considering him a pawn in the hands of the more sophisticated New Yorkers. George Meade voiced this view in a letter to his wife. Although he considered Hooker a good soldier, "the danger he runs is of subjecting himself to bad influences, such as Dan Butterfield and Dan Sickles, who, being intellectually more clever than Hooker, and leading him to believe they are very influential, will obtain an injurious ascendancy over him and insensibly affect his conduct."[38]

Still, Hooker needed Butterfield's administrative expertise as much as he craved the companionship of the dissolute but warm-hearted, life-loving Sickles. With his chief of staff's ready support, he began to tackle the many problems that plagued the army, problems that would prevent it from achieving peak performance in its first campaign under him. Believing that the quickest way to a soldier's heart was through his stomach, Hooker began by streamlining the army's commissary department to ensure that everyone was issued rations of better quality, greater quantity, and richer variety. This change worked wonders in quick time. By mid-February soldiers were writing home in glowing terms about their improved diet. A New York infantryman spoke for many when he declared that "Fighting Joe Hooker is . . . becoming [a] favorite with us because he has ordered that we shall have fresh bread four days a week . . . Bravo for Joe Hooker." By early April, a cavalry officer, previously critical of the army leader, was admitting that "I like old Joe Hooker better now than I did two months ago. . . . We get more potatoes in a week now than we used to get in a month." Still another frequent critic of the high command paid a backhand compliment to Hooker when he wrote: "Soft bread, Potatoes, onions, Molasses, beans, beef, and butter are among the things we now eat. Like a herd of poor oxen they are fattening us for the slaughter."[39]

Another way Hooker sought to improve the army's health was by upgrading its medical care and promoting soldier hygiene. These goals he attained with the unflagging support of his medical director, Dr. Jonathan Letterman. According to one historian, Letterman, "mandated the rotation of campsites, improvement of drainage ditches, removal of latrines from living areas and the vicinity of water supplies, and the regular airing of tents, huts, and bedding. In early April he even persuaded Hooker to order every soldier in the army to wash both their clothes and themselves." To complement Letterman's reforms, Hooker approved the convening of examining boards to weed out inefficient or lax surgeons just as similar panels had rid the army of line officers who failed to measure up to their responsibilities. These efforts served to produce a dramatic decrease in the army's sick rate. During the three months prior to Hooker's assumption of command, more than 134,000 soldiers had reported sick, and 1,500 of them had died of noncombat-related causes. Through the first three months of Hooker's regime, the sick roll contained fewer than 90,000 names, and only 1,068 of them succumbed to disease.[40]

If the army had unmet physical needs, its psychological and emotional requirements were just as serious, if not more so. Angered and dispirited by its treatment under Burnside, the men showed their dissatisfaction by dropping out of the ranks at an alarming rate, many never to return. Soon after taking command, Hooker studied the absenteeism problem and was shocked to find that the army was short 81,964 enlisted men and 2,922 officers, about half of whom apparently had deserted or were absent without leave.[41]

This drain could not be permitted to continue, and so Hooker applied himself diligently to reversing the trend. He instituted a variety of reforms aimed at raising esprit de corps and appealing to a soldier's self-respect and his sense of responsibility to his comrades. One affirmed a basic and yet often-neglected right. When Hooker took over, most of the army had not been paid in six months or more. As one historian writes, "men who had enlisted under the conviction that their pay would enable them to support their families were daily receiving letters from the latter representing their destitution and distress." For his part, Hooker saw to it that paymasters made more regular visits to regiments and batteries, even those on the outermost lines. When the army took the field in the spring of 1863, the paymasters accompanied the troops even to the front lines, sometimes distributing pay under fire.[42]

Another morale-building effort melded inspections and furloughs. Hooker increased the army's inspectors to cover fully every arm of the service. Each brigade was assigned an inspector who reported regularly on deficiencies in equipment, arms, ammunition, and other areas and made certain his recommendations were acted on by the headquarters staff. Formal inspections of brigades, divisions, and corps were conducted more frequently and were extended to the previously neglected picket lines of the army.

On occasion, Hooker personally conducted unit inspections. On a particularly cold night in the dead of winter, he visited the far picket lines of the army. Appalled to find half-frozen men shivering in a snow bank, he ordered them back to camp and berated their commander for not relieving them in timely fashion. One officer who observed the incident called it "a small & a transparent act" but admitted that it made a positive impression on the men, who began to feel that someone at headquarters—*the* man at headquarters—was looking out for them.[43]

The revamped inspection process not only made the soldiers believe the army was concerned with their welfare but provided a fair and regular basis for awarding furloughs. Under Burnside, furloughs had been issued infrequently and inequitably. Under Hooker they were made more available and, to ensure impartiality in their allocation, were linked to the inspection process. As General Butterfield testified before Congress, "a system of furloughs to deserving men was instituted, giving to regiments that bore proper inspection and were in good condition leaves of absence for ten days to two officers of each regiment; and furloughs for ten or fifteen days, according to the State from which the men came, to two out of every one hundred men present for duty." He added, unnecessarily: "The order gave great satisfaction."[44]

Hooker further tackled the morale problem by reinstating a drill and instructional program that had lapsed under his predecessor. By increasing a soldier's workload this effort risked incurring the army's displeasure, but once they returned to regular drill most men saw the benefit of it, especially since hundreds of recruits joined the army at Falmouth, threatening to lower a unit's tactical proficiency. Then, too, drill combated idleness, which Hooker called "the great evil" of soldiers everywhere. Therefore, "whenever the weather would permit it, they were engaged in field exercises . . ."[45]

Small, seemingly trivial, measures as well as large, highly visible ones helped raise spirits throughout the ranks, stimulate unit pride, and create a sense of corporate identity. Hooker gave new impetus to an old but neglected program to allow units to inscribe their flags with the names of battles they had taken part in. "No better incentive," he believed, "could be given in this army for future effort than this honorable recognition of their past services." He also permitted each corps to have its own flag, a hitherto-dormant means of increasing large-unit identity.[46]

By far the most popular of Hooker's small-scale attempts to raise morale was his adoption in mid-March 1863 of a plan developed by Butterfield, under which each corps would be identified by its own insignia: a roundel (the symbol of the First Army Corps), a trefoil (Second Corps), a diamond (Third Corps), a Maltese cross (Fifth Corps), a Roman cross (Sixth Corps), a half moon (Eleventh Corps), and a star (Twelfth Corps). The badges were colored red, white, or blue depending on whether they indicated the corps' first, second, or third division. Each soldier would wear the insignia in the form of a cloth badge sewn on the crown of his hat or cap. In time, the badges became so popular that men purchased nonregulation copies made of brass or copper, which they wore on the breast pockets of their uniforms or affixed to some item of equipment.

The idea of corps badges appears to have originated with Phil Kearny during the Peninsula campaign. Hooker's old comrade-in-arms (who had fallen mortally wounded after Second Bull Run) had instituted an informal system of badges so that he might identify at a glance the men of his own division, especially those who merited punishment for misdeeds. When Butterfield moved to make the issuance of badges armywide, he envisioned the practice as a means of enhancing battlefield control and discouraging straggling, but it was soon perceived as increasing unit morale. Twenty years after the war Hooker observed that their issuance had a "*magical* effect on the discipline and conduct of our troops. . . . The badge became very precious in the estimation of the soldier, and to this day they value them more than anything beside."[47]

Hooker's reforms extended to headquarters support organizations and entire branches of the service. One of the most valuable of these special departments did not exist prior to his assumption of command. As his chief of staff observed, before Hooker took over "there was not a record or document of any kind at headquarters of the army that gave any information at all in regard to the enemy. There was no means, no organization, and no apparent effort to obtain such information."[48]

All that changed when Hooker established a Bureau of Military Information headed by Col. George H. Sharpe. This organization systematically gathered, interpreted, and disseminated intelligence on enemy troop strength, movements, and intentions. Sharpe and his handpicked subordinates operated a network of military scouts, civilian informants, and spies from all walks of life, one that coordinated its functions, more or less closely, with General Patrick's provost command.

Through the diligent and imaginative efforts of Sharpe and his officers, army headquarters was continuously supplied with remarkably accurate data on the strength and organization of Lee's army. Thanks to the assistance of local Unionists, the bureau also provided Hooker with what later generations would call real-time strategic intelligence. Sharpe was even able to plant false information that Confederate signalmen intercepted and relayed to their army's headquarters, contributing to operational miscues that furthered Hooker's strategic and tactical designs.[49]

Hooker's intelligence-gathering efforts were aided by an aerial observer corps headed by the nation's foremost civilian "aeronaut," Professor Thaddeus Sobieski Constantine Lowe. The professor's two helium-filled observation balloons had been supporting the Army of the Potomac, with a fair degree of effectiveness, since McClellan's tenure. Because military ballooning was in its infancy, however, Lowe's ability to observe and report accurately on enemy positions and movements was inconsistent and sometimes erratic, dependent as it was on clear weather, calm winds, and the talents of his ground support personnel. Lowe was also hamstrung by the controlling tendencies and obstructionist tactics of the army officer to whom Hooker subordinated him, Lt. Col. Cyrus B. Comstock. More dependable was the communications support provided by the army's network of flag- and torch-bearing signal officers, and by the civilian telegraphers who accompanied the maneuver elements of the army, filling the distances between them with miles of insulated wire connected to 150-volt wet batteries.[50]

One of Hooker's most sweeping reforms, one that brought him quick and consistent returns, involved upgrading the effectiveness of his cavalry. Under McClellan, Pope, and Burnside, the army's horsemen had been largely neglected, their special needs ignored, their unique talents untapped. Until Hooker's ascendancy, the cavalry had been utilized at less than maximum strength, usually reduced to companies, squadrons (composed of two companies), or battalions (two squadrons) for field service. Denied effective organization and commanders of their own, the arm had degenerated to a mere

Prof. Thaddeus S. C. Lowe and his observation balloon

appendage of the army, derided by infantrymen and artillerists as summer-soldiers or comic-opera warriors (a prevalent taunt being the sarcastic inquiry, "Whoever saw a dead cavalryman?").

Hooker strengthened the arm both materially and psychologically. He made sure it received remounts on a regular basis as well as sufficient tack and equipment to do its job. He provided it with state-of-the-art weaponry that included the single-shot breech loading carbine and repeating rifles that cavalry needed to make an effective showing against enemy troops of all arms. Perhaps his most far-reaching cavalry reform, however, was his grouping of more than ten thousand officers and troopers into a single, separate corps. He placed over it a poker-playing cohort from his Sonoma days, Brig. Gen. George Stoneman, for whom Hooker procured the second star that gave him the authority he needed in his dealings with his infantry colleagues.[51]

Hooker's reforms were not universally successful. By moving so quickly and so drastically to improve the proficiency of the command he made a few notable missteps, the effects of which would not become evident until active

108

campaigning began. By ordering the widespread substitution of slower and less reliable pack mules for mule- and horse-drawn supply wagons, he compromised the efficiency of army transportation. By abolishing in early February his predecessor's grand division organization, he decentralized command and control. Instead of the three subordinates with whom Burnside had to deal, Hooker would have to communicate his orders to the leaders of eight corps. This would prove cumbersome at best. General Howard offered one explanation for the change: Hooker's sense of power and control would be enhanced by "maneuvering several independent bodies."[52]

Perhaps Hooker's greatest mistake in the name of operational efficiency was to demote the army's long-tenured and highly respected chief of artillery, Brig. Gen. Henry J. Hunt. Prior to Hooker's coming, Hunt had served as both administrative head and tactical commander of the army's batteries. By aligning Hunt's units with the army's infantry divisions, whose commanders thereby gained effective control over them, Hooker stripped Hunt of most of his operational responsibilities. In effect, the latter was reduced to command of the army's eleven-battery Artillery Reserve. This was bad enough, for Hunt's expertise was critical to the smooth functioning of his arm, but Hooker made things worse by assigning no more than four batteries to a division. This move lowered the chances that his army would dominate a battlefield with massed firepower.[53]

These miscues notwithstanding, by the end of the winter of 1862–63 Joe Hooker had done much to change the Army of the Potomac for the better. When warm weather returned to the Rappahannock basin and with it the imminence of active operations, the main Union fighting force in the eastern theater was better equipped than ever before to meet on an equal footing its highly vaunted enemy across the river. The army's physical and moral revival was evident to all who had a modicum of perceptivity, and the majority of those who benefited from Hooker's reforms appreciated his efforts in their behalf. One of them, a field-grade officer in Stoneman's cavalry, expressed the thoughts of many comrades when writing home from Falmouth in mid-March 1863: "Gen[eral] Hooker took this army in the gloomiest moment, when discouragement prevailed, when demoralization was apparent to any one, when no one thought it could be rescued from being disbanded . . . and by unceasing toil, by severity and kindness, he has rebuilt its foundation, extracted the rotten beams and replaced them by sound ones."[54]

No wonder that Hooker, reviewing the effects of his rebuilding program, pointed to the future with exuberant optimism, declaring that Robert E. Lee and his troops would prove no match in an open fight against "the finest army on the planet."[55]

Plans and Preparations

I n mapping out his strategy for the spring campaign, Joe Hooker had a great deal of leeway. The only instructions governing his future movements given him by Washington had come in the form of a communiqué from Halleck's office five days after Hooker assumed command of the army. The letter, which Hooker assumed bore the imprint of Lincoln himself, merely informed the new leader that "you can best judge when and where it [the army] can move to the greatest advantage, keeping in view always the importance of covering Washington and Harper's Ferry, either directly, or by so operating as to be able to punish any force of the enemy sent against them."[1]

By late March or early April Hooker had a pretty good idea of what he wanted to accomplish when active campaigning resumed, but how to pull it off was the sticking point. He wanted to confront the enemy directly, but a wide river separated them and the other side was lined with observant sentinels and combat troops strongly entrenched. Obviously he could not cross in the Confederates' immediate front, but outflanking them would be a difficult and delicate business especially if the weather turned bad as it had during Burnside's swan song of an advance last January.

Burnside's attempt at passing Lee's left flank having failed, his successor considered turning the enemy right by throwing pontoon bridges across the river downstream from Fredericksburg. A crossing there would be effectively shielded by the army's artillery, and once on the other side he might maneuver in such a way as to threaten Lee's railroad link to Richmond, causing him to pull up stakes and relocate closer to his capital. The latter prospect remained Hooker's objective, but he finally decided that the strong line of works Lee had extended all the way to Port Royal would prove too tough a nut to crack. By early April he had given up that idea and was planning anew.[2]

The concept of striking Lee's lines of communication remained a good one, and this furnished a basis for Hooker's second plan of operations. The mighty corps of horsemen he had created and placed under George Stoneman was eager and willing to take on a major operation, its first at full strength. Hooker believed Stoneman's command capable of getting into Lee's rear quickly and once there wrecking the Richmond, Fredericksburg & Potomac Railroad, Lee's principal line of supply. The spies and scouts employed by Colonel Sharpe's intelligence bureau, who included a loyalist resident of the region beyond Fredericksburg, one Isaac Silver, had brought word that Lee had not stockpiled supplies in the immediate vicinity of his army. If cargo traffic on the R, F & P could be disrupted for any length of time, Lee would have to retreat, either straight to Richmond or southwestward in the direction of the railhead at Gordonsville. Once in motion, he would be easy prey to the mobile elements of Hooker's main army, which their commander considered capable of a devastating pursuit. In fact, the army had organized a fast-reaction force tailored to just such an operation, the so-called "Light Division" (actually a large brigade of infantry, complete with artillery support), a component of Maj. Gen. John Sedgwick's Sixth Corps.[3]

On April 12 Hooker sent his revamped plan to the White House via General Butterfield. The commanding general's appreciation of the need for operational secrecy was such that he would permit only the president to examine the document—even Secretary of War Stanton was left out of the loop. Lincoln saw promise in the plan and

Maj. Gen. George Stoneman, USA

112

approved it. The very next day Hooker sought to put it in motion. Stoneman, whose troopers had been placed in readiness for marching at a moment's notice, started out in good style. He planned to cross the Rappahannock at Kelly's Ford, scene of General Averell's St. Patrick's Day success over Stuart and Fitz Lee. But after one brigade had waded across there, beyond the left flank of Lee's main body, rain, sleet, and even hail came down to raise the river and make everyone involved absolutely miserable—a scene eerily reminiscent of the Mud March. Stoneman's operation came to a dead halt and remained suspended for two weeks.[4]

Not until April 27 did the river recede sufficiently to permit a crossing. By then Hooker had been forced to reshape his plan of campaign yet again. Although he assured the anxious Lincoln that the failure of the thirteenth was not Stoneman's fault, Hooker would no longer rely on his mounted arm to turn Lee out of his position. When the army was able to march, it would move out in full strength. Stoneman would precede it, crossing in the same locale, but now he would clear a path for the infantry and artillery, which would also move below the Rapidan River and into Lee's rear behind Fredericksburg.

As Hooker saw it, the threat this movement would pose to the health of the Army of Northern Virginia would be so serious that as soon as Lee detected the enemy's presence in his rear, he would abandon his long-held position and head south. En route, if Stoneman had done his job properly, the Confederates would be caught between the cavalry and the main army.

Given its potent combination of size and speed, Hooker expected the mounted wing to play a large role—even if no longer the primary one—in this pincers movement. Stoneman's revised orders would expand on those originally assigned him. Instead of merely hammering at a single communications line, he would split his force into raiding parties charged with striking various and sundry targets, most of them of a logistical nature. As before, the mounted leader would be expected to lay a heavy hand on the railroad to Richmond. But as soon as he learned of Lee's fallback, Stoneman would recall his detachments and get "in position with your full force to cut off the retreat of the enemy by his shortest line. In all other respects your instructions as before referred to will remain the same." In those earlier instructions, Hooker had told his cavalry chief to "let your watchword be fight, and let all your orders be fight, fight, fight, bearing in mind that time is as valuable to the general as the rebel carcasses."[5]

Hooker was correct to direct Stoneman's attention to the matter of timing, always a critical element in any plan but even more so in this one. In enlarging Stoneman's mission, enjoining him to disperse and destroy, then reconcentrate and block Lee's path of retreat, Hooker would be complicating matters for his cavalry. Stoneman would have to keep a close eye on the clock; otherwise his mission would degenerate into a mere raid, scattering destruction across a wide area instead of focusing it where liable to do the most harm.

To the extent that it would support the main effort around Lee's left, Hooker clung to his original idea of laying pontoon bridges downstream of Fredericksburg. Two of his army corps, Sedgwick's and the First Corps of John Reynolds, plus one of General Couch's Second Corps divisions, that of Brig. Gen. John Gibbon, were in such proximity to the Rebels opposite Falmouth that they could not shift position without giving away Hooker's plans. Thus he would leave them where they were, at least at the outset. When the flanking movement began, he would send them across floating bridges to be erected near the point where General Franklin's Grand Division had crossed on December 13—a place now known, logically enough, as Franklin's Crossing. Once on the far side, the troops, under Sedgwick's overall command, would demonstrate against Fredericksburg, holding Lee's troops in place and distracting his attention from the flank drive.[6]

The feinting operation below Fredericksburg would improve the chances of the turning movement, but the latter, the cornerstone of Hooker's new strategy, remained a risky and delicate maneuver. It would entail moving five army corps—Meade's Fifth, Howard's Eleventh, and Slocum's Twelfth, to be joined in motion at some point by Couch's Second and Sickles's Third—a distance of twenty miles across the enemy's left flank along a stream so narrow in places that it invited opposing pickets to fraternize by wading across it.[7]

Hooker's intelligence-gathering apparatus had been the determining factor in his new plan. Not only had Colonel Sharpe compiled a remarkably accurate order of battle for the Army of Northern Virginia, he had determined how many troops under Longstreet had left the Fredericksburg front, as well as the location of the gaps thus created in Lee's defenses. By ascending high above the opposing lines, Professor Lowe had given army headquarters a fairly clear picture of Lee's dispositions, at least those south of Fredericksburg, the line held by Jackson's corps. The positions occupied by what remained of Longstreet's command west of the town in the direction of a giant forest known as the

Wilderness were more difficult to survey. But in mid-April, even as Hooker was rethinking his plans in the wake of Stoneman's failure to cross at Kelly's Ford, Isaac Silver brought Colonel Sharpe news of great importance. Silver, whose farm lay three miles east of Chancellorsville, a crossroads clearing along the eastern edge of the Wilderness, reported that the large force of infantry and artillery that had occupied his neighborhood as recently as six weeks ago had decamped for points unknown. The only units of any size below the Rappahannock in the vicinity of Silver's farmstead were portions of three brigades from the division of Maj. Gen. Richard H. Anderson. They covered two crossing sites on the Rappahannock not far from that river's confluence with the Rapidan: United States Ford and, almost three miles closer to Fredericksburg, Banks's Ford.

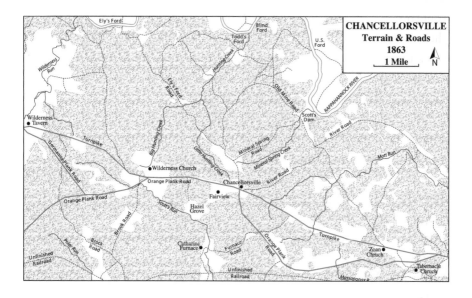

Most of the troops hugged the riverbank, although a large detachment was stationed three miles farther inland. Silver estimated the total force at fewer than forty-five hundred foot soldiers, supported by a couple of light batteries. Thus, no Confederates covered two of the three roads that ran through the Wilderness toward Fredericksburg and which could be easily reached via Kelly's Ford: the Orange Turnpike and the Orange Plank Road. Hooker saw at once that he could use those virtually unobstructed thoroughfares to sneak up on Lee from his blind side.[8]

There was still the problem of getting to Kelly's Ford unobserved, which involved a long, roundabout march to escape detection by cavalry pickets patrolling the length of the riverbank. If the tread of shod feet and the clouds of dust they would generate did not catch the Rebels's attention, then the passage of artillery teams, pack mules, and ammunition wagons would. This gloomy prospect threatened to ruin Hooker's strategy yet again. Before all was considered lost, however, another fortuitous piece of information reached army headquarters. By interrogating a captured signalman, Colonel Sharpe's people learned that the Rebels had broken the Army of the Potomac's signal code. This intelligence enabled Hooker's signal stations, under the guidance of Lt. Samuel T. Cushing, the army's chief signal officer, to wig-wag a report that Stoneman's troopers were embarking on a raid through the Shenandoah Valley. To permit immediate interpretation by the enemy, the message was sent not in the compromised cipher or in the form of an official message that would necessarily have been encoded, but in an uncoded, conversational manner that gave the impression of a chat between signalmen. The Confederates perceived it as such and regarded the message as authentic.

The effect of this stratagem was twofold. It permitted Stoneman to cross the river without unduly arousing the suspicions of enemy scouts and pickets. Of greater advantage to Hooker, the hoax prompted Lee to counter the phantom movement by directing Stuart to detach Fitz Lee's brigade from its position along the river and send it to the Shenandoah. Thus, when the turning movement got under way, that portion of Lee's cavalry normally in position to observe it would be far away and looking in the wrong direction.[9]

Even with these advantages, Hooker's offensive entailed risk. Had he his druthers, he would have preferred to cross his flanking column over the river at United States Ford or Banks's Ford, which lay far enough in Lee's rear to permit a devastating attack from an unexpected quarter but one delivered on mostly open ground that would promote unit cohesion and facilitate communication. But because these fords, as Mr. Silver confirmed, were still held in some force, Hooker could not use them without alerting the enemy to his intentions. By swinging far upstream and crossing at Kelly's Ford he would protect the element of surprise, but the need for secrecy would increase the distance to be covered and thus the time required to get into the enemy's rear.

Once below the Rappahannock Hooker's troops would proceed south across the Rapidan River at Ely's and Germanna Fords—twelve and seventeen miles, respectively, from Fredericksburg. Those crossing sites provided entrance to the Wilderness. If Lee should receive timely warning of Hooker's advance and move to counter it before the Federals cleared the forest, all bets would be off. In that event, the advantage would probably shift to the Confederates who, having occupied that wooded region for months, had a much better knowledge of the local topography than anyone in Hooker's columns. Hooker pushed those unpleasant considerations out of mind as he mapped out the details of his proposed movement.

His strategy, as embodied in this, his third and final plan of operations, appeared to pivot on his determination to attack and destroy Lee before he could reach the defenses of his capital. This is the light in which historians have long viewed Hooker's intentions. Typical is the commentary of one of the most recent students of the Chancellorsville campaign, who has termed Hooker's plan "the boldest and most daring" operation he ever undertook, one far more innovative than anything any of his predecessors had conceived of.[10]

Bold and daring it was in conception, but it did not even need to be fully executed to gain the objective Hooker had in mind. For he was not planning to engage Lee in full-scale battle between Fredericksburg and the forest to the west. Rather, his strategy was predicated on Lee's turning and running the minute he discovered himself outflanked and caught between two fires. Hooker believed his plan so powerful that Lee could not oppose it effectively—he would have no other course than to flee south in full retreat. When that occurred, Hooker would pursue but without expectation of bringing Lee to bay short of Richmond, although he might attempt a stand along the North Anna River, only fifteen miles above the capital. In effect, then, the plan itself—not Stoneman's cavalry, not the multicolumn turning movement— would evict Lee from his formidable position and send him scurrying toward a city that could be besieged into submission. McClellan had had the means to effect a successful siege in the summer of '62, but had lacked the heart, or the intestinal fortitude, to pull it off. Joe Hooker was certain that he himself had the nerve to succeed where the Young Napoleon had failed.

The repercussions of a successful investment of the enemy capital—and Hooker could envision nothing short of Richmond's surrender and occupation—would surely occur in time to influence the 1864 presidential election.

Hooker was no politician, and he had no overwhelming desire to unseat Abraham Lincoln, whom he sincerely admired and respected. But Salmon Chase, who had hitched his star to Hooker's success in the field, had such a desire. If Hooker helped put the treasury secretary in the White House, Hooker could expect certain favors—for starters, his replacement of his hated rival, Henry Wager Halleck, as General in Chief of all the Union armies.[11]

THROUGH MOST of the winter, Robert E. Lee had been unimpressed, although occasionally provoked to mirth, by the fitful stirrings of his opponent across the river. As late as April 24, in a letter to his wife at her residence-in-exile in Richmond, the Confederate leader derided Hooker's preparations for the coming campaign: "The enemy is making various demonstrations either to amuse themselves or deceive us, but so far they have done us little harm."[12]

He enumerated some of Hooker's stranger movements. The previous week his soldiers had "infested" the upper Rappahannock fords, including Kelly's, and a few days later had abandoned them. Next, the Yankees "sent down the river their infantry & artillery & with their cavalry swept around by Warrenton towards the Blue Ridge as if intending to visit the Valley. Day before yesterday they made their appearance on the lower Rappahannock. Formed in line of march, threw out skirmishers, advanced their artillery, brought up their wagons, built up large fires, & after dark commenced chopping, cutting, & sawing as if working for life till midnight, when the noise ceased & at day light all had disappeared but 8 or 10 men keeping up the fires. I suppose they thought we were frightened out of all propriety & required refreshment."[13]

Lee could see no strategic value in these maneuvers—they could scarcely be called operations—but he doubted that would dissuade the enemy from crowing over their effectiveness: "Their expeditions will serve for texts to the writers for the [New York] *Herald, Tribune* & *Times* for brilliant accounts of grand Union victories & great rejoicings of the saints of the [Republican] party. I hope God in His own time will give us more substantial cause for rejoicing & thankfulness."[14]

Within three days of writing Mary, however, Lee's attitude toward what his enemy was up to had changed markedly. On the twenty-seventh he sent a dispatch to James Longstreet, then well into a siege of the Union garrison at Suffolk even as his foragers continued to harvest the abundant farmlands of the region. Lee had been apprised by the head of the Confederacy's small but resourceful secret service bureau in Richmond that Hooker's army recently had been reinforced to a total of about one hundred sixty thousand officers and men. Lee did not credit this figure—which, as it turned out, was a reasonably accurate estimate of the aggregate present and absent strength of the Army of the Potomac—but the reinforcement operation concerned him a great deal: "This looks as if he intended to make an aggressive movement, but by what route I cannot ascertain."[15]

Other recently received intelligence had only deepened the mystery. The previous day J. E. B. Stuart had reported the presence of a large body of Stoneman's cavalry near Warrenton Junction on the Orange & Alexandria Railroad several miles northwest of Kelly's Ford. Unknown to Stuart, Stoneman had massed there in preparation to cross at and near the ford, in advance of Hooker's flanking column, on the morning of the twenty-ninth. Then, too, a brigade of Yankee infantry had been observed in the vicinity of Rappahannock Bridge, which carried the tracks of the O & A across the river toward Brandy Station and Culpeper Court House. The foot soldiers had taken position on both sides of the bridge, as if to prevent interference with the operation of the railroad on the north side.

Although Stuart had failed to determine that troops were being shuttled down to the river, Lee was concerned that Hooker intended to use the railroad to threaten the far end of the Confederate left. He had been suspecting a movement of some sort in that general vicinity. Four days earlier he had informed Stonewall Jackson that despite Hooker's recent raid on Port Royal, "I think that, if a real attempt is made to cross the river, it will be above Fredericksburg." How far above remained the vexing question.[16]

The portents looked ominous enough to make Lee think about reinforcing his own army. In his letter to Longstreet he asked: "Can you give me any idea when your operations will be completed and whether any of the troops you have in Carolina can be spared from there?" While he hoped he had sufficiently conveyed his concern, he was not ready to put a stop to a foraging operation ordered by Richmond and that seemed so vital to the welfare of the Army of Northern Virginia. "As regards your aggressive moment upon Suffolk," he added tamely enough, "you must act according to your good judgment."[17]

This same day Lee warned Jefferson Davis in an official dispatch that in his present position he did not feel entirely secure from attack, "and from the condition of our horses and the amount of our supplies I am unable even to act on the defensive as vigorously as circumstances may require." In the light of the enemy's recent buildup, and given Lee's doubt that the Federals would move against Charleston in the wake of Flag Off. Samuel F. Du Pont's failed attack on Fort Sumter, he sounded out Davis about the return of Brig. Gen. Robert Ransom Jr.'s division, which had been sent to North Carolina after Fredericksburg to free up troops for the defense of Charleston.[18]

That afternoon Lee shared with one of his officers some thoughts on Hooker's intentions, thoughts he had not put into his communications with Longstreet and Davis. Capt. James Keith Boswell, Stonewall Jackson's engineer officer, paid a visit to army headquarters at Hamilton's Crossing along the railroad four miles south of Fredericksburg. There he had a brief conversation with Lee, who enjoyed chatting with young subordinates. At one point the army commander expressed his belief that "Hooker was intending to advance, and would have done so on Friday [the twenty-fourth] but for the rain." This was a reference to the storm that had broken on the thirteenth and which had continued, almost without interruption, to the present. Until it stopped entirely, the roads would be too soggy to permit a forward movement of any size by Hooker.[19]

But where, when the weather cleared, would that advance come? The cavalry buildup around Warrenton Junction—even though Lee had been led to believe that its destination was the Valley—and the recent infantry movements in the same vicinity suggested that Hooker intended to cross the river beyond Lee's upper flank. Of course, it was quite possible that these movements were feints calculated to divert attention from a crossing somewhere else, perhaps downstream from Fredericksburg, or perhaps in the same general area where Burnside had crossed his main army in December.

The range of possibilities was troubling, but it had been so, it seemed, since Genesis, and so Lee decided to expend no additional energy attempting to sort them out. He trusted, as always, that Stuart's troopers would provide timely warning of an enemy advance. In that event, he surely would have the time he needed to concentrate against any threatened point, making a crossing—even multiple crossings—difficult and dangerous, and perhaps impossible. In his almost sixteen months in army command, Lee had never found himself at a loss to counter any move his many opponents had attempted. He had no reason to believe otherwise now for, as he had so pungently observed, the Lincoln government had yet to oppose him with a general he did not thoroughly understand.

HOOKER HAD PUT the final touches to his strategy, but he was wary of sharing it with anyone—not with his own generals, not even with his president. On the nineteenth, Lincoln and Halleck had made a quick trip to Aquia Landing to meet with Hooker, but at the brief conference the army commander had failed to communicate the substance of his latest and finest plan. By the twenty-sixth—two days after the incessant rains appeared to have run their course at last—Hooker had put the army under notice to march at any time. But he had yet to tell his corps commanders—even those who would conduct the all-important flanking march—their roles in the grand scheme

Maj. Gen. George G. Meade, USA

of things. That same day, George Meade complained in a letter to his wife in Philadelphia that "Hooker seems very confident of success, but lets no one into his secrets. I heard him say, that not a human being knew his plans either in the army or at Washington. . . . All I ask and pray for is to be told explicitly and clearly what I am expected to do, and then I shall try, to the best of my ability, to accomplish the task set before me."[20]

Hooker's mania for secrecy had its roots in the frequency of information leaks throughout the army, which had warned Lee of Union dispositions, movements, and objectives. Some of this intelligence came from those pickets who crossed the river to trade coffee beans for plugs of Confederate tobacco. The unlicensed press, however, was a bigger culprit in the spread of information regarding the army. Those big-city newspapers with the wherewithal and the influence to place reporters inside the army regularly printed stories that gave away military secrets, speculated dangerously on plans under development, and released statistics on army strength and composition. Seeing at first hand the results of this incautious reporting, Hooker had tightened control over the reporters traveling with the army, and he forbade his staff from divulging any information that the enemy could use against it. Still, Hooker was haunted by the prospect that someone, whether private soldier or gentleman of the press, might release word of the coming movement. He knew that gaining and maintaining surprise would be critical to the success of his strategy.[21]

Hooker on this day, April 27, did permit himself to divulge the substance of his offensive plan to two people. He sent a letter, by one of his staff officers, to the White House. The letter conveyed Hooker's appreciation of the president's anxiety to know what was about to happen on the Rappahannock. Therefore it disclosed the basic outline of the offensive. Though Hooker provided few details, he did enclose some maps for the president's perusal. Even this limited information pleased Lincoln, who expressed his gratification at having been taken into his general's confidence. He added that Hooker should not suppose that he was "impatient, or waste a moment's thought on me, to your own hindrance, or discomfort." Abiding by Hooker's wish for secrecy, Lincoln agreed to show the communiqué to neither Stanton nor Halleck.[22]

Maj. Gen. Darius N. Couch, USA

National Archives

Late that same day, with some of the troops involved in the flanking column already in motion, Hooker called his senior subordinate, Darius Couch, to his headquarters, where he carefully explained his plan of campaign. He appears to have done so because, as Couch recalled, "under certain contingencies, the right wing [i.e., the flanking column] would be placed at my command." Presumably this would occur should

Hooker be killed or disabled in the fighting. In that event Couch would also assume control of Sedgwick's diversionary operation.[23]

The forty-year-old Couch, who had graduated from West Point nine years after Hooker, had fought ably in the Mexican War, and had made a name for himself on the Peninsula and other fields, was not a great admirer of Hooker. While he himself did not want the job, Couch believed Lincoln could have done better when choosing a successor to the admittedly incompetent but poorly served Burnside. For this reason he might have been expected to be critical of Hooker's plan—which he was, but only to a degree. Overall, he thought it "brilliantly conceived," although the prospect of dividing the army into two segments separated by enemy forces worried him.[24]

Of greater concern to Couch was the role Hooker's plan assigned the force under Sedgwick. Although only one-third of Couch's command would be held opposite Fredericksburg when the right wing headed for Kelly's Ford, the corps leader feared for its safety when told that Sedgwick was obliged to threaten an attack, and perhaps execute one, over the same ground that had become a graveyard of Union lives and hopes.

The prospect of committing a second debacle at Fredericksburg when the effects of the first still seared the mind was more than Couch wished to contemplate. The impact of that prospect struck him fully only after he had left Hooker's headquarters: "When riding back to camp, and revolving over what had been imparted to me, I said to myself, that Sedgwick could never carry out such impracticable conditions as were imposed upon him, and I pitied him from the bottom of my heart."[25]

THE ARMY OF THE POTOMAC took to the roads, in accordance with its leader's plan, at sunrise on the twenty-seventh. The day before, Howard's and Slocum's corps had received orders to move at dawn from their long-held positions north of Falmouth—the Eleventh Corps near Brooke's Station on the railroad to Aquia Landing, the Twelfth Corps farther north at Stafford Court House. Meade's Fifth Corps was issued its marching orders at 1:00 A.M. on the twenty-seventh. They called on the command to move at an unspecified hour that day—early enough to reach Kelly's Ford, the same destination as the other commands, by 4:00 P.M. on the twenty-eighth.[26]

An early version of Hooker's plan had called for Meade to delay his march until after Slocum and Howard passed the Rappahannock. They would then push toward Fredericksburg, thus uncovering United States Ford, where the Fifth Corps would cross. That idea, however, was abandoned when Meade complained of difficulties likely to ensue, presumably those that would cost the army the element of surprise. The security-conscious Hooker would have appreciated such a concern.[27]

Other worries nagged the army leader even at this late date. Two-thirds of the units involved in the turning movement were not his choice to carry the burden of the most critical element of his plan, but there had been no help for it. Meade's corps was a veteran command that had forged a record of solid performance on the march and in battle, but the Eleventh and Twelfth Corps had no such history to recommend them. They had been with the Army of the Potomac only since the previous September, having come over from Pope's stigmatized army following its drubbing at Second Bull Run. Prior to that questionable period of service, they had been part of the luckless force over which Stonewall Jackson had ridden roughshod during his Valley campaign. The military ancestry of neither corps had endeared it to the army it had since joined.[28]

Then there was the issue of ethnic identity, which in the minds of many native-born soldiers called into question the fighting ability of the Eleventh Corps. This corps, the smallest of any under Hooker (little more than twelve thousand officers and men, half the size of the Sixth Corps) was widely perceived to be the army's weak link, primarily because its ranks abounded with German immigrants and second- and third-generation German-Americans ("Dutchmen," as the non-immigrants contemptuously referred to them). Its brigade and division commanders had names like Schurz, von Steinwehr, Krzyzanowski, and Schimmelfenning, although its leaders also included the scions of several-generation Americans including Howard, Brig. Gen. Charles Devens Jr., of Boston, and Brig. Gen. Francis C. Barlow of New York. In fact, foreigners predominated in less than half the regiments that made up the corps, but that fact did not sway the thinking of those in other organizations who believed that soldiers who spoke German or whose English came with an accent were somehow lesser humans. For their part, the "Dutchmen" resented their second-class status, believing the army had treated them with less respect and consideration than units with fewer foreign-sounding names. However, this present operation—whatever it would bring, wherever it would lead—appeared to offer an opportunity for the officers and men of the corps to prove themselves worthy comrades of the doubters and perhaps even the bigots in the ranks.[29]

Drawing of the Army of the Potomac on the march

The men of Hooker's right wing might not know where they were heading, but they must have suspected that, after a long winter of picket duty, drill, target practice, reviews, and inspections, they were finally moving out in strength against the enemy. Their impedimenta—the allocation of which showcased Hooker's attention to logistical details—would have confirmed the fact. Each soldier carried eight days' worth of field rations—five carried in his haversack, three in his knapsack. This complement did not include the men's beef ration—a cattle herd was being driven along in rear of the columns. This was a greater supply of rations than the men had ever carried on the march, but it was not the extent of their food supply. At the end of eight days it was supposed that the army's main supply train would catch up with the moving columns. As these vehicles carried an average of five days' worth of field rations per man and two days of grain for the horses of the officers and the cavalry detachments that guarded the flanks of each column, Hooker had provided enough victuals to support almost two weeks of campaigning. Of equal or greater importance, he had decreed that enough ammunition be on hand to provide each man with 140 rounds, 60 to be carried in pockets and cartridge boxes, 20 borne by the columns' pack mules, and 60 hauled by the ammunition wagons that were a part of the main supply train.

In addition to the wagons of the general train, each division in the column was accompanied by two ambulances and a line of pack mules carrying small-arms ammunition. The baggage wagons of each corps were stationed at points where they would be easily accessible once the columns reached Kelly's Ford. The Fifth and Twelfth Corps were represented by about thirty baggage wagons each, while Howard's corps, despite its small size, was accompanied by almost sixty vehicles. The columns also included artillery units—one six-gun battery per division. To speed the marching pace, the bulk of the artillery had been left at Falmouth, to be forwarded to the front, as needed, once the envelopment of the Confederate left flank was complete.[30]

The route of march took the marching columns up the northwestward-leading roads to Hartwood Church, seven miles out of Falmouth and four miles above United States Ford. This road was far enough above the river to permit the soldiers to escape detection by however many pickets remained on the south bank. And yet, even as the right wing continued on to Kelly's Ford, Hooker directed other troops to converge on the open areas north of Banks's Ford and United States Ford. He wished these forces—two regiments at each site—to be observed by Lee's pickets, not to compromise secrecy but to strengthen the impression created by Sedgwick's diversion by making the operations there appear supportive of it. Hooker intended to utilize both fords to further his turning movement. When the flanking column was well advanced, he would send Couch and Sickles across them via pontoon bridges. The pontoons would not be laid, however, until late on the twenty-ninth, by which time the enemy on the opposite shore would have detected the envelopment, but too late to halt it.[31]

The march to Hartwood Church, scene of Fitz Lee's embarrassing dash on the Union cavalry's picket lines, was neither particularly long nor rough even for troops stiff-legged after months in winter quarters. Nor did the men seem to mind the chilly drizzle that fell on them throughout the operation. In fact, the day was warm enough and the travel brisk enough that many tossed aside overcoats and other bulky articles of clothing suddenly made to appear expendable.

Some time in the afternoon of the twenty-seventh, the three columns converged on Hartwood Church, where they bedded down for the night. The men were tired after their outing but not exhausted. In fact, they had enough energy left to serenade their leader, who appeared among them suddenly and unexpectedly. Hooker had spent the better part of the day at Falmouth reviewing the Second Corps in company with distinguished guests including Secretary of State William Seward, diplomatic officials from Sweden and Prussia, and the governors of Maine and New Jersey. After the ceremony he had had his heart-to-heart with General Couch. Then he had departed his headquarters to overtake the marching men. Surprised and pleased to meet the architect of their army's revival, the troops greeted him with "deafening cheers." Some broke into a song one of their own, a would-be musician, had composed under the title "Hooker Is Our Leader." Hooker had heard the song so often he knew it by heart. But his soldiers had never sung it with the enthusiasm they put into it this day. They belted out the chorus with particular gusto:

> The Union boys are moving on the left and on the right,
> The bugle-call is sounding, our shelters we must strike;
> Joe Hooker is our leader, he takes his whisky strong,
> So our knapsacks we will sling, and go marching along.[32]

Quite obviously, the men were in high spirits. Hooker was pleased, for he knew they had to be in peak condition, physically, mentally, and emotionally, to perform the critical work that lay ahead.

Crossing Over

Before daylight on the twenty-eighth Hooker's right wing resumed its march, leaving Hartwood Church for Kelly's Ford, seventeen miles to the southwest. Howard's corps led the movement by the direct route to the ford, while Slocum's and Meade's soldiers angled their march farther north and west to Mount Holly Church, within easy reach of Kelly's. The marching pace being slow, the head of Howard's column did not reach the vicinity of the ford until about four in the afternoon, where it awaited the arrival of a canvas-topped pontoon train that had been ordered up from Washington the previous morning.[1]

Upon reaching Mount Holly Church Hooker left the column and rode northeastward to Morrisville. There, as per an order sent to General Stoneman the day before at Warrenton Junction, he met and conferred at length with his cavalry leader. Only now was Stoneman enlightened as to his command's role in the offensive. He was surprised to learn, among other things, that Howard's foot soldiers planned to cross at Kelly's Ford before the day was out. Now that the river had fallen, Stoneman had expected to wade across at or near Kelly's Ford but not until the morning of the twenty-ninth. Revised instructions now called on him to pass over that night, completing the operation by eight o'clock the next morning. Stoneman was not certain he could meet this requirement: "From Morrisville to where the Cavalry Corps lay was 13 miles, from there to where some of the extreme pickets were was 13 more."[2]

By dint of great effort, he made it—barely. His scattered command was not massed along the river, ready for crossing, until after dark, "owing to the state of the roads, the result of the recent heavy rains, and the darkness of the night, rendered doubly obscure by a dense fog." The crossing was not completed until the deadline had nearly passed.[3]

Stoneman was surprised not only by the brief preparation time imposed on him but also by the revamped orders governing the balance of his mission, which bore the handwriting of Capt. William L. Candler of Hooker's staff. Instead of making directly for the railroad from Fredericksburg to Richmond, the cavalry was to advance south in two columns, the smaller of which would veer west toward Louisa Court House via Raccoon Ford on the Rapidan. No doubt this was intended to fool J. E. B. Stuart's scouts into supposing Stoneman was heading for Gordonsville. The larger column was not only to operate against the R, F & P but also to threaten enemy forces along the O & A. Hooker recommended that the columns rendezvous at some unspecified hour on the Pamunkey River or some other stream within striking range of the Confederate capital, where they would be in position to cut off Lee's retreat from Fredericksburg. Thus, Stoneman's mission had been expanded to include simultaneous movements in widely divergent directions, attacks on at least two railroads, and a concerted effort to confront Lee.

To accomplish these objectives Stoneman could call on the services of 90 percent of his command. He was to leave behind a single brigade to reconnoiter for, and guard the flanks and front of, the turning column. This force, barely thirteen hundred strong, Stoneman entrusted to his senior division leader, Brig. Gen. Alfred Pleasonton. Stoneman and Pleasonton were not on cordial terms, which may explain the former's decision to leave the latter at the head of an inferior command with Hooker when the first large-scale movement of the rejuvenated cavalry corps went forward. Ironically, this situation would redound to Pleasonton's benefit and Stoneman's detriment, for reasons neither officer could foresee. Both, however, must have wondered why Hooker had elected to send almost his entire mounted force so far from the scene of his most important maneuvers, while the main army made do with so few mobile reconnaissance assets. In effect, Hooker was ensuring that at the critical hour of his offensive he would lack the powers of perception—the "eyes and ears" that only horse soldiers could provide.[4]

If Stoneman was concerned that his mission had become more complicated than he had bargained for, he gave no hint of it during his confab with Hooker at Morrisville. In fact, as Hooker recalled years later, the cavalry leader suggested adding a mission, one that fueled his superior's "distrust of the want of zeal in this officer, to execute my wishes." Stoneman, Hooker claimed, handed him "a written application, for his command to visit Staunton, ostensibly to break up some Shoe Manufactory, which I declined, saying that it was too small a matter for his whole force to be employed in." Hooker added disdainfully that on Stoneman's return from his mission "he asked for this paper to be returned to him, anticipating I suppose that its ghost, might appear to him again when he would not want to see it."[5]

If Stoneman's eccentricities bothered Hooker, so did the loping pace of the right wing, which by the time it reached Kelly's Ford was so far behind schedule that Hooker had to wire Falmouth to delay similarly Sedgwick's river crossing. The rear of the column, Meade's corps, did not close within striking distance of the ford until some time after ten o'clock. The army's support units, however, had made good time. At approximately five thirty, only an hour and a half after Howard's arrival, the lead section of the pontoon train had reached the ford. Within ninety minutes members of the Fifteenth New York Engineers, a part of the brigade commanded by Hooker's studious but libationary West Point classmate, Brig. Gen. Henry W. Benham, began laying the canvas boats across the river, which at that point was about one hundred yards wide. The engineers worked in close cooperation with one of Howard's brigades that had been pre-positioned at the crossing site. Hooker, having left Stoneman at Morrisville, was on hand to oversee the work, which progressed with gratifying speed.[6]

The general was pleased to reflect that, by all indications, the march from Hartwood Church had attracted no unwanted notice. In furtherance of his security-first program, he had seen to it that every house along the route of march was placed under guard to prevent Southern sympathizers from spreading an alarm. Nothing that could compromise the operation appeared to have been neglected, meaning that the critical advantage of surprise remained intact. Not only Hooker but everyone involved in the operation believed so, including those still at Falmouth. These included Dan Butterfield, whom Hooker had left behind to man a communications link between the already widely dispersed wings, one that the army's telegraph operators would continually extend as the flanking column advanced. Writing by lamplight in his tent near Butterfield's command post, General Patrick noted in his diary that "So far, I think the rebels have not the slightest idea what we are about today."[7]

AT HIS HEADQUARTERS below Fredericksburg, Lee noticed no appreciable change in the enemy lines across the river. Neither did word of any untoward movement come to his attention beyond the usual reports of Stoneman's comings and goings in the Warrenton area. There were indications of activity along the river toward the far left of the army, but nothing out of the ordinary. The forces opposite Banks's and United States Fords appeared to have increased slightly, but that fact failed to suggest a pattern of reinforcement.

Indications of a Union movement toward the Shenandoah were no longer discernable. Still, Lee kept alert to the possibility of an incursion into that region. By now he had recalled most of Fitz Lee's troopers from Fauquier County, where they had been sent seventeen days earlier in preparation for a possible transfer to the Valley. Many of his nephew's outposts on the river, however, had not been fully reoccupied—others had not been manned since Averell's attack on them six weeks ago. Fitz's brigade, which was headquartered at Culpeper Court House, twelve miles from Kelly's Ford, was stretched more thinly than ever before, the result of the continuing absence of Wade Hampton's brigade, south of the James.[8]

Robert E. Lee realized that the country beyond his twenty-five-mile-long defensive line deserved heavier protection and greater vigilance but, as always, his resources were critically limited. What forces he could spare for picketing, scouting, and reconnoitering must be husbanded to confront the Yankees in the army's immediate front. As Lee saw it, optimum allocation of resources was akin to the perfection of mankind—a goal devoutly to be pursued but never to be realized.

AROUND SIX IN THE EVENING on April 27 Hooker lowered another of his carefully placed security barriers by issuing John Sedgwick the orders that would govern his operations over the next several days. Calculating that his flanking column would be across the river early on the twenty-ninth, Fighting Joe desired that in preparation for the crossing of the left wing, the river opposite

Fredericksburg should be spanned by or before 3:30 A.M. on the twenty-ninth. Once the four bridges allocated to the operation were down, Reynolds's corps would cross near the mouth of Pollock's Mill Creek, Sedgwick's people about a mile and a half farther north at Franklin's Crossing. Sickles's Third Corps, to which Hooker had assigned a supporting role—one not necessarily confined to Sedgwick's operations—was to cross at either bridgehead by 4:30 A.M. Almost one hundred cannons including those of the batteries attached to the Sixth Corps—the whole under General Hunt, recently returned from an inspection tour of Banks's Ford—would cover the crossings from atop 150-foot-high Stafford Heights.[9]

The demonstrations Sedgwick was to make, once his troops were safely ensconced on the Fredericksburg side, were aimed at occupying the historic Telegraph Road, which ran south toward Richmond. Sedgwick's instructions provided for a very real possibility: "In the event of the enemy detaching any

Maj. Gen. John Sedgwick, USA

considerable part of his force against the troops operating at the west of Fredericksburg," the left wing commander was to "attack and carry their works at all hazards, and establish his force on the telegraphic road, cutting off all communication by the enemy, in order to prevent their turning his position on that road." If, as Hooker hoped and anticipated, the Rebels reacted to the demonstrations by abandoning their positions, the wing commander should pursue "with the utmost vigor, fighting them whenever and wherever he can come up with them."[10]

Sedgwick was eager to contribute his share to the army's great offensive, but he got off on the wrong foot. His orders called on him to break camp on the morning of the twenty-eighth, but the continuing rain and other, unspecified hindrances combined to delay a general movement until near noon. At the dinner hour, Reynolds's corps finally took to the road, followed about three hours later by Sedgwick's troops. Sickles's command began heading for the river at about 5:00 P.M. The First Corps reached its assigned position behind the bluffs that shielded Pollock's Mill Creek by 5:30, but the Sixth Corps, followed by the Third, did not arrive at Franklin's Crossing until 9:00 P.M. Sedgwick's late start and slow progress presaged other delays of a more serious nature.

Upon reaching Franklin's Crossing, Sedgwick was met by couriers bearing dispatches from Chief of Staff Butterfield as well as from Brig. Gen. Seth Williams, Hooker's adjutant general. The first provided general information on enemy dispositions; the second reminded Sedgwick that "your operations for tomorrow are for a demonstration only, to hold the forces of the enemy while the operations are carried on above [i.e., behind Lee's left] unless the enemy should leave the position, or should weaken his force materially by detachments."[11]

Once in position, Sedgwick tried to meet Hooker's stipulation that the left wing be concealed, as much as possible, from Rebel view. He complied to the extent of outlawing fires in his bivouacs throughout that bone-chilling evening. Even as he took this precaution, Sedgwick realized the futility of it— the men were too close to the enemy's pickets to escape detection. Other high-ranking officers, however, were willing to pretend that absolute secrecy was attainable with a little effort. General Benham, whose men would lay the bridges upon which the left wing would cross, ordered that the pontoons be brought down to the river quickly but stealthily. Rather than transport them aboard the noisy horse-drawn wagons that had conveyed them to the river bluffs, he demanded that all forty-four pontoons—each weighing upwards of fifteen hundred pounds—be hauled forward by fatigue parties detailed from Sedgwick's wing.

Sedgwick was willing to humor Benham, whom Hooker had invested with control over all aspects of bridge construction. He did not know what one of Benham's subordinates later reported: the chief engineer was drunk this evening and barely coherent. As a sober observer would have anticipated, the labor proved too difficult to be accomplished by manpower alone. The boats were so heavy that every attempt to manhandle them down to the river—even with seventy men assigned to each pontoon—failed.

General Reynolds, whose corps was waiting to cross near the creek mouth via two of Benham's bridges, lost his temper over the extended delay. Determined to expedite progress no matter the cost to operational secrecy, he had his men return the pontoons to the wagons and wheel them into position at water's edge. Observing the results born of Reynolds's exasperation, Sedgwick resorted to the same expedient, over the spluttering objections of General Benham.

Troops from the Sixth Corps division of Brig. Gen. William T. H. Brooks, USA

Benham's differences with his infantry colleagues had just begun. Due to miscommunication and jealousy over prerogatives, he failed to enlist the support of Brig. Gen. William T. H. Brooks, whose Sixth Corps division supposedly had been placed at Benham's disposal. Brooks's refusal to obey the drunken engineer denied the bridge builders the crossing squads whose service in clearing the far shore of defenders was absolutely critical to the safe laying of the pontoons. Sedgwick had neglected to pass the word to his subordinates that Benham was in command of the evening's operations. Benham, however, believed he had the power to compel obedience, and he was not hesitant to use it. When one of Brooks's brigade leaders, Brig. Gen. David A. Russell, not only refused to make crossing squads available but insulted the engineer officer, Benham tried to have him arrested for insubordination. A disgusted Russell ignored him and went about his business.

Not only did Benham fail to gain satisfaction from the Sixth Corps, neither Reynolds nor his ranking subordinate, Brig. Gen. James S. Wadsworth, was willing to provide guards. The problem was not resolved and the squads not made available until some time after sunrise. In the interim, Benham, his engineers, oarsmen, and loading crews sat "inactive and perfectly powerless." Sedgwick finally intervened in Benham's behalf, but by the time Brooks and Wadsworth had been compelled to assign their troops to the operation—upwards of sixty armed men to each of the pontoons to be piloted across—it was 5:00 A.M., well past the hour Benham's orders called for him to finish laying all four bridges.[12]

The time lost to high-level foul-ups might have proved fatal to the success of the crossings, but it did not. As soon as the pontoons carrying the covering details bumped to a halt against the south bank, the boats emptied and their passengers moved into position opposite the nearest rifle pits. Their movements masked by darkness, the attackers struck with enough suddenness to clear the trenches in minutes. Those Rebels not felled by the first volley scrambled from their holes and raced up the riverbank, many being shot in the back as they fled.

As soon as the victors signaled their success to comrades on the other shore, Benham's engineers got to work with speed born of pent-up anxiety. As the general reported, before 7:15 both bridges were up at Franklin's Crossing. Construction of the lower bridges was slowed by heavier resistance from the far shore, which prevented the timely launching of the crossing squads. Once those squads finally forced their way across the steam, the bridge building commenced there, although it was close to noon before both spans near Pollock's Mill Creek were in operation. By then a third bridge had been laid at Franklin's Crossing in response to the demands of Brig. Gen. John Newton, in charge of the crossing of Sedgwick's corps.[13]

The bridges down and secure, John Sedgwick readied his men for the diversion designed to arrest the attention of the Confederates in front of Fredericksburg. He did not look forward to the mission, which, being a mere simulation, was fraught with risk and devoid of glory. The fact that he was committed to such a thankless operation while colleagues in Hooker's flanking column were preparing a real assault, one that might win the war in a single stroke, may have gnawed a little at Sedgwick's pride. Even so, this general whom his troops affectionately called "Uncle John" was determined to play his part, however small in the scheme of Hooker's overall strategy, to the best of his ability. He would do his utmost to confront, threaten, and confound Robert E. Lee long enough to enable the turning movement to triumph. Unlike his West Point classmate, John Sedgwick's sense of self-worth did not depend on a star turn; a successful supporting performance would satisfy him just as well.

AT 10:00 P.M. on the twenty-eighth the canvas-covered pontoons were in place at Kelly's Ford and the head of Howard's column began crossing the Rappahannock. The main body had been preceded by members of Col. Adolphus Buschbeck's brigade of New York and Pennsylvania Infantry, which had been occupying the Kelly's Ford area for almost two weeks. Buschbeck's men had paddled across the stream in pontoons in the manner of Brooks's and Wadsworth's troops on the far left. Seeing the Yankees come, the sentinels across the way fled after getting off only one shot. Howard, having just rejoined the column after a conference with Hooker at Morrisville, supervised the securing of the Rebel shore. The corps commander had been briefed on Hooker's broad strategy and the role of the Eleventh Corps in it. He had learned, among other things, that Slocum's corps would lead the march to and across the Rapidan at Germanna Ford, followed by his own troops. Meade's command, which was just then closing up on Kelly's Ford, would move to the Rapidan by a more easterly route, crossing that stream at Ely's Ford.[14]

After Howard's advance reached the south side of the Rappahannock, the rest of the corps crossed over, screened by the Seventeenth Pennsylvania Cavalry. Once on dry ground, the troopers trotted down the darkened roads toward Fredericksburg. The Seventeenth was one of three regiments that made up Pleasonton's command. The brigade's titular commander was Col. Thomas C. Devin, an able veteran of long and varied service. The other components of Devin's command were likewise assigned the mission of closely supporting the infantrymen of the right wing. The Sixth New York was attached to Slocum's corps, while the Eighth Pennsylvania, along with a single company of the First Michigan Cavalry, would cover the front and left of the Fifth Corps as it moved to the Rapidan.[15]

While Pleasonton supported the main army, Stoneman was preparing to head south with the balance of his corps. By now he had gotten his last trooper over the river via the fords west of Kelly's, but he was not yet ready to move out. Although he had enjoyed two weeks of relative inactivity during which to plan his next moves, he had received his final orders from Hooker only hours ago. Thus Stoneman "assembled the division and brigade commanders, spread our maps, and had a thorough understanding of what we were to do, and where we were each to go."[16]

Stoneman's raiders on the march

They were to go many places and do many things. General Averell's division, along with the brigade of Col. Benjamin F. "Grimes" Davis and Horse Battery A, Second U. S. Artillery, under Capt. John C. Tidball, would constitute the westerly column, the one bound for Culpeper Court House. Stoneman would personally command the second, larger column, consisting of Brig. Gen. David M. Gregg's division, Brig. Gen. John Buford's "Reserve Brigade," and combined Batteries B and L, Second Artillery, under Capt. James Madison Robertson. This latter force would make for Stevensburg, southeast of Culpeper, before descending on the line of the South Anna River above Richmond.

Each column was expected to inflict major damage to Lee's supply lines prior to linking on or near the Pamunkey. Thereafter they would coordinate operations in the direction of the capital. Stoneman would head south in company of several officers who had performed capably on previous campaigns, especially Gregg, Buford, and the battery commanders. Having been kept as active as possible in the aftermath of their failed crossing, the entire command was in good spirits and looking forward to the coming expedition.

Stoneman appeared to lack nothing required to make a success of his interdiction mission. Yet the cavalry chief's ability to clamp a secure hold on Lee's retreat route once Hooker dislodged him from Fredericksburg was another matter entirely. Hooker appeared to believe that such an objective was easily attainable, a mere matter of cutting a railroad here, demolishing a bridge there. But if Lee were truly intent on reaching the defenses of his capital, as Hooker was certain he would be, it was doubtful that any mounted column—even one as large, as well-equipped, and as high-spirited as Stoneman's—could bar his path for an appreciable period.[17]

THE TASKS HOOKER ASSIGNED to his mounted arm presumed little or no interference from Stoneman's natural opponent, J. E. B. Stuart's division of Confederate cavalry. Yet that truncated but aggressive command would prove a formidable obstacle not only to Stoneman but to his infantry comrades. Stuart had his faults, including a disrespect for his enemy that sometimes bordered on contempt and a penchant for courting a fight against heavy odds. But if he occasionally performed erratically in combat, he was a vigilant and skillful gatherer of intelligence, which he had the ability to place in the hands of a superior while still warm. But on this damp and foggy morning of April 29, 1863, it remained to be seen whether Stuart was up to the challenge posed by a mounted force that seemed to have materialized like a blue miasma on the upper Rappahannock.

Stuart's forward vedettes (mounted pickets) had failed to detect the crossing of the first wave of Federals at Kelly's Ford. This lapse was understandable, for the movement that secured the south bank had been conducted by Buschbeck's brigade, which had occupied the area so long without making threatening moves that Stuart's scouts had been lulled into thinking that nothing the Yankees did was cause for alarm. Buschbeck's lengthy presence had been another of the many imaginative efforts Hooker had made in the name of secrecy.[18]

Before 9:00 P.M. on the twenty-eighth, however, Rooney Lee's scouts were acutely aware that a major fording operation was in progress at Kelly's. A courier rushed the news to J. E. B. Stuart's headquarters at Culpeper Court House. After the messenger galloped off, the scouts crept closer to Kelly's in order to gain a closer view of the local situation. They were fortunate to cut off a few members of Howard's command who had proceeded inland incautiously and alone. One captive, a Belgian-born officer on the staff of Howard's ranking subordinate, Maj. Gen. Carl Schurz, proved to be an especially valuable prize. In thickly accented English, and perhaps at gunpoint, he confirmed that the troops who had crossed were members of the Eleventh Corps. When pressed for strength estimates, he exaggerated the size of the column as twenty thousand.[19]

When the officer's story was relayed to Culpeper, J. E. B. Stuart astutely lowered the manpower figure to fourteen thousand but incorrectly assumed that it embraced only a division. Based on the incomplete reports of his scouts, he made an even greater error that found its way into the dispatch he tried to transmit to army headquarters that evening. In his mind Stuart coupled the sightings of Yankee infantry with Stoneman's widely observed crossing farther west. Stoneman's position and presumed heading confirmed Stuart's earlier expectations of a cavalry raid on Gordonsville. When the initial direction of the Union infantry below the river was found to be slightly southwesterly, he assumed that it too was moving toward the railhead almost thirty miles away.

Through its erroneous inference, Stuart's message would mislead Robert E. Lee and stay his response to Hooker's advance for almost twenty-four hours. Moreover, Lee did not receive it until 10:00 A.M. the day after it was sent. The delay stemmed from Stuart's decision to send the message not by courier but by telegraph. The inadequacies of the Confederate field telegraph were such that a communiqué from Stuart's sector traveled to Fredericksburg by a roundabout circuit through Staunton and then Richmond. One or both of these relays was incapable of twenty-four-hour operation, which held back transmission until well after daylight on the twenty-ninth. By then the Confederate commander had been alerted to events unfolding in front of Fredericksburg that had occurred hours after those Stuart had reported.[20]

BEFORE DAWN on the twenty-ninth, the passage of Sedgwick's troops over Franklin's Crossing came to the attention of Maj. Gen. Jubal A. Early, whose division of Jackson's corps occupied the line of defenses to the north of Hamilton's Crossing, not far from its position during the battle of December 13. Almost as soon as the first infantry-occupied pontoons reached shore near the mouth of Deep Run, Early was rushing word of the lodgment to Jackson's headquarters. Jackson, whose position extended downriver as far as Port Royal, saw immediately that he must concentrate for defensive action, a move he quickly communicated to each of his division commanders, Maj. Gen. Ambrose P. Hill and Brig. Gens. Robert E. Rodes and Raleigh Colston.[21]

At Jackson's direction, Lt. James Power Smith of his staff rode a mile across the fields to bring the disturbing news to army headquarters. Arriving there, the youngster found both Lee and his adjutant general, Lt. Col. A. Reid Venable, slumbering in their adjacent tents. Upon Smith's arrival, however, Venable awoke and when he learned the reason for the staff officer's coming he told Smith to wake the army commander. Years later Smith recalled that under gentle prodding Lee slowly placed his feet on the ground beside his cot, sat up, and came fully awake. To Smith's surprise, the army leader greeted the news he conveyed by playfully remarking: "Well, I thought I heard firing, and was beginning to think it was time some of you young fellows were coming to tell me what it was all about. Tell your good general that I am sure he knows what to do. I will meet him at the front very soon."[22]

Lee threw on his uniform, assembled his staff, and under a misty rain rode down to the river to confer with the commander there. From a hilltop he observed—as much as the continuing fog would permit—Federal troops moving inland from their lodgments on the south bank. Thousands of the enemy's troops were congregating there, but they appeared content to remain in place, building breastworks and digging rifle pits. From the crest across the river, Union cannons continued to pound the ground in the infantry's front, forcing Early's defenders to hunker down behind their own works.

The static nature of the operations at the river did not suggest to Lee that this was a mere diversion. Once the Federals—whom captured comrades had identified as members of Hooker's First and Sixth Corps—firmed up their hold on the south bank, they undoubtedly would advance in force, perhaps over the same ground they had failed to carry in December. It seemed to Lee a curious strategy, but perhaps the new commander wanted to prove that he could succeed where his discredited predecessor had come up short.

After several minutes spent in quiet observation, Lee rode to the outskirts of Fredericksburg. The Yankees had laid no bridges opposite the town and no attempts to force a crossing were in evidence. Even so, efforts had begun to evacuate the town of its civilian population, women and children first. Satisfying himself that all was quiet in that sector, Lee returned to his original position, to be joined there by Stonewall Jackson.[23]

The commanders conferred briefly on what must be done to hold the ridges along the river and prevent a further advance by the enemy. To concentrate opposite the point of occupation, Lee ordered that outlying units be drawn in. These included elements of the two divisions Longstreet had left behind when moving to the Southside, those commanded by Maj. Gens. Richard H. Anderson and Lafayette McLaws. Jackson's troops, the divisions of Hill, Rodes, and Colston, were moved closer to Early's right flank. The contraction left Jackson's command holding a perimeter that stretched for about a mile and a quarter, from Deep Run on the north to Massaponax Creek on the south. Lee ordered two of Anderson's brigades—Brig. Gen. Ambrose R. Wright's and Brig. Gen. Joseph B. Kershaw's—to close up on Early's left. In the latter sector Early could also draw support from the balance of McLaws's command, the brigades of Brig. Gens. Paul Semmes and William T. Wofford.[24]

As yet Lee had drawn no conclusion as to whether he was facing the main Union effort, or whether a heavier blow might fall elsewhere. However, as the hours passed, the work on the bridges continued, and pontoons passed from shore to shore conveying Federal soldiers to the south bank, he began to believe that the operation under his eye constituted Hooker's primary offensive.

At about 10:00 A.M., while still at the river, Lee received Stuart's dispatch of the previous evening. Soon afterward he wired a message of his own to the Richmond office of Adj. and Insp. Gen. Samuel Cooper. He reported the crossings south of Fredericksburg and, despite the failure of the enemy to move inland from his bridgehead, opined that "he is certainly crossing in large force here, and it looks as if he was in earnest." Lee treated the news from Stuart that other Yankees had crossed the upper Rappahannock as something of an afterthought. Repeating the erroneous information sent him, he added that "I hear of no other point at which he is crossing except below Kelly's Ford, where Genl Howard has crossed with his division, said to be fourteen thousand, six pieces of artillery, and some cavalry. Stoneman will probably cross about the Warrenton Springs, and I fear will make for Gordonsville and may destroy our [rail]roads."[25]

Having recently complained that with Longstreet, Hood, and Pickett away he lacked the manpower for proper defense, Lee now extended his concern to the crossing at Kelly's Ford: "I have nothing to oppose to all that force up there except the two brigades of cavalry under Genl Stuart. All available troops had better be sent forward as rapidly as possible by rail and otherwise."[26]

For hours after receiving Stuart's wire, Lee heard nothing from him or his subordinates. At first puzzled by the silence, he began to suspect that the Federals who had crossed at Kelly's had cut the cavalry leader off from the main army. Not until after dark did Lee learn that his supposition was correct. Some of the general's men trickled into army headquarters to report they had gotten separated from Stuart when the Yankees moved down from Kelly's Ford. They reported further that both Union cavalry and infantry were en route to the Rapidan. Later reports confirmed that the enemy had crossed at Germanna Ford. The news gave Lee his first real inkling that some Yankees might be heading toward Fredericksburg as well as toward Gordonsville.[27]

THE UNION ADVANCE from Kelly's Ford to the Rapidan, which began at daylight on the twenty-ninth, was led by Slocum's corps, preceded by the cavalry assigned to it, the Sixth New York. Behind the horsemen marched Brig. Gen. Thomas H. Ruger's brigade of Alpheus S. Williams's division, followed at a distance of three miles by the main body of the corps. By 10:30 A.M., the Twelfth Corps had cleared the bridgehead, enabling Meade's people to begin crossing the pontoons. As the Fifth Corps reached the other side and began to veer east toward Ely's Ford, Howard's command filed in behind it and started toward its designated crossing site on the Rapidan.

Unexpectedly, the men were joined on the march by their leader, Hooker having arrived from Morrisville. Again he stirred the men to demonstrations of regard for his stewardship, cheering Fighting Joe "to the echo." Hooker's sense of self-esteem had never been so robust, his confidence never so high.[28]

LESS THAN THREE MILES below Kelly's Ford, Slocum's cavalry encountered some of Stuart's troopers, a detachment of Rooney Lee's Thirteenth Virginia, supported at a distance by part of the Ninth Virginia (the remainder of the brigade was off on a foraging expedition and inaccessible to its commander).

The Virginians fell back to avoid being overwhelmed; a running fight continued all the way to the Rapidan.

While Rooney Lee tangled with infantry and cavalry on the right flank of Slocum's column, Stuart learned that additional troops were coming down from the river along a more easterly track. Leaving Robert E. Lee's son to keep an eye on the enemy, the "Beau Sabreur of the Confederacy" galloped in the direction of the new threat at the head of Fitz Lee's brigade. Near Madden's Tavern, about four and a half miles from Germanna Ford, he encountered the right flank of Slocum's wing, en route to the Rapidan. He found that a large portion of the column had already passed that point, heading south. Boldly attacking, Stuart took prisoners from all three Union corps. The interrogation process that followed not only gave him a better idea of the scope of the enemy advance, it provided more than a hint of where it was headed. It seemed clear that the foot soldiers were not advancing toward Gordonsville in company with their cavalry friends, but eastward in the direction of Fredericksburg.[29]

Stuart's first impulse was to rush the news to army headquarters via courier, but the Federals had solidly interposed between him and the main army. The cavalry leader had been cut off from contact not only with Robert E. Lee but also with a fatigue party, some engineers, and members of Stuart's staff, who had been at Germanna Ford, where a burned bridge was being repaired.

Stuart decided to reunite with Lee by crossing the Rapidan west of the enemy and looping south and east around their flank. But at the same time he had to deal with other Yankees who did indeed appear to be heading for the Gordonsville vicinity—Stoneman's troopers, whose movements were now being monitored by Rooney Lee. As he started off on his roundabout route to Lee's headquarters, Stuart ordered Rooney to head for Gordonsville with the Ninth Virginia and four pieces of horse artillery. He was to defend the rail junction and, as much as possible, shield the line of the Virginia Central, the army's link to its main source of rations and forage, the Shenandoah Valley. Once the Thirteenth Virginia disengaged from its clash with Slocum's cavalry, it, too, would join the pursuit of Stoneman's raiders.[30]

BECAUSE STUART WAS PREVENTED from alerting them to the enemy's approach, the Confederates at Germanna Ford were easy pickings for Slocum's

Maj. Gen. Henry W. Slocum, USA

advance echelon. The fatigue detail of about eighty men, supported by about fifty combat troops occupying rifle pits on both sides of the stream, was surprised by Ruger's stealthy advance and was captured nearly intact. The POWs, when escorted to the rear, were plainly astonished by the size of the enemy column they passed. Their reaction told Slocum that word of his advance had not penetrated this far south. The advantage of surprise continued to hold, even at this late stage of the game when Lee's enemy was turning to confront him.[31]

Pleasonton, whose cavalry had taken part in the attack on the force at the bridge, believed the milestone of the day was not the revelation that the right wing had escaped detection but the capture of a diary left behind by one of the escapees, Stuart's aide Thomas R. Price. Pleasonton claimed he spent most of that night searching the "very bulky volume" for clues to Stuart's dispositions and intentions. The only tidbit he gleaned from the document was a reference to a meeting at Stuart's headquarters the previous month, attended by Jackson and some of his subordinates. "They were in conference over five hours," Pleasonton related, "and came to the decision that the next battle would be at or near Chancellorsville, and that the position must be prepared." What advantage could come from this information, he did not explain. It appears, rather, that the diary was more notable for its droll and often unflattering descriptions of Stuart, which cost Lieutenant Price his position when excerpts found their way into the pages of the *New York Times*.[32]

Potential opposition at Germanna Ford having been removed, Slocum sent his troops across the Rapidan without further delay. Because the burned bridge had been only partially replanked, the soldiers had to wade the deep stream, whose current was so strong that several of the shorter men were swept downstream, saved from drowning by cavalry comrades mounted on the largest horses and positioned in the middle of the river. As the crossing continued, engineers in blue replaced those in gray. They completed the replanking, enabling the bridge to convey Slocum's rear ranks over the ford. The quickly rebuilt span, however, proved insufficiently sturdy to bear the weight of Slocum's wagons, pack mules, and artillery teams, which joined the majority of the column in fording. The Twelfth Corps finished crossing about an hour before midnight, at which time Howard's men began to join them on the south bank.[33]

While the crossing continued, Slocum received a message from General Butterfield at Falmouth. Hooker's chief of staff announced that all the bridges on Sedgwick's front had been laid and that Lee's and Jackson's attention was riveted on the operations in that sector. The flanking column's success appeared assured; Slocum was in a position to command the only roads by which Lee could escape the pincers now closing upon him. Slocum was urged to press on, uncovering United States Ford. There he would connect with the two divisions under Darius Couch.[34]

While Slocum's column headed for Germanna Ford, Meade's troops spent most of the twenty-ninth marching to Ely's Ford. Two-thirds of the command, the divisions of Maj. Gen. George Sykes and Brig. Gen. Charles Griffin, had begun crossing the Rappahannock, in rear of the Twelfth Corps, at about 11:00 A.M. As soon as they were on the south side, the foot soldiers, preceded by the Sixth New York Cavalry, moved toward the Rapidan via Richardsville, crossing ground alternately wooded and open. Throughout the day Meade had lacked the services of Brig. Gen. Andrew A. Humphreys's Third Division, which had remained on the Rappahannock to escort the corps' wagons and to assist the engineers in taking up the bridge at Kelly's Ford, a project not completed until well after dark.

By midnight the men of Sykes and Griffin had bivouacked below the Rapidan, where their cavalry comrades had made contact with the troopers escorting Slocum and Howard. Meade intended that Humphreys's men would be on hand by the time he resumed his advance, but due to the darkness of the night and the incompetence of some local guides, the Third Division would not reach Ely's Ford until the next morning. By then the rest of the corps would have moved on, but no longer in a southward direction. They had at last turned east toward Fredericksburg and Lee's army.[35]

BY THE FORENOON of the twenty-ninth Lee had completed the dispositions he considered vital to shoring up his lines south of Fredericksburg. When, late in the afternoon, he received solid information that two columns of Federal infantry had crossed the Rapidan and were moving toward him in the direction of a crossroads named Chancellorsville, he took steps to strengthen his defenses in that area as well. By then his subordinates west of Fredericksburg had been alerted to the advance. Brig. Gen. William Mahone, commanding a brigade of Virginians in Anderson's division, had learned of Meade's arrival at Ely's Ford, and soon afterward of Slocum's and Howard's advance from Germanna Ford. Within an hour of the receipt of this intelligence, Mahone's soldiers were breaking up the encampment opposite United States Ford that they had occupied since the battle of Fredericksburg.

Mahone's main body was still striking tents (about six hundred men would remain near the ford until further notice) when orders from army headquarters sent the brigade leader toward Chancellorsville in cooperation with another of Anderson's brigades, Brig. Gen. Carnot Posey's. Reaching his

assigned position just north of the crossroads, Mahone erected a line that covered the approaches from Ely's Ford on the south and United States Ford to the north. Posey's Mississippians, accompanied by a two-gun section of a light battery, advanced deeper into the Wilderness. They staked out a position just west of Chancellorsville, blocking the road from Germanna Ford.[36]

Near Fredericksburg, Lee was ordering other forces to the suddenly threatened sector—Wright's brigade of Anderson's division and Semmes's brigade from the division of McLaws.

Maj. Gen. Lafayette McLaws, CSA

Lee also called on General Pendleton to send up the bulk of the army's artillery, which had been wintering well to the south. This force embraced the Artillery Reserve as well as the guns

Longstreet had left behind when sent south of the James—both organizations were stationed at Chesterfield Station on the R, F & P. Also called up were the cannons of Jackson's corps, which its commander, Col. Stapleton Crutchfield, had massed north of Richmond at Bowling Green. Finally, McLaws was put on notice to add other elements of his division, as needed, to Jackson's line as well as to the new front in the Wilderness.[37]

Lee personally delivered his instructions to McLaws. The forty-two-year-old Georgian later recalled that the two had "a long conversation" in which Lee expressed quiet confidence he could hold back the enemy in all quarters "should our troops behave as well as they have usually done." Lee had words of counsel for those troops, which he wished McLaws to convey to them as forcefully as possible: "Let them know that it is a stern reality now, it must be, Victory or Death, for defeat would be ruinous."[38]

These steps taken, Lee could do little but wait for the fighting to come—the next move was up to Joe Hooker and the commanders of his widely separated forces. Lee's hope was that come morning he would not be so hard-pressed in front and rear that he could not defend both sectors effectively. His view of the relative danger posed by those threats had slowly but firmly shifted. He no longer believed that the landings below Fredericksburg signaled Hooker's main offensive. As he informed Jefferson Davis in a message whose matter-of-fact tone belied the gravity of the situation it conveyed, the Yankees' apparent intention "is to turn our left, and probably to get into our rear. Our scattered position favors their operations. I hope if any reinforcements can be sent, they may be forwarded immediately."[39]

Yet Lee must have suspected that any additions would prove too little, too late. Increasingly, he considered the expedient of retreating before he could be hammered on two sides at once. For this reason he added to his dispatch a significant, and perhaps an ominous, suggestion: "The bridges over the [North and South] Annas ought to be guarded, if possible."[40]

A Most Extraordinary Twenty-Four Hours

On the south side of the Rapidan, the men of Hooker's right wing entered a forest the likes of which most had never seen. Covering more than sixty square miles, this blasted-looking expanse of scrub oak, cutover pine, and rank undergrowth had the ability to inspire fear in the hardiest traveler. One who passed through in the spring of 1864 at the outset of another campaign fraught with promise and risk spoke for many comrades when he pronounced it "a region of gloom and the shadow of death."[1]

Almost as soon as one entered this dark and foreboding expanse, he felt constricted, trapped, imprisoned. The gnarly, second-growth pines—the original tree cover had been denuded to supply charcoal to feed the fires of an iron foundry, now semiabandoned, known as Catharine Furnace—were in such profusion that they blotted out the sky. The claustrophobic effect was not relieved by the few clearings that broke the monotony of trees and brush. The most extensive of these was Chancellorsville, which, despite its name, was not a village but a seventy-acre tract surrounding a two-and-a-half-story brick house with a large open porch, the habitation of one Frances Chancellor and her large family. Mrs. Chancellor was renting from a Mr. Guest, the owner of the dwelling; her mother had operated the tavern around which the structure had been erected in 1816. Other notable expanses of open ground included Fairview, the original Chancellor farmstead, now the home of the family's overseer, which sat a few hundred yards south and west of Chancellorsville; and Hazel Grove, a little over a mile to the southwest, until

149

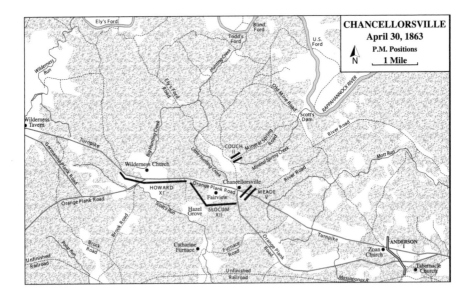

recently the property of the Reverend Melzi S. Chancellor, Baptist clergyman and pastor of nearby Wilderness Church.[2]

A narrow passageway through the forest stretched from Wilderness Tavern eastward through Chancellorsville to Tabernacle Church and adjacent Zoan Church. Where trees and brush did not cover it, the ground was rough in places and spongy in others, riven as it was with low, sharp ridges and criss-crossed by a spidery network of creeks, runs, springs, and marshes. Few roads of substance had been cut through the woodland, but three were commodious enough to facilitate east-west travel. The River Road (or Shore Road) followed the lower bank of the Rappahannock to and below Fredericksburg, where its name changed to the Bowling Green Road. The other two major thorough-fares, the Orange Turnpike and Orange Plank Road, ran parallel for a portion of their length, the distance between varying from a half-mile to a mile. They came together south of Wilderness Church, met the road from Ely's Ford at Chancellorsville, then forked and ran east for another four miles before reunit-ing northeast of Tabernacle Church.[3]

By no stretch of the imagination was this gloomy woodland a fit place to fight a battle. The dearth of roads would impede the passage of infantry, pre-vent the deployment of cavalry, and deny fields of fire to artillery. By his own admission, Joe Hooker had not given proper attention to the influence the

Wilderness would exert on his strategy. His plans, and his army, would suffer for that neglect.

BEFORE DAWN ON APRIL 30, General Meade turned his soldiers out of their bivouacs and started them marching southeastward down the Ely's Ford Road and through the forest toward Chancellorsville. His supporting cavalry, the Eighth Pennsylvania, preceded the advance. A three-squadron detachment of the regiment, under Maj. Pennock Huey, probed gingerly toward United States Ford, where Meade was to make contact with Couch's Second Corps. Showing commendable stealth, the horsemen sneaked up on and captured a picket force left behind by General Mahone. Continuing onward, however, they blundered into a fight with Rebel infantry not far from United States Ford.

Fearing that the enemy would dispute his effort to connect with the Second Corps, Meade sent only half of his force, Sykes's division, in that direction, while intending to proceed to Chancellorsville with Griffin's division. Meanwhile, farther west, Slocum's column was also on the march down the road from Germanna Ford that intersected the Orange Plank Road southwest of Wilderness Church. The Twelfth Corps had the advance, with the division of Brig. Gen. John W. Geary out in front and Howard's corps bringing up the rear.[4]

At an early hour reports of the Federals' progress reached General Anderson, the ranking Confederate commander west of Fredericksburg. Lee had sent Anderson to the Chancellorsville

Maj. Gen. Richard H. Anderson, CSA

vicinity the previous evening to monitor the threat emanating from that sector. Although Anderson had his faults, including an occasional need to be prodded, he was an effective combat commander and had the rank Lee wanted on the scene. Having arrived there around midnight, Anderson at once huddled with

Mahone and Posey and later with the newly arrived General Wright. He then questioned the leaders of the various scouting details that had ranged westward. After receiving their reports, Anderson made the only decision possible under the circumstances—to retreat before he could be confronted and overwhelmed. At his order, Mahone fell back via the turnpike, Posey and Wright by the plank road.

A detachment of the Eighth Pennsylvania Cavalry, riding at the head of Meade's column, observed the rather precipitate withdrawal. Led by Major Huey, the outfit pursued to and beyond Chancellorsville—and into the teeth of a volley from Mahone's rear guard. The troopers recoiled and staggered backward. After this check, they decided to hold the crossroads until their infantry comrades came up and secured the position.[5]

Anderson, at about nine o'clock, halted his retreat at the very edge of the forest, some three and a half miles southeast of Chancellorsville. He was met there by engineer officers dispatched from Fredericksburg by General Lee. They had come to lay out a defensive line that would cross both the turnpike and the plank road. The perimeter would extend as far south as the bed of an unfinished railroad that paralleled the plank road. Anderson was soon joined by additional help from the rear, the twenty-four cannons of Col. E. Porter Alexander's artillery battalion.[6]

After the engineers finished laying out Anderson's line, the division commander received an extraordinary order from army headquarters. He was to dig in, preparing a line not only for the three brigades currently at his disposal but for additional troops to be sent up by Jackson and McLaws. It was difficult to believe that a disciple of Jomini could have issued such a directive. As Freeman observes, this marked the "first time, in open operations, that Lee had ordered the construction of field fortifications. He had thrown up works at Fredericksburg when he thought that he might wish to hold the heights with a small force, while keeping the rest of his troops for manoeuvre, and now he reasoned that he could increase his defensive power on the left by putting his men under cover."[7]

Another factor in Lee's decision was his growing awareness of the nature of the enemy's operations below Fredericksburg. Early that morning he had accompanied Jackson to the bluffs overlooking the Union lodgment, where the skirmishing remained desultory. Although Lee was becoming less and less concerned with the threat in that quarter, Jackson had favored a full-scale offensive aimed at driving the Yankees back across the river. Lee did not reject the thought out of hand, but neither did he approve it. He calmly replied that a full-scale advance would fail just as signally as it would have had Lee attempted it—as some believed he should have—following Burnside's repulse in front of Marye's Heights. If the effort were made and had to be aborted, the attackers would find it equally perilous to fall back and to go forward under the murderous fire from the cannons on the Fredericksburg heights. Even so, Lee was willing to consider an assault if Jackson insisted. Stonewall noted his superior's objections, then asked for time to consider them. He left Lee to

Lt. Gen. Thomas J. ("Stonewall") Jackson, CSA

make a personal reconnaissance of the ground in front, only to return later that morning to report his conversion to Lee's point of view. He had concluded that an attack would risk too much and gain too little.[8]

If there would be no offensive in front, Lee had to consider what to do about the enemy in the rear. Returning to his tent, he reexamined the reports of scouts who had observed Slocum's and Meade's movements. Lee no longer believed he was confronted in that sector by a single division fourteen thousand strong. There was growing power in the Yankee buildup that appeared to be centered a few miles from the eastern boundary of the Wilderness.

Weighing the danger posed by this concentration against the risk of denuding his lines opposite Falmouth, he finally decided that "the main attack will come from above"—i.e., from the rear. He could respond to this threat in either of two ways. He could retreat, which he was prepared to do if the enemy maneuvered in such a way as to threaten his supply line to Richmond. If, however—as seemed more likely at this point—the Yankees intended to challenge him in the Wilderness, Lee would oblige them.[9]

If he advanced against the enemy to the west, Lee would not wait to receive an attack. He would seek to take the offensive, to shape the battle even if it must be fought on ground selected by his opponent. As badly outnumbered as he knew he would be in that event, he could not afford to react to events controlled by an army able to strike him at many points simultaneously. That was one maxim Lee could not afford to violate.

His options carefully considered, he spent the rest of the morning working out the details of the movement. He would leave Early's division to confront the Yankees who continued to maneuver, but not advance, on the river. Early would be augmented by the Mississippi brigade of William Barksdale, perhaps McLaws's most combative brigadier, as well as by Pendleton's reserve artillery. The rest of McLaws's command would march after dark to Anderson's prepared line of defense, which it would help secure. If Sedgwick's response to the redeployment was as mild as Lee suspected it would be, soon thereafter Jackson would lead the rest of his corps to the threatened point. Lee himself would not be far behind.[10]

JOE HOOKER SPENT MOST of the twenty-ninth not at the front but in the rear, having returned to his headquarters at Falmouth to confer with his chief of staff and study the latest reports from the field. Although the U.S. Military Telegraph had established a communications link between Sedgwick's wing and the flanking column, the army leader believed it imperative that he personally review the latest message traffic and render any decisions that seemed called for.

One report that caught his eye suggested that troops were moving west from Lee's headquarters, while the forces opposing Sedgwick appeared to have diminished, if only slightly. Hooker could not determine if this meant Lee had intuited his strategy or was simply taking prudent measures to build up his western flank. He reacted by ordering General Couch to move his two divisions from Banks's Ford to United States Ford and to put himself in communication with the right wing. Hooker then gave Sickles notice to ready his corps for a march to United States Ford preparatory to joining the flanking column.[11]

While at headquarters, Hooker sent a dispatch to Slocum, who as senior officer had been given command of Howard's corps as well as his own. Slocum was informed that after reaching Chancellorsville he would be joined not only by Meade but also by Couch and quite possibly by Sickles as well. He assured

Slocum that Lee was counting on the Army of the Potomac delivering its main attack at Fredericksburg.

In sending this message, Hooker may have reflected that the critical hour of the campaign was drawing near, when his carefully crafted offensive would be put to the test. For the first time since putting his army in motion on the twenty-seventh, he seems to have entertained a doubt that, when the armies came to grips, all would go as he had hoped and anticipated.

He conveyed a sense of this concern in a dispatch that Butterfield relayed to Sedgwick late on the twenty-ninth. The left wing commander was informed of the gratifying progress Slocum and Meade had made. Then followed an especially meaningful sentence: "The manoeuvers now in progress, the general hopes, will compel the enemy to fight him on his, Hooker's, own ground."[12]

Many historians have interpreted this passage as hinting at a drastic change in Hooker's strategy, a switch from the bold offensive to the timorous defensive. John Bigelow, one of the first historians to study the campaign in minute detail, claims that Hooker had begun to consider "renouncing the initiative and relying for successful achievement upon the enemy's doing what he wanted him to do; that is, attacking him . . . in a position of his own choice, and against such part only of his line as should be suited and prepared to receive an attack. . . ." Other historians have expanded on Bigelow's observation to suggest that Hooker had begun to display a basic weakness in his character, one that would color his strategic and tactical planning throughout the campaign.[13]

This view is sustainable only if Hooker's primary intention was to attack Lee and force him to fight. But Hooker never thought in these terms—his plan all along had been to succeed through maneuver, not fighting. All he needed to do was to show Lee the peril facing him, squeezed as he was on two sides, and the Confederate leader would strike his tents and flee to Richmond. That Hooker did not mean to stand and fight is indicated by his refusal to advance on Lee from the south, cutting his line of communications and closing off his route of retreat. Hooker's true intent was expressed in a swaggering pronouncement recently delivered before newspaper reporter William Swinton: "The rebel army is now the legitimate property of the Army of the Potomac. They may as well pack up their haversacks and make for Richmond. I shall be after them."[14]

This example of wishful thinking wrapped in braggadocio can be viewed as yet another expression of Hooker's generous quota of self-confidence. But what he conveyed in his April 30 message to Sedgwick was his concern—a concern growing by the hour, as the showdown approached—that when Lee finally learned what his enemy was up to, he would choose to fight rather than run. In that event, all Hooker could do was to assume the defensive "on his own ground."

That had always been his fall-back position, but now, as the press of time forced him to consider the option in all its implications, he may have begun to worry that he would be unable to pull it off. Lee's reputation as a brilliant tactician and dogged fighter especially when his back was to the wall would have added to the doubt that had begun to gnaw at Hooker's peace of mind. Fighting Joe may not have slept soundly that night.

Refreshed or not, he was up and about at an early hour on the last day of April. Reacting, perhaps, to the stress he was under, he determined that Sedgwick should wait no longer to launch his diversion. In an eight thirty dispatch to the left wing commander, Hooker decreed that the operation commence promptly at one o'clock, that it be conducted in corps strength, and that it be directed toward Hamilton's Crossing, "the object being simply to ascertain whether or not the enemy continues to hug his defenses in full force." The logical implication was that if those lines were found to be weak, it meant that Lee had detached to counter the right wing. Sedgwick was not to butt his head against heavy fortifications; in fact, he had the option to call everything off if he found himself facing heavy opposition. As Butterfield had informed him the previous evening, Hooker "has no desire to make the general engagement where you are, in front of Brooks and Wadsworth."[15]

John Sedgwick could not have agreed more. He had no intention of confronting earthworks or gun emplacements unless ordered to do so as a part of a general offensive, in which event he could hope for material support. He could not determine if troops had been drawn from his front because fog and mist were hampering the observations of Professor Lowe, whose balloons had remained at Falmouth where ground support was immediately available. Nor had more down-to-earth reconnaissance been of much help. For all Sedgwick knew, his opponents had been reinforced, not weakened.

His subordinates agreed that a demonstration could prove as deadly, and as futile, as an all-out attack. Their leader seems to have decided to submerge his own opposition beneath theirs. About two hours before he was scheduled to go forward, he informed Butterfield that "General Reynolds is satisfied that the enemy have not weakened their forces either in infantry and artillery; and that a demonstration will bring on a general engagement on the left. General Brooks thinks the infantry force in his front is undiminished and strong. . . ." A half-hour later Sedgwick received from headquarters the reply he wanted: "Let the demonstration be suspended until further orders."[16]

Hooker kept the army telegraph clicking throughout the afternoon. He instructed General Benham (presumably sober by now) to take up two of the bridges on Sedgwick's front, one each from Franklin's Crossing and Pollock's Mill Creek, and move them to Banks's Ford, by which reinforcements would be sent to the right wing. This work was not to commence until after dark, as it was to be concealed from Rebel view. Hooker then directed General Gibbon to prepare to move to United States Ford at daylight on May 1, joining Couch. Hooker's plans had advanced to the point where it was no longer necessary to hold Gibbon stationary for fear of compromising operational security. Hooker even messaged Brig. Gen. Herman Haupt, the engineering genius who served (without pay) as chief of construction and transportation for the U.S. Military Railroads. In a display of confidence—or false bravado—the army leader told Haupt to stand ready to begin repairing the half-destroyed R, F & P trestle over the Rappahannock between Falmouth and Fredericksburg. This bridge would play a major role in Hooker's pursuit of his fleeing enemy, an event he expected to come to pass within days.[17]

The general next turned to the task of augmenting the right wing for the coming confrontation with Lee. He ordered Couch, as soon as the bridges were laid at United States Ford, to cross and join the two columns that would have united in the Wilderness under Slocum's command. Sickles he ordered to move with the utmost stealth to United States Ford, where he was to fall in behind Couch and cross the Rappahannock by seven o'clock the next morning.[18]

At 2:15 P.M. Hooker sent out his most important dispatch of the day. It instructed Slocum, then at or near Chancellorsville, to refrain from advancing any part of the right wing beyond the Chancellor House clearing until all the forces ordered to his support had reached him. Hooker must have known the directive would have a sobering, if not a disheartening, effect on the troops involved in the turning movement, as many were yearning to pitch into Robert

E. Lee while his back was turned. Yet the implications of Hooker's message tallied perfectly with his strategic intentions. Any disappointment the men experienced at being halted short of contact with the enemy would dissipate once Lee probed their lines, found them too strong and the Wilderness too constricting, and then turned and fled.[19]

The least meaningful communiqué Hooker composed while at Falmouth (which bore the purple prose of Dan Butterfield) was a congratulatory order that he would personally carry to the right wing. General Order No. 47 informed everyone under Hooker's command that their unstinting labor had ensured them of victory: "The enemy must either ingloriously fly or come out from behind his intrenchments and give us battle on our own ground, where certain destruction awaits him."[20]

Hooker departed Falmouth some time after four o'clock, leaving Butterfield to sit by the telegraph, and rode hard to overtake soldiers who were about to reap the fruits of their commander's strategic vision.

ONE RESULT of the Eighth Pennsylvania Cavalry's encounter with the Rebel infantry on the road to United States Ford was the dispatching of George Sykes's division of the Fifth Corps in that same direction. Sykes's command, which comprised the only Regular infantry units in the Army of the Potomac— albeit units skeletonized by lax recruiting and detachments to the volunteer service—looked forward to chastising the Confederates they expected to find at the ford. As it happened, however, they found none; by the time they arrived, as one soldier lamented, "the rebels had flown." The Regulars at least had the satisfaction of linking with the volunteers of the Second Corps on the north bank. One of the engineers stationed there was surprised and overjoyed to find "our own men . . . on the *rebel shore.*" He and his comrades hallooed across, and for the next several minutes raucous greetings were exchanged.[21]

Sykes stationed enough men at this ford to secure its south side, then turned his division about and countermarched to rejoin Meade. By 2:00 P.M. the bridge-builders had begun to lay plain-wood pontoons across the river. Unlike their colleagues below Fredericksburg, they would labor contentedly, beyond rifle range of the enemy. Both spans would be ready for use by Couch's soldiers by 3:30.[22]

Meade had halted Griffin's division at Big Hunting Run, about a mile and a half short of Chancellorsville, pending the outcome of Sykes's mission. When he learned United States Ford was in friendly hands, he resumed the march, reaching the crossroads at about 11:00 A.M. A novel sight presented itself there: "Four ladies in light, attractive spring costumes" standing on the upper veranda of the Chancellor house. These were members of Mrs. Chancellor's extended family, which included cousins and in-laws who lived locally. The home also housed refugees from areas overrun by the armies; this may explain the ladies' pronounced displeasure at having been overtaken once again. "They were not at all abashed or intimidated," one of Meade's soldiers recalled. In fact, they "scolded audibly and reviled bitterly. They stated they had assurances from General Lee, who was just ahead, that he was there anxiously awaiting an opportunity to extend the 'hospitalities of the country.' They had little conception of the terrors in store for them."[23]

While waiting for Sykes to join him and for General Humphreys to arrive from Ely's Ford (the latter had been relieved of his mission to escort the corps trains), Meade had his cavalry picket every road radiating from the clearing. An especially strong force was stationed on the plank road to the south; another detachment reconnoitered northeastward toward Banks's Ford. Via pontoons to be thrown across there, the troops at Chancellorsville could be reinforced by Gibbon's division and perhaps also by Sickles's corps if for some reason either command did not cross at United States Ford.

Orders had called for an early advance from the crossroads but they had been overtaken by recent events—more accurately, by second thoughts on Hooker's part. This became clear to everyone near Chancellorsville when Slocum's column arrived there. Slocum had resumed his march from Germanna Ford some time after 6:00 A.M., his own corps still in the advance, Howard's second-class citizens bringing up the rear. The march was unimpeded except by the jungle-like undergrowth the column's pioneers had to pole through to clear a passageway not only for the men but for the artillery teams lumbering along in the rear.[24]

The head of the column established contact with Meade's rear echelon near the crossroads at about 2:00 P.M. One hour earlier, Sykes's soldiers had come in from United States Ford. The concentration had a powerful effect on George Meade. Although not known for displays of ebullience, when Slocum joined him at the Chancellor house, some time after 2:30, the Fifth Corps commander greeted him with a boisterous shout: "This is splendid, Slocum, hurrah for old Joe; we are on Lee's flank, and he does not know it. You take the Plank Road toward Fredericksburg, and I'll take the Pike, or vice versa, as you prefer, and we will get out of this Wilderness!"[25]

The habitually reserved Slocum quickly put a damper on his colleague's enthusiasm by showing him a copy of Hooker's order, received only minutes before. As senior officer on the ground, he was directed to assume command of the Fifth, Eleventh, and Twelfth Corps and to withhold any advance from Chancellorsville until the reinforcements en route to that point—Humphreys's division, Couch's two divisions, and Sickles's corps—arrived. Meade, who had intended to push hard for Fredericksburg, was openly incredulous. Surveying the trees that loomed up on all sides, he warned that "we ought to get into the open country beyond."[26]

Slocum sympathized, but orders were orders. A disgusted Meade promptly recalled Griffin's division, which had been dispatched to Banks's Ford. The order was not well received. While moving out the turnpike preparatory to turning north on the ford road, Griffin had encountered what appeared to be a fairly sizeable force of Rebel infantry holding commanding terrain inside a clearing—this probably an advanced detachment of Anderson's force. Hoping to secure the position for himself, Griffin had sent back for reinforcements only to be met by an aide from corps headquarters conveying Meade's instructions. Griffin, whose emotions always ran close to the surface, treated the aide to a barrage of expletives. Finally, over the protests of Brig. Gen. James Barnes, the commander of his First Brigade, Griffin turned his command about and marched back to Chancellorsville, muttering incoherently.[27]

Once at Chancellorsville, Slocum began to deploy in response to his new orders. He informed Howard that his corps, which had closed up at Dowdall's Tavern on the Orange Plank Road a little over a mile west of the crossroads, would form the right flank of the wing's position. The Eleventh Corps was to extend westward, passing beyond Big Hunting Run, the distance from there to Dowdall's being about three and a half miles. At first Howard believed that his left would connect with the right flank of the Twelfth Corps, but he learned he would have to cover another three-quarters of a mile in a southeastward direction to meet Slocum.

Attending to his own dispositions, Howard placed Charles Devens's division

Maj. Gen. Oliver O. Howard, USA

on his right—the far right flank of the Union army at Chancellorsville. One of Devens's brigades was deployed facing south, the other west. Farther east, Howard stationed his Third Division, commanded by Carl Schurz, also facing to the west. Brig. Gen. Adolph von Steinwehr's Second Division constituted the left flank of the corps. Anchored at Dowdall's, its line extended east for a mile. The distance to be covered rendered the line quite shallow—perhaps too shallow to provide adequate defense. Much better situated were the other corps of the right wing. The line of the Twelfth Corps curved through the woods south and east of Chancellorsville, abutting Meade's right flank on the plank road just below the crossroads. The balance of Meade's line ran northward, covering the River Road and the Orange Turnpike, both likely avenues of enemy advance.[28]

EN ROUTE FROM FALMOUTH to the right wing, Hooker crossed at United States Ford, where he lingered to confer with General Couch and observe the passage of his corps. He then continued on to Chancellorsville, passing the upper flank of Meade's troops north and east of the crossroads. He arrived at his destination at about six in the afternoon. Within minutes his aides were distributing to the commanders of divisions and brigades copies of General Order No. 47, which was read aloud in the various camps that night. The message had already made the rounds of Sedgwick's and Couch's troops, but Hooker's presence ensured that the response of the right wing would be more demonstrative than anywhere else. It was observed that most of the soldiers wildly cheered the proclamation; some tossed their caps in the air as if the campaign had already been won. This was the impression Hooker had intended to give.

Not every member of the army was captivated by the bombastic confidence expressed in Hooker's message. As Bigelow puts it, "here and there an old soldier went on smoking his pipe in silence, and when reproached for his seeming apathy would reply to the effect that Lee had never been known to ingloriously fly, that it would be better to wait until after the battle to do one's cheering."[29]

Drawing of Hooker's headquarters at the Chancellor House

As soon as he dismounted at the Chancellor House Hooker appropriated it for his headquarters. Before his arrival, the dwelling had been the scene of conviviality and even merriment. One observer recorded that "general officers, with their staffs, as their troops approached the vicinity, gathered about and occupied the porches. It was a lively and inspiring scene . . . the presence of the ladies adding a spicy sprinkling of society and domestic life."[30]

That changed abruptly when Hooker took over the house. Most of the ladies were unceremoniously confined to their rooms and later to the cellar, where they huddled for safety when, in later days, the house became a target of Confederate artillery. By the afternoon of May 1 the dwelling had been transformed into a field hospital where grisly sights abounded. One of Mrs. Chancellor's daughters, a teenager at the time of the battle, never forgot "the horror of that day! The piles of [amputated] arms and legs outside the sitting room window and the rows and rows of dead bodies covered with canvas!"[31]

At his new headquarters Hooker conferred with his ranking subordinates. One imagines he had to use all his powers of persuasion to convince them of the efficacy of his decision to suspend the forward movement. One of those who argued with him over the halt was Alfred Pleasonton, whose troopers had nabbed a courier bearing a message sent early that afternoon from Robert E. Lee to Lafayette McLaws, relaying word that the Federals were in force at Chancellorsville. The movement had taken Lee by surprise but he intended to counter it through troop transfers to that sector.

Pleasonton handed the captured dispatch to Hooker along with the seized diary of Stuart's aide. When Hooker displayed little interest in the items, Pleasonton urged him to resume his movement out of the Wilderness: "A march of three or four miles would take us . . . where we could form our line of battle, and where our artillery could be used to advantage; we would then be prepared to move on Fredericksburg in the morning. Besides, such a movement would enable us to uncover Banks's Ford, which would shorten our communications with General Sedgwick over 5 miles, and bring us within 2 1/2 miles of Falmouth by that Ford."[32]

How much of this little speech Pleasonton actually delivered and how much was the product of a self-serving postwar memory is impossible to determine. The brigadier, a self promoter to rival Hooker, claimed to have imparted sage advice to other superiors on other occasions. Each episode appeared calculated to make Pleasonton look prescient and combative and his commanders unimaginative and lethargic. This time it was Hooker who came off looking badly, Pleasonton claiming that his superior, "who up to that time had been all vigor, energy, and activity, received the suggestion as a matter of secondary importance, and that he considered the next morning sufficiently early to move on Fredericksburg." Pleasonton's tale is not corroborated by evidence; moreover, it is contradicted in part by a more detailed, and more fanciful, account of the conversation that Pleasonton inserted into his subsequent testimony before the Joint Committee on the Conduct of the War. [33]

One reason why Hooker may have ignored Pleasonton is that he faced more pressing concerns just now. After reaching Chancellorsville he had received, via Butterfield, a dispatch from General Reynolds south of Fredericksburg claiming that Confederate troops had moved across Massaponax Creek toward his right flank. Reynolds described the moving column as between three to five thousand infantry, then added the alarming suggestion: "I think it must be troops from Richmond." This information raised the possibility that Longstreet and his two divisions had arrived from Suffolk to add their weight to Lee's defense and perhaps enable him to take the offensive.[34]

The return to Lee of his most trusted subordinate and the veteran troops of Hood and Pickett was one prospect that had long weighed on Hooker's mind. If the report proved accurate, it would change the complexion of Hooker's offensive, but to what degree he could not say. Hooker's mind eased a bit when he recalled the communiqué he had received the previous day from Maj. Gen. John J. Peck, commanding the garrison that Longstreet was besieging: "I think I can hold Longstreet here for some time, which will favor your operations very materially." Peck's remark suggested that Longstreet was still below the James. If so, Hooker could rely on his inability to join Lee before the drama west of Fredericksburg played out. Recovering his equilibrium, and his capacity for bravado, Hooker had Butterfield inform John Sedgwick, who had forwarded Reynolds's dispatch, that "General Hooker hopes they [the newly arrived Confederates] are from Richmond, as the greater will be our success."[35]

Hooker had additional information and instructions to give Sedgwick, whose lines had sustained "considerable cannonading," as if in preparation for an attack, during the army leader's journey from Falmouth to United States Ford. He had Butterfield inform the wing commander that come morning the Second, Fifth, Eleventh, and Twelfth Corps would make contact with the enemy at Fredericksburg. When the encounter took place, Sedgwick should observe the movements of the enemy opposite him, "and should he expose a weak point, attack him in full force and destroy him." If the Confederates appeared to fall back, Sedgwick was to pursue "with the utmost vigor" down the Bowling Green and Telegraph Roads, "turning his fortified positions. . . . until you destroy or capture him."[36]

Despite the disturbing possibility of Lee's reinforcement and the knowledge that the hour for action was almost at hand, Hooker, when he turned in for the night, could comfort himself with the knowledge that the numbers appeared to be on his side. As of midnight, more than fifty thousand Federals were concentrated around Chancellorsville with another twenty-two thousand en route there. Beyond Fredericksburg some forty-seven thousand additional troops were engaged in a holding action that could be converted into an all-out attack in a matter of hours. In between was Robert E. Lee, whose army—thanks to Colonel Sharpe's accurate calculations—Hooker knew to be less than half as large as his own. Of course, he had no inkling that in the small hours of May 1, even as he slumbered, Lee was rushing to meet him at the head of even fewer troops but planning to fight him on a battlefield that would make the disparity in numbers all but meaningless.[37]

BACK AT FALMOUTH, Provost Marshal General Patrick sat up late in his tent, scratching out a journal entry. The day now ending, had been "a most extraordinary 24 hours. . . . When I rose from making my last entry [in midafternoon] I was sure that the Ball would be well opened before this time, but, save a little cannonading in front of Sedgwick & Reynolds, I have heard nothing at all. . . . So far as we can see, or judge, they [the Confederates] still believe that we are making all our arrangements for a ground attack in front of Sedgwick & Reynolds. . . . We cannot understand *how* they are so blinded and that is all that makes us afraid some deep plan is laid for us."[38]

Confidence Lost

etween midnight and one in the morning of May 1, Lafayette McLaws moved two of his brigades, Kershaw's and Wofford's, whose men had been supplied with two days' cooked rations, from their entrenchments south of Fredericksburg and out the Orange Turnpike and Orange Plank Road to Tabernacle Church. Semmes's brigade of McLaws's command already had moved to Anderson's support, reaching his defensive line by seven on the evening of the thirtieth. In taking his leave of the Fredericksburg front, McLaws's left behind only William Barksdale's brigade, which remained in close support of Early's division opposite Sedgwick and Reynolds.[1]

When the Yankees below Fredericksburg failed to press their opponents on the thirtieth, Lee decided that it was Sedgwick who was playing the "Chinese Game." By evening he was making preparations to send Jackson's Second Corps, minus Early, to Tabernacle Church. The only orders he gave Jackson were to "repulse the enemy."[2]

Stonewall hauled his command—the divisions of Hill, Rodes, and Colston—from the front lines and sent it westward behind McLaws. As the troops departed, Early's division, Barksdale's brigade, and Pendleton's batteries shifted under cover of darkness to fill the void thus created. Although Jackson and McLaws had left behind most of the batteries attached to their commands, Lee ordered additional cannons sent to the front. One battery he sent downriver in response to reports that Union gunboats were shelling his far right at Port Royal.[3]

Lee was comforted by the knowledge that the ten thousand troops remaining at Fredericksburg would be under Jubal Early. Since First Manassas, the grizzled,

gruff, forty-six-year-old West Pointer—Joe Hooker's classmate—had been a sturdy cog in the machine that was the Army of Northern Virginia. Aggressive and enterprising when on the offensive, at Fredericksburg he had turned in a defensive performance that more than met the exacting standards of Lee and Jackson. Known for his crusty demeanor and rich vocabulary of profanity (Lee fondly called him "my bad old man"), of the army's many division commanders Early was probably best suited to engineer a defensive effort that smacked of a forlorn hope.[4]

Maj. Gen. Jubal A. Early, CSA

Early deserved to know exactly what his superior needed from him on this occasion. Lee, who had remained at Fredericksburg following Jackson's departure but expected to be at Tabernacle Church by late morning or early afternoon, gave his soon-to-be embattled subordinate a detailed list of instructions. To the extent possible, Early was to conceal his strength from Sedgwick; he was to hold his position even under duress; and if forced to fall back he should head south in the wake of the supply trains Lee had already put in motion in that direction. Should he learn that Sedgwick had detached to reinforce his comrades in Lee's rear, Early was to send as many of his own troops as he could spare to augment Jackson. And if Sedgwick returned to the north side of the river, Early, with his entire command, should make for Tabernacle Church with all haste. Early understood his orders and had no illusions about his situation. He knew he was being asked to perform a minor miracle—the tactics involved in holding in place almost fifty thousand Federals with a force one-fifth as large were not a part of any textbook he had ever read—but he vowed to succeed, or die trying. He knew that his men, if the proposition were put to them, would vote the same way.[5]

From the same vantage point he had occupied on December 13, Lee was surveying the last phase of Jackson's transfer operation when he was joined by J. E. B. Stuart, just back from his circuitous detour around Slocum and Meade. After crossing the Rapidan at Raccoon Ford, the "Beau Sabreur," at the head of Fitz Lee's main body, had fought his way past numerous enemy forces to rejoin the army. He had descended to Todd's Tavern, along the southern edge of the Wilderness, where he had a sharp encounter with the cavalry attached to Meade's column, before curving north on his homeward leg. After an all-night ride, he had reached Anderson's position east of Chancellorsville, whose flanks and front were now guarded by Fitz Lee's troopers. Fitz's uncle was plainly relieved to have his cavalry back at his side. Mounted reconnaissance would play a large role in the confrontation to come—in fact, a larger role than either he or Stuart could anticipate.[6]

After Stuart left him to return to Tabernacle Church, Lee spent the balance of the morning conferring with Early and some of his subordinates and reading dispatches that Jackson had sent in after reaching his new station. Some time after noon, Lee collected his staff and his escort unit and rode out the plank road toward the sounds of musketry and artillery fire.

By two in the afternoon. he was at the side of the usually drab and sometimes shabby Jackson, whom he was amused to find clad in his finest dress uniform. Lee was even more impressed by the decisions and dispositions Jackson had made upon reaching Anderson's defensive line at eight that morning. A quick survey of the local situation had convinced Stonewall that he could not permit the Yankees to advance beyond the Wilderness and gain the open ground in front of Anderson's breastworks and entrenchments. The enemy's great advantage in men and artillery would make the ensuing battle a brief, lopsided test of strength. The Confederates had to force a fight among the trees, where those advantages would be negated. Thus Jackson had uprooted the troops of Anderson and McLaws, had joined his men to theirs, and had ordered an advance.[7]

The troops had gone forward in two columns, one on the turnpike, the other on the plank road. Mahone's Virginia brigade of Anderson's division took the former path, followed closely by McLaws's command and accompanied by twenty-four guns. Farther to the rear came two more of Anderson's brigades, the Alabamians of Cadmus Wilcox and the Floridians of Edward A.

Perry. The column, whose upper flank was protected by Fitz Lee's Third Virginia cavalry, consisted of approximately twelve thousand officers and men.

The lower column, some twenty-eight thousand strong, its left flank guarded by the Fourth Virginia Cavalry, was led by the balance of Anderson's command, the Mississippians of Posey, the Georgians of Wright, and the fourteen guns of Alexander's battalion. Then came Jackson's corps—Hill's division in front, followed by Rodes's. Far to the rear on the plank road trudged Colston's division, in company with Jackson's artillery. When it came up, the infantry and artillerists of this rear echelon would add almost eight thousand men and fifty-six cannons to the forces opposing the Yankees at Chancellorsville.[8]

Upon arriving at Tabernacle Church, Lee conferred with Jackson and approved his dispositions. Then the two trotted forward side-by-side out the plank road as if drawn by the racket of battle. At the sight of the famous duo, whose very

Brig. Gen. Robert E. Rodes, CSA

Photographic History of the Civil War

presence had the ability to inspire and cheer, officers and men shouted out a greeting. "What spirit was imparted to the line," recalled Lieutenant Smith of Jackson's staff, "when Jackson and then Lee himself, appeared riding abreast of the line. . . !" Suddenly the odds facing these soldiers became less of a concern, and an image of victory began to take shape in their minds and hearts.[9]

BY 11:00 A.M. ON MAY 1, when Hooker issued orders covering the day's operations, almost twenty hours had passed since he had ordered the army to cease its advance and halt in place. At least the delay had brought the better part of two more army corps within Hooker's reach. Couch's two divisions had joined him at 10:00 P.M. on the thirtieth, and Sickles's entire corps had arrived at Chandler's house, about a mile north of Chancellorsville, at 9:00 this morning. Hooker was confident that he now had the manpower to deal the stunning blow that would awaken Lee to his dire situation, from which he had no recourse except to run.[10]

Hooker had kept his men so closely in hand that none had ventured far enough eastward to detect Anderson's presence, let alone observe the coming of Jackson, McLaws, and Lee himself. Hooker was so ignorant of the situation in his immediate front that his objectives for the day included points well within the enemy's lines. Slocum's corps, trailed by Howard's, was to advance on the Orange Plank Road to Tabernacle Church, where Hooker planned to relocate his field headquarters. The movement would escape detection through the employment of "small advance parties." It was to be completed by noon. Meade's command was to march along the River Road to a point just short of Banks's Ford, arriving by 2:00 P.M. One of Couch's divisions would extend the advance southward, taking position at the crossroads adjacent to Todd's Tavern. The balance of the Second Corps, along with Sickles's infantry and all of the cavalry, would remain at Chancellorsville as a reserve force.[11]

His biographer believes that Hooker was so confident of advancing unopposed that his orders failed to address action to be taken in the event the enemy interfered. At least one historian, however, theorizes that while Hooker's instructions to his units gave the impression of a decisive forward movement, he had already decided that he must go over to the defensive; thus the day's operation "was more for the record than a bona fide offensive gesture."[12]

If Hooker were going to assume the defensive, his left wing must take some of the pressure off his troops. Early on May 1 he wired Butterfield to have Sedgwick launch at 1:00 P.M. the demonstration he had deferred the previous day. This morning, however, the military telegraph was experiencing transmission problems; Sedgwick did not receive his orders until almost 6:00 that evening.

Sedgwick got his columns in motion within an hour of his delayed receipt of the order, but little came of it. Perhaps because Professor Lowe had reported "a large force of the enemy . . . digging rifle-pits extending from Deep Run to down beyond the lower crossing," the left wing—mainly Reynolds's part of it—went forward with extreme caution. After drawing enough fire to suggest that the enemy in their front remained strong and vigilant, the troops returned to their starting point, having achieved nothing of value to the right wing. Hooker would not have been pleased, but he had no time to lodge a complaint, for he soon found he had more pressing concerns.[13]

171

The initial fighting this day began at about 11:15 along Mott Run, which crossed the Orange Turnpike about three-quarters of a mile from Chancellorsville—i.e., about two and a half miles inside the Wilderness. The opening shots of the battle sounded during an exchange between the vedettes of the Eighth Pennsylvania Cavalry and skirmishers in advance of McLaws's division. Major Huey sent forward the main body of his regiment, which, fighting dismounted, held the Confederates at bay for a short time. Eventually, however, the troopers were forced back on the infantry in their rear, Sykes's division of Meade's corps. Sykes ordered his Regulars forward and managed to drive the Rebels before him. But approximately halfway between Chancellorsville and Tabernacle Church— still within the constricting embrace of the forest—resistance stiffened to the point that Sykes could make no additional progress. This was troubling enough, but within minutes gray-clad soldiers were moving up on his flanks. Sykes attempted to dig in, but the opposition kept mounting and his men began falling in alarming numbers. He asked that reinforcements be sent him at the double-quick. [14]

Word of Sykes's check was carried to Chancellorsville by Brig. Gen. Gouverneur K. Warren, chief engineer of the Army of the Potomac, who had accompanied the head of Meade's column out the turnpike. Hooker was as stunned by the news as if struck in the face by a saber. He had not expected a strong enemy response—in fact, he had expected no response at all except retreat. More to the point, he had not expected to be struck while on this ground, so incompatible with the free movement of units that defined warfare as Hooker knew it.

The blow that had been dealt him—so forcefully delivered as to bring a division of Regulars to a halt—had come from a powerful source, one not lacking in depth or breadth. That suggested that the Army of Northern Virginia—if not its entire force, then its main element—was confronting him. Did this mean Lee was not going to retreat although he must know the odds against him? Did Lee expect to give battle *here*, on this godforsaken ground? What was he thinking? What manner of gamble was he taking? [15]

Suddenly the awful possibilities, the confidence-shattering imponderables, began to overwhelm Joseph Hooker. In an instant he knew the unreasoning fear that is the enemy of all men who risk everything on the turn of a card or the roll of a dice but cannot afford to lose, cannot bear even the prospect of losing. The mantle of responsibility, which he had worn so lightly and so stylishly since his earliest days in the army, became a boulder of crushing size and weight. He tried to throw it off, but it remained fixed to his shoulders. Hebert observes that "in the past, when he had been in command of a division or corps, there had always been someone else to make the decisions and someone for him to criticize later. Now it was all Hooker. The self-confidence fostered since boyhood was ebbing fast." In fact, it was gone in the blink of an eye. As Hooker later admitted in a rare moment of self-awareness, painful in its honesty and intensity, from the moment of that first check in the Wilderness, "for once I lost confidence in Hooker."[16]

Now he began to act reflexively, bereft of the ability to reason, to consider the repercussions of the decisions he must render and enforce. After a long moment of hesitation, he sent out an order recalling Sykes's division to Chancellorsville. When his brain again began to function more or less normally, Hooker realized that this move had been a mistake. He had intended, if and when he assumed the defensive, to make Lee fight him on his own ground. But the Wilderness was not ground of his own choosing. It offered as few advantages to a defender as it did an attacker—fewer, perhaps, because the trees would prevent a man from detecting an advance until the enemy was at his throat. Having occupied the area for the past several months, the Rebels had a working knowledge of this immense growth of natural cover and knew how to use it to advantage. Hooker and his men knew only what they saw—everywhere trees and underbrush, barriers to advance and retreat, obstacles to the free employment of cavalry and artillery. Quite simply, there was no room for an army here, no field for a battle.

The impulse Hooker had acted on—to recall not only Sykes but every other force that had begun to advance and to hunker down to fight amid this brown and green maze—was the product of panic. Later, when he had the time to cloak his actions in words and phrases that made some tactical sense, he would claim that he ordered a fall-back because "as the passage-way through the forest was narrow, I was satisfied that I could not throw troops through it fast enough to resist the advance of General Lee, and was apprehensive of being whipped in detail. Accordingly, instructions were given for the troops in advance to return and establish themselves on the line they had just left, and to hold themselves in readiness to receive the enemy."[17]

This was the only attempt he ever made to explain—and explain away—his urge to run and hide. All he told Butterfield at Falmouth was that he had suspended his advance "from character of information." He added, obscurely: "The enemy may attack me—I will try it." In a later, handwritten dispatch he informed his chief of staff that he hoped "the enemy will be emboldened to attack me. I did feel certain of success. If his communications are cut [presumably by Stoneman's raiders] he must attack me. I have a strong position."[18]

The nature of the "information" Hooker referred to remains elusive. It may have related to a report sent from Falmouth—the fruit of ground reconnaissance, prisoner interrogation, and Professor Lowe's observations—that several thousand troops had passed from the Fredericksburg front toward Hooker's position but that the forces opposite the left wing showed no signs of having diminished. From this Hooker may have inferred that reinforcements had reached Fredericksburg from Richmond. If so, they must be Longstreet's troops, just up from Suffolk. A little after 2:00 P.M. Butterfield had informed Hooker that a couple of deserters from Early's command (one "an intelligent man" of Northern birth) had reported the arrival at Fredericksburg, the previous day, of Hood's division. The deserters' story, which also purported to supply information on other enemy units both at Fredericksburg and on the march toward Chancellorsville, was riddled with inaccuracies and apparent falsehoods, but Butterfield had passed it along as credible and Hooker apparently accepted his assessment.[19]

Copies of Hooker's message recalling every component of the right wing went out at 2:00 P.M. The order provoked an immediate and furious response. If his subordinates had been disappointed by yesterday's halt, they were incensed by today's fallback to that congested and indefensible position. According to Bvt. Brig. Gen. Francis A. Walker, the historian of the Second Corps, "so manifest and so monstrous was the blunder, that the officers who were sent with the message could not bear to carry it, nor could the officers to whom it was sent bring themselves to believe that General Hooker had such an intention."[20]

Darius Couch, who had sent Hancock's division to Sykes's support before the withdrawal order reached him, was furiously upset at having to relinquish a position on favorable terrain that would be impossible to reclaim. Conferring hastily with Hancock, Sykes, and Warren, Couch found the consensus to be "that the ground should not be abandoned, because of the open country in front and the commanding position." The surrounding terrain "was high ground, more or less open in front, over which an army might move and artillery be used advanta-geously; moreover, were it left in the hands of an enemy, his batteries, established on its crest and slopes, would command the position of Chancellorsville."[21]

In desperation, Couch petitioned Hooker to reconsider his decision, but his courier returned with a positive order to fall back. Every officer in the group expressed his disgust and Warren went so far as to suggest the order be ignored. Couch, however, decided that "nothing was to be done but carry out the com-mand," and he made preparations to do so.[22]

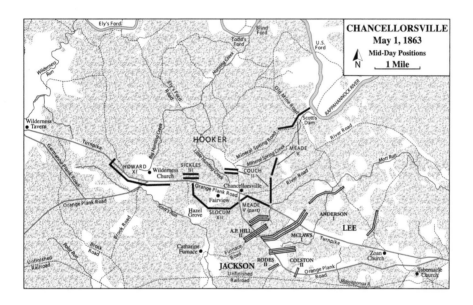

The corps leader found, however, that he could not disengage until other troops who had advanced far enough to become involved in heavy skirmish-ing pulled back first; these included the men of Slocum's corps, who had moved up on Couch's right. Sykes's division was the first to withdraw, fighting as it went, followed by Hancock's, and then by Slocum's troops. As the last seg-ment of his command began to move to the rear, Couch received a message from Hooker urging him to hold his position for three hours longer. The vac-illation conveyed in the message—undoubtedly the result of the storm of protest Hooker's original directive had created—prompted Couch to reply "with warmth unbecoming a subordinate." He added that it was too late for holding the line: "I am in full retreat."[23]

The position to which the army returned offered none of the advantages of that it had given up. According to General Walker, "the new line was drawn through low and largely wooded ground, commanded here, enfiladed there, by the batteries which the advancing enemy were already establishing on the high ground which had been abandoned in obedience to the fatal orders." Hastily laid out by Warren and his subordinates, the perimeter described a semicircle running north, east, and south of Chancellorsville. Most of the troops of the Second, Third, and Fifth Corps were positioned above the Orange Turnpike. Slocum's men had dug in below the pike, separated by a quarter-mile from Howard's corps, which extended the line westward. The Confederates commanded almost every portion of this line. Above the turnpike, a mix of McLaws's and Anderson's units faced the Union left, while Jackson's corps, supported closely by two of Anderson's brigades and one of McLaws's, opposed the Union right between the turnpike and the plank road. The nature of the terrain they occupied appeared to give the Confederates a decided advantage. Referring to the high ground he had been forced to hand over to the enemy, General Meade was heard to exclaim: "My God, if we can't hold the top of a hill, we certainly cannot hold the bottom of it!"[24]

Couch had not finished his critique of Hooker's generalship. After falling back, he galloped to the Chancellor house and confronted his superior. He had barely begun his tirade when Hooker, who had regained at least a portion of his earlier aplomb, stopped him with the assurance that "it is all right, Couch, I have got Lee just where I want him. He must fight me on my own ground." Couch was stunned into silence. He turned on his heel and stalked off without another word. Later he explained that "the retrograde movement had prepared me for something of the kind, but to hear from his own lips that the advantages gained by the successful marches of his lieutenants were to culminate in fighting a defensive battle in that nest of thickets was too much, and I retired from his presence with the belief that my commanding general was a whipped man."[25]

AFTER THEIR INITIAL ENCOUNTER with the troops of Sykes and Hancock, Lee's soldiers were surprised to observe their opponents cease their advance, then retire. At approximately 3:00 P.M. Jackson sent three of A. P. Hill's brigades, under Brig. Gen. Henry Heth, from the Orange Plank Road to the

Orange Turnpike and ordered them to move up the latter road until forced to halt. As Heth advanced, the Yankees continued to withdraw. Slocum's corps,

National Archives

Maj. Gen. Ambrose P. Hill, CSA

which had taken up a forward position on the turnpike, was so hard pressed it was thrown into temporary confusion but managed to regain cohesion and reach the safety of breastworks hastily constructed at the crossroads. Heth continued on till he encountered Hancock's division north of the pike, which he engaged until darkness compelled him to withdraw.[26]

Other elements of the Confederate line, including McLaws's entire command, also advanced. Some made indifferent progress, but one movement paid handsome dividends. At about the time Heth went forward on the plank road, Wright's Georgians advanced south of it.

Wright had been instructed to locate and envelop Hooker's lower flank. His line of march skirted the bed of the unfinished railroad that paralleled the plank road. Encountering little opposition, the brigade crossed the road to Catharine Furnace; some time in late afternoon, it reached the furnace itself. There Wright met J. E. B. Stuart, accompanied by his staff and some horse artillery batteries under Maj. Robert F. Beckham.

Wright had intended to turn north toward Hazel Grove, which, because it enclosed high, cleared ground, would provide a critical foothold in rear of the Union right. Stuart cautioned his colleague that Yankees—Slocum's troops—occupied the woods north of the furnace and also Hazel Grove. Wright decided to press ahead anyway. Resuming his march, he soon encountered a Twelfth Corps outpost, whose occupants—two regiments—offered spirited resistance. Bringing up his reserves, Wright drove the Federals from their position and into some recently completed entrenchments on the northern edge of Hazel Grove.

When halted by the fire from the occupants of these trenches, Wright called on Stuart for artillery support. But as soon as Beckham opened fire, he drew a deadly barrage from undetected positions not only at Hazel Grove but also farther to the northeast, at Fairview. Wright, Stuart, and Beckham beat a hasty retreat, as did Stonewall Jackson, who had reached the scene with his staff as the Union guns started in.[27]

Before being chased from his forward position, Stuart had been gathering intelligence on the lay of the Union right flank, which he found to extend up the turnpike past Hunting Run. Fitz Lee's brigade had been especially active in that area, during which it had a sharp encounter with some of Howard's troops. What Fitz's scouts learned in the course of this reconnaissance would have a major impact on everything that transpired at Chancellorsville over the next three days.

As yet ignorant of his cavalry's findings, Robert E. Lee had been assiduously planning to take the offensive. His initial intent was to assail the Union left in an effort to cut Hooker off from United States Ford, by which he might gain additional forces. Lee went forward on a personal reconnaissance in that direction, but his findings were inconclusive. The closer he got to the Union line, however, the more surprised he was, and to a certain extent troubled as well, by the enemy's behavior. Lee's troops were sweeping forward on all sides, pressing the enemy backward with relative ease. Was Hooker deliberately falling back, hoping to lure him into a trap of some sort? Perhaps the man had prepared formidable defenses deep in the forest, against which an attacking force would bleed itself white.

As yet Lee had no answers, but he was willing to take a gambler's chance—he knew of Hooker's tendency to "flunk" when the chips were down. First, however, he needed more information about his enemy's dispositions. That was why Heth, Wright, and the leaders of various other advances had been sent out along, above, and below the roads that wound through the trees to Chancellorsville.[28]

Some time before sunset Jackson reported that the Federal withdrawal had ceased and his own advance had been checked. Shortly after dark Lee rode out the plank road and met his subordinate returning from Catharine Furnace. They talked strategy, Lee stressing that a point must be found that could be attacked successfully. As a Jominian, he preferred a flank assault, thus minimizing casualties, but if he must attack Hooker's center he would do so.

He had come to doubt that the Union left was a viable objective. Although he did not know for a certainty which elements of Hooker's army were at Chancellorsville (he had not learned of Couch's or Sickles's arrival on the scene), he had a fairly clear picture of how many troops held Hooker's left. He had been informed that those soldiers had built breastworks and dug entrenchments, which they continued to improve. Later Lee would discover that some Federals had fashioned abatis (baskets of sharpened stakes) and had felled trees to clear fields of fire for their cannons.[29]

If the Union left was a known quantity, the right flank was something of a mystery to Lee. He did not know where Howard's people had taken position—he was not even certain the Eleventh Corps was on the ground. Lee told Jackson that he must have a better idea of the defenses Hooker had constructed in that sector. While their staffs milled about at a respectful distance, the generals dismounted and sat on pine logs under the darkened trees. As their conversation continued, Lee perceived that Jackson thought success virtually assured. The ease with which Hooker had been driven to his crossroads suggested that his entire movement was a feint. Having been countered, Hooker would have to withdraw across the Rappahannock. "By tomorrow morning," Jackson predicted, "there will not be any of them this side of the river."[30]

Lee hoped his subordinate was correct but did not share his optimism. Having worked so hard to bring so much force to bear on his enemy, Hooker could not afford to pack up and leave without making an effort to engage Lee. Undoubtedly Hooker hoped to persuade his adversary to attack him behind his strong works. Lee was entirely willing to take the initiative Hooker was relinquishing, but he was determined to use it properly. At length he sent for a couple of trusted engineer officers including Captain Boswell of Jackson's staff and ordered them to make a thorough reconnaissance of the ground in front of Hooker's position. If, afterward, the two advised against a frontal assault, and Lee could find no other place to strike, he would give up the offensive, at least temporarily, and try to maneuver his way into the Union rear—wherever it was.

The officers saluted and rode off, to be replaced by General Stuart, who had an important finding to divulge. Before the sun went down some of Fitz Lee's scouts had penetrated so deeply into the woods that they had located the extreme Union right on the turnpike beyond Big Hunting Run. They had found that flank to be unanchored on a natural defensive point. Nestled inside a thick grove of pines, the position could be approached without detection. Not only would the defenders' visibility be limited, but few cavalrymen appeared to be stationed anywhere in the area. In fact, Union cavalry had been in short supply wherever Fitz Lee had looked. Their scarcity increased the prospect that the position would be taken by surprise.[31]

The intelligence stimulated the conversation between Lee and Jackson, especially after the engineers returned with a negative assessment of a frontal assault. Thereafter Lee only considered attacking on the right. He wondered if it were practicable given the distance to be covered, which included a long detour to the southwest in the interest of escaping detection. Then, too, the operation would entail a division of forces for the second time in as many days. A fraction of a fraction of the army would have to pass the enemy flank unseen and take position on the west side of Hooker's line so as to strike it squarely from the rear. Having the assault column face in that direction—toward the rest of the army—would improve the chances of the two segments reuniting before either could be crushed by the enemy's preponderance of strength.

After further discussion, Lee decided that the gamble should be taken. His mind was eased somewhat when the "chaplain general" of Jackson's corps, the Reverend B. T. Lacy, reported to Lee just before the latter turned in for the night. Stuart had sent him, having learned that Lacy had once ministered to a congregation in the area to be covered by the flank column. The clergyman confirmed to Lee's satisfaction that good roads gave access to that section of the turnpike on which Hooker's flank rested. An attacker could expect to make steady progress en route to the objective. The point eased Lee's worry that the movement called for endurance beyond that of most soldiers.

The information Lacy imparted, although important, was not the deciding factor in Lee's decision. By the time the minister joined him, the army leader had made up his mind. Already he had instructed Jackson to launch the operation as early as possible in the morning.

Stonewall's reply had been concise: "My troops will move at 4 o'clock."[32]

WHILE LEE PLANNED BOLDLY and confidently, his opponent—uncertain of, and apprehensive about, the future—waited uneasily for events to unfold. His carefully laid and well-executed strategy having unraveled in the face of circumstances beyond his control, there seemed nothing to do but hope that Lee would assault him in the morning, bashing his brains out against the heavy defenses

Hooker's troops had constructed all along their tree-sheltered line. Their general continued to cling to the chimera that—as he informed Butterfield in a dispatch sent just before he turned in for the night—"the enemy in his desperation will be compelled to attack me on my own ground." To this feeble boast, he added a strange and plaintive postscript: "I am all right."[33]

It was a statement that Joseph Hooker would not be able to make the next day, or for many days thereafter.

Trusting to an Ever Kind Providence

W hen the guns quieted and the stirrings around the campfire ceased, Lee snatched at sleep in his pine-shaded sanctuary. Some time before dawn, he was again awake. Discovering that Jackson had already arisen, Lee joined him by the fire. Perhaps an hour earlier, Jackson had conferred with Chaplain Lacy, whom he had dispatched, in company with Capt. Jed Hotchkiss, Jackson's topographical engineer, to find an alternate route toward

Drawing of the final conference between Lee and Jackson

183

the Union right, one farther removed from Hooker's lines than the one that the clergyman had recommended the night before. Now Lee and his subordinate sat on some cracker boxes abandoned by the enemy and awaited the men's return. They discussed the general plan of attack, which they agreed must be put in motion at an early hour lest the enemy make bold to attack the part of the army that Jackson would leave behind. Jackson believed that Hooker had been cowed into immobility, but Lee suspected that even a poor poker player could nerve himself to call a bluff now and then.[1]

When Lacy and Hotchkiss returned, the engineer officer perched on a box between the generals and oriented them to a map of the area that he had sketched. He indicated where he and the chaplain had located a recently hewn trail through the woods that led from Catharine Furnace to the Brock Road, the thoroughfare Jackson expected to take to his objective. One of the proprietors of the furnace, who had brought the obscure route to Hotchkiss's attention, had agreed to provide Jackson with a guide—his own son. This seemed to assure all concerned that the movement had sufficient chance of succeeding, even with the distance to be covered and the presumed proximity of enemy sentinels at various points along the route.

After several minutes of concentrating on the map, Lee turned to his subordinate, and in a quiet voice asked what he proposed to do next. "Go around here," Jackson replied, tracing with his finger the roundabout path Hotchkiss had mapped. Lee had not specified how many troops Jackson should take. Now he asked, "What do you propose to make this movement with?" Stonewall believed it would not do to march with only a portion of the twenty-six thousand troops under his command. A lesser force would rob the attack of the crushing force it must deliver in order to be effective. "With my whole corps," he answered.[2]

In fact, he would take not only his own command, including the eighty-eight cannons attached to it, but an additional regiment—the Eighth South Carolina of Kershaw's brigade—and fourteen of the guns allocated to the First Corps. To keep watch over the enemy as he marched, as well as to guard his flanks and rear, he would also be accompanied by three and a half regiments of Stuart's cavalry and the ten horse artillery pieces commanded by Major Beckham. The total force would consist of more than twenty-eight thousand troops of all arms and 112 guns.

Jackson would leave behind the bulk of Anderson's and McLaws's commands, approximately thirteen thousand infantry and twenty-four cannons. This force—only one-third of the infantry and 20 percent of the artillery available to Robert E. Lee this morning—would have to hold the line against four times as many Yankees in position around Chancellorsville. Lee calculated that the thirteen thousand would have to maintain their position, commanding Hooker's attention without giving him an opportunity to attack, for seven or eight hours, perhaps longer. Lee would command the force, for he considered the operation too important to be entrusted to any subordinate. Anderson and McLaws were capable enough at carrying out orders but neither had demonstrated the capacity to shoulder independent command, at least not one of this magnitude.[3]

Lee and Jackson shared the map for a few minutes longer, discussing logistical issues with Hotchkiss. While they talked, Lee took notes on the composition and position of the forces to be left in his charge. Finally, he turned back to his trusted lieutenant and gave official approval to the mission: "Well, go on." Jackson stood up, saluted, mounted, and rode to the bivouac area of his corps. The men, just now coming awake, were partaking of a scant breakfast.

It took some time for the division and its attached forces to break camp and assemble on the road to Catharine Furnace. Preliminary actions had to be attended to before the march began. At Lee's order, Wilcox's brigade of Anderson's division, supported by two batteries, returned to its former mission of guarding Banks's Ford. Shifts of position necessitated by Jackson's leave-taking involved three more brigades: Wofford's, Posey's, and Wright's. A brace of rifled guns commanded by Maj. William J. Pegram advanced toward the left flank of Hooker's line at Chancellorsville and began shelling the nearest Federals to keep them from detecting Jackson's pull-out. The twenty-minute barrage attracted the fire of at least a dozen Union guns. Undaunted, a line of skirmishers from McLaws's division moved up on the turnpike, probing the lines opposite them. The movement disclosed that Hooker's troops continued to hug their works due east of the crossroads. They showed no inclination to assume the initiative—a finding that eased Lee's concern about the precarious position in which he was about to place the army.[4]

These several actions had the effect of delaying Jackson's departure until at least five thirty, ninety minutes behind the schedule he had set. At about that hour, the head of his column, Brig. Gen. Alfred H. Colquitt's Georgia brigade, left its bivouac near Alrich's farm at the intersection of the plank road and the Catharpin Road. Other units slowly fell in behind Colquitt and the line began to lurch forward. The still-forming column moved northwestward as far as the Decker farm and the head of the road to Catharine Furnace. There it swung due west past Robert E. Lee, who was observing the march from atop a hill on the Decker property. When Jackson rode up, he engaged his superior in brief conversation—the last words they would ever exchange.[5]

After a few minutes Stonewall moved on and Lee stood watching the men go by, whom he gestured into silence every time they sent up a cheer. By eight o'clock or a little later, the column, which included the cannons and ammunition wagons attached to each division, had passed the Decker farm and was lost to Lee's view. Only the main supply train was still visible as it trundled down the Catharpin Road toward Todd's Tavern. This route, which reached farther south than the road taken by the infantry, would ensure the wagons' ability to evade detection and perhaps seizure.

Well before the column had passed, Lee turned to the task of redeploying Anderson's and McLaws's men. He instructed Wilcox that if the Yankees opposite Banks's Ford showed signs of forcing a crossing in his front, he was to hasten to the support of Lee's main body with all but a small segment of his command. Lee then moved Wright's brigade down the road to the furnace, where it formed on the right flank of Posey, whose position extended nearly to the line of the unfinished railroad. Finally, Kershaw's brigade was brought up from the rear to plug the gap between Anderson's right and McLaws's left.

When the dispositions were complete, Lee's defensive perimeter stretched for three and a half miles from the furnace on the southwest to Mine Road on the northeast. Skirmishers were placed well in advance and the gaps between regiments and brigades were filled with artillery pieces positioned to cover all avenues of approach. Despite every effort to maximize its strength, however, the line was so elongated as to be thin in many places and threadbare in more than a few. If attacked in force anywhere, the entire position might quickly cave in. Hooker certainly had enough men to make this a reality if he should go over to the offensive even in a limited way. Lee was fully aware of his vulnerability but could do nothing to remedy it.[6]

He was likewise aware that should Jubal Early—facing the same lopsided odds at Fredericksburg—be driven from his position, Anderson and McLaws would be in mortal danger. Especially if Hooker coordinated an advance with Sedgwick, Lee would have no hope of holding either the line facing Chancellorsville or that at Fredericksburg. In that event Jackson's force would also be subject to annihilation. Focusing on the critical nature of Early's defensive role, Lee sent to Fredericksburg his chief of staff, Col. Robert H. Chilton—West Point classmate of both Early and Hooker—to impress on Early what he must do if attacked by Sedgwick or if the latter should abandon the Fredericksburg front to reinforce his superior.[7]

Having done what he could to contain Hooker with the meager resources at hand, Lee sent a communiqué to Jefferson Davis in which he endeavored to explain what he intended to do and the risks it entailed. He described the enemy's position, which Hooker evidently intended to hold indefinitely and which he already may have reinforced from the troops facing Early. That position was so inherently strong that Lee could not strike it directly. Even an indirect attack might not succeed, in which case "I shall have to fall back and Fredericksburg must be abandoned. If [I am] successful here Fredericksburg will be saved and our communications retained. I may be forced back to the Orange and Alexandria or the Virginia Central [Railroad], but in either case I will be in position to contest the enemy's advance upon Richmond."[8]

He mentioned the success gained the previous day in repulsing the enemy's advance from Chancellorsville and his inability to drive the Yankees from the position to which they had withdrawn. Mention of Jackson's flank movement was confined to a single sentence: "I am now swinging around to my left to come up in his [Hooker's] rear." He closed the body of his message by lamenting that he must fight with less than his entire command, for he held out no hope of Longstreet's rejoining him in time to deal with the bluecoats who opposed him in such overwhelming strength.[9]

It was not the most optimistic message Jefferson Davis ever received from a field commander, but it gave him a realistic picture of Lee's situation, one lacking in the hyperbole and bombast with which his opponent's dispatches habitually overflowed.

O N   T H E   M O R N I N G   of May 2 Joe Hooker awoke from a restless sleep to contemplate anew his army's situation. Although he outnumbered his enemy on the present line by at least two-to-one and probably by an even wider margin, he was concerned that he lacked the manpower to make his position as strong as it should be. Just before seeking sleep, he had messaged Butterfield to order the First Corps to leave Sedgwick and join the right wing via United States Ford. One of the first matters Hooker attended to upon arising was to determine if Reynolds had begun the transfer operation. He learned that the corps was shifting positions with the Sixth Corps prior to withdrawing; the march to the ford would commence by 8:00 A.M.

Hooker knew that the unexpected transfer of Reynolds's troops would weaken Sedgwick's hold on the Fredericksburg line, but the left wing commander still had his own corps, the largest in the army, and it was entirely possible that the Confederates facing Sedgwick had been reduced over the past day or so. Sedgwick retained the strength to break through to Chancellorsville if he tried, which is what Hooker expected him to do this day.[10]

Fighting Joe spent the early morning observing from a safe distance the progress of the skirmishing that had been going on east of Chancellorsville since sunrise. The sleep he had gotten, brief as it was, had refreshed him to the point that he knew at least what had to be done to prepare his army to receive Lee's assault. Gathering up his staff including Lieutenant Colonel Comstock, the engineer officer who oversaw Professor Lowe's operations, and accompanied by some high-ranking subordinates including Dan Sickles, at about 7:00 A.M. Hooker left headquarters on his white charger to inspect his defensive perimeter and shore up any parts of it that appeared weak.

Probably he first visited the extreme left of his line, which now extended all the way from Chancellorsville to Scott's Dam on the Rappahannock, just over a mile downriver from United States Ford. This sector was occupied by Meade's corps, which formed a continuous, densely packed line. During the night Griffin's division had moved into position between Humphreys's division, on the far left, and Sykes's troops, on the Mineral Springs Road. After inspecting this position, Hooker ranged south to examine the works built by Couch's command. Hancock's division was in front on this line, its lower flank extending to the Orange Turnpike, where it was refused at a ninety-degree angle to the west, before bending backward. French's division he found dug in about a mile northwest of Hancock, along the road to Ely's Ford.

Hooker and his entourage would have continued their tour by riding south as far as the Orange Turnpike, then turning toward Chancellorsville. A short distance southeast of the Chancellor house Hancock's right flank connected with the left of Slocum's corps—the divisions of Geary and Brig. Gen. Alpheus S. Williams. Slocum's semicircular line curved southwestward from the intersection of the turnpike and plank road to a point on the latter where stood two adjacent buildings known locally as the Old Schoolhouse; this line enclosed the fortified clearing of Fairview. The Hazel Grove salient, to the south and west of Slocum's position, was occupied by Maj. Gen. David Bell Birney's division of Sickles's command, which was detached from the rest of the corps. The divisions of Brig. Gen. Amiel W. Whipple and Maj. Gen. Hiram G. Berry (the latter being the command Hooker had led on the Peninsula and at Second Bull Run) had taken position in a narrow field behind the Chancellor house, where they were kept in reserve for quick transfer to the front line as needed.[11]

From Hazel Grove, Hooker's tour of inspection proceeded out the plank road past the Old Schoolhouse to the bailiwick of the Eleventh Corps. On the far left of the corps's line sat Dowdall's Tavern, a wooden structure one and a half stories tall, which since 1859 had been the home of the Reverend Melzi Chancellor (despite its local designation, the place had not served as a watering-hole for several years). Currently it housed the headquarters of Oliver Otis Howard, who had inherited it from its previous tenant, General Slocum.[12]

At Dowdall's the one-armed Howard (he had lost his right limb at Seven Pines/Fair Oaks) joined Hooker and retinue in inspecting the Eleventh Corps defenses, which Colonel Comstock found wanting in some respects. Although Hooker ordered Howard to carry out the engineer's recommendations, nothing appears to have been said or done about the weakest points on the line, its far flanks. To the east a considerable gap continued to separate Howard's left and Slocum's right. Theoretically, the space was bridged by Birney's salient at Hazel Grove, but the nearest troops lay a good mile from Dowdall's Tavern. Even more vulnerable was the far right of the Eleventh Corps. Immediately south of Dowdall's Tavern, along what Howard called a "curving ridge," he had positioned the division of Brig. Gen. Adolph von Steinwehr, a veteran of the Prussian army. Farther to the right was the division of Carl Schurz, who had fought the Prussians during the revolutionary conflicts of the 1840s. Schurz's line, which now faced southwestward, hugged the pike as far as the Talley farmstead, where General Devens, who commanded the division on Howard's far right, had his headquarters. Devens had refused his flank by placing Col. Leopold von Gilsa's brigade at a right angle to the northward, but only two of its regiments faced west toward the rear of the corps.

As Howard later observed, von Gilsa's brigade originally had been deployed well out along the turnpike with only a thin skirmish line connecting it with the brigade east of it, that of Brig. Gen. Nathaniel C. McLean. Perhaps as a result of Hooker's inspection, von Gilsa's men were drawn in closer to McLean, "so as to make a more solid connection, and so that, constituting as it did, the main right flank, the reserves of the corps could be brought more promptly to its support . . . should an enemy by any possible contingency get so far around." To be sure, this was a contingency that neither Howard nor any of his subordinates expected to face. The fact remained, however, that Devens's position in the woods, where trees and underbrush would obscure an attacker from view, was quite precarious.[13]

Moreover, the refused sector of Devens's flank was barely four hundred yards long and a half-mile or more distant from the nearest supports, the reserve brigade of Francis Barlow. Hooker and Comstock ought to have detected this vulnerability and taken steps to rectify it. The army's left was comparatively strong, resting as it did upon the Rappahannock near Scott's Dam, but no such barrier anchored the far right, which lay four miles from the south bank of the Rapidan. Hooker's intention in ordering the First Corps to join him from Fredericksburg had been to cover the gap between Howard and the river, but events would conspire to prevent this step from being taken.[14]

Although hopeful of bolstering it, Hooker did not consider Howard's position especially vulnerable. To the end of his days, the army leader rejected the criticism that, because it lacked a natural anchor, Howard's right was "in the air." He wrote fifteen years after the battle: "When we consider the dense forest in which the Corps was enveloped I do not think the suggestion a credible one to either the manhood or soldiership of those officers [whose units held the flank].

It seems to me that that 11 or 12 thousand men should be able to make a *point d'appui* of themselves without any additional accessory, if their officers were imbued with the proper feeling. . . ." Thus, the caliber of his subordinates, not the condition of the flank, was the key to holding it.[15]

Despite some misgivings about a sector here and there, Hooker believed the position he had staked out around Chancellorsville was strong enough to resist any blow Lee could deal it. At one point in his tour, he was heard to exclaim about the breastworks and rifle pits confronting him at every turn: "How strong, how strong!" He also believed that the morale of the defenders remained high— perhaps higher than his own this morning. As he rode along the line the men greeted him with what Sickles described as "hearty and prolonged cheers," as they had over the past several days. The object of their enthusiasm recalled his frame of mind at this juncture: "I felt confident . . . that I had eighty chances in a hundred to win."[16]

On his way back to headquarters, he stopped at the position held by Sickles's reserves and chatted briefly with division, brigade, and regimental commanders as well as with some staff officers. To many observers, he appeared his old self, exuding confidence and poise. He assured General Patrick, just arrived from Falmouth, of the correctness of his plans: "All were working admirably and . . . the game was in our hands." Another spoken to, Col. Robert McAllister of the Eleventh New Jersey, reported in a letter to his family that "Genl. Hooker is in fine spirits and says our success is assured. I hope it is so." Yet Hooker's highest-ranking companion cautioned McAllister that much hard work lay ahead: "Genl. Sickles says that we will be engaged this afternoon. Another report says that the Rebels have been reinforced, and it is also said that they are falling back some ¾ of a mile." Uncertain who or what to believe, the colonel prepared his regiment for a host of contingencies including repelling an assault at any point on the army's line.[17]

JOE HOOKER FOREVER REGARDED Jackson's flank march as a suicide mission, one that should never have been attempted under the best of conditions and certainly not under those obtaining on May 2, 1863. Years later he would complain that "Jackson's movement if not an accident was eccentric, and reprehensible, as no one would be justified in anticipating [its] success. . . .

the movement was an unheard [of] one, and under the circumstances admitted of not a ray of probability of successful execution. Ninety nine chances out of a hundred, Genl Jackson's Corps would have been destroyed."[18]

For attempting such a long shot, Hooker held Jackson solely responsible: "It is for such movements that Jackson will ever be considered as an unsafe person to place in command of Armies." The low probability of success "should furnish abundant evidence of his imprudence and madness, as it doubtless will . . . [when] human opinion is matured and crystallized on this subject."[19]

In lodging his ironic complaint, Hooker failed to fault the man most responsible for the risky operation. It was Lee who had determined to make the movement in violation of every military principle dear to his heart. Jomini, for one, was clear on this point: "It may be laid down as a principle, that any movement is dangerous which is so extended as to give the enemy an opportunity, while it is taking place, of beating the remainder of the army in position." Lee's decision to fragment his already fragmented army and send almost half of it in broad daylight on a roundabout march across the extended front of the enemy's position was a classic example of risking everything because half-measures would not suffice.[20]

In fact, Lee was taking a double gamble. Not only was he betting that Jackson could move undetected or at least unimpeded to a distant objective, he was gambling that Hooker would not advance against the remnant Jackson had left behind. Lee made the move because he believed he knew enough of his opponent's character and personality to predict his action (or inaction) in response to it. Everything indicated that Hooker had hunkered down behind woodland defenses so well crafted and formidable he could not bear to leave them. Quite simply, it was not in Hooker's nature to take a risk now that his plan to sneak up on Lee had been detected and countered. By deciding to stay put and fight it out in the Wilderness, Lee had robbed his opponent of the will to take the initiative. The next move was Marse Robert's, and it would be throughout the day.

Few events threatened the peace of mind Lee had achieved once he determined to play the gambler. The morning passed in desultory exchanges of rifle fire, shell, and canister. As Freeman writes, "the early hours were such as the army might have spent during the weeks of waiting in front of Richmond, eleven months before." Now more certain than ever that Hooker would not assail him, Lee turned his attention to the flanking maneuver, a source of greater concern. Beginning at about 10:00 A.M., artillery fire erupted from the general direction of Jackson's march. Over the next hour or more, it grew steadily before abruptly ending without any indication of its result.[21]

Then, shortly after noon, volleys of musketry could be heard coming from Catharine Furnace. Lee learned that a Yankee force had attacked one of the wagon trains trailing Jackson's artillery. Although he lacked the resources to cover the flanking column, Lee moved two of Anderson's brigades closer to the threatened sector to provide remote support. Lee was concerned that Hooker had gathered the nerve to make at least a brief attempt to oppose Jackson's march. At length, however, word reached him that the Yankees had withdrawn and the wagons were resuming their movement toward a place beyond range of assault.

After these anxiety-stirring events, Lee's mind was eased by a return to the featureless skirmishing that had occupied the morning hours. In midafternoon activity flared on the right, where Wofford's brigade reacted strongly to an aborted enemy advance, but the pattern of listless exchanges of musketry and artillery quickly resumed.[22]

Some time after 3:00 P.M., a courier handed Lee a message he welcomed. Jackson had taken time on his march to report that he was making good progress and hoped "as soon as practicable to attack. I trust that an ever kind Providence will bless us with great success." Stonewall added a postscript that confirmed his favorable situation: "The lead[in]g division is up & the next two appear to be well closed."[23]

Lee made preparations to support his subordinate's assault, although to what degree and in which form remain unknown. Some postwar accounts claim that as soon as Jackson's artillery was heard, McLaws's division was to make a vigorous attack on Hancock's position, while Anderson attacked with Wright and Posey those Third Corps units at and near the furnace. Anderson's biographer notes only that Wright and Posey were expected to make "a show of force and a threat of attack" against Birney, "which last was to be increased when Jackson's guns were heard. They were not to make an actual assault unless some unexpectedly favorable opportunity should offer."[24]

For the rest of the afternoon Lee waited—as the shadows lengthened, with mounting impatience—for those cannons to speak. Only then would he begin to learn whether his gamble had paid off or whether it would doom his army to defeat.

UPON RETURNING to his headquarters at the end of his inspection trip, Joe Hooker learned that "a continuous column of the enemy had been marching past my front since early in the morning, as of a corps with all its *impedimenta*. This put an entirely new face upon the problem, and filled me with apprehension for the safety of my right wing, which was posted to meet a frontal attack from the south, but was in no condition for a flank attack from the west."[25]

It would appear that Hooker's concern was not a contemporary reaction but the product of twenty-twenty hindsight, for at the time—shortly after nine that morning—the nature of the movement that had been brought to his attention was ill defined. The troops who had been spotted were so strung out and so far to the south that none of Hooker's men could have identified them as a corps. Nor could Hooker have known that this force, whatever its size, was moving to strike from the west. At this point Jackson's column was heading toward the southwestern extension of the Orange Plank Road, which would carry it in the general direction of Gordonsville. This would have been Lee's initial objective had he chosen to abandon his positions at Fredericksburg and east of Chancellorsville and retreat to Richmond. This possibility tallied with Hooker's concept of the choices facing his opponent. Although he had adopted the notion that Lee would attack him, Hooker had never given up his initial hope and belief that his opponent would shun a confrontation and withdraw to a better position closer to his capital.

Whatever the state of his mind upon receiving it, the report of an enemy movement prompted Hooker to warn Generals Slocum and Howard to be alert to it and prepared to meet any contingency. In a joint message dated nine thirty in the morning, he reminded both subordinates "that the disposition you have made of your corps has been with a view to a front attack by the enemy. If he should throw himself upon your flank, he wishes you to examine the ground and determine upon the position you will take in that event, in order that you may be prepared for him in whatever direction he advances." Hooker had come to believe that the army's far right was insufficiently strong to withstand an attack, lacking as it was in "artificial defenses" and manpower. Both generals should have "heavy reserves well in hand" and should advance their pickets to points where they could gather "timely information" of an enemy approach.[26]

More than anything else, the sighting of a Rebel column south of Chancellorsville told Hooker that John Sedgwick had failed to pin Lee's army to the Fredericksburg area and suggested that recently received reports of Jackson's entire corps being in Sedgwick's front were exaggerations. Soon after his warning to Slocum and Howard, Hooker directed Butterfield to instruct Sedgwick, "if an opportunity presents itself with a reasonable expectation of success, to attack the enemy in his front. We have reliable information that all the [Confederate] divisions known to us . . . except Ewell's [i.e., Early's] are in this vicinity." Hooker told Butterfield to stress that it was impossible to judge at such distance whether or not it was "expedient" for Sedgwick to attack: "It must be left to his discretion."[27]

HOOKER'S DESIRE that his subordinates probe any nearby Rebels extended to Dan Sickles. At about ten o'clock he ordered the Third Corps leader to advance eastward on the plank road toward a portion of Lee's line where an artillery barrage had recently commenced. Calling up his reserves, Sickles dispatched to that sector a couple of regiments from Brig. Gen. Joseph B. Carr's brigade of Berry's division, accompanied by a detachment of Col. Hiram Berdan's sharpshooters from the division of Whipple. The reconnoitering force saw little action but did nab a couple of stragglers from Jackson's column, who informed their captors that numerous comrades were marching toward the Union right.

About eleven o'clock Sickles received additional information in the form of "several reports in quick succession" from General Birney at Hazel Grove, whose pickets had sighted Rebel infantry moving toward the right. Sickles believed the force to be retreating in the direction of Gordonsville or maneuvering to strike Howard's flank—"perhaps both, for if the attack failed the retreat could be continued." Sickles had Birney shell the passing troops, which caused consternation and confusion but failed to halt their westward movement. Sickles reported the activity to army headquarters, which Hooker interpreted as evidence that Lee was averting rather than seeking a collision. Late that afternoon he had Butterfield inform John Sedgwick that "we know that the enemy is flying, trying to save his trains."[28]

Sickles asked Hooker's permission to probe the enemy force with his entire command. He went so far as to message both Slocum and Howard, seeking their support in his forward movement. Unwilling to commit all his reserves to such an operation, at noon Hooker granted Sickles's request but authorized him to take only Birney's and Whipple's divisions. The politician-general was ordered to "advance cautiously toward the road followed by the enemy, and harass the movement as much as possible."[29]

Accompanied partway by Pleasonton's brigade of cavalry and a battery of horse artillery, Sickles moved Birney's men through the forest toward Catharine Furnace, which the tag end of the gray column was then passing. Birney's troops crossed Scott's Run on two hastily thrown bridges and on the other side encountered a Confederate skirmish line from the Twenty-third Georgia Infantry of Colquitt's brigade, which Jackson had left behind to discourage interference with his movement. Birney's advance drove the regiment's skirmishers to the grounds of Catharine Furnace. Their assailants pursued, only to be halted, at about two o'clock, by the fire of Capt. James Brooke's Virginia battery, which had been detached from the rear of Jackson's column to counter Sickles's advance.

Lacking enough room to employ it profitably, Sickles returned the cavalry and its attached battery to Scott's Run. Then he called up enough of his own artillery to silence the enemy guns. At this point, Berdan's sharpshooters advanced on the Twenty-third Georgia and captured almost sixty of its men. The furnace area now secure, Sickles went forward on a personal reconnaissance that made him believe he could reach the road on which the enemy was moving. At the same time, he witnessed a sight that startled him: a line of wagons and artillery units heading not westward—the direction in which Jackson was reported to be moving—but southward. The corps commander leapt to a fateful conclusion, which he at once communicated to army headquarters: "I think it is a retreat, sometimes a regiment, then a few wagons—then troops then wagons."[30]

Sickles asked permission to pursue, although he admitted that in doing so he would probably encounter stubborn resistance. For that reason, he decided not to advance unless closely supported by Slocum and Howard. Slocum responded more or less helpfully, ordering Williams's division to take up a position on Sickles's left. Howard, however, was unwilling to assist his colleague until Hooker belatedly ordered him to shift Barlow's brigade toward Sickles's right flank. This move, which Howard personally accompanied, was not completed until after four o'clock.

Thus augmented, if incompletely and slowly, Sickles resumed his advance. Reaching the road Jackson's column had taken, Sickles placed a battery in it and shelled the rear of "the retreating column of the enemy." Subsequently, he tangled with Rebel infantry that he took to be from Jackson's column. Yet not everyone agreed with him. Howard, for one, forever believed that Sickles's barrage was directed not against the flanking column but at Anderson's troops, who had advanced toward Catharine Furnace from their original position near Decker's. "It was General Lee himself," Howard claimed, "who, during Jackson's wonderful march, by means of Anderson and McLaws and part of his artillery, took care of Sickles's whole line. . . . They were engaged, not as Hooker telegraphed, with Lee in full retreat, but with Lee himself staying behind after Jackson's departure."[31]

Howard was correct, but his conclusion failed to tell the whole story. The fighting that Sickles precipitated around Catharine Furnace attracted elements of Anderson's division—Posey's Mississippians and Wright's Georgians—which Lee sent over from the north and east. Also drawn by the fighting were four Tennessee companies from A. P. Hill's division, which had failed to keep up with Jackson's column. Additionally, the brigades of Brig. Gens. James J. Archer and Edward L. Thomas had countermarched from the rear of Jackson's column to challenge Sickles's advance.[32]

Rather than Jackson's main body, Sickles had detected the passage of its reserve artillery and the ammunition train attached to it. To escape his advance, these units had turned off the Furnace Road onto a narrower and rougher path that bypassed the furnace. Initially this road ran southward, which made Sickles believe he was witnessing a retreat toward Gordonsville. With the exception of Archer and Thomas, by the time Sickles reached the road Jackson's column had passed off to the west, home free on its excursion toward the Union right.[33]

How long the fighting around the furnace went on is uncertain, but it must have lasted two or three hours, for not until some time after six o'clock did

Sickles believe he had enough support on hand to advance farther. Somehow the corps commander determined that within minutes "five or six regiments would be cut off and fall into our hands. Regarding the moment opportune . . . I was about to dispatch a staff officer to bring him [Pleasonton] forward when it was reported to me that the Eleventh Corps had yielded the right flank of the army to the enemy, who was advancing rapidly, and, indeed, was already in my rear. I confess I did not credit this statement until an aide-de-camp of General Warren, of General Hooker's staff, confirmed the report."

That ended any further efforts at pursuit. Sickles spent the last hour of daylight recalling Birney and Whipple and leading them back to Hazel Grove "for the purpose of making disposition to meet and arrest this disaster."[34]

BEYOND THE STRIKE against his reserve artillery, Jackson encountered few impediments in moving toward his enemy's right rear. Saturated by the recent rains, the road his men traveled was soft to the touch and all but bereft of the dust that, if kicked up, would have bedeviled the marchers and perhaps given away their position. Opposition consisted of a cavalry vedette or two and a couple of infantry outposts that seemed to melt away when confronted, even at considerable distance.[35]

The advantageous conditions did not stop Jackson from pushing the column forward with an almost frantic urgency. He seemed to believe that mortal danger lurked behind every bend in the road and in every woodlot the column passed. Not even the presence of Stuart's vigilant horsemen guaranteed safe passage across the front of a force several times as large as Jackson's. Stonewall's demeanor reflected the gravity of the situation. His medical director, Dr. Hunter McGuire, was struck by the general's "eagerness and intensity. . . . His face was pale, his eyes flashing. Out from his thin, compressed lips came the terse command: 'Press forward, press forward!' In his eagerness, as he rode, he leaned over on the neck of his horse as if in that way the march might be hurried. 'See that the column is kept closed and that there is no straggling,' he more than once ordered, and 'Press on, press on,' was repeated again and again. Every man in the ranks knew that we were engaged in some great flank movement, and they eagerly responded and pressed on at a rapid gait. . . . The fiercest energy possessed the man, and the fire of battle fell strong upon him."[36]

Near the intersection of the Furnace Road and the Brock Road, the column swung abruptly to the northwest. Although the Brock Road was the most direct route to his destination, Jackson did not take it at this point but shunted his troops onto a narrower road that paralleled the first. This route placed an additional half mile between the column and the nearest Federals. The marchers continued on this track, passing the railroad cut and a byroad just above it, until they regained the Brock Road about a mile short of its junction with the Orange Plank Road. Jackson intended to follow the plank road to its intersection with the Orange Turnpike near Dowdall's Tavern. By turning right at that point, he expected soon to be in a position from which he might roll up the Union right like a long blue carpet.

The only problem was that Jackson had an imperfect conception of the location of his objective. No one else in the column had a better understanding—not even the horsemen of Fitz Lee, whose business it was to know the lay of the land they traversed. Upon reaching the plank road some time after one in the afternoon, Lee's Second Virginia, riding well in advance of the infantry, turned and followed the byway as far as Hickman's place, where the Germanna Ford Road snaked off through the trees to the northwest. While waiting for Jackson's men to catch up, most of the troopers dismounted and caught some rest. One squadron of the Second, however, proceeded up the plank road.

Encountering an enemy picket, the Virginians chased it toward the turnpike. Unable to overtake the well-mounted Federals, the squadron rejoined its comrades at Hickman's. There one of the men informed his immediate superior that he had ranged close enough to gain a view of the Union line. That line, he said, extended west of Dowdall's Tavern, well beyond the point at which Jackson expected to strike it.[37]

The man's finding was brought to the attention of Fitzhugh Lee, who, accompanied by a single staff officer, proceeded up the plank road as far as the Burton farm, about three-quarters of a mile short of the turnpike intersection. Ascending a knoll on the edge of the farmstead, the brigade commander peered northward through his field glasses and confirmed the trooper's report. As he recalled years later, "What a sight presented itself before me! Below, and but a few hundred yards distant, ran the Federal line of battle. I was in rear of Howard's right. There were the lines of defense, with abatis in front, and long lines of stacked arms in rear. Two cannon were visible in the part of the line seen. The soldiers were in groups in the rear, laughing, chatting, smoking, probably engaged, here and there, in games of cards, and other amusements indulged in while feeling safe and comfortable, awaiting orders. In rear of them were other parties driving up and butchering beeves."[38]

Fitz Lee knew what Jackson did not: the enemy's position extended out the turnpike for nearly a mile west of its junction with the plank road. Had Jackson taken the latter to his destination, he would have struck not the flank of the Eleventh Corps but its midsection. Fitz galloped back to the intersection with the Brock Road, where he found Jackson riding at the head of his column. Almost breathless with excitement, the cavalryman gasped out an invitation to accompany him to the Burton farm. After a brief hesitation, Jackson followed the cavalryman to the knoll, where he could appreciate what Fitz called "the great advantage of attacking down the Old turnpike instead of the Plank road."[39]

Like Dr. McGuire, Robert E. Lee's nephew studied the corps commander's visage as he reacted to the imminence of combat: "His eyes burned with brilliant glow, lighting up a sad face. His expression was one of intense interest, his face was colored slightly with the paint of approaching battle, and radiant at the success of his flank movement."

After a few minutes lost in thought, Jackson turned and calmly instructed the courier who had accompanied him to inform the officer at the head of the column to continue up the Brock Road to its junction with the turnpike. At that point, just east of Wilderness Tavern, the head of the column should be about a mile and a half beyond the end of the Union line. There it could turn, unobserved, toward the enemy's rear.[40]

Without so much as a word of thanks to his benefactor, Jackson left Fitz Lee and galloped up the road ahead of his troops. En route, or soon after reaching the turnpike, he penned his three o'clock dispatch to Robert E. Lee. It took another two hours or more for the column to reach him, turn onto the pike, and take position among the trees surrounding the Luckett farm. With some difficulty—the product of the constricting forest—Jackson's subordinates formed the men into three lines of battle, Rodes's division in front and Colston's division about one hundred paces behind. The third line was to consist of A. P. Hill's troops, many of whom were still on the pike, waiting to be deployed, when the rest of the column prepared to go forward to the attack.[41]

Rodes's and Colston's commands presented a front two miles long, extending more than a mile north of the pike. Out in front was a force of skirmishers consisting of the best marksmen in Rodes's division. Jackson's strictures on preserving security were so carefully followed that although his lines were dressed within striking range of the Union works, Howard's men remained blissfully unaware of their proximity. A member of that unobservant force later wondered how it was that "an army of thirty thousand men could be moved directly past the front of a much larger force, and arrange itself in three lines of battle, within half a mile of the force to be attacked!"[42]

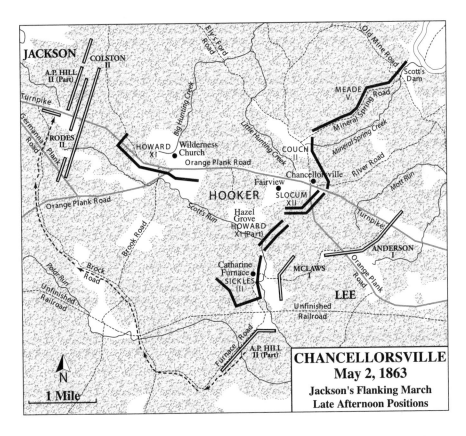

CHANCELLORSVILLE
May 2, 1863
Jackson's Flanking March
Late Afternoon Positions

Just shy of six o'clock, with less than an hour's daylight remaining, Jackson asked Robert Rodes if his division was prepared to go forward. Rodes replied in the affirmative, and at Jackson's order the skirmish line began to crunch through the forest, the main body following closely behind.[43]

My God, Here They Come!

I f, as Hooker complained after the war, Jackson's flank march was so flawed in its conception that it should never have succeeded, he refused to admit that he himself was the reason the law of probability failed to snare Stonewall and his men. Although alerted to the maneuver at an early hour on May 2, the Union commander did almost nothing to counter it. Nor did he ensure that his army was prepared to receive Jackson's blow.

Despite his later claims that he did not credit Sickles's prediction of a Confederate retreat toward Gordonsville, Hooker did believe a Confederate withdrawal was underway by the early hours of May 2. Not only did the heading of Jackson's column appear to bear this out, a retreat would have represented a logical reaction to Stoneman's raid. As of that time Hooker had yet to receive word of the progress and results of the cavalry expedition on which he had pinned so many of his strategic hopes. By the same token, he had no reason to doubt that Stoneman was laying a heavy hand on the Richmond, Fredericksburg & Potomac and other communication lines in the enemy's rear. With his lines of supply damaged and disrupted Lee would have to fall back on Gordonsville, which afforded access to a secondary line of supply, the Orange & Alexandria.[1]

But if Hooker believed the Rebels were retreating, why did he not advance against Jackson's column? Strung out as it was for over ten miles along a single, narrow track, the flanking force was extremely vulnerable at almost every point. Even a limited strike against its head or rear might have transformed the march into a chaotic reprise of First Bull Run. A general of another era, Edward J. Stackpole, described Jackson's predicament: "Weighted down by his division trains, unable to effectively deploy his troops if attacked, incapable of utilizing his artillery, Jackson was courting disaster every step of the way from early morning until late in the day. . . ." Yet Hooker not only failed to attack, he did not even probe the enemy column until noon, four hours after it was first sighted. And when he finally authorized Sickles to go after it, Hooker stipulated that his subordinate should "advance cautiously," merely in order to "harass the enemy."[2]

The blame for this masterful inactivity must be shared by several of Hooker's subordinates, notably Generals Howard and Devens. Both officers afterward claimed they had taken effective precautions against the possibility of an attack on any sector of their line. The evidence suggests, however, that neither gave credence to the numerous reports that reached them, warning of substantial numbers of foot soldiers, supported by horsemen and cannoneers, marching across their front from midmorning through late afternoon of May 2.

The earliest warnings came to Howard direct from army headquarters. The first, from Hooker himself, triggered by his inspection tour of that morning, advised Howard to examine the ground south and west of his position and determine how he would counter an attack on his flank. Soon after this message went out, Hooker dispatched a circular to Howard and Slocum (the latter no longer in charge of the Eleventh Corps as well as his own) cautioning both generals that the army's right did not appear strong enough to withstand an attack.

Both orders were dated nine thirty in the morning; couriers carried them to Eleventh Corps headquarters at Dowdall's Tavern by ten o'clock or shortly thereafter. The first arrived while Howard, having stayed up late the previous night, was sleeping. General Schurz received and read the dispatch, woke his superior, and discussed its contents with him. As they conversed, a messenger delivered the circular, which Howard read. Later the corps leader claimed he had received neither message, but his self-serving recollection is disputed by incontrovertible evidence to the contrary.[3]

Schurz recalled that while discussing the first dispatch with Howard, a report came in of an infantry column marching across the front of the corps, about two miles off. The sighting was, apparently, of that part of Jackson's column then passing through the clearing near Catharine Furnace. Just short of eleven o'clock Howard relayed this information to army headquarters along with his claim that "I am taking measures to resist an attack from the west." Yet all he did was to post the signal corps officer attached to his headquarters, Capt. Davis E. Castle, out on the turnpike a mile west of corps headquarters with instructions to alert by flag Lt. Charles W. Keen Jr., who was stationed at Dowdall's Tavern, should Castle discern any suspicious movements in that quarter. It appears that Howard also faced some pieces of his corps' reserve artillery, then arriving from the rear, toward the west.[4]

If Howard responded to Hooker's warnings through half-measures, he totally ignored other reports of Jackson's passage toward his rear. Soon after he set up his signal station, Captain Castle observed the enemy's approach and began to contact Lieutenant Keen, "reporting constantly all movements of the enemy as far as I could see them from my position." Keen relayed Castle's sightings to Eleventh Corps headquarters but nothing was done in response.

Between eleven o'clock and noon, scouts who had advanced south from the position of General McLean's brigade spied enemy cavalry, followed at some distance by a column of infantry, moving toward the Union right. Two of these scouts personally reported their findings to Howard, who merely instructed them to go to army headquarters with the story. The Chancellor house was a mile and a half from Dowdall's Tavern, and apparently the men failed to reach there in time for Hooker to act upon their information.[5]

General Devens proved to be as unresponsive as his superior. Early in the afternoon reconnaissance missions conducted by the small cavalry force at Devens's disposal, and later by infantry units of his division, detected Jackson's approach. In one case, a scouting party was fired on by the Rebels. The fact was reported to division headquarters but was not acted upon. On two other occasions between one and two o'clock, the commander of an Ohio regiment in McLean's brigade reported to Devens that his pickets had detected Jackson's movement. The brigadier merely replied that he had received no information about it from higher headquarters, which led him to doubt the accuracy of the report. Apparently Devens failed to pass on the sighting to corps headquarters, nor did he relay a later, similar report brought to his attention by his officer of the day. The officer, apparently on his own initiative, carried the information to corps headquarters, but Howard or members of his staff, believing an unsubstantiated report of this sort could create a panic, turned the man away with words of rebuke. When the officer returned to Howard's headquarters at about two o'clock with further evidence of a movement toward the right, he was told to shut up—the Rebels were withdrawing, not advancing.[6]

The calls to action became not only more numerous but also more strident. Close to three o'clock the officer in charge of the picket line of Colonel von Gilsa's brigade informed his superior that "a large body of the enemy is massing in my front. For God's sake, make disposition to receive him." Von Gilsa thought the warning so important that he personally relayed it to Howard. Reportedly, the corps commander not only rebuffed his subordinate but accused him of faintheartedness. Other German-born officers who conveyed reports of enemy sightings, including Capt. Hubert Dilger, commander of Battery I, First Ohio Light Artillery, one of the most celebrated German-American units in the army, were treated similarly either by Howard or Devens, or their staffs. The prevailing attitude at corps and division headquarters was very much in keeping with the army's lack of regard for the Eleventh Corps as a unit: foreign-born soldiers were excitable dolts who need not be taken seriously.[7]

Of course, not every bearer of calamitous news deserved to be taken seriously. Unverified sightings of enemy troops passing across the front of the corps stimulated similar reports by soldiers who were too distant from Jackson's route of march to have detected his approach or to have identified his column as friend or foe. Many of the supposedly contemporary observations that worked their way into the history of the battle were actually postwar recollections based on a knowledge of events not available on the morning or afternoon of May 2, 1863.

And yet enough pickets and vedettes came into contact with outlying detachments of Jackson's force to spawn credible reports of an ominous-looking movement toward the army's unanchored flank, and these were not only disbelieved but rejected out of hand as panic-driven fabrications. Reportedly, General Devens indulged in some serious drinking this day; when some of those reports reached him he may have been sleeping off the effects. Such behavior does not excuse his conduct but it may offer an explanation for it. Howard, however, could not plead impaired mental capacity.

For this reason, his failure to credit the many sightings of Jackson's approach and his stubborn inaction throughout the day defy rational analysis.[8]

EVEN BEFORE they heard the firing of Jackson's guns, the Federals on the far right knew that a storm was about to engulf them. From out of the trees to the west bounded deer, rabbits, squirrels, and other animals flushed from their forest homes by masses of advancing men. Then, carried on the still evening air, came the spine-tingling falsetto of the Rebel Yell, the music of thousands of voices merged into a single, lingering cry of exhilaration and terror. In an instant the woods were alive with running, screaming men in gray and butternut, swarming over the enemy they had taken unawares, shooting down men unable to reach their stacked guns, chasing fugitives from tree to tree, bayoneting those who would not or could not run. Like a raging tide Jackson's corps flooded over the two regiments Howard had faced westward, sweeping up and carrying along everything in its path—men, guns, limbers, caissons, wagons. As quickly as these went under, they were tossed aside, dead and broken, the pitiful flotsam of war.

Battles and Leaders of the Civil War

Drawing of Jackson's attack on the Eleventh Corps, May 2, 1863

The exultant Confederates swept onward, not stopping to secure captured camps or cannon, to gather up spoils, even to take prisoners. Intent on riding their momentum as far as it would carry them, they surmounted successive lines of defense, reducing to human debris companies and batteries, whole regiments, entire brigades. Because the attackers overlapped Howard's line on both north and south, virtually no one who lacked the time to run escaped the onslaught.

Units farther east received a few minutes' warning of impending doom. Although a number of officers and enlisted men attempted to make a stand, most availed themselves of the opportunity to flee. Panicked by the onrush of bodies, the spiteful crack of rifle fire, and the terrible keening that seemed to rise above the trees, rank upon rank of Howard's men threw down their arms and raced wild-eyed to the rear as if pursued by the legions of darkness.[9]

Not only the rank-and-file were caught up in the frenzied search for sanctuary. Having just returned from a visit to Dan Sickles at Hazel Grove, General Howard had topped a rise on the Talley farmstead when hundreds of panicked troops came hurtling at him. Runaway artillery units and wagons hauled by frightened teams were careening wildly through the mass of humanity. The clogged roads were further congested by fugitive beeves from the cattle herd that had accompanied the army, felling and trampling everyone in their path.

Howard saw at a single glance that he had no hope of holding back this sea of demoralization and defeat. Jerking on his horse's reins, he turned about and joined the exodus. Farther up the road, having temporarily outdistanced the mob, he snatched a national standard from the color-bearer of an undemoralized regiment. Tucking the banner under what remained of his right arm, he rode the length of his rear guard, calling on every man near him to stand firm and arrest the flight of the corps. The gesture was commendable but it achieved indifferent success. Even before the body of fugitives reached them, most of Howard's reserves turned to the rear in order to get a head start on their frightened comrades.[10]

The efforts of other officers to stop the panic were just as ineffective but more belated. An acoustical quirk—the deadening of the sounds of fighting by the densely packed trees that covered the right flank—prevented the troops around Chancellorsville from learning of the rout for more than an hour after it began. Strange to tell, no one alerted to the panic seems to have made his way to army headquarters to sound the alarm.

Battles and Leaders of the Civil War

Drawing of the retreat of the Eleventh Corps, May 2, 1863

Not until the stampede of the Eleventh Corps spread to other units closer to the crossroads clearing did Hooker get an inkling of what was happening farther west. The general and his staff were lounging on the porch of the Chancellor house. He appears to have been in a good humor, probably because John Reynolds had just arrived to report that the First Corps was crossing the river at United States Ford, almost within supporting distance of the main army.

The corps' move from Fredericksburg had been delayed almost three hours by problems either with the field telegraph at United States Ford, which relayed the transfer order to Falmouth, or with the courier who had brought the written message from Hooker's headquarters to the telegraph station. Hooker had thought the delay strange but not serious—plenty of time remained for Reynolds's men to take position on Howard's flank and shore up the army's right.[11]

At approximately a quarter past seven, Hooker's aide, Capt. Harry Russell, thought he heard a distant tumult. He stepped down from the porch and trained his field glass out along the plank road. What he saw drew from him a startled exclamation: "My God, here they come!" A minute or two later, the crossroads was alive with the same sights and sounds that Howard and his

209

subordinates had beheld over the past hour or more: frightened troops running for their lives, shouting—often in German—as Rebel bayonets jabbed their backs and buttocks.[12]

To his credit, Hooker did not react with the panicky indecision he had displayed the previous day when apprised of Sykes's repulse on the plank road. He threw himself into the saddle and, trailed by Russell and the rest of the staff, galloped into the midst of the fugitives, hoping to block their escape, corral them, and face them toward the enemy. Like Howard, however, he saw at once that his every effort would be unavailing. The men would have to outrun the enemy before they could outrun the panic. Overcome by a dreadful sense of futility, the army leader, his face flushed from stress and worry, rode back to Chancellorsville. There he called up his only reserves, his old division, now Hiram Berry's.

Berry's troops responded with an alacrity and a resolve that made its commanders, past and present, proud. With demoralized comrades rushing past it, the division marched out the plank road with steady tread, bayonets fixed. Despite the equanimity thus displayed, the officers feared that the panic would communicate itself to their men. Berry's artillery chief, Capt. Thomas W. Osborn, hoped that the sights he saw this day "may never again be seen in the federal army of the United States. The Eleventh Corps . . . were fleeing to the river like scared sheep. The men and artillery filled the road and the skirts of the field. . . . Aghast and terror-stricken, heads bare and panting for breath, they pleaded like infants at the mother's breast that we should let them pass to the rear unhindered."[13]

Berry halted his men about a half mile west of Chancellorsville, where they formed a line along a stream bed and began to entrench. They were joined by a brigade-size force of undemoralized members of the Eleventh Corps that the resolute General Schurz had cobbled together. These troops added weight to Berry's right flank, but it appears that someone on high doubted their fighting spirit; at some point, Schurz's men passed to the rear, replaced by a Second Corps brigade.

Some time after eight o'clock more help arrived—Williams's troops of Slocum's corps, who went into position on Berry's left, extending the new line toward Fairview. As soon as Rebels came into view from the west, they blasted them back with volley after volley of musketry. The opposition they generated was magnified by the fire of several artillery units, which Hooker and his staff had collared while heading to the rear. Complementing these guns were some twenty others belonging to the Third Corps, which Dan Sickles had emplaced farther south and west, at Hazel Grove.

The overall effect of these hasty but determined efforts to shore up the army's position west of Chancellorsville was most gratifying to Hooker. Before nine o'clock Jackson's attack had been mostly contained, its damage limited to the loss of the Eleventh Corps's position. Most of the credit was given to the troops who had rushed into the breach at the critical hour, especially Berry's division. Some credit was due to Hooker, for he had been responsible for Berry's timely intervention at the point of greatest need.[14]

Other officers claimed a share of the reward for helping stanch the retreat. One of the loudest voices was that of Alfred Pleasonton, whose cavalry, along with Sickles's foot soldiers, had been ordered back to Hazel Grove from Catharine Furnace shortly before Jackson attacked. En route, Major Huey's Eighth Pennsylvania was twice ambushed by some of the deepest penetrating attackers, who tried to prevent the regiment from reaching the Orange Plank Road. Huey had his men draw sabers and smash through the roadblocks. In the process his second-in-command, Maj. Peter Keenan, was killed along with two other officers and thirty enlisted men; seventy other members of the Eighth fell into enemy hands. By wild riding and sabering right and left, Huey and the remainder made it to safety inside a clearing southwest of Chancellorsville. Their ordeal would become one of the best-known episodes of the day's fighting.[15]

Pleasonton later maintained he had ordered Huey's charge with a view to preventing Jackson from striking Hooker's main body before it could re-form and halt his attack. This was just so much balderdash, as was Pleasonton's contention, voiced loudly and often both at the time and in postwar writings, that he had saved the Hazel Grove salient from being overrun. Arriving at that position ahead of Sickles, Pleasonton had taken charge of a battery of horse artillery that had unlimbered there. He claimed responsibility for directing the fire not only of this unit but of several guns attached to the Third and Twelfth Corps, in the process repulsing several thousand Rebels. In truth, the attackers had been so few—no more than two hundred members of Brig. Gen. George Doles's brigade—that they were recalled shortly after reaching Hazel Grove for fear they would be quickly overwhelmed. This did not stop Pleasonton from promoting himself as the savior of a critical sector of the Union position. He so fully convinced his superior that when President Lincoln visited the army ten days later, Hooker introduced Pleasonton to him as the man "who saved the Army of the Potomac the other night."[16]

Individual claims of having stopped Jackson notwithstanding (Sickles, who upon reaching Hazel Grove took charge of the defensive effort there, would also take credit for the outcome), the Confederate assault ceased due to dwindling momentum, gathering darkness, the opposition not only of Berry's and Williams's divisions but also of Amiel Whipple's men, and the faulty design of the attack formation. Jackson had deployed his second line so close behind his first that when terrain, fatigue, and Union resistance combined to slow the advance of Rodes's troops, Colston's men slammed into them from the rear, causing a massive traffic jam. Furthermore, because A. P. Hill's men were still dressing ranks when the charge began, they failed to add their weight to the initial attack, thus limiting its staying-power. For these reasons, not because of the single-handed heroism of a few general officers, the attack that had undone an entire army corps had shuddered to a halt about a mile and a half west of Chancellorsville.[17]

WHETHER OR NOT it ended prematurely, Jackson's assault had been wildly successful. By half past seven, full darkness having settled over the field of battle, the position of the Army of the Potomac was three and a half miles shorter than it had been ninety minutes earlier. A major defensive position had been lost; almost one-sixth of the defenders of Chancellorsville had been felled or disabled by demoralization; and their able-bodied comrades had been squeezed inside a four-mile-long line that ran from Scott's Dam south to Hazel Grove.

These achievements were not sufficient to satisfy Stonewall Jackson, who was determined to turn rout into ruin. If the attack could be renewed, he believed it possible to isolate the Yankees at United States Ford and to cut Hooker's main body off from the Rappahannock River. Although weary from their ten-hour march, the attack, and the full-tilt pursuit of Howard's "flying Dutchmen," Jackson's troops considered themselves capable of overwhelming anyone who stood in their way. Jackson believed that their lofty spirits, their fixed purpose, and the pride aroused by their accomplishments this day would help them conquer their fatigue and get the drive moving again. Conversely, he considered the entire Army of the Potomac, not merely Howard's corps, to be downcast and demoralized and thus susceptible to further manhandling. Moreover, a full moon had risen, providing enough light to support a further advance. Stonewall believed Lee expected him to keep going.

At about eight o'clock, he called up A. P. Hill, four of whose six brigades were well in hand, and ordered the commander of the Confederates' own Light Division to resume the advance. Hill was to pass through the stalled and intermingled lines of Rodes and Colston, advance along the plank road and then along the northeastward-leading Bullock Road, and interpose between the river and the Union left flank. A bystander noted that Jackson "manifested great impatience to get Hill's troops into line and ready to move promptly." It was late and everyone was tired, but rest would have to wait.[18]

After Rodes and Colston fell back from their advanced positions to reorganize, Hill's division went forward on the plank road, the brigade of Brig. Gen. James H. Lane in the van. Jackson's artillery chief, Colonel Crutchfield, covered Lane's movement with a barrage that drew a sharp response from the batteries clustered around Chancellorsville; the counterbattery fire brought Lane's column to a halt. At Hill's order, Crutchfield's cannon ceased shelling, whereupon the Yankee guns quieted and Lane went forward once again.

By now it was close to nine o'clock. Jackson, who had observed the stop-and-start motion, was fretting over the slowness of the advance. Meeting Hill on the plank road in advance of its junction with the turnpike, he urged the division leader onward: "Press them, General Hill! Press them and cut them off from the United States Ford!"[19]

As Hill moved off, Jackson, accompanied by Captain Boswell and other members of the corps staff, passed through the ranks of Lane's North Carolinians to take the advance. Several officers whom he met en route urged the general to proceed with caution, but he dismissed the suggestion with a wave of his hand. "The danger is all over," he declared, "the enemy is routed. . . . Go back and tell A. P. Hill to press right on!" He did the same, continuing up the darkened road until, accompanied by his little party, he veered into a stand of pines that separated his corps from the nearest Yankees.[20]

AFTER WITHDRAWING from Catharine Furnace, Dan Sickles became concerned about his ability to hold Hazel Grove, which he perceived to be critical

213

to keeping the wings of Lee's army well apart. To take pressure off its defenders, he petitioned Hooker for authority to attack westward against Jackson's right flank. Early in the evening, the Rebels had penetrated to within three hundred yards of the clearing, but by ten o'clock they appeared to have fallen back to occupy the breastworks and rifle pits they had wrested from the Eleventh Corps.

It was difficult to size up the opposition for, as Sickles reported, the enemy's line "could only be defined by the flash of his musketry, from which a stream of fire occasionally almost enveloped us." Those salvos were usually followed by an attack on a part of Sickles's line. His infantry and artillery beat back each effort, but the corps commander was concerned that unless he took decisive action he would eventually be overrun. He was also interested in retrieving some resources—two or three cannons, a few caissons, and some ammunition-laden mules from the pack train of Whipple's division. These had been abandoned in the woods to the west of Hazel Grove, too close to the enemy's assumed line to recover by anything short of a major attack. The latter might also enable the Third Corps to regain part of the army's lost position along the Orange Plank Road.[21]

Some time around ten o'clock Sickles received the requisite authority for his night attack. By then he believed he had secured the close cooperation of Berry, whose men would sidle down from Chancellorsville, and Williams, whose division would go forward on Sickles's right. Garbled communication, however, crippled the operation and limited it to something less than full success. Berry failed to get the word to advance, and the too-eager Sickles started off before Williams—who was reluctant to cooperate until his superior, Slocum, consented to it—could advance in conjunction with him.

Sickles moved out shortly after midnight, Birney's bayonet-wielding troops in advance. They were aiming at the enemy line thought to be near the Old Schoolhouse on the plank road, almost a mile away. From the outset, foul-ups ensued. Instead of striking the target squarely, the units on Birney's north flank blundered into Williams's lines. Believing themselves under attack, the latter fired wildly in the dark, killing and wounding several of their Third Corps comrades. Other members of Birney's command fell victim to an artillery barrage that Slocum—who had yet to be informed of Sickles's movement—laid down on the plank road. These errors, combined with the stout fighting of the Confederates on the plank road, forced

Sickles to withdraw after having engaged only a couple of the enemy's regiments at close range.[22]

Such meager accomplishments did not deter Sickles from claiming credit for an operation whose "brilliant execution" had driven the enemy from his captured breastworks, which Birney's men now occupied. Sickles's assertions were outlandishly exaggerated—for openers, Birney's men never got within a mile of Howard's old works. Still, Birney had secured a foothold within rifle range of the plank road; moreover, his aggressiveness served to impede Jackson's effort to cut the Army of the Potomac off from the Rappahannock. Eventually—for reasons that no Yankee understood at the time—that effort came to a halt and was not resumed.[23]

ALTHOUGH THE RACKET generated by Jackson's assault did not penetrate to Union headquarters, Robert E. Lee heard it in time to order Lafayette McLaws to demonstrate against the left flank of Hooker's lines east of Chancellorsville and Anderson to press their center. The coordinated effort was designed not only to dampen opposition to Jackson's strike but to prevent Hooker from shoring up his embattled right. Both Anderson and McLaws were encouraged to incline their movements toward the left so they might link with Jackson's forward units. In his after-action report Lee observed that "these orders were well executed, our troops advancing up to the enemy's intrenchments, while several batteries played with good effect upon his lines until prevented by the increasing darkness."[24]

The movement did, however, cause some problems. The general inclination to the left caused a gap to open on McLaws's front, which might have endangered his upper flank. As Lee had foreseen, however, Hooker was too intent on maintaining the defensive to sally forth and exploit the error, which eventually was filled by the skirmishers of Semmes's brigade. And although they advanced "up to the enemy's intrenchments," neither McLaws nor Anderson could break through, thanks primarily to the stubborn defense of Hancock's troops, who, holding the center of that line, bore the brunt of the attacks delivered by both divisions.[25]

Lee had personally supervised the advance of Mahone's and Posey's brigades of Anderson's division. Once he felt certain no reinforcements could be sent from

Chancellorsville to oppose Jackson, he withdrew Mahone, along with the better part of McLaws's division, to their original lines. After that, the Confederate commander became a spectator listening to the ebb and flow of battle, able to do nothing to influence its outcome. It was a trying, anxious time for the chess master who had staked the life of his army on a most un-chesslike series of moves.

Freeman waxes poetic in describing this interval, when Lee could only wait and hope: "Soon the moon rose above the trees in a sky of floating clouds and vaguely illuminated the landscape, but the western horizon was covered with a fiery curtain, draped into fantastic, ever-changing folds by the lighted fuses of the flying shells—a dazzling, awesome sight. Now the din diminished, now it rose again; salvoes and volleys, the nervous, uneven fire of scattered, frantic batteries, the rattle of long lines of muskets. Hour after hour the night battle continued, slowly drawing nearer and shifting southward. At eleven o'clock it was still in its fury; not until midnight did it die away into silence."[26]

In the wee hours of May 3 Lee, who had bedded down on the hard ground inside a pine thicket, fell into an uneasy sleep. After perhaps an hour, he awoke at the arrival of Capt. R. E. Wilbourn of Jackson's staff, who had ridden at breakneck speed from the far side of the Yankee army with news of Jackson's success. Lee listened intently to the aide's report of the collapse of Hooker's flank and the shameful flight of the Eleventh Corps. Although the assault finally bogged down in the shadowy forest, the enemy held a most precarious position. This was, of course, good news, but Wilburn ended on a disturbing note. While attempting to restart the offensive in the direction of the Rappahannock, Jackson, along with a scout and a few staff officers, had ridden in advance up the Bullock Road toward the river. After a brief reconnaissance, Jackson had turned about to rejoin his troops. In the dark, his party had been mistaken for Yankee cavalry and was fired on by members of a North Carolina regiment in Lane's brigade. The errant fusillade killed Captain Boswell and one other man, while stampeding Jackson's horse. Regaining control of the beast, Jackson again rode back toward his lines when a second misdirected volley rang out. Two bullets had struck the general's right hand and left wrist, while a third passed through his left arm, shattering the humerus between elbow and shoulder.[27]

Wilbourn downplayed the severity of the injuries and stressed that Jackson had been carried to the rear, where Dr. McGuire was, or would soon be, attending to him. The messenger's attempt to ease Lee's mind, however, proved ineffective. At the first mention of Jackson's wounding, a stricken look had crossed Lee's face as if he were the one who had been shot. He told Wilbourn that "any victory is dearly bought which deprives us of the services of General Jackson, even for a short time!"[28]

Although too overcome to bear the details of Jackson's ordeal ("thank God it is no worse!"), Lee wished to know the position of Jackson's men and who had command of them. The captain explained that A. P. Hill had taken over only to be struck by a piece of shell and temporarily disabled. General Rodes had then assumed command, but as a brigadier he had lacked the rank to maintain it. On Hill's initiative, J. E. B. Stuart, the only unwounded major general west of Chancellorsville, had been sent for. Leaving his blocking position on the road to Ely's Ford, the cavalryman had taken charge of the troops his friend and colleague Jackson had already led to storied triumph.[29]

Lee approved of Stuart's elevation—on several occasions the Beau Sabreur had demonstrated skill in command of combined arms—and he dashed off a letter to the officer he had known fondly since Stuart's West Point days: "It is necessary that the glorious victory thus far achieved be prosecuted with the utmost vigor, and the enemy given no time to rally." Stuart should direct his efforts at capturing Chancellorsville, "which will permit the union of the whole army." Lee would join him as soon as possible, "but let nothing delay the completion of the plan of driving the enemy from . . . his position." To emphasize the importance of immediate action, Lee repeated these instructions in a second dispatch sent barely a half hour after the first. This communiqué he entrusted to Capt. Hotchkiss, who had reached Lee's headquarters with further details of Jackson's condition and the disposition of his command.[30]

No longer able to sleep, Lee spent the next several hours wide awake and hard at work. He informed Jubal Early of the activity planned for that day and issued orders to govern the movements of his troops. To support Stuart and exploit any breakthrough he might achieve, McLaws and Anderson were directed to press the eastern and southern sides of the enemy's line between Hazel Grove and the Rappahannock. Preparatory to this operation, Lee had Anderson extend his lower flank to Catharine Furnace. The detached brigades of Wright and Posey were instructed to advance in conjunction with the rest of their division. With these important issues attended to, Lee rode off to observe from a better vantage point the operation that he hoped would drive the Yankees from their last line of defense, while also uniting his own dangerously divided army.[31]

EARLY MORNING of May 3 found Joe Hooker downcast and fretful. To an outside observer, his mood would seem unjustified. After all, Jackson's attack had been contained, and although a several-mile stretch of the army's original line had been lost, an equally formidable perimeter had been hacked out of the forest. That line had been strengthened by the recent arrival of Reynolds's corps, which was taking position along the east bank of Little Hunting Run and from there southeastward along the Ely's Ford Road, thus connecting the army at Chancellorsville with the south bank of the Rapidan. The regrouped (but not rejuvenated) fugitives of Howard's corps performed a similar function farther east, linking the troops around Chancellorsville with the Rappahannock and covering United States Ford. Howard's right flank abutted the left of Couch's two divisions, whose convex position touched the upper flank of Slocum's southwest-curving line. Farther west, Sickles's corps, holding the position it had gained after midnight, completed Hooker's formidable defensive circle by stretching from Hazel Grove to the Bullock house, more than a half mile above Chancellorsville.

By calling in the First Corps, Hooker had expanded the force under his immediate command to almost ninety thousand, about twice the number available to Lee in two widely separated bodies. Hooker also had Sickles's supposedly masterful night attack to soothe his jangled nerves. He might further console himself with the knowledge that more than half of his army—the First, Fifth, and Twelfth Corps and most of the Second—had seen little or no action thus far, leaving them not only fresh but eager to punish the Confederates for their sneak attack.[32]

An artilleryman attached to Hancock's division spoke for many in the army in proclaiming his morale to be high despite the enemy's recent success: "The Rebels have got a good position but we think we will make them skedadle by tomorrow night. . . . our men made two splendid charges last evening. We are all in good spirits. The Boys all go into it [battle] with a cheer. They go on for victory or death. . . ." He added that his comrades still expressed "great confidence in Fighting Jo. Hooker." A reference such as this, however, would soon disappear from soldiers' letters to their families at home.[33]

Despite these many strengths and advantages, early on this Sabbath morning "Fighting Jo." was desperately concerned about the situation on Sedgwick's front, especially about Sedgwick's belated responses to a series of urgent messages sent him over the past twenty-four hours. The same order that had detached the First Corps from the wing commander also instructed him to take up the bridges laid at Franklin's Crossing, a task that had not been attended to until 4:00 A.M. on May 3.[34]

About two hours before Jackson's flank attack struck home, Hooker had also ordered Sedgwick to capture Fredericksburg, "with everything in it, and vigorously pursue the enemy." This was the message in which Hooker described Lee as "fleeing, trying to save his trains." He had heard nothing from Sedgwick on the subject until 3:00 A.M. on the third, when Butterfield wrote to confirm that Sedgwick had begun his assault.[35]

Only thirty minutes later, however, Hooker learned that the wing commander was making slow progress in driving Early from his five-mile-long line of defense. In fact, Early was threatening his left flank, preventing Sedgwick from complying with yet another order—sent by Hooker on the evening of the second—to cross the Rappahannock at Fredericksburg and march to Chancellorsville in time to reach the crossroads by daylight on the third. Hooker had added that "you will attack and destroy any force you may fall in with on the road. . . . You will probably fall upon the rear of the force commanded by General Lee, and between you and the major general commanding he expects to use him up." Hooker's state of mind in the jarring aftermath of Jackson's assault was such that he had forgotten Sedgwick had already crossed the Sixth Corps to the Fredericksburg side of the river. The dispatch would only create confusion and misunderstanding.[36]

The worries that beset Hooker upon arising on the third drove him to issue Sedgwick still another order, more strident and demanding than its predecessors. By 2:35 A.M. a courier was galloping to Falmouth with a dispatch that began: "Everything in the world depends upon the rapidity and promptness of your movement. Push everything."[37]

It had come to this: Hooker, with almost four times the troops available to his subordinate, was counting on Sedgwick to fight his way through the lines of Early, McLaws, and Anderson and rescue the main army at Chancellorsville.

AFTER DARK on the second, while engaging Federal troops along the road to Ely's Ford, J. E. B. Stuart had been sought out by a member of A. P. Hill's staff who galloped up with word of Jackson's wounding and Stuart's appointment to succeed him. Within minutes the cavalry leader was accompanying the aide through the woods to the Orange Plank Road. Even before he reached Hill's side, Stuart had made up his mind "to press the pursuit already so gloriously begun."[38]

Upon his arrival, about ten o'clock, Stuart held a hurried conference with Hill, who had turned his division over to his senior brigadier, Henry Heth. At the same time, Stuart sent a staff officer to inform the fallen Jackson that "he would cheerfully carry out any instructions he would give" (his wounded friend merely replied that Stuart should trust to his own good judgment). Then the cavalry commander sought to familiarize himself with the dispositions of the Second Corps. He found Heth's troops holding both sides of the Orange Plank Road about half a mile from Chancellorsville and learned that Sickles's men had attacked the right of the line but had been repulsed. Concerned about a second assault, Stuart immediately retracted the right.[39]

Sickles's offensive and the confusion it had generated, which had caused Hill's troops to fire on one another just as Slocum had fired on Birney, prompted Stuart, "much against my inclination," to wait for daylight to renew the assault intended to block the enemy's access to the Rappahannock. After receiving Lee's back-to-back dispatches early on the third, however, he abandoned any thought of resuming Jackson's attack. Lee had emphasized the need for a quick reuniting of the army rather than a push toward the river.[40]

Many historians believe that Lee personally agreed with Jackson's philosophy but was unwilling to execute it with a cavalry general in charge of an infantry corps and a brigadier in command of its most advanced division. Then, too, while Jackson's plan might have succeeded in the immediate aftermath of his flank attack, before the enemy could regroup and strengthen his lines, the opportunity had passed by the time Stuart took over.[41]

In preparation for the less complicated offensive he intended to launch before dawn, Stuart conferred with Jackson's artillery chief, Col. E. Porter Alexander, who informed his temporary superior that a ridge running through Hazel Grove, if occupied, would enable him to enfilade the Federals opposite, paving the way for an infantry assault. When Stuart ordered Heth's men forward just before sunrise, he had Alexander direct his fire against the salient, where Sickles's men continued to hold on for dear life. The focal point of Stuart's assault, however, was the clearing around Fairview, which enclosed a line of log breastworks manned by the divisions of Berry and Williams. In response to his orders from Lee, when the attack rolled forward, Stuart swung Archer's brigade, on Heth's far right, toward the southeast in hopes of making contact with Anderson's troops, who were thought to be approaching from the vicinity of Catharine Furnace.

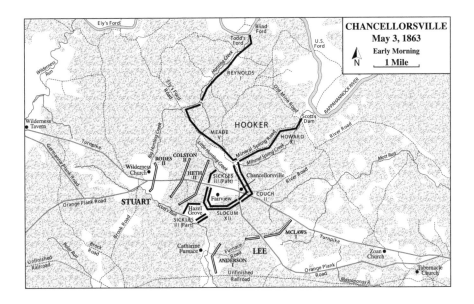

Due to some crowding and confusion in the ranks, Heth's initial attack, which overlapped the plank road, was repulsed, as were subsequent assaults against many points on the enemy's line at Fairview. Stuart, however, kept ordering up regiments and brigades, supported in the rear by the divisions of Colston and Rodes. Alexander's guns continued to hammer not only Berry's and Williams's positions but also Hazel Grove. At the height of the fighting Stuart, famous for his buoyant demeanor under fire, rode along the lines, singing a ditty based on a camp-meeting song, "Old Joe Hooker, Get Out of the Wilderness!"[42]

His panache was rewarded when, some time after five o'clock, the lines around Hazel Grove began to empty. In less than two hours, the strategic clearing was devoid of enemy troops. Ignorant of the reason why but thankful for large favors, Stuart directed Alexander to lose no time taking possession of the ridge. Lee's recent reorganization of the army's artillery facilitated this maneuver. "Under the happy effects of the battalion system," dozens of guns were soon crowning the high ground. At Alexander's expert direction, they began throwing shells at those Yankees withdrawing to Chancellorsville, whose artillery, hobbled by the lack of a directing hand such as General Hunt's, had difficulty replying. Stuart thought the overall effect "superb."[43]

So did Robert E. Lee, who had ridden as far toward Stuart's lines as he dared. From a vantage point near Catharine Furnace he studied the gratifying results of Stuart's offensive through his field glasses. Beside him sat a foreign observer, Capt. Justus Scheibert of the Prussian army, just then "making [a] sketch of the assault before my eyes in order to give permanence to the unforgettable impression." A warm admirer of the Confederate leader, Scheibert was astonished when Lee, with shells and rifle balls screaming overhead, delivered a fervent lecture on the importance of self-control to a soldier: "He fervently deplored war and bloodshed as usual, [and] he said that his chief aim was to keep the men morally disciplined and to guard against barbarianism."[44]

Then Lee ranged beyond the war to speak of life in the South to come: "You have before you the elite of our people from sixteen to forty-five years of age. The state is to be made up of them in the future—they are later to resume peaceful occupations and to practice quiet civic virtues. War is a savage business, and one must accustom the men as well as possible to self-control."[45]

Even under fire, Robert E. Lee felt impelled to pass on life's lessons that an all-wise mother had ingrained in him fifty years earlier.

SHORTLY BEFORE STUART'S ATTACK got underway, Hooker rode out to inspect Hazel Grove, whose defensive potential filled him with worry. That position on the far southern end of the Union line was defended not only by the divisions of Birney and Whipple but also by Barlow's brigade, the only element of the Eleventh Corps that had escaped being caught up in the rout of the previous day.

Although Sickles's midnight attack out of the salient appeared to be a stepping-stone to a further advance, Hooker considered it vulnerable in light of more recent events. Sedgwick's inability to link with him had foiled Hooker's plan to catch Lee's army in a pincers. Now he feared he had to remain on the defensive, warding off the blows he knew his opponent would deal him this day. Yet he considered his troops too strung out to offer effective resistance, especially should Lee unite his army and put its full weight into a knockout punch. Hooker believed he must contract his lines and husband his strength before calamity overtook him.

Drawing of Union troops under fire at Hazel Grove, May 3, 1863

With this in mind, the army leader called on Dan Sickles and ordered him to withdraw his divisions, as soon as possible, to Fairview. There they would join with forces such as Berry's in occupying a new line of trenches in the woods southwest of Chancellorsville. Sickles, who more fully appreciated the strategic importance of Hazel Grove, did not think much of this idea, and apparently argued against it. Had a colleague with a highly regarded eye for terrain such as Henry J. Hunt been on the scene to back him up, Sickles might have prevailed. As it was, Hooker silenced him with an abrupt gesture, turned about, and rode back to his headquarters.

By five o'clock, the corps' artillery, followed closely by Whipple's division, was evacuating the wedge between Robert E. Lee's wings. Birney's troops, bringing up the rear, relinquished their works more gingerly than their comrades. The evacuees passed to the north under cover of rear-guard musketry and an artillery barrage. Crossing a swampy branch of Scott's Run that had been corduroyed with pine planks, the Federals topped the heights in front of Fairview. Not far behind, they hunkered down in trenches and behind breastworks, shielded by an imposing array of cannons.[46]

No sooner was the evacuation complete than Stuart's troops poured into the strategic clearing, occupying the deep and intricate works Sickles had left behind. By seven o'clock no fewer than thirty-one guns were pounding away at the lines at Fairview and Chancellorsville from the high ground Stuart had coveted. The elevation enabled them to throw shells at the brick dwelling that was reported to house Hooker's headquarters.

His gunners' aim was true. About nine thirty, a 12-pounder cannon sent a solid shot through a wooden pillar on the porch of the Chancellor house. It struck directly next to the spot where Hooker was standing. The shell split the column in two, hurling half of it lengthwise at the general, who had been in the act of reaching for a dispatch handed up to him by a member of Sickles's staff. The force of the blow sent Hooker crashing to the floor of the porch, where he lay crumpled and unmoving, as if dead.[47]

Attack and Counterattack

For Jubal Early, the past three days had been a time of planning, posturing, and watchful waiting. Since midnight of April 30–May 1, he had been opposing with approximately 12,700 troops (his own division, Barksdale's brigade of McLaws's division, and, in remote support along the road from Banks's Ford, the troops of Brig. Gen. Cadmus Wilcox, of Dick Anderson's command) more than twice as many Federals on both sides of the Rappahannock below Fredericksburg. Any commander in such a situation would have been forgiven had he given way to the jitters, but the irascible Early, while quick to anger, was slow to react to stress and impervious to panic.

The first thirty-five hours of his confrontation with Sedgwick's wing had passed without undue strain. The only tense moments occurred in the early afternoon of May 1 when Sedgwick massed his own corps as well as John Reynolds's troops for an apparent assault on Early's lines. Before an advance commenced, however, the blue columns stood down and the movement was canceled—the result, Early believed, of the vigilant, resolute appearance of his well-entrenched riflemen and the batteries that supported them under the supervision of General Pendleton.[1]

The tension appeared to ease on May 2, when a considerable portion of Sedgwick's command could be seen passing to the rear, evidently bound for the north bank of the Rappahannock. Precisely at this juncture, however, Early found himself in the midst of a baffling crisis, one that threatened the security not only of his own command but of the entire Army of Northern Virginia.

At approximately eleven o'clock that morning he and Pendleton were standing on Lee's Hill—Robert E. Lee's favorite vantage point—watching Reynolds's troops withdraw under cover of the guns on the river bluffs. The two generals were suddenly joined by Lee's chief of staff, Colonel Chilton, sent from the lines opposite Chancellorsville. Chilton brought a verbal order from his superior: Early was to march at once with his main body to join the rest of the army. He was to leave behind as a rear guard one brigade and eight to ten pieces of artillery. The rest of Pendleton's cannons were to return to the depot in the far rear from which they had been sent up four days ago.

Union battery supporting Sedgwick's troops near Fredericksburg, VA, May 2, 1863

Early and Pendleton were equally shocked by Chilton's message, which seemed to suggest that the army was in dire straits—in need of immediate support, perhaps in preparation for a retreat. Early tried to discern if Chilton was truly conveying Lee's intent or whether he had misconstrued it. He reminded his West Point classmate that a large-scale withdrawal in broad daylight would be quickly detected by the signalmen on Stafford Heights as well as by Professor Lowe. As soon as Early's men had departed, the enemy would occupy Fredericksburg and the territory above and below the town.

Chilton was aware of all this, but he was adamant that he was conveying Lee's urgent need for Early's presence. He opined that Reynolds's recent departure presaged Hooker's reinforcement. Obviously, Lee was reacting in kind.[2]

Early, still doubtful that Chilton had interpreted Lee correctly, continued to argue the point for some time. Finally he decided he had no recourse but to obey the unwanted order. Leaving the Louisiana brigade of Brig. Gen. Harry T. Hays to hold what remained of the line behind Fredericksburg, and one of Barksdale's regiments to occupy the town itself, Early began the ponderous process of evacuating his forces.

The withdrawal was not complete until two that afternoon. By then Chilton had returned to army headquarters and the head of Early's column was well on its way up the Orange Plank Road. At this critical point, a courier from army headquarters galloped up with a handwritten order from Lee canceling the operation now underway. As Early had predicted, Lee's chief of staff had misquoted him, an error Lee had discovered after Chilton returned to report the upshot of his errand. The army commander had intended that Early should join him only if the enemy opposite his lines withdrew completely— the same instructions Lee had given Early upon leaving Fredericksburg to take charge of the troops facing Hooker.[3]

Early's mind was relieved but he faced a new dilemma: Should he continue his march to join Lee or attempt to regain the position he had evacuated, which must now be in enemy hands? Fearing the latter effort would prove a forlorn hope, he resumed his march in the direction of Chancellorsville. He halted only when a courier from General Barksdale, at the rear of the column, pounded up to report that the abandoned ground had not been occupied, although a large force of blue-coats appeared ready to cross the river to strike at Hays. The situation had prompted Barksdale on his own initiative to lead his brigade back to the river.

After a brief deliberation, Early decided that his subordinate had acted correctly. He turned the rest of the column about and had it countermarch. It did not reach its former position until after dark. Amazed by the enemy's failure to seize a commanding position offered to them as if on a platter, Early spent the evening reoccupying and building up every sector of the defensive perimeter.

If Early had heaved a sigh of relief, it would have been appropriate to his situation, for his return had been a near thing indeed. Had the enemy moved promptly to take advantage of his departure, he would not have recovered his foothold on the river except at a heavy cost in casualties—perhaps not even then. Apparently, his old classmate, John Sedgwick, continued to deserve the reputation he had gained at West Point, that of a slow but steady performer. Fortunately, the emphasis remained on "slow."[4]

HAD SEDGWICK BEEN AWARE of the ordeal his opponent had gone through thanks to conflicting and confusing orders, he would have been able to empathize. He, too, had been plagued by orders from army headquarters that had been delayed in transmission and that failed to take into account the tactical realities of Sedgwick's situation.

On the evening of May 1 came the order to make a demonstration in force at one o'clock that afternoon. Sedgwick responded as quickly as his deliberate and exacting nature would permit, but while preliminary maneuvers were underway, Hooker called off the operation. After sunup the next morning, Sedgwick received a communiqué, sent shortly before two o'clock, ordering him to detach Reynolds's corps and forward it to United States Ford. He complied with alacrity, but due to the delay in the message's receipt it was now daylight. Thus Sedgwick could not obey Hooker's additional demand that he take up and move upriver two of the pontoon bridges at Franklin's Crossing.[5]

Just before dark on May 2, Sedgwick was handed the dispatch in which Hooker crowed that Lee was fleeing. The Sixth Corps was now to "cross the river as soon as indications will permit; capture Fredericksburg, with everything in it, and vigorously pursue the enemy"—meaning Early's command, whose evacuation of its lines Professor Lowe had reported but which was already returning to its works. Hot on the heels of this message, another arrived. Now Sedgwick was to pursue the enemy on the road to Bowling Green. As quickly as he was able, he collected the two divisions still on the Falmouth side of the river—Maj. Gen. John Newton's and Brig. Gen. Albion P. Howe's—and sent them across to join Brooks's soldiers on the south bank.

Soon after reaching dry land, Newton's advance guard encountered skirmishers from Early's command; in sharp, seesaw fighting, they drove some of the Confederates from the Bowling Green Road. The fracas was still in progress that night when, at eleven o'clock, Sedgwick received yet another insistent order from army headquarters, enjoining him to "cross the Rappahannock at Fredericksburg . . . and at once take up your march on the Chancellorsville road until you connect with him [Hooker]. You will attack and destroy any force you may fall in with on the road"—a reference to Lee, McLaws, and Anderson.[6]

Understandably, the order to cross the river puzzled its recipient, who could obtain no clarification from army headquarters. Not realizing that Hooker believed most of the corps to be on the north side of the stream, Sedgwick interpreted the directive as requiring him to return to that side, lay a pontoon bridge opposite Fredericksburg, and cross over it into the town. This would consume an inordinate amount of time, which conflicted with the peremptory nature of the order. Sedgwick was also surprised and upset by the requirement to march at once to join Hooker. He calculated the distance from his present position to army headquarters as fourteen miles, ground he would have to cover in the dark.[7]

Sedgwick realized that thousands of Rebels separated him from Hooker, and he had received no assurances that the latter would support him in any way that required assuming the offensive. Furthermore, now that Early had reoccupied his lines, Sedgwick found himself opposed by a long but discontinuous line of well-defended breastworks, trenches, and artillery positions that stretched from a point above the perversely memorable Marye's Heights on the north, to Hamilton's Crossing on the south—a distance of more than five miles.

The corps leader responded to these unrealistic demands in the only way that made sense to him. About one in the morning of May 3, he led Newton's division, followed by Burnham's mobile reserve and the troops under Howe, up the Bowling Green Road toward Fredericksburg. Brooks's division he left behind to guard the bridgehead at Franklin's Crossing. The movement immediately attracted opposition from skirmishers posted at the Bernard house, in front of Early's right flank. The Federals responded warmly, but the gray skirmishers continued to lash their flanks and rear as they moved up the riverbank.[8]

Reaching the outskirts of Fredericksburg, Sedgwick quickly drove out Barksdale's rear guard, then posted Newton's troops in the streets of the town. After daylight they would be joined by two-thirds of Gibbon's division (one of its brigades had been transferred to Banks's Ford). This command—the addition of which would give Sedgwick more than twenty-seven thousand troops and around sixty artillery pieces with which to oppose the badly outnumbered Early—had finally been ordered to leave its holding position at Falmouth. It would cross the river upon one of the floating bridges Sedgwick belatedly moved from Franklin's Crossing to a point near the Lacy house (also known as "Chatham"), directly across from the town.[9]

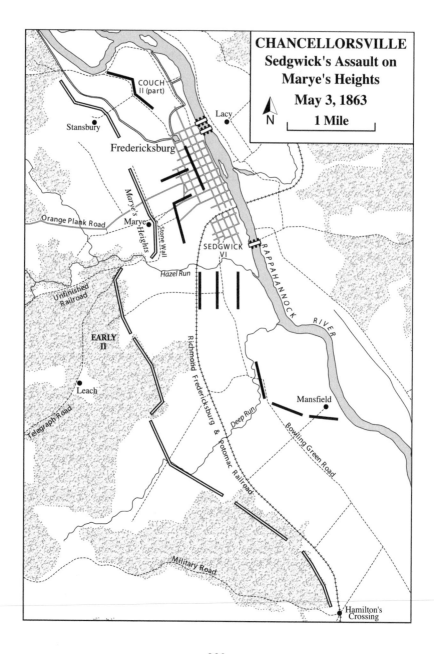

CHANCELLORSVILLE
Sedgwick's Assault on
Marye's Heights
May 3, 1863

N | 1 Mile |

When dawn provided enough light to operate by, Sedgwick had Newton moved elements of Brig. Gen. Frank Wheaton's and Col. Alexander Shaler's brigades toward a heavy line of rifle pits immediately behind Fredericksburg. Rebel muskets went to work by the hundreds, and the attackers were driven back with heavy loss. "The force displayed by the enemy," Sedgwick wrote, "was sufficient to show that the intrenchments could not be carried except at great cost." The setback made him reluctant to order another head-on attack. Instead, he devised a plan under which Gibbon would turn Early's left above Marye's Heights and Howe would outflank the high ground to the south. While waiting for Gibbon, whose arrival was delayed by difficulties in laying the bridge at Chatham, Sedgwick located positions for cannons whose fire would cover the movement. In case the operation failed and another attack on the Confederate center were required, he formed a storming party, composed of units from Newton's and Burnham's troops, hoping he would not have to use them.[10]

Launched at 9:30 A.M.—about an hour and a half behind Sedgwick's schedule—the flank drives immediately encountered trouble. Gibbon was denied access to the enemy left by a canal thirty feet wide, which Sedgwick knew was there but had not taken into account.

there but had not taken into account. Meanwhile, Howe found his path to the lower end of Marye's Heights blocked by a deep ravine formed by the waters of Hazel Run. To cross the ravine Howe would have to expose his left flank to the rifles and cannons of Brig. Gen. Robert F. Hoke, whose North Carolina brigade held the right-center of Early's line astride Deep Run.

Obstructed on the right and left, Sedgwick prepared his storming parties for another assault on Marye's Heights. A terrible sense of déjà vu assailed the wing commander, who vividly recalled the carnage of December 13, but he had no alternative. He had been ordered to

Brig. Gen. Robert F. Hoke, CSA

fight his way through to Hooker as quickly as possible, and straight ahead up the heights was the most direct route.[11]

Whether or not he fully appreciated them, Sedgwick enjoyed two advantages. Because Jubal Early refused to believe that his adversary would repeat the mistake Burnside had made five months ago, he concentrated his strength, and his attention, between Hamilton's Crossing and Lee's Hill, giving special attention to the gap that separated Barksdale's right from Hoke's left along Deep Run. Then, too, Sedgwick's troops had discovered a weak point in the Rebel position. Following the unsuccessful assault on the rifle pits, one of his subordinates had requested a local truce in order to bring off wounded men. Without seeking the approval of his superior, General Barksdale, the commander of one of the two regiments that held the stone wall at the base of Marye's Heights had acceded to the request. When advancing to gather up their fallen comrades Newton's men scrutinized the position and noted how

The stone wall along Marye's Heights after Sedgwick's attack, May 3, 1863

few troops defended it. This was the point at which Burnham's storming party would direct its attack.[12]

Confounding John Sedgwick's worst fears, the attack succeeded admirably. Burnham's men double-quicked to the vulnerable position, cut a jagged swath through its defenders, scaled the stone wall, and swept up the heights, killing, wounding, or capturing everyone in their path. On the left, Howe's troops, which were formed into three columns, managed to ford Hazel Run without suffering crippling losses. They took the position in flank and rear at the same time that Burnham smashed through frontally. The principal fighting lasted all of fifteen minutes. Their success cost the Federals upwards of eleven hundred casualties, but the Confederates had suffered almost as many. The psychological effect of having surmounted an obstacle of such symbolic importance was alone worth the cost.[13]

Observing the breakthrough, which included not only Marye's Heights but elevations on either side of it, Jubal Early gave vent to his anger in a string of pungent oaths. With its left flank gone, his entire position was compromised. The irascible Virginian quickly withdrew the troops who had held his right and center and marched them down the Telegraph Road. About three miles southwest of Fredericksburg, he was joined by Barksdale's survivors, who had scrambled cross-country from the scene of their defeat. Somehow Early would have to reconstitute his command and lead it back into action against Sedgwick. For now, however, he had to mend its shattered ranks and try to restore lost morale. That would take time, perhaps twenty-four hours, perhaps longer.

Early's opponent had no time to savor his costly but gratifying victory. After telegraphing word of his success to Falmouth, he replaced the captors of Marye's Heights with Gibbon's division. Then he called up Brooks's men from Franklin's Crossing and placed them at the front of a column facing west. By 2:00 P.M., he was ready to start for Chancellorsville, prepared, as Hooker had warned him, to "attack and destroy any force you may fall in with on the road."[14]

THE CANNONBALL that knocked Joe Hooker senseless struck at a particularly inopportune time for the Army of the Potomac, which was left leaderless as the fight for possession of Fairview and Chancellorsville neared its climax.

That battle—a frenetic succession of attack and counterattack—had been building for at least two and a half hours before Hooker was rendered hors de combat. After his occupation of Hazel Grove, J. E. B. Stuart had concentrated his firepower against Fairview, where the troops of the Third and Twelfth Corps occupied a line of log breastworks that ran for about one thousand yards and in places rose to a height of three feet. The front of this line was defended by the divisions of Berry and Williams. Farther to the rear, trees had been felled to open a field of fire for artillery and to facilitate the passage of reinforcements to the front.

Advancing under a devastating barrage from the batteries at Hazel Grove, Confederate infantry pressed all sectors of Sickles's and Slocum's lines. One particularly aggressive assault, launched at about seven thirty that morning, targeted the log works on either side of the plank road. Under unrelenting pressure, an inexperienced regiment in the Twelfth Corps gave way. Its flight exposed the left flank of Berry's position, which also began to waver. While attempting to shore up the endangered sector, Berry was mortally wounded by a sharpshooter. When Fighting Joe—then two and a half hours away from being injured— heard that the friend who had succeeded to the command of his old division had fallen, he was inconsolable.[15]

Brig. Gen. William D. Pender, CSA

He was similarly shocked to learn that another long-time subordinate, Brig. Gen. Joseph W. Revere—a direct descendant of Paul Revere of Revolutionary War fame—had of his own volition removed Dan Sickles's old Excelsior Brigade from the front lines and led it to United States Ford, where it sat out the rest of the battle. Revere would be court-martialed and sentenced to dismissal from the service, but that did nothing to repair the damage done to another sector of the Union line. There, above the plank road, Brig. Gen. William Dorsey Pender's North Carolina brigade made substantial inroads. It not only dislodged

Brig. Gen. William Hays's Second Corps brigade but also captured Hays and most of his staff.[16]

Just before his upper flank could give way, Hooker threw into the breach Maj. Gen. William H. French's division of Couch's corps. Surging forward north of the plank road, French's fresh troops thrust back many of Pender's North Carolinians. It also drove to the rear almost every Georgian in Brig. Gen. Edward L. Thomas's brigade, which had carried Stuart's first wave of attack as far as the Bullock house. Eventually, French's people were thrust back in turn by Pender's and Thomas's supports, but then reinforcements arrived to stabilize the Union right, at least temporarily.[17]

While the fighting raged north of the all-weather road, units under Robert E. Lee's personal direction were battering the eastern flank of Hooker's lines around Chancellorsville. In support of Stuart's offensive, McLaws's division assaulted the troops of Hancock and Geary, who were covering the road to Fredericksburg. At the same time, Dick Anderson's soldiers sidled up from the southeast in response to an order that they join hands with their comrades under Stuart. Anderson's men put tremendous pressure on the Federals holding the log works south of the plank road. One result was the forced withdrawal of Williams's division, which had run out of ammunition—sixty rounds per man was insufficient to support a battle of this magnitude with its relentless pattern of thrust and parry.

Before falling back, Brig. Gen. Thomas H. Ruger's brigade of Williams's division had given a splendid account of itself, repulsing successive charges by three brigades in Stuart's first wave—those of Lane, Heth (this day under Col. J. M. Brockenbrough), and Brig. Gen. Samuel McGowan. Units from Sickles's corps moved up to take Williams's place and the frantic struggle on the Union left continued without interruption.[18]

To the west, Stuart kept pushing forward, hoping to gain at Fairview a foothold at least as advantageous as the one he had secured at Hazel Grove. His first line of attack having lost momentum, the dashing Virginian— resplendent in a gilt-spangled uniform of blue liberated from a Yankee supply depot—summoned to the front his next division, Raleigh Colston's. This command—originally commanded by Maj. Gen. Isaac R. Trimble of Maryland, a mustachioed sexagenarian whose name continued to cling to it—had not been quite the same since the combative old fellow's wounding and disabling at Second Manassas. Colston sometimes seemed beyond his depth in the role of

Trimble's replacement, and his brigade leaders—two of whom were substituting for brigadiers wounded the previous day—were no great help to him.

To Stuart's dismay, Colston's troops were late in coming up, and when they advanced they achieved indifferent success. Brig. Gen. Elisha F. Paxton, commanding the Stonewall Brigade of First Manassas and Valley campaign fame, quickly fell mortally wounded. Denied his leadership, the brigade penetrated to within seventy yards of the position still held by Ruger's brigade before being forced to retreat with heavy loss. At least Paxton's men advanced; another of Colston's brigades, Brig. Gen. John Robert Jones's, could not be forced to pass a line of captured breastworks behind which it huddled for an hour or more. The brigade's behavior was due at least in part to the absence of its commander, Jones having gone to the rear with a spurious ailment. After the battle he would be quietly dropped from the rolls of the Army of Northern Virginia along with his superior, Colston.

Stuart's offensive received an infusion of energy when Robert Rodes's division came up behind Colston's and entered the fray. North of the plank road Rodes's former brigade, today led by Col. Edward A. O'Neal, and the North Carolinians of Brig. Gen. Alfred Iverson tangled with a mingled mass of Third and Twelfth Corps units that slowed but did not halt their advance.

On the opposite side of the road, Brig. Gen. George Doles's Georgians and Brig. Gen. Stephen Dodson Ramseur's North Carolinians made greater headway. Although Doles's drive was eventually blunted, Ramseur got much the better of Brig. Gen. Charles K. Graham's Third Corps brigade, which had replaced Ruger's men behind the log works west of Fairview. To reach his objective Ramseur had to "run over the troops in my front"—the huddled masses of Jones's leaderless command. With a shout, the North Carolinians topped the captured works and drove Graham's New Yorkers from a parallel line of defenses. Ramseur claimed that his men held those works "under a severe, direct, and enfilading fire, [while] repulsing several assaults on this portion of our front."[19]

Ramseur's thrust had opened a gap in the lower end of the Union line that widened as fresh troops rushed up to support his brigade. The penetration exposed to attack the flank of Geary's division southeast of Fairview, which had been facing south against the forces of Anderson. It also speeded up the transfer of Union batteries from Fairview to Chancellorsville. This process, which proceeded clumsily in the absence of General Hunt's directing hand (the artillery chief remained on the north side of the river as if in quarantine), had been ongoing ever since Alexander's gunners at Hazel Grove began to shower Fairview with shot and shell. Those salvos took what one of Stuart's subordinates called "a ghastly & sickening" toll: "Brave men were laying everywhere . . . some with the backs of their heads blown off, others with their faces gone & still others with no heads at all."[20]

The fighting along the Union center and right continued at full fury through the morning. As afternoon approached, however, Stuart began to husband his dwindling resources to devote them to seizing and occupying Fairview. His task was made easier by the increasing support he received from Anderson. The brigades of Posey, Perry, Wright, and Mahone, along with Kershaw's brigade of McLaws's division, kept shifting to the left as they advanced against the Union south flank. At length, Posey's column made contact with Archer's brigade of Heth's division, reunifying the largest fragments of the Army of Northern Virginia. As soon as the merger was complete, a relieved and gratified Lee ordered Stuart to press his attack all along the enemy line, an effort in which Anderson's entire division would participate. With so many Yankees moving to the rear, the seizure of Fairview—the key to Hooker's complete overthrow—seemed a matter of time.[21]

THE SHELL THAT STRUCK the pillar against which Hooker had been leaning left him insensible for upwards of an hour. When he finally regained consciousness, the right side of his body was livid and wracked with pain, the result of being struck by the splintered beam, and he had trouble clearing his mind, the result of a severe concussion. He attempted heroically to throw off the effects of both injuries. In an effort to dispel rumors, already rampant, that he had been fatally injured, he insisted on being lifted into the saddle and rode his white charger along the lines nearest the Chancellor house. Soon, however, "the pain from my hurt became so intense that I was likely to fall, when I was assisted to dismount, and was laid upon a blanket spread out upon the ground, and was given some brandy. This revived me."[22]

Numerous officers and men witnessed the administering of the medicinal stimulant. The act would give rise to charges that Hooker had been felled by drunkenness. One rumor had it that he had been imbibing heavily through-out the battle, which was not the case. Other critics attributed Hooker's evident loss of will, nerve, and coherence not to his drinking but to his abstinence during an unusually trying period. They professed to believe that had he indulged his habitual thirst for alcohol, he would have handled better the mental and physical stress the fighting inflicted on him.

Feeling somewhat better after consuming the brandy, Hooker again insisted on being helped to mount. He recalled that "scarcely was I off the blanket when a solid shot, fired by the enemy at Hazel Grove, struck in the very center of that blanket, where I had a moment before been lying, and tore up the earth in a savage way."[23]

While in the saddle he spoke with General Couch, who had rushed to his side upon learning of Hooker's injury. Finding his boss in better shape than he had expected, Couch congratulated him on his narrow escape and returned to his command. Hooker's senior subordinate recalled that "this was the last I saw of my commanding general in front. . . . He probably left the field soon after his hurt, but he neither notified me of his going nor did he give any orders to me whatever."[24]

After inspecting his own lines, Couch visited John Geary's embattled position farther south, then subjected to a murderous shelling. Its commander was pacing along his line, exclaiming, "My division can't hold its place!" His visitor saw at once that this was so. Although "everything was firmly held except-ing Geary's right, which was slowly falling to pieces," Couch realized that "Lee by this time knew well enough, if he had not known before, that the game was sure to fall into his hands, and accordingly plied every gun and rifle that could be brought to bear on us."[25]

While trying to bolster Geary's line, and his confidence, Couch was flagged down by a courier from army headquarters with word that Hooker wished to see him at once. Returning to the Chancellor house, Couch found it afire, Alexander's cannons having struck it time and again. Hospital inmates and terrified civilians were being evacuated in great haste. Hooker had relo-cated his headquarters to a row of tents in the back yard of the Bullock house. Galloping there, Couch found General Meade, whose corps was positioned nearby, as well as other high-ranking officers whom Hooker appeared to have summoned.

As Couch approached one of the tents, Hooker, who had suffered a relapse in his executive officer's absence, motioned him inside. He promptly informed Couch that command of the army was being transferred to him. Couch was not, however, to use his discretion in directing its operations: "You will withdraw it and place it in the position designated on this map." Hooker ran his finger across a sketch map drawn by General Warren or one of his subordinates. The designated position described a half-circle that began as a salient at the Bullock house and ended on the south bank of the Rappahannock, its left covering Scott's Dam and its center United States Ford. It was not a position out of which an army could easily attack; its obvious function was to protect the two pontoon bridges that had been laid across the upper ford on April 30 (a third bridge would be laid in the same vicinity on May 4). Although Couch had suspected as much, the map told him that the last ounce of fight had gone out of his superior. Hooker no longer intended to wage a defensive struggle on ground of his own choosing, or anywhere else for that matter—he was interested only in retreating.[26]

Twenty years later, when he put his recollections of the campaign on paper, Couch remained convinced that as of that hour—late in the morning on May 3, 1863—"it was not then too late to save the day. Fifty pieces of artillery, or even forty, brought up and run in front and to the right of the Chancellor House, would have driven the enemy out of the thicket, then forcing back Geary's right, and would have neutralized the thirty guns to the right [at Hazel Grove] which were pounding us so hard. But it is a waste of words to write what might have been done. Hooker had made up his mind to abandon the field."[27]

In retrospect, the Army of the Potomac would have been better off had the solid shot struck Hooker instead of the porch. While the general's demise would not have guaranteed a turn of the tide of battle, it would have resolved an uncertain command situation. Although Hooker appeared to have recovered physically from the effects of the shell blast, his mental condition continued to be adversely affected by his injuries. Yet his outward ability to function more or less normally stayed the hands of those who otherwise might have taken steps to transfer command authority to Couch or some other subordinate. Not even Dr. Letterman, Hooker's medical director, could say definitively that the army leader was incapacitated to the point of being unable to perform the duties of his position. Nor could he have said that Hooker understood the consequences of the actions he would force upon his executive officer and, by extension, on the army itself.[28]

His hands tied by the instructions given him, Couch saw no recourse but to withdraw the army preparatory to crossing to the north bank of the river and returning to Falmouth. Upon departing Hooker's tent, he encountered Meade, who before Couch's arrival had unsuccessfully importuned Hooker to order a counterattack from the north. A member of Meade's staff quoted his superior as having insisted that "his troops were in fine condition and spirits, and that he had reason to think that he would meet with success. General Meade said this more than once, but General Hooker positively refused to accede to his proposition, insisting that he should remain on the defensive where he was."[29]

Meade had been hoping that Couch would succeed where he himself had failed. Similarly hopeful was Col. H. N. Davis of the army headquarters staff, who, as Couch departed Hooker's tent, exclaimed: "We shall have some fighting now." Instead, Couch gave both men a disgusted look and explained the facts of the case. Then he set out for Geary's position to begin the lengthy and delicate process of pulling back the army from its forward position. As he rode south, Couch may have reflected upon the fact that neither Meade's nor Reynolds's corps had been engaged on this bloody and fateful morning. He may have reflected, as well, on the words Lincoln had imparted to him and his superior when taking leave of the army at Falmouth: "In your next fight, *put in all of your men.*"[30]

THE PRESIDENT WOULD have more to say about the performance of the army and its commander, but for now he was very much in the dark as to its movements, even as to its location. Nor was he aware that a battle was in progress in the Virginia Wilderness. Despite the easy accessibility of the military telegraph, Hooker had not seen fit to send even a brief report of operations to the White House. Of course, he had no intention whatsoever of keeping General Halleck informed of events.

Hooker was no longer tight-lipped for reasons of military security—he appears to have been reluctant to contact anyone up north unless or until he could report a victory, or at least some semblance of success. Hooker had so often and so loudly boasted of his ability to outthink, outmaneuver, and outfight his enemy that he could not bear to admit to official Washington that his operations were going less well than he had anticipated.

Apparently his chief of staff had a sense of propriety and compunction that Hooker did not share. At 8:50 A.M., only a half hour or so before Hooker was knocked sprawling, General Butterfield wired Lincoln, giving him the first inkling that an event of importance was underway: "Though not directed or specially authorized to do so by General Hooker, I think it not improper that I should advise you that a battle is in progress."[31]

Such a brief and perfunctory dispatch would have only aroused the president's anxiety. Even this much information, however, was more than Hooker cared to release. Four hours after Butterfield's telegram went out, Brig. Gen. Rufus Ingalls, chief quartermaster of the army, who had assumed the duty of communicating with Falmouth while Hooker recuperated, informed Butterfield that "I think our victory will be certain, but the General told me he would say nothing just yet to Washington, except that he is doing well. In an hour or two the matter will be a fixed fact."[32]

This was a remarkable statement in any context, the more so because by the time Ingalls composed it his boss had decided to break contact and fall back. Before Butterfield received the wire, however, he sent a second, more detailed report to the White House, meditating on the uncertain outcome of the "fierce and terrible" battle and mentioning Hooker's injury, which he described as not severe. Almost apologetically, the chief of staff added that Hooker "has preferred that thus far nothing should be reported, and does not know of this, but I cannot refrain from saying this much to you."[33]

Butterfield did not know it at the time, but Hooker had screwed up enough courage to send a personal telegram to the president. Composed at 1:15 P.M., it informed Lincoln that the army had been involved "in a desperate fight yesterday and today, which has resulted in no success to us, having lost a position of two lines which had been selected for our defense. We may have another turn at it this P. M. I do not despair of success." So far, so good—he had been candid about his less than desirable situation. Then, however, he fell back on his old habit of blaming it on the failings of others: "If Sedgwick could have gotten up, there could have been but one result. As it is impossible for me to know the exact position of Sedgwick as regards his ability to advance and take part in the engagement, I cannot tell when it will end."[34]

If Hooker imagined this dispatch would set its recipient's mind at rest, he was badly mistaken. Rather than relieve Lincoln's anxiety over the outcome of the fighting, Hooker's attempt to make it look as if he was keeping his superior informed without actually telling him anything drove the president toward panic. At 4:30 P.M. he shot Butterfield a desperate telegram: "Where is General Hooker? Where is Sedgwick? Where is Stoneman?"

Butterfield was at a loss to answer.[35]

HOOKER MAY NOT HAVE KNOWN John Sedgwick's whereabouts, but he could have told Lincoln where Stoneman's cavalry was—a large portion of it, at least. The previous morning he had learned from scouts that General Averell's column of thirty-four hundred troopers and horse artillerymen was at Rapidan Station, the Orange & Alexandria depot along the north bank of the river of the same name. Hooker had no idea why this force remained in an area it should have departed more than twenty-four hours earlier to join Stoneman in operating against other, more important targets in Lee's rear.

Although he could not say with certainty, Hooker wondered if Averell's dawdling had something to do with the army's inability to certify that Stoneman's raiders had accomplished its objectives. Lee's army had not reacted noticeably to any untoward event in its rear, nor had it shown an inclination to fall back to protect an asset under attack or threatened with attack. Moreover, in several dispatches to Butterfield, Sedgwick had remarked on the regular arrival of northbound trains at Hamilton's Crossing, which suggested no disruption of service on the all-important Richmond, Fredericksburg & Potomac. Hooker had the nagging suspicion that Stoneman had made a botch of his operation, and he intended to find out how and why.[36]

At 6:30 A.M. on May 2, Averell received an order to report to army headquarters without delay. The nonplussed brigadier pulled up stakes and led his men, horses, guns, and pack mules up the north bank of the Rapidan to its confluence with the Rappahannock. At 10:30 P.M., some three hours after Jackson's attack on Howard's corps had run its course, Averell drew rein at Ely's Ford. Apparently unable to locate Hooker that night—and possibly made nervous by his recall—Averell determined to make himself useful by reconnoitering toward the left flank of Jackson's exhausted but exhilarated troops in the

Wilderness. Before he could do so, however, he had to counter an attack on his bivouac, launched just before midnight by foot soldiers whom Averell identified as members of a regiment in Pender's brigade.

The assault was repulsed, but nothing came of the attempted reconnaissance. The officer in charge of the operation returned to report the country in that direction "almost impracticable for infantry and impassable for cavalry—a thick black jack jungle." Thus Averell had few visible accomplishments to report when, after moving on to United States Ford, he reached army headquarters at the Bullock house late on the morning of the third.[37]

He found Hooker "prostrated in energy" from the lingering effects of his close encounter with the solid shot. Though hobbled, the army leader listened intently to Averell's oral report of his command's operations—a tale of missed opportunities, exaggerated dangers, and slow, halting movement toward the Confederate rear. His column had left the Rappahannock early in the evening of April 29, bound for Brandy Station on the O & A. Stoneman had expected him to reach the depot before dark, but Averell went into camp several miles short of his objective.

He pushed on next morning, having parted ways with Stoneman although obliged to communicate with an element of the latter's main body at Stevensburg, five miles southeast of Brandy Station, later that day. After the brief reunion, Averell would again go his own way to Culpeper, then south to the Rapidan. En route he was expected to encounter Stuart's cavalry, which he was to prevent from hindering Stoneman's operations against the R, F & P and the Virginia Central. After delaying Stuart as long as possible, Averell was to join his superior on the Pamunkey River. Thereafter their columns would team to destroy critical points on Lee's communication line with Richmond.[38]

Instead of meeting Stuart's entire command, en route to Culpeper Averell found himself opposed by a single regiment (later augmented by a second) under Rooney Lee. He drove the small force through the courthouse village and toward the river. But Averell moved warily, having been duped by prisoners and deserters into crediting reports that Stuart, with four brigades and fifteen pieces of horse artillery, was hovering near Culpeper. Averell considered a force of that size too large to contend with. He decided not only to ignore his orders to engage Stuart but to pursue Rooney Lee toward the Rapidan. In so doing, he also ignored his orders to meet Stoneman's emissary at Stevensburg. The change of itinerary had fateful consequences. By not communicating with his superior, Averell failed to receive instructions clarifying his role during the balance of the expedition. Clarification was vital, for due to an egregious breakdown in communication, Averell had no inkling that now he was to join the main body on the South Anna River.[39]

Reaching Rapidan Station about eight o'clock in the evening of April 30, Averell found Rooney Lee's few hundred troopers, backed by a single piece of horse artillery, guarding the south side of the bridge that carried the O & A across the river. The raiding leader spent the rest of the day as well as the morning and afternoon of May 1 trying half-heartedly to cross the stream, threaten Lee's flank, and gain his rear. Robert E. Lee's son was too nimble to be pinned down; by shuttling his small force back and forth across the riverbank, he not only eluded capture but avoided casualties.

Rooney's inspired maneuvering prompted Averell to consider burning the bridge, as if his mission were a defensive one. Late in the day, his opponent saved him the trouble, torching the span in response to orders from his father's headquarters. Then he slipped away to challenge Stoneman, leaving Averell stymied on the north bank—but not because the bridge had been destroyed. Soaked by recent rains, only a portion of the trestle had burned; most of it remained standing. Apparently Averell considered the span too weakened to attempt a crossing upon it. Unable to decide what else to do, he remained immobile for another twelve hours, until recalled by Hooker. All he had to show for his mission was the destruction of miscellaneous property, chiefly supplies stored at Brandy Station and Culpeper, but little or no damage to the O & A.[40]

Evidently Hooker, during Averell's summary of operations, said nothing to suggest disapproval or displeasure. When permitted to return to his command, the brigadier believed all was well. He was astonished when, early the next day, he was handed an order relieving him of command and transferring his division to Alfred Pleasonton. Hooker never explained this action, and Averell professed to be ignorant of the reason for it. The following day he was permitted to leave the army for Washington, where he made the rounds of the White House and the War Department. Although granted interviews with Lincoln and Stanton, he learned nothing about his case, a situation that rankled him furiously.[41]

Had he been privy to Hooker's subsequent correspondence with the adjutant general of the army, Averell would have been enlightened to his superior's view of the facts of his case. Hooker explained that he had dismissed his subordinate for irresponsibly disregarding his orders, the result being that "the services of nearly 4,000 cavalry were lost, or nearly lost, to the country during an eventful period, when it was his plain duty to have rendered service of incalculable value. . . . [Averell] seems to have contented himself between April 29 and May 4 with having marched through Culpeper to Rapidan [Station], a distance of 28 miles, meeting no enemy deserving the name, and from that point reporting to me for instructions."[42]

To this harsh but valid indictment, Hooker appended a stinging rebuke: "This army will never be able to accomplish its mission under commanders who not only disregard their instructions, but at the same time display so little zeal and devotion in the performance of their duties. I could excuse General Averell in his disobedience if I could anywhere discover in his operations a desire to find and engage the enemy." Although he had no intention of preferring charges against the man, "in detaching him from the army my object has been to prevent an active and powerful column from being paralyzed in its future operations by his presence."[43]

Averell would never again serve in the Army of the Potomac, a victim not only of his own incapacity but of his branch's inability to perform at a level that gave an honest return on Joe Hooker's investment in its rejuvenation. Hooker's penchant for hurling blame had never been more clearly displayed, but at least in Averell's case he appears not to have overshot the mark.

AT OR CLOSE TO THE TIME Averell reported to him, Hooker was in the process of withdrawing the army from Chancellorsville to his new line of defense. In actuality, only half of the army had to move any distance to reach this, the last position it would assume during the campaign. Reynolds's and Meade's troops were already holding the right flank of the line along Big Hunting Run and the road to Ely's Ford. The men of the Eleventh Corps—the still-demoralized as well as the able and willing—had entrenched along the other flank, astride the Mineral Springs Road. Only the Second, Third, and Twelfth Corps had to disengage from close contact with the reunited wings of Lee's army. Those wings were pressing every sector of the Chancellorsville enclave with energy and enthusiasm born of recent success and impending triumph.[44]

On May 3, before the final fall-back commenced under Darius Couch's supervision, Sickles's troops, low on ammunition and bereft of support, held the west flank of the Chancellorsville plateau, including what remained of the Fairview salient, against Stuart's troops. To the south and east, Geary's division was opposing Anderson's division, which overlapped its flanks and was pressing it on all sides. On Geary's left, Hancock's Second Corps was fighting in two directions at the same time—parallel lines facing west against Stuart as well as east against the comparatively fresh troops of McLaws. All of these commands had been fiercely engaged since five o'clock that morning. Their men were exhausted, nearly fought out, and on their own, thanks to Hooker's unwillingness to commit Reynolds and Meade. Most of the men were willing to fall back if they could do so without causing half the army to come crashing down before it could reach safety. That, as Couch understood all too clearly, was the rub.[45]

Sickles's corps was the first to withdraw. Even before the word came down, substantial numbers of its soldiers, forced from their works by the inexorable advance of Anderson, had begun to fall back. As they retreated, cheering Rebels seized the Fairview clearing and Colonel Alexander rushed up as many batteries as he believed needed to secure it. The guns were soon throwing solid shot and shrapnel well to the north of Chancellorsville, raking the ground between the Chancellor and Bullock houses. When they struck the dead wood and dry leaves that abounded in that section of the forest, the projectiles ignited fires that spread rapidly in all directions. Numerous Federals and a few Confederates, disabled by wounds and unable to crawl to safety, were engulfed in the flames, adding a horrific touch to a day already awash in human suffering.[46]

After Sickles's men made their way, as best they could, from their collapsing line, Geary's division got the word to follow. This was the second time it had withdrawn from its forwardmost positions. Some time after eight o'clock Geary, nearly surrounded by surging Rebels, pulled his men out of their trenches west of Fairview to a spot just below the Chancellor house, where he formed a new line at right angles to the old. At this point, an as-yet-uninjured Hooker had ridden up to demand that Geary reoccupy his old position "and hold it at all hazards." Against mounting odds and his better judgment, Geary, accompanied by Col. Charles Candy's brigade, two regiments from the brigade of Brig. Gen. George S. Greene, and six cannons, fought his way back to the trenches. The rest of the division, "in the confusion of the moment and the conflict of orders," had been cut off and forced to take position in a woods north of Chancellorsville.[47]

Against Geary's truncated command, "the whole fury and force of the enemy's fire seemed to be concentrated." Somehow the men of Candy and Greene held on for another ninety minutes or so, before obeying a final order to retire by the left flank. In language hinting at his prewar political career, Geary described the withdrawal as "executed in excellent order . . . even at that time the parting volleys of this brigade were given with an earnestness of will and purpose that showed their determination to avenge the death of their comrades if they could not avert the issue of the day."[48]

Geary's departure left Hancock's division, stationed above the plank road and east of the Chancellor house, to hold back the enemy long enough to permit their comrades to reach safety. The steady, profane, and dapper Hancock responded with one of the most resolute and effective rear-guard actions of the war. He did so without close support from any quarter and despite being assailed by McLaws on the east, Anderson on the south and southwest, and Stuart on the west. Against tremendous pressure, his command fought by brigades separated from each other by gaps more than a quarter-mile wide.

Not only were Hancock's men opposed by charging infantry, they were subjected to a murderous fire from Alexander's guns in their newly secured position at Fairview. "What wild eyes and blanched faces there were," recalled one of Hancock's lieutenants, "when the shells and solid shot came in from the right front and rear of us." The division had been subjected to cannonading on many fields, but, as another officer noted: "Old soldiers say that the firing . . . was heavier than any they ever heard. Antietam was surpassed. Malvern Hill was cast into the shade."[49]

By holding on to the bitter end, the division suffered terribly. Its highest ranking casualty was General Couch, who took a slight wound; more severely injured was Col. Nelson A. Miles of the Sixty-first New York, who, while steadying his regiment against a particularly strong attack, took a bullet through the abdomen. Two days before, when fending off McLaws's attack in support of Jackson's rout of the Eleventh Corps, the colonel had performed so superbly under fire that Couch himself had described him as "worth his weight in gold." Miles would survive his wound to be awarded a Medal of Honor for his performance on this field and to become, thirty-four years after the battle, commanding general of the United States Army.[50]

A little after ten o'clock, Couch gave his subordinate the word to pull back to the Bullock house clearing. The order came none to soon; as one of Hancock's subordinates claimed, "had we delayed *five* minutes more we should have been taken prisoners or cut to pieces." As they withdrew, the troops not only held their shouting, surging enemy at arm's length but helped drag off some of the eighteen guns that had been supporting the division from Chancellorsville, most of whose teams—and many of whose crews—had been killed or disabled.[51]

Last to disengage were the members of Hancock's skirmish line, whose rock-solid resistance had been a key to the division's ability to avoid being surrounded and cut off. Thanks to their efforts and those of embattled but tenacious comrades who had supported the command at a distance, the First Division, Second Corps, returned relatively intact from the last sector of the position its army had occupied over the past five days. The Army of the Potomac's hold on the Chancellorsville battlefield had been broken as fully and as irretrievably as the spirit and will of its commander.[52]

AS THE LAST ABLE-BODIED DEFENDER pulled out of Chancellorsville, the forces of McLaws and Anderson, soon joined by those under Stuart, converged in the clearing that surrounded a once-comfortable house now fully engulfed in flames. Exhausted by hours of close-up skirmishing and attacks large and small, the Confederates attempted to catch their breath, straighten out their jumbled ranks, and orient themselves to their enemy's new position. Thoughts of victory were not uppermost in their minds. It would take time to appreciate the importance of the capture of this position and the heroic nature of the exertions that had forced the enemy to give it up.

The mood changed dramatically, however, when Robert E. Lee rode through the clearing astride Traveller. Bone-weary men surmounted their fatigue to salute the architect of their victory. Lee's aide, Charles Marshall, recalled the scene: "The fierce soldiers with their faces blackened with the smoke of battle, the wounded crawling with feeble limbs from the fury of the devouring flames, all seemed possessed with a common impulse. One long, unbroken cheer, in which the feeble cry of those who lay helpless on the earth blended with the strong voices of those who still fought, rose high above the roar of battle, and hailed the presence of the victorious chief. He sat in the full realization of all that soldiers dream of—triumph; and as I looked upon him in the complete fruition of the success which his genius, courage, and confidence in his army had won, I thought that it must have been from such a scene that men in ancient days rose to the dignity of gods."[53]

A modest man to the core, the demonstration humbled the army leader even as it warmed his heart and touched his soul. He bowed and doffed his hat in recognition of the honor thus bestowed on him. At this moment he knew more genuine adulation than Joe Hooker would experience in a lifetime of seeking it.

What Will the Country Say?

I n the immediate aftermath of the greatest victory of his career, Lee was struck twice in rapid succession by potentially disastrous news. On the heels of a note dictated by General Jackson congratulating his superior on his triumph, Lee learned that Stonewall's "flesh wounds" had necessitated amputation of his left arm. Shaken by the prospect of losing indefinitely the services of his most combative lieutenant, Lee dashed off a reply in which he attributed the victory to Jackson's splendid offensive and declared that "could I have directed events, I should have chosen for the good of the country to be disabled in your stead."[1]

After Lee returned to the enemy now ensconced northeast of Chancellorsville, he was met by Lt. Andrew L. Pitzer of Jubal Early's staff, who had galloped up from the Fredericksburg front to announce the capture of the town, the loss of Marye's Heights, the forced withdrawal of Early's command, and the approach of Sedgwick by the Orange Plank Road. Surprised but not stunned, the army leader promptly laid aside his plan to finish off Hooker and, trailed by his staff and escort, spurred Traveller cross-country to the headquarters of Lafayette McLaws. The latter's division had seen less action today than any of the others engaged and was thus available for immediate service. At Lee's order, the Georgian dispatched Kershaw's brigade, accompanied by Mahone's (which remained attached to his command) out the Orange Plank Road to meet Sedgwick. Once they had cleared the road, McLaws himself followed with the troops of Semmes and Wofford.

As the four brigades moved out, couriers raced ahead to inform Early, who was still attempting to regroup his scattered ranks along the lower reaches of the Telegraph Road, that troops were being sent to confront the victors of the second battle of Marye's Heights. Old Jube was to cooperate with them in barring Sedgwick's path, bringing him to battle, and shoving him back to Fredericksburg and, if possible, across the Rappahannock. Together McLaws and Early would bring some eighteen thousand troops to bear against the twenty-four thousand members of the Sixth Army Corps. Lee feared the odds against him were even greater, for he believed that Gibbon was advancing in company with Brooks, Newton, and Howe.[2]

McLaws's detaching left Lee facing an even more lopsided equation: with thirty thousand officers and men he would have to hold at bay more than eighty thousand. The disparity promised a most uneven fight, but this was nothing new. Once again, he must play David to the blue-clad Goliath. Once again he must violate the rubrics of his profession by splitting his army to counter two larger forces, either of which could do him grievous harm and which, if they united, might crush him to death.

Against any opponent except Joe Hooker, Lee might not have undertaken such a daunting task with the poise and confidence he displayed that day to all about him. When the chaplain of one of Barksdale's regiments arrived from the scene of Early's defeat, "gasping for breath, his eyes starting from their sockets," and tried to convince Lee that doom was approaching in the guise of John Sedgwick, the army leader reacted with an equanimity remarkable even by his standards. An artillery officer marveled at his response: "Something like a grave, sweet smile began to express itself on the General's face, but he checked it, and raising his left hand gently, as if to protect himself, he interrupted the excited speaker, checking and controlling him instantly." In a calm, even voice Lee explained that the situation was being dealt with as they spoke and begged the good chaplain not to worry himself about it.[3]

But the man appeared not to have heard. When he repeated his tale of woe in the same excited tone, Lee tried a different approach. Speaking of the John Sedgwick he had known in the prewar army, he declared that "the major is a nice gentleman; I don't think he would hurt us very badly, but we are going to see about him at once. I have just sent General McLaws to make a special call upon him." With a polite nod, he turned at last from his anxious informant and rode off to do battle with another opponent, one not so estimable as former Maj. John Sedgwick of the Second United States Cavalry.[4]

SEDGWICK'S INITIAL OBSTACLE on his way to join Hooker was not McLaws but Cadmus Wilcox, whose brigade, alone of all the forces available to Jubal Early, was in a position to oppose the advancing column. Having reached Marye's Heights too late to prevent the enemy's breakthrough, Wilcox had preceded the victors along the plank road in the direction of Chancellorsville. About midway between the latter place and Fredericksburg, he halted to give battle. About one thousand yards east of Salem Church, a small, one-story chapel of red brick that topped a densely wooded ridge crossing the plank road, the brigadier dug in.

Drawing of Salem Church

Wilcox, who had as sharp an eye for terrain as anyone in Lee's army, had determined that this position commanded not only the Orange Plank Road but also the River Road and the few other approaches from Fredericksburg.

Until forced to give it up, he intended to hold the ridge with his five Alabama regiments, four cannons, and small force of cavalry. Sedgwick's characteristically deliberate pace enabled him to throw up a tree-shrouded line of earthworks that stretched across the road.[5]

Thanks to time lost to some confusion in the ranks at the outset of the march from Marye's Heights, Brooks's division, leading Sedgwick's column, did not make contact with Wilcox until almost 3:30 P.M. on May 3. By then McLaws had arrived from Chancellorsville via the Orange Turnpike. He had deployed atop Salem Heights behind an abatis-protected line of works to which Wilcox fell back when finally driven in by Brooks's skirmishers. At about 4:00 Wilcox went into position on the left of Kershaw and Wofford and to the right of Mahone and Semmes. The twenty-two cannons that had accompanied McLaws, including fourteen pieces from Alexander's battalion, bolstered the hastily erected line.[6]

Determined to break through this roadblock as he had the one on Marye's Heights, Sedgwick deployed Brooks's division across the road, two brigades above and two below it, and placed Newton's just-arriving troops in their right rear. Howe's division, which had brought up the rear, fending off jabs from Barksdale's re-formed Mississippians, did not get up until around sunset.

About 5:30 P.M., before the sun could go down, Sedgwick decided to attack. This was a mistake, since not only was Howe still to the rear, so was most of the corps' artillery. With no means of softening up the enemy position, he ordered Brooks to advance. His First and Second Brigades—mostly New Yorkers and New Jerseymen—rushed forward and clambered up the east slope of the ridge, which was covered with brush and vines. According to Brooks, "immediately upon entering the dense growth of shrubs and trees which concealed the enemy, our troops were met by a heavy and incessant fire of musketry; yet our lines advanced until they had reached the crest of the hill in the outer skirts of the wood." There they were met by "fresh and superior numbers of the enemy"— mostly members of Wilcox's Ninth Alabama, which had rushed to the defense of other regiments that had been driven in by the impetus of the assault.[7]

After Brooks's men swept forward, Wheaton's brigade of Newton's division belatedly advanced farther north. The disjointed nature of the attack and the fact that Sedgwick threw barely five thousand troops against a line of defense held by at least as many Confederates spelled defeat. Wheaton's troops crossed a wide ravine, then ascended Salem Heights "under a terrific fire of musketry from a hidden foe." Seeing that his men could not hold the crest without support, Wheaton sent back for reinforcements. Before they could arrive, Brooks's men, forced from the high ground, retreated into and through Wheaton's ranks. By the time Wheaton restored order, Billy Mahone's Confederates were crossing the same ravine from the other side, threatening his right and rear. To avoid being cut off, Wheaton fell back but clung tenaciously to his side of the ridge. He was still holding it when darkness ended the fighting for the day. During the night Wheaton's men withdrew from their exposed position, a tacit admission of defeat by Sedgwick.[8]

When Howe finally reached the scene some time after six o'clock in the evening, Sedgwick placed his troops in line of battle facing to the rear and also southward. The position enclosed Banks's Ford, where communication was opened with infantry and artillery units on the north bank. During the night, Sedgwick inspected his works and attempted to reconnoiter the enemy's. The effort convinced him that, although he now outnumbered his opponents and held a well-anchored line, his position was precarious. Absent an effort by Hooker to break through to him, the Sixth Corps might have to cross the river to safety.

The fighting around Salem Church resumed shortly after dawn on May 4. If Sedgwick thought himself in trouble before, he was in mortal danger now, opposed not only by McLaws but also by most of Jubal Early's and Dick Anderson's troops. Having finally regrouped, early that morning Early had returned to Marye's Heights with the intention of wresting the position from Gibbon's men. But when he sent John Gordon's brigade to retake the high ground, it was found to have been abandoned. Through miscommunication, Gibbon had fallen back to Fredericksburg. Having reoccupied its old works, Barksdale's brigade attempted to recapture the town, only to be sent reeling by Gibbon's skirmishers. Thereafter the Mississippian's mission was reduced to keeping the Yankees bottled up in the town. In the end, he did not have to: before daylight on the fifth Gibbon would recross the river to guard the army's camps at Falmouth and protect Hooker's line of supply to Aquia Creek.[9]

The recapture of the high ground lost the previous day left Early feeling vindicated. Full redemption, however, depended on the successful execution of the plan Robert E. Lee had outlined for him by courier the previous evening. Early was to strike the Union left rear at Salem Church in conjunction with a frontal assault by McLaws, a maneuver that Lee believed would "demolish" Sedgwick. But McLaws was not so sure. When details of the plan reached him, he expressed doubt that he had enough troops to execute his role in it. This was not the sort of response Lee expected from his subordinates, but he took McLaws's concern to heart and set about reinforcing him with what remained of Anderson's division. By midmorning on May 4 Anderson was heading out the plank road at the head of Wright's, Posey's, and Perry's brigades.[10]

Once again Lee had weakened one of his wings to bolster another. Here was a gamble more worthy of a poker sharp than a devotee of chess, but Lee felt comfortable betting on Joe Hooker's chronic inability to take the offensive. That gamble had paid off time after time over the past week; Lee believed he could pull it off at least once more.

What Lee did not count on was inertia in his own ranks. Both before and after Anderson reached Salem Church, Lafayette McLaws displayed the kind of studied inactivity that Lee's opponents were famous for. McLaws's and Early's divisions lay a mile and a half apart, making communication between them irregular and chancy. Having heard nothing from Early, McLaws waited for his colleague to attack before he committed his own command. For his part, Early believed that McLaws, as senior division leader on the ground, should make the first move.

While the standoff ensued, Early harassed the position of Howe's division, hoping to find a way to slip between it and Banks's Ford. Every attempt failed, but at least Old Jube kept active; McLaws showed little inclination to do more than hold his ground and skirmish a little.[11]

When Robert E. Lee saw no signs of decisive activity at Salem Church even after Anderson should have reached there, he began to display symptoms of the anger that occasionally seized him uncontrollably. By late in the morning his unrest prompted him to suspend his watch over Hooker's quiescent troops and gallop to Salem Church. Upon arriving, he conferred with Early and McLaws and personally directed the placement between them of Anderson's supports, including the just-arrived artillery of Alexander.

The additions gave the Confederates a slight numerical edge over Sedgwick. Lee considered the advantage more than sufficient to execute the operation, which was to begin with a movement by Early against Sedgwick's left rear. This movement, it was believed, would dislodge Howe's defenders and shove them into the path of Anderson's attack farther west. As the pincers closed, McLaws would maneuver so as to prevent an enemy breakthrough toward Chancellorsville as well as any effort by Hooker (however unlikely) to reinforce his left wing.[12]

Lee expected that the necessary dispositions would be complete by the middle of the afternoon, if not sooner. Anderson, however, experienced some difficulty in getting his brigades into position for the assault. The ground in his sector was as rough and as entangled as the Wilderness itself, and no road ran the length of his position. The time thus lost consumed the entire afternoon. As the sun steadily lowered, Robert E. Lee looked on helplessly, his frustration mounting, his temper flaring.[13]

JOHN SEDGWICK BELIEVED himself to be heavily outnumbered, the result of an exaggerated report of enemy strength sent him that morning by Professor Lowe. As a result, during the night of May 3 he had General Howe contract his left flank toward the river. The maneuver left the Union line resembling a giant horseshoe, both of its prongs resting on the Rappahannock. In this position Howe parried several advances by Early that imperiled Banks's Ford and, farther downriver, Scott's Ford. Howe's stubborn defense eased Sedgwick's worried mind, but only to a degree. He remained concerned about the fifteen thousand Rebels Professor Lowe had spotted moving toward his rear—presumably, Early's command, its size magnified by inexpert estimation.

The only good news Sedgwick had received this morning left him believing that he was no longer under an obligation to fight his way through to Hooker. At six thirty on May 4 he had received a dispatch sent at midnight from army headquarters by General Warren, who had been shuttling back and forth between Hooker and his left wing. Hooker, Warren reported, had contracted the army's lines "a little" and was hoping that Lee would attack him in his new position. If Lee obliged, Sedgwick was to refrain from attacking the enemy at Salem Church unless he learned that Hooker had changed his mind and was lashing out at Lee.

Later Warren blamed the dispatch's lack of clarity on mental fatigue, the result of many sleepless hours. Less confusing was the engineer's injunction that

Sedgwick "look well to the safety of your corps, and keep up communication with General Benham at Banks's Ford and Fredericksburg. You can go to either place, if you think it best. To cross at Banks's Ford would bring you to supporting distance of the main body, and would be better than falling back to Fredericksburg."[14]

Thus Sedgwick could now act solely in the best interests of his own command, which included, presumably, giving up any attempt to bull his way through the roadblock to the west. On the other hand, he could not afford to remain indefinitely in his present position, nor—if Lowe's sighting had been accurate—could he fall back. Certainly he could not return to Fredericksburg, which he now knew to be occupied by Early, not Gibbon. The only viable option was to retreat to the north side of the river via Banks's Ford.

The wing commander did not know that Warren's order expressed the chief engineer's own position, not that of his superior. The previous evening Warren had rejoined the main army to find its commander asleep. When awakened, Hooker, still suffering from the effects of the near-miss at the Chancellor house, was too groggy and incoherent to impart instructions to Sedgwick. Warren had acted strictly on his own when sending the dispatch. Thus Sedgwick may well have been confused when he received a message from Hooker—sent at 11:00 A.M. on the fourth but not received until sev-

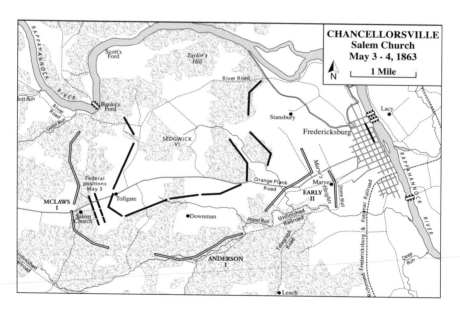

eral hours afterward—urging him not to cross the river unless compelled to do so: "It is very important that we retain [the] position at Banks's Ford."[15]

By the time he got this message, Sedgwick seemed to have little choice in the matter. At 6:00 P.M., as the sun was beginning to set, Lee finally assaulted the positions of Brooks and Howe. Although begun in promising fashion, the attack quickly bogged down. Anderson drove in Brooks's skirmishers, but well-entrenched infantry, supported closely by cannons, sent his division staggering backward. Had McLaws thrown his weight into the contest at this point it might have proven decisive, but the Georgian withheld a blow until it was too late. Later he blamed the quick descent of darkness and a vision-obscuring fog that rolled off the river.

The assault against the other end of Sedgwick's line also faltered—not from a lack of coordination but from misdirection. Some of Early's brigades failed to pivot according to the rather complicated plan of attack. Instead, they stumbled into each other's lines and became disastrously entangled. Once the movement lost cohesion, Union reinforcements—several regiments and a battery under Wheaton—rushed up to contain it. The battery proved especially effective; as Sedgwick observed, within minutes "the advance of the enemy was checked, his troops were scattered and driven back with fearful loss, and the new position was easily maintained until nightfall."[16]

Sedgwick may have repulsed a mismanaged attack, but he feared he could not withstand a more closely coordinated one such as Lee was liable to deliver come morning. Under cover of darkness, he emulated Joe Hooker by drawing his troops inside an even more compact line at the river. By 10:30 P.M., his men had secured the heights overlooking Banks's Ford, and Sedgwick was preparing for a crossing to the north side.

Before he retreated, however, he decided he had better gain Hooker's approval, even if he had to stoop to pleading. In a message sent just short of midnight he informed his superior that "my army [corps] is hemmed in upon the slope, covered by the guns from the north side of Banks' Ford. If I had only this army to care for, I would withdraw it tonight. Do your operations require that I should jeopard[ize] it by remaining here? An immediate reply is indispensable, or I may feel obliged to withdraw." In other words, he would consider withdrawing even without formal permission.[17]

To his chagrin, Hooker was unwilling that he should retreat just yet. Late on

May 4 the army leader had informed some of his officers that he had a plan for attacking out of his bridgehead. The next morning he would cross a part of the army over United States Ford, march down to Banks's Ford, slip over the river there, and strike Lee in flank and rear. For the plan to have a chance of succeeding, Sedgwick would have to hold his position until it was well underway.[18]

While it is doubtful that he was privy to the details of this strategy, Sedgwick got the impression that he was wanted to remain on the south bank at least until morning. He also understood that disobedience might have career repercussions. Soon after sending in his request for permission to cross the river, he had welcomed a visitor from the north bank, his West Point classmate and friend Henry Benham. When he learned of the request, Benham urged Sedgwick to retract it lest he be made to look fainthearted as well as insubordinate, behavior that could be held against him should the campaign end as badly as it appeared to be ending and should Hooker decide he needed a scapegoat. Appreciating the logic in this advice, Sedgwick quickly sent Hooker a second message indicating his willingness to "hold my position, as ordered, on south of Rappahannock."[19]

The second communiqué reached Hooker's headquarters by telegraph only ten minutes after the first. By then, however, the army leader reluctantly had sent Sedgwick the permission he craved. Happy to learn that his subordinate had changed his mind, Hooker immediately countermanded the authority to withdraw. This action should have been decisive, but although transmitted only twenty minutes after Hooker's initial reply it reached Sedgwick an hour and a half later.

The transmission delay, the origin of which was never determined, effectively quashed Hooker's plan to attack Lee via Banks's Ford (if in fact there had been such a plan). Upon receipt of Hooker's permission to withdraw, Sedgwick began to cross his men over the ford. By the time the countermand reached him the operation was too far advanced to be halted, a retrograde being, in Sedgwick's words, "wholly impracticable, and I telegraphed that fact to General Hooker."[20]

The last major action of the Chancellorsville campaign was history. It had ended on May 4, fittingly enough, with a Union retreat in the wake of the repulse of a spirited but flawed Confederate assault.

IN LATER DAYS, when the officers and men of Hooker's army began to question the tactical basis of the decisions he had rendered during the campaign, he was especially criticized for spending Monday, May 4 idle inside his new line of works while enemy forces converged on Sedgwick's corps from three sides. Colonel Wainwright, for one, believed "there was no reason for not attacking on Monday afternoon, when Lee had gone to pitch into Sedgwick; which is the time, it has always seemed to me, Hooker was most to blame for not taking advantage of. This reason of his for keeping so many men out of the fight [at Salem Church] makes me think of Sumner's holding his 30,000 in reserve at Williamsburg. . . . From all that I can learn, so far from any blame resting on Sedgwick, he deserved the highest commendation; and all the glory of the late engagements belongs to him and his corps."[21]

Hooker would offer a number of explanations for failing to assist Sedgwick. The one he gave Wainwright stressed his concern that Jackson (whose disabling had not come to Hooker's attention) was about to assault his right flank. Hooker added that Sedgwick was largely to blame for his own predicament—the corps commander had flouted his orders to move expeditiously to Chancellorsville once Marye's Heights had been taken, and, although well equipped to defend himself, he had been "afraid to fight" at Salem Church, even when opposed only by McLaws and Wilcox. Wainwright said nothing in rebuttal, "but my feelings were divided between shame for my commanding general, and indignation at the attack on so true, brave, and modest a man as Sedgwick."[22]

The following year Hooker, testifying before the Committee on the Conduct of the War, came up with another explanation for his inertia: a reconnaissance he had caused to be made on the morning of the fourth had demonstrated convincingly that the lines confronting him were too strong to risk a sortie. Lee and Stuart had "thrown up heavy defensive works from a half a mile or more in advance of me in the forest."[23]

After the war, when visiting the sites of his most celebrated defeat, Hooker declared to his literary executor, Samuel P. Bates, that he had wanted to go to Sedgwick's assistance but had been prevented by the terrain: " . . . we were in this impenetrable thicket. All the roads and openings leading through it the enemy immediately fortified strongly, and planted thickly his artillery, commanding all the avenues, so that with reduced numbers he could easily hold his lines, shutting me in, and it became utterly impossible to manoeuvre my forces." Presumably, these disadvantages explained how Stuart, with one-fourth as many troops, had pinned down Hooker's army throughout one day and well into a second.[24]

In reality, Hooker had been fought out—exhausted physically by fatigue, stress, and the effects of his injury, and mentally and psychologically by Lee's apparent ability to divide and reconstitute his army at will, moving portions of it hither and yon with a deftness that dazzled and confounded his adversary. Hooker also continued to be consumed by the fear—continually fed by second- and third-hand reports forwarded from Falmouth by Dan Butterfield— that Longstreet had rejoined Lee. (In reality, Longstreet would not depart Suffolk in advance of his troops until May 6 and would not alight from the train at Hamilton's Crossing until the ninth.)

Hooker's mindset was such that throughout May 4 he rejected repeated requests from Reynolds, Meade, and other subordinates to attack out of his bridgehead. Reynolds was so incensed by Hooker's recalcitrance that on his own he strongly probed Stuart's lines in hopes of provoking a response that would involve the army in a major fight. Hooker's studied determination to avoid taking the offensive strongly suggests that his plan to outflank Lee was so much wishful thinking. This view tallies perfectly with his chronic tendency to propose bold action, then withhold it for one trumped-up reason or another.[25]

Even had Sedgwick maintained his grip on the Banks's Ford salient, it seems doubtful that Hooker would have been more amendable to taking the offensive on May 5 than he had been on any day since April 30, when Lee first turned and confronted him. More likely, he would have remained immobile inside his new defenses, which he dared not leave for any reason short of his enemy's complete withdrawal. This Hooker did not anticipate; in fact, he expected Lee to strike him at some point during the fifth, probably on his right flank.[26]

Hooker would always claim that he had hoped Lee would attack. This probably is true, for by the morning of the fifth his perimeter had been improved to the point of near-impregnability by almost forty-eight hours of trench-digging, breastwork building, and artillery emplacement. The left of that sharply angled line was held by the Second and Eleventh Corps, the right by the troops of Reynolds and Meade (it made sense that the freshest units should defend the sector Hooker considered most likely to be attacked). The

Third Corps, situated between the Second and Fifth, covered the apex of the angle at and near the Bullock house, while the Twelfth Corps was held in the middle of the formation as a reserve.[27]

The entire position was fairly smothered with artillery—initially, more than 100 guns up front and 140 others closer to the river. Skillfully arranged and carefully supervised, the cannons commanded every possible line of approach. For this mighty bulwark the army could thank Hooker's reinstatement of General Hunt to tactical control of the army's artillery.[28]

The impetus behind this dramatic reversal was Charles Wainwright, who on May 3 had been appalled to find batteries moving about the Fairview salient helter-skelter. Many had unlimbered in the thickest reaches of the Wilderness, where they were denied fields of fire. Others had not been supplied, or lacked proper direction. As Wainwright discovered during an impromptu inspection, "several artillery officers from other batteries came up to me, asking where they could procure ammunition; no one appeared to know anything, and there was a good deal of confusion." One reason for the chaos was that every division commander kept those guns attached to his command on a short tether; their officers were expressly forbidden to assist colleagues in other units. [29]

When granted an audience with Hooker, Wainwright brought the situation forcefully to his attention. His earnest entreaties to return Hunt to field command certainly helped resolve the problem, but it appears that the clumsy transfer of batteries to Chancellorsville following Fairview's evacuation had been the deciding factor in Hooker's decision to take remedial action.[30]

IF HOOKER WAS CONTENT to remain on the defensive to the last, his opponent was determined to land a final, devastating blow. Early on the fifth, after Sedgwick was found to have escaped across the river, Lee ordered Early, with his own division and Barksdale's brigade, back to Fredericksburg, while recalling McLaws and Anderson to Chancellorsville. But the troops had become scattered, especially where the attacking columns had become intermingled. The time lost to sorting them out—reminiscent of the delay that had caused the previous day's attack to be made in gathering darkness—meant that the return march did not begin until about 4:00 P.M.

At first, the movement went smoothly, but then a sudden and violent storm turned the road into soup. Sensing imminent and final victory, the men seemed not to mind. A British journalist described them as "splashing through the mud in wild, tumultuous spirits, singing, shouting, jesting, heedless of soaking rags, drenched to the skin, and burning again to mingle in the wild revelry of battle." But the revelry had to wait—although McLaws reached Chancellorsville by nightfall, Anderson did not.[31]

A disappointed Lee contented himself with the knowledge that, with his eastern flank and rear no longer under threat, he could maneuver freely in the morning, bringing his full weight to bear on Hooker's last line of defense. Lee did not share his adversary's belief in the impregnability of that position. In spirited skirmishing throughout the fourth, Stuart had probed it for weak points and believed he had found a few. Stuart's aggressiveness not only inhibited the Yankees from launching sorties but took a human toll. Among the casualties this day was General Whipple, mortally wounded by a sharpshooter in the act of dispatching marksmen of his own to suppress the harassing fire.[32]

Another factor in the restoration of Lee's characteristic equanimity was the news he received on the fifth that Stonewall Jackson was recuperating nicely from his wounds. Earlier, when it briefly appeared that Hooker might sally forth to strike the Confederate left, Lee had removed Jackson and his medical team to Guiney's Station, the army's transportation hub on the R, F & P eighteen miles from Chancellorsville. The groggy but cheerful patient now lay abed in a plantation manager's office on the estate of a family named Chandler. He had withstood the journey well; his wounds appeared to be healing, and he—along with Lee—was hopeful of a speedy return to active duty.[33]

When Lee retired on the evening of the fifth, he was in good spirits, his descent into frustration and anger a thing of the past. Come morning, the army would attack all along the line, driving Hooker's soldiers from their last refuge into the roiled waters of the Rappahannock. Stuart would strike from the west, Anderson and McLaws from the east, their lines converging toward the salient at the house where Hooker had made the decision to break contact with the enemy.[34]

Lee had no doubt that Hooker, despite his evident lack of steadfastness, would remain to receive the blow. Lee was ignorant of the nature of the malaise that gripped his opponent, but the man appeared incapable of moving of his own volition. Already, however, Lee had taught him how to run. Now he would teach him how to swim.

BUT LEE HAD UNDERESTIMATED the general once known as Fighting Joe. Before the close of May 4, Hooker decided he had overstayed his time south of the Rappahannock. Ever since his withdrawal from Chancellorsville, his ultimate goal had been to retreat over United States Ford and return to Falmouth, where he might rest, recuperate, and plan anew. But although fully committed to a withdrawal, at the last minute he saw the value of calling together his senior subordinates and making them a party to his decision.

Just before midnight, every corps commander except Sedgwick and Slocum (the latter being on an inspection tour of the farthest extent of his own position) converged on Hooker's tent at the Bullock house. There their common superior summarized the army's situation as he saw it. He mentioned the possibility of an attack on Lee's forces but gave his audience to understand that its chances of success were slim indeed. He reminded them of the army's overriding mission to cover Washington and to avoid jeopardizing the government's safety. In the end, he asked them to vote on whether the army should take the offensive or end the campaign. Presumably to avoid influencing the outcome, before a show of hands was taken he left the tent in company with Dan Butterfield, whom he had called in from Falmouth the day before.[35]

In their leader's absence, the generals discussed the situation at some length, then made their preferences known. Howard and Reynolds were for staying and fighting. Meade was also, but he made the mistake of voicing doubt that the army could safely retreat in the face of a vigilant and aggressive foe. He thus gave the impression that his vote was based solely on that consideration. Darius Couch voted to withdraw but only because (as he later claimed) he had no confidence in Hooker's ability to execute any maneuver except a retrograde. Politician-general Sickles favored withdrawal out of concern that should Lee parry their offensive and strike a damaging blow of his own, the capital would be endangered and the Union cause would suffer disaffection.

When Hooker rejoined the gathering and learned the results of the vote—three to two in favor of remaining and attacking—he immediately overturned the decision. He announced that unless assaulted, the army would retreat across the bridges at United States Ford after dark on May 5. It would join Sedgwick on the north bank and return to Falmouth to fight again another day. Hooker would take full responsibility for this decision, which he considered in the best interests of the army. He dismissed his subordinates before any could lodge a protest, although after being shooed outside, the crusty John Reynolds wondered aloud why Hooker had called them together, having made up his mind in advance.[36]

For his part, Hooker never second-guessed himself. Later, however, he would claim that his decision had pivoted on the receipt of word that Sedgwick had retreated across Banks's Ford, an act that made a new offensive impracticable. The only flaw in Hooker's assertion was that he did not learn of Sedgwick's withdrawal until hours after the war council broke up.

Even if Sedgwick's retreat did not influence Hooker's determination to follow suit, it seems to have depressed the army commander. After the meeting broke up, he confided in George Meade that he had had enough of army command and "almost wished he had never been born." Perhaps he truly believed that had the Banks's Ford salient remained in friendly hands he could have nerved himself to take decisive action against Lee. If so, he was almost certainly deluding himself.[37]

BEFORE THE DAY WAS DONE, General Warren and Lieutenant Colonel Comstock laid out a third set of defensive works, this covering the bridges at United States Ford. The position was to be occupied shortly before the army began crossing. In designing the new bridgehead, the engineer officers undoubtedly conferred with General Hunt, whose expertise in selecting the most advantageous positions for artillery was legendary. Under his guidance, cannons were emplaced not only inside the perimeter but also on the north bank above the ford. No fewer than forty-four guns covered the crossing site, positioned to sweep every yard of open ground surrounding it.

Throughout May 5 army headquarters saw to the implementing of preliminary actions. All wagons and pack mules and most of the ambulances were assembled at the ford and then led across the pontoons. The brawnier members of Reynolds's corps were put to work felling trees to block enemy access to the army's flanks. Sedgwick, to whom Gibbon's division had again been assigned, was instructed to bolster his picket lines in the direction of United States Ford. He was informed that the crossing would probably begin shortly after dark.[38]

It did. About 7:10 P.M. artillery units began to cross the floating bridges under a rain that had been falling more or less steadily since midafternoon. The downpour combined with the darkness of evening to mask the movement, while foilage spread atop the pontoons helped deaden the sound of battery wheels and shod hooves. The rain had a negative effect as well, for it made Hooker fear the rising river would imperil the crossing and perhaps prevent it. His concern appeared well-founded, for by 10:00 P.M. the north end of both spans had gone underwater, bringing the crossing to a temporary halt. Perhaps for this reason, when the operation resumed Hooker became one of the first soldiers to cross. The blatant act left many of his subordinates scratching their heads—it stood in such contrast to Hooker's normal behavior that one aide speculated he had not fully recovered from his concussion.[39]

When General Couch, who had not been informed of Hooker's departure, found him gone, he considered himself acting commander of the army. Believing he had the authority to suspend the crossing, he announced to George Meade that "we will stay where we are and fight it out." Although Meade shared Couch's sentiments, he did not think it proper to overrule an absent superior; thus he sent a staff officer to locate Hooker and inform him of Couch's intentions. The aide crossed the river to find Hooker and his chief of staff asleep on the floor of a house by the ford. Upon waking Butterfield, the officer was advised that the retreat must and would continue. A rather sharply worded dispatch from Hooker informed Couch of this decision. Hooker would not delay the operation even for a few hours. When General Hunt, who doubted that the entire army could cross before daylight, advised a twenty-four-hour suspension, he was abruptly turned down.[40]

Hunt was proved right, but his concern was misplaced. Soon after dawn on May 6, the last artillery unit having reached the north bank, the infantry began crossing. Covered by Meade's troops, huddled inside Hooker's third and last line of defense, the main army encountered few difficulties as it trod the pontoons throughout the early morning hours. Picket firing was sporadic and did little damage even after Meade's corps began to withdraw. Covered by Hunt's guns, the rear guard of the command made it to the north bank by 9:00 A.M.

As was true of the rest of the army, some of Meade's troops believed they were merely shifting into a position from which to retake the offensive. The majority of the rank-and-file, however, had no illusions about a quick return to action, especially when, after reaching the north bank, they were marched downstream toward Falmouth. As one enlisted man recalled of his comrades, "the muttered curses were prolonged and deep as they plodded back in the mud to their old camps."[41]

LEE WAS PREPARED TO ATTACK Hooker's bridgehead shortly after dawn. He expected to find Hooker at home when he came calling; as he informed Secretary of War Seddon, the Union commander "is now fortifying himself, with a view, I presume, of holding a position this side of the Rappahannock. I understand from prisoners that he is awaiting re-enforcements."[42]

Lee had already deployed for the attack that he believed would send Hooker and his men diving into the river in chaos and panic. He was in the midst of a last-minute review of his dispositions when William Dorsey Pender galloped up to army headquarters at Fairview to report that his skirmishers had probed the enemy's lines and had found them empty. The Army of the Potomac had moved out and gone home.

Lee was incredulous. After a few moments of stunned silence, he regained his voice with a vengeance, exclaiming, "Why, General Pender! That is the way you young men always do. You allow those people to get away. I tell you what to do, but you don't do it!" His subordinate stood uneasily before him, hesitant to reply to those words that smoldered with barely suppressed rage. Finally, Lee barked, "Go after them, and damage them all you can!"[43]

But nothing could be done—the bird had flown. Safely ensconced on the far side of a major river, the Federals were beyond Lee's reach; additional damage was not possible. At long last, Joe Hooker had stolen a march on his opponent.

AT ELEVEN O'CLOCK on the morning of May 5 Dan Butterfield had sent a dispatch to the White House that, due to the vagaries of the military telegraph, took twenty-four hours to reach Lincoln. The news was not good. By all indications Stoneman's raid had failed; Sedgwick's hold on Banks's Ford had been broken and he had crossed the river; the situation of the main army was so critical it might have to join Sedgwick on the north bank. And yet General Hooker was reported as hopeful Lee would attack, the implication being that he expected not only to absorb the blow but deliver one of his own.

The president replied to this dire news calmly enough, informing Hooker that, at least as reported in the Richmond press, Stoneman had not failed but had done Lee's communications much harm. "This," wrote Lincoln hopefully, "with the great rain of yesterday and last night, securing your right flank, I think, puts a new face upon your case, but you must be the judge."[44]

Lincoln's optimistic pronouncement failed to mask his fear that, as he confided to Noah Brooks, Hooker had been beaten. Still, he appears to have hoped to the last that he would be proven wrong. When, later that day, confirmation of Hooker's crossing and return to Falmouth reached him, the Commander in Chief was reduced to abject despair. "Never, as long as I knew him," Brooks recalled, "did he seem to be so broken up, so dispirited, and so ghostlike. Clasping his hands behind his back, he walked up and down the room, saying, 'My God, my God, what will the country say? What will the country say?' He seemed incapable of uttering any other words than these, and after a little while he hurriedly left the room."[45]

EPILOGUE

Out of the Woods

Hooker would claim that he did not feel that he had been beaten at Chancellorsville because when he withdrew north of the Rappahannock, his army was largely intact and many of its components had not seen heavy action at any point in the campaign. In fact, as he told the Joint Committee on the Conduct of the War, "when I returned from Chancellorsville, I felt that I had fought no battle; in fact, I had more men than I could use, and I fought no general battle for the reason that I could not get my men in position to do so. . . ." This, of course, begs the question of why he felt compelled to break contact with Lee and force those fresh troops of his to relinquish the battlefield to the enemy.[1]

Hooker's belief that his army had emerged from the campaign as something more than a loser has a statistical basis of sorts. Those troops that had been engaged had suffered a total of 17,300 casualties, most of them in the ranks of the Third and Sixth Corps. In contrast, the Army of Northern Virginia lost almost 13,500 men killed, wounded, or missing, more than 60 percent of them in the Second Corps minus Early's division. Both sets of statistics indicate heavy loss, but the major difference was not in killed or wounded but in men missing and presumed captured, the largest loss in this category having occurred, not surprisingly, in the ranks of the Eleventh Corps on May 2. Remove this element from the equation, and the two armies suffered almost equally. The comparison actually tilts in the Federals' favor when one considers that Hooker's losses constituted about 13 percent of his total force, while

271

Lee lost 22 percent of his available manpower. The disparity suggests the cost of Lee's determination to carry the offensive to a stronger enemy and to maintain it against all odds.[2]

Hooker was not alone in his belief that his army had been neither fought out nor defeated. As a body, his troops appeared to feel that on every day of the campaign and on virtually every part of the field, they had given at least as good as they got and, in many instances, better than they got. As a Wisconsin officer put it, "the men were absolutely astonished at our move [i.e., retreat] for every one felt that we had the best of the Rebs and could hold our position . . . till Hell froze over." An Indiana soldier lamented that "we marched, we fought, we failed. We were not defeated but we did not defeat."[3]

The army may not have felt beaten, but it had given up the fight and had quit the field. If the rank-and-file was not to blame for this undesirable outcome, who was? In the minds of many, the man at the top was solely responsible. A Pennsylvanian asked sarcastically of a civilian friend: "What is thought of Hooker's retreat? Do you not think he covered Washington well?" The average enlisted man, however, seemed inclined to blame not Hooker himself but external factors such as the size and unwieldiness of the command he had led into battle for the first time. A typical private concluded that "Gen Hooker is a bold and a fighting Genl, but not one to plan out maneuvering of a large army."[4]

The officer corps was much less inclined to make excuses for their commander. Charles F. Adams Jr., never one to suppress his indignation at high-ranking ineptitude, called Hooker "the least able commander we have had" and attributed the army's defeat to his flawed character, especially his weakness of will: "Hooker got frightened and, after Sedgwick's disaster, seemed utterly to lose the capacity for command. . . . Two thirds of his army had not been engaged at all, and he had not heard from Stoneman, but he was haunted with a vague phantom of danger on his right flank and base, a danger purely of his own imagining, and he had no peace until he found himself on this side of the river. Had he fought his army as he might have fought it, the rebel army would have been destroyed and Richmond today in our possession."[5]

The loss-of-confidence theme was especially prominent in the writings of Hooker's senior subordinates. Alpheus Williams believed that "we have lost physically and numerically, but still more morally . . . by a universal want of confidence in the commanding officer. . . . I have not met the first officer who does not feel this, from the highest to the lowest." Within days of the army's return to Falmouth, General Patrick was reporting that "no confidence is felt in Hooker," and that "there is a feeling of universal disgust among the Officers as to the management of Gen. Hooker." The letters he received from friends at home told the provost marshal general that "the loss of confidence in Hooker . . . is now beginning to be understood" throughout the North. General Warren did not have to name the object of his criticism when he described the campaign as having been lost due to "a want of nerve *somewhere*."[6]

Even George Meade, who had tried to think well of Hooker even when the man's words and deeds made it difficult, was forced to admit that the campaign "was a miserable failure" and that it had "shaken the confidence of the army in Hooker's judgment. . . ." He elaborated on this issue in a letter to his wife: "General Hooker has disappointed all his friends by failing to show his fighting qualities at the pinch. He was more cautious and took to digging quicker even than McClellan, thus proving that a man may talk very big when he has no responsibility, but that is quite a different thing, acting when you are responsible and talking when others are."[7]

Meade was especially critical of his commander's handling of the midnight council of war: "Who would have believed a few days ago that Hooker would withdraw his army, in opposition to the opinion of a majority of his corps commanders?" Hooker had added to his transgressions when he later accused Meade of double-dealing—voting to recross the river but telling others he desired to stay and fight. The doubt Meade expressed over a safe evacuation of the army had furnished Hooker with grounds for contending that his subordinate had supported the decision to withdraw. When Meade bristled at this self-serving interpretation, his friendship with Hooker came to an abrupt end.[8]

And yet, during the weeks following the army's return to Falmouth, Meade refused to join Generals Couch and Slocum in a clandestine campaign, one reminiscent of Hooker's intriguing against Burnside, to persuade Lincoln to oust the army leader in favor of Meade himself. Denied Meade's participation, this effort—which began on May 7 when the president and his general-in-chief made a quick trip to Falmouth to measure the fallout of the defeat, assess the mood and morale of the army, and speak candidly with some of its principals—slowly flickered and died out. Hooker would retain his command until late in June, when a new round of questionable decisions and inept moves forced Lincoln—even as the army prepared to fight a critical battle in southern Pennsylvania—to replace Fighting Joe with Meade.[9]

If his own generals were quick to indict Hooker for the army's defeat, Fighting Joe had his own ideas as to where the blame should rest. Topping his list of culprits were Howard and Sedgwick. In Hooker's mind, the culpability of both was as obvious as it was egregious. He held Howard personally responsible for his corps' being taken by surprise on the second, resulting in the loss of a critical defensive position, the damaging of the corporate morale, and the near-destruction of the army. Sedgwick he blamed for numerous sins of omission and commission—his apathetic attempts to demonstrate against Early, his initially ineffectual efforts to seize Marye's Heights, the unconscionable slowness that prevented him from carrying the position at Salem Church before Lee could secure it, and his inability to hold his strong position at Banks's Ford in the face of virtually even odds.[10]

To this roll of blame Hooker might have added the name of Dan Sickles, whose slow and ineffectual attempts to cut off Jackson's flanking movement on May 2 overshadowed his determination to hold Fairview against enemy encroachment and Hazel Grove against Hooker's misguided opposition. Hooker, however, was loath to fault a subordinate who also happened to be a friend and kindred spirit. He might have distributed blame as well among the army's staff of couriers and civilian telegraphers, whose lapses delayed the receipt of orders critical to coordinating the operations of Hooker's disparate units.

HOOKER WAS PRIVY to these blameworthy actions because they occurred under his gaze or quickly came to his attention. In later days, when details of the cavalry's operations in the Confederate rear became widely known, he added a third name to his list of those responsible for the army's retreat— George Stoneman.

Hooker's mounted commander had fallen into error from the outset of his expedition. From the moment he crossed the Rappahannock after midnight on April 28–29, Stoneman ought to have pressed his efforts to wreck Lee's communications, then block his anticipated retreat to Richmond. Instead, he lost precious time by calling in his senior subordinates, spreading his maps, and outlining everyone's role in the operation—something he should have attended to days earlier. Even then Stoneman failed to clarify details of Averell's mission, ensuring that the brigadier's column would go astray. Subsequent attempts to communicate with Averell and coordinate his movements with those of the main body proved unavailing. The proximate fault may have been Averell's, but Stoneman, as overall commander, bore a greater share of the blame for the miscommunication.[11]

Stoneman and the main body dawdled on the south bank of the Rappahannock for a full day after Averell cut loose from them. As a long-time sufferer from hemorrhoids, Stoneman may have delayed his own march in order to limit his time in the saddle. He finally got underway on the last morning in April, even as J. E. B. Stuart, accompanied by Fitz Lee's brigade, was straining to get ahead of Hooker's right wing as it moved between the Rappahannock and Rapidan, and while Rooney Lee was setting out to harass Averell.

Stoneman's path led to Raccoon Ford on the Rapidan, which John Buford's brigade took from the rear, capturing a picket party. The main column remained in the area until the next morning, in order to verify reports that Stuart's horsemen, instead of heading its way, had galloped toward Fredericksburg for a link-up with Robert E. Lee. While he waited, Stoneman forced his troopers to endure a cold and rainy night without campfires while standing "to horse" beside their fully saddled mounts.[12]

On May 1 Stoneman finally descended upon the railroads he was supposed to damage critically. His original orders had directed him to concentrate on wrecking Lee's main supply line, the Richmond, Fredericksburg & Potomac. Hooker's revised vision for his cavalry had extended Stoneman's and Averell's labors to the Virginia Central Railroad—which crossed the R, F & P at Hanover Junction, two miles above Richmond—and the Orange & Alexandria. By expanding Stoneman's area of operations and adding to his target base, Hooker ensured that there would be little concentration of time, resources, and effort against a single, major objective. Stoneman should have focused his attention on Hanover Junction and the railroad bridges north of it. By choosing to head for points south and west of the depot, he ensured that his raiders would strew sporadic, random damage across a wide area—damage susceptible of rapid repair.

Over the next several hours, Stoneman's thirty-five hundred-man column laid a light hand on Confederate communications. The advance echelon of David Gregg's division captured a small picket at Orange Springs, about eleven miles north of Louisa Court House, but did no harm to the nearby O & A. Moving to Louisa Court House, Gregg charged through the village in three columns only to find the place empty of enemy soldiers. There, at least, his command tore up a small stretch of track and cut the telegraph line. Simultaneously, detachments of Stoneman's column struck the Virginia Central, demolishing rolling stock and burning a bridge over the North Anna.[13]

Only after reaching Thompson's Cross Roads on the South Anna late on May 2 did Stoneman attempt a systematic destruction of enemy resources. Addressing his brigade and regimental commanders, he announced that they had struck the region "like a shell, and that I intended to burst it in every direction . . . and thus magnify our small force into overwhelming numbers." This was an impressive boast, but the raiding leader failed to follow through. The four detachments he sent in as many directions from Thompson's early on the third performed more like a dud than an artillery projectile scoring a direct hit on Rebeldom.[14]

A two-regiment force under Col. Percy Wyndham of the First New Jersey Cavalry galloped to Columbia, seventeen miles to the southwest. Wyndham's troopers burned a few bridges and some boats on the James River Canal. They were prevented, however, from doing material damage to the stone aqueduct that carried the canal over the Rivanna River (Stoneman had failed to provide the detachment with the requisite explosives).

Two other columns struck the R, F & P several miles north of the Confederate capital. Neither inflicted substantial damage but the one led by Col. H. Judson Kilpatrick of the Second New York penetrated the outer works of Richmond, throwing the local populace into a panic. The other detachment, under Lt. Col. Hasbrouck Davis of the Twelfth Illinois, ranged toward Hanover Junction but did not reach it. Had it damaged the depot, it might have disrupted the flow of rations, forage, and supplies to the fighting front from the Shenandoah Valley. Prevented by pursuers from rejoining Stoneman, Kilpatrick and Davis retreated by separate routes, looping around Richmond and seeking refuge inside Union lines on the York River.[15]

Meanwhile, David Gregg led a strike against Ashland Station, twelve miles above Richmond, but failed in an effort to destroy a target of considerable value, the R, F & P trestle over the South Anna. While awaiting Gregg's return, Stoneman's escort units left Thompson's Cross Roads to burn some bridges and inflict minor damage on a few other easy targets. The troopers who had remained at the side of their leader tangled with the roving Confederates of Rooney Lee, who had ridden more than seventy miles from the Rapidan—where they left Averell's column stranded on the north bank—to harass Stoneman.[16]

Although his badly outnumbered opponents eventually drew off, the raiding leader began to feel "no little anxiety" to rejoin the main army before larger numbers could converge against him. As if forgetting that he was supposed to monitor and then hinder the retreat of the Army of Northern Virginia, almost as soon as he heard a rumor that Hooker's offensive had been repulsed (no official word ever reached him from army headquarters), Stoneman made preparations to return home. By the evening of May 6 he was heading north, and before daylight on the seventh he was crossing the Rapidan at Raccoon Ford. By now he had gotten some details of Hooker's retreat, so he speeded up his own. At this juncture, Stoneman's primary emotion was depression, brought on by the realization that the damage his men had inflicted on three railroads would count for nothing in the long-range, strategic view.[17]

By late on May 8 the raiders were back within supporting distance of the main army, where Hooker promptly assessed the results of their expedition as embarrassingly meager. Later he would claim that had Stoneman taken a heavy toll of Confederate railroads, supply depots, and other rear-echelon resources, the army would not have relinquished its foothold on Chancellorsville but would have fought Lee to the bitter end. Whatever the likelihood of that prospect, Hooker was deeply disappointed by Stoneman's failure to put the R, F & P out of commission, at least to the point of disrupting service between Richmond and Hamilton's Crossing. As it was, within forty-eight hours of the raiders' departure labor crews were repairing the last of the damage done the railroad, even in those few places where the tracks had been torn up for several hundred yards. Although he did not regard Stoneman's culpability on a par with Averell's, Hooker not only lambasted him in both official and private correspondence but also maneuvered him into taking leave in Washington, ostensibly for treatment of his hemorrhoids. But Hooker had no intention of recalling his old army colleague. Like Averell, Stoneman would never again have a command in the Army of the Potomac.[18]

Despite the failure of Stoneman's raiders to do lasting damage to any of Lee's communications, they had displayed daring, combativeness, and an extraordinary amount of endurance during the long and taxing expedition. They were, and they remained, fiercely proud of their accomplishments on this, the first large-scale, independent maneuver of the army's cavalry corps. For this reason they bristled at any suggestion they had not performed to the utmost of their ability. They took particular offense at Hooker's publicized criticism of Stoneman and, by extension, his command. Typical of their reaction was the sarcastic comment of a trooper from Maine: "Whether he [Hooker] was dissatisfied or not with our raid . . . I think we accomplished as much as he did."[19]

WHILE HOOKER WAS CAREFUL to give Lincoln, both before and during his flying visit to the army, the impression that he intended to take the offensive at the earliest opportunity, upon reaching Falmouth he did little more than compose an address to his troops. In fulsome language, he congratulated them (and himself) on a phantom victory. The soldiers who had endured quite the opposite at Hooker's hands must have rolled their eyes and wagged their heads when assembled in their camps for a reading of General Order No. 49, which claimed, among other things:

> " . . . the events of the last week may swell with pride the heart of every officer and soldier of this army. We have added new luster to its former renown. We have made long marches, crossed rivers, surprised the enemy in his intrenchments, and whenever we have fought, we have inflicted heavier blows than those we have received. We have taken from the enemy 5000 prisoners [actuality, about half that many, plus] fifteen colors; captured and brought off seven pieces of artillery; placed *hors de combat* 18,000 of his chosen troops [in truth, about 11,000]; destroyed his depots filled with vast amounts of stores; deranged his communications; captured prisoners within the fortifications of his capital; and filled his country with fear and consternation. We have no other regret than that caused by the loss of our brave companions; and in this we are consoled by the conviction that they have fallen in the holiest cause ever submitted to the arbitrament of battle."[20]

More becoming in their simplicity and modesty were the words of Robert E. Lee, embodied in a congratulatory address disseminated to his troops one day after Hooker's proclamation. General Order No. 59 gave most of the credit for the great triumph to a power higher than Lee and Jackson:

> With heartfelt gratification, the general commanding expresses to the army his sense of the heroic conduct displayed by officers and men during the arduous operations in which they have just been engaged. . . . While this glorious victory entitles you to the praise and gratitude of the nation, we are especially called upon to return our grateful thanks to the only Giver of victory, for the signal deliverance He has wrought. It is therefore earnestly recommended that the troops unite, on Sunday next, in ascribing to the Lord of Hosts the glory due unto His name. . . .[21]

The two addresses, markedly different in tone if not in style, suggest the contrasting outlooks of their authors. Joseph Hooker appeared to remain in the grip of that mental paralysis that beset him following his May 3 injury. He had been effectively reduced to reacting to events set in motion by decisions made by his opponent. He did not quickly recover from his malaise; as late as six weeks after the return to Falmouth, he appeared to his subordinates "like a man without a plan"—lost and drifting, incapable of learning from the past and unable to face the future head-on.[22]

In stark contrast, Robert E. Lee had a plan, one he intended to implement as soon as he patched the holes rent in his army by a week of desperate struggle in a forbidding woods. Hooker's offensive had forced Lee to postpone his intention to return his troops to Maryland with a view to moving across the Mason-Dixon Line. Now he could make that move secure in the knowledge that his army was at the peak of both its efficiency and its morale. As his inadequately fed, poorly clothed, indifferently equipped soldiers had proven, even when contending against superior numbers in a movement-hindering, vision-obscuring forest, they could not be beaten. It followed that such a force could not be stopped—even seriously threatened—whether operating in friendly territory or in the far-off country of the enemy.[23]

With an engine such as this to attach himself to, Lee was confident of going anywhere and of doing whatever needed to be done when he got there. He had achieved not only freedom of movement but the ability to realize his every objective—including, perhaps, making real the bright and captivating vision of Southern independence. All he asked was that the stalwarts who had helped him get this far be allowed to accompany him the rest of the way. These included his "War Horse," James Longstreet, whose counsel and support Lee had missed dearly during the campaign, and Stonewall Jackson, whose tactical genius Lee had only recently come to appreciate fully. Fortunately, as of May 6 Longstreet was on his way back to the army and Jackson was convalescing rapidly enough to satisfy even his most cautious attendants. Surely the God who had granted Lee such a complete and satisfying victory would not deny him the personnel he needed to transform that victory into final triumph.[24]

IN ITS CHEERLESS CAMPS opposite Fredericksburg, the Army of the Potomac awaited the opportunity to redeem itself for its error-riddled performance below the Rappahannock. Its only hope was that its next field of battle would lack the obstacles that at Chancellorsville had canceled out its native advantages of size and resources. Moreover, it hoped to fight under someone without Joe Hooker's tactical ineptitude, infirmity of purpose, and emotional fragility. If only to keep from sinking into despair, many officers and men dwelled on the thought that such a day would surely come. Others, however, could see only a long, tortuous road that stretched off into the dark unknown. General Patrick was one of these; in his diary entry for May 6 he lamented that "I feel perfectly disheartened and cannot see the end of this war—it is now in the hands of gamblers."[25]

In fact, it had been in the hands of gamblers throughout the campaign just ended. At its outset, Lee had committed himself to maneuvering and fighting with chesslike precision according to cherished maxims that had won historical acceptance. Before the contest was well advanced, however, he abandoned the chessboard to join Hooker, an inveterate card sharp, at the poker table. The game that followed was a classic test not only of strategies but of contrasting visions and clashing personalities. It began with Hooker halving his main army with the intent of crushing Lee between its formidable parts. Lee saw Hooker's bid and raised the ante by splitting his own army into no fewer than three parts, on no fewer than two occasions. Quickly nearing his break point, Hooker put on his best poker face. But Lee saw his aggressive-looking move for what it was—a bluff. He called the bluff and his opponent promptly folded. From that moment on, the game was in Lee's hands.

Notes

One

1. James Longstreet, "The Battle of Fredericksburg," *B&L* 3: 76.

2. Ibid., 79.

3. Ibid., 81.

4. John Esten Cooke, *A Life of Gen. Robert E. Lee* (New York, 1871), 184.

5. Thomas L. Connelly, *The Marble Man: Robert E. Lee and His Image in American Society* (Baton Rouge, La., 1977), 206–07.

6. Ibid., 205; Douglas Southall Freeman, *R. E. Lee: A Biography.* (4 vols. New York, 1934–35), 1: 11–12.

7. Freeman, *R. E. Lee*, 1: 9; Charles Royster, *Light-Horse Harry Lee and the Legacy of the American Revolution* (New York, 1981), 106–36.

8. Burton J. Hendrick, *The Lees of Virginia: Biography of a Family* (Boston, 1935), 377–79, 392; Freeman, *R. E. Lee*, 1: 33–34; Connelly, *Marble Man*, 169.

9. Freeman, *R. E. Lee*, 1: 6–14, 31–32; Hendrick, *Lees of Virginia*, 384–93; Royster, *Light-Horse Harry Lee*, 63–64, 66–83, 100–04, 156–61; Thomas Boyd, *Light-Horse Harry Lee* (New York, 1931), 245–48, 285–88, 293–98, 309–10; Emory M. Thomas, *Robert E. Lee: A Biography* (New York, 1995), 31–32.

10. Royster, *Light-Horse Harry Lee*, 161–68; Boyd, *Light-Horse Harry Lee*, 310–27, 331–32; Freeman, *R. E. Lee*, 1: 14–17; Connelly, *Marble Man*, 169.

11. Thomas, *Robert E. Lee*, 40, 44–45; Connelly, *Marble Man*, 177; Freeman, *R. E. Lee*, 1: 22–23.

12. Connelly, *Marble Man*, 169; Freeman, *R. E. Lee*, 1: 30, 33–34, 36–37; Mary G. Powell, *The History of Old Alexandria, Virginia, from July 13, 1749, to May 24, 1861* (Richmond, Va., 1928), 152–57; Mollie Somerville, *Washington Walked Here: Alexandria on the Potomac . . .* (Washington, D.C., 1970), 170–71.

13. Freeman, *R. E. Lee*, 1: 33, 37–39.

14. Ibid., 36, 40, 44.

15. *Register of the Officers and Cadets of the U. S. Military Academy . . .* (West Point, N.Y., 1829), 19; Eben Swift, "The Military Education of Robert E. Lee," *Virginia Magazine of History and Biography* 35 (1927): 102; Freeman, *R. E. Lee*, 1: 48–60, 74.

16. Freeman, *R. E. Lee*, 1: 55, 60–61, 65, 82–83; Francis B. Heitman, comp., *Historical Register and Dictionary of the United States Army . . .* (2 vols.

Washington, D.C., 1903), 1: 694; A. L. Long, *Memoirs of Robert E. Lee: His Military and Personal History . . .* (Philadelphia, 1886), 71.

17. Freeman, *R. E. Lee*, 1: 62; Swift, "Military Education of Robert E. Lee," 102–03; David H. Donald, "Refighting the Civil War," in David H. Donald, *Lincoln Reconsidered* (New York, 1956), 88–89.

18. Donald, "Refighting the Civil War," 89–90.

19. Ibid., 90; Michael L. Handel, *Masters of War: Sun Tzu, Clausewitz and Jomini* (Portland, Ore., 1992), 4, 8, 142–43.

20. Antoine Henri Jomini, *Summary of the Art of War*, trans. G. H. Mendell and W. P. Craighill (Westport, Conn., 1977), 328–31.

21. Handel, *Masters of War*, 42–44, 59, 106–07; Grady McWhiney and Perry D. Jamieson, *Attack and Die: Civil War Military Tactics and the Southern Heritage* (University, Ala., 1982), 41–43.

22. Donald, "Refighting the Civil War," 92–93.

23. McWhiney and Jamieson, *Attack and Die*, 48–58.

24. Freeman, *R. E. Lee*, 1: 87.

25. Ibid., 99–107; John Ball Osborne, *The Story of Arlington: A History and Description of the Estate . . .* (Washington, D.C., 1899), 21–22; Randle Bond Truett, *Lee Mansion, Arlington, Virginia* (New York, 1943), 4–6; Murray H. Nelligan, *Custis-Lee Mansion: The Robert E. Lee Memorial* (Washington, D.C., 1962), 1–9; Connelly, *Marble Man*, 165, 171–72.

26. Connelly, *Marble Man*, 165–77; Freeman, *R. E. Lee*, 1: 379.

27. Connelly, *Marble Man*, 177–60, 190–91.

28. Freeman, *R. E. Lee*, 1: 200–19; K. Jack Bauer, *The Mexican War, 1846–1848* (New York, 1974), 145–51.

29. Freeman, *R. E. Lee*, 1: 218–72; Winfield Scott, *Memoirs of Lieut.-General Scott, LL. D., Written by Himself* (New York, 1864), 432, 444, 446, 450, 471, 475, 479–80, 484–85; Bauer, *Mexican War*, 246, 248, 250, 264, 288–95; Alfred Hoyt Bill, *Rehearsal for Conflict: The War with Mexico, 1846–1848* (New York, 1947), 210, 214, 216, 225–26.

30. Scott, *Memoirs of Lieut.-General Scott*, 508–37; Bauer, *Mexican War*, 311–17; Bill, *Rehearsal for Conflict*, 292–97; Freeman, *R. E. Lee*, 1: 294.

31. Freeman, *R. E. Lee*, 1: 294.

32. Connelly, *Marble Man*, 167–68, 176–80; Edward G. Longacre, *Fitz Lee: A*

Military Biography of Maj. Gen. Fitzhugh Lee, C.S.A. (New York, 2005), 9–12; Thomas J. Fleming, *West Point: The Men and Times of the United States Military Academy* (New York, 1969), 130–36; James L. Morrison, Jr., *"The Best School in the World": West Point, the Pre-Civil War Years, 1833–1865* (Kent, Ohio, 1986), 77, 115; George S. Pappas, *To the Point: The United States Military Academy, 1802–1902* (Westport, Conn., 1993), 273–75, 288–307.

33. Freeman, *R. E. Lee*, 1: 353–59; Morrison, *"Best School in the World,"* 96.

34. Freeman, *R. E. Lee*, 1: 349–50; James R. Arnold, *Jeff Davis's Own: Cavalry, Comanches, and the Battle for the Texas Frontier* (New York, 2000), 11.

35. Freeman, *R. E. Lee*, 1: 360–64; Arnold, *Jeff Davis's Own*, 37–38, 79–81, 85–90, 159–62; Longacre, *Fitz Lee*, 15–25.

36. Freeman, *R. E. Lee*, 1: 377.

37. Ibid., 370.

38. Ibid., 371–73; Thomas, *Robert E. Lee*, 173, 184.

39. Freeman, *R. E. Lee*, 1: 394–402; Allan Keller, *Thunder at Harper's Ferry* (Englewood Cliffs, N. J., 1958), 68–69, 98–99, 125–27, 137, 141–49, 151, 153–57, 162; Stephen B. Oates, *To Purge This Land with Blood: A Biography of John Brown* (New York, 1970), 290–301.

40. Freeman, *R. E. Lee*, 1: 410–12.

41. Ibid., 413–30.

42. Ibid., 425–37; Thomas, *Robert E. Lee*, 186–88.

Two

1. Freeman, *R. E. Lee*, 1: 444.

2. Thomas, *Robert E. Lee*, 188–89.

3. Ibid., 189–90; Connelly, *Marble Man*, 201–02; Alan T. Nolan, *Lee Considered: General Robert E. Lee and Civil War History* (Chapel Hill, N.C., 1991), 42–44.

4. Freeman, *R. E. Lee*, 1: 472–509; Thomas, *Robert E. Lee*, 195; *OR*, I, 2: 37–44; Osborne, *Story of Arlington*, 26.

5. Connelly, *Marble Man*, 34; Nelligan, *Custis-Lee Mansion*, 26; Freeman, *R. E. Lee*, 1: 511.

6. *OR*, I, 2: 44–52, 64–74, 77–104, 123–24, 193–293.

7. Ibid., 156–87; William C. Davis, *Battle at Bull Run: A History of the First Major*

Campaign of the Civil War (Garden City, N. Y., 1977), 17–22, 80–88; David Detzer, *Donnybrook: The Battle of Bull Run, 1861* (New York, 2004), 26–32, 54–64.

8. *OR*, I, 2: 303–18; Davis, *Battle at Bull Run*, 90–131; Detzer, *Donnybrook*, 110–204.

9. Freeman, *R. E. Lee*, 1: 537–40; Steven E. Woodworth, *Davis and Lee at War* (Lawrence, Kan., 1995), 39–42.

10. *OR*, I, 2: 202–08, 220–27, 285–88; Freeman, *R. E. Lee*, 1: 532–34, 541–44.

11. *OR*, I, 5: 192.

12. Ibid., 184–93, 842, 846; Freeman, *R. E. Lee*, 1: 545–78.

13. Freeman, *R. E. Lee*, 1: 588–601; *OR*, I, 5: 615; 51, pt. 2: 335.

14. Freeman, *R. E. Lee*, 1: 602–27; Thomas, *Robert E. Lee*, 211–13; *OR*, I, 6: 357.

15. Freeman, *R. E. Lee*, 1: 614–31; Thomas, *Robert E. Lee*, 213–16.

16. Woodworth, *Davis and Lee at War*, 104–05; Stephen W. Sears, *To the Gates of Richmond: The Peninsula Campaign* (New York, 1992), 11–14.

17. *OR*, I, 11, pt. 1: 5–19, 279–423; Sears, *To the Gates of Richmond*, 23–62.

18. Sears, *To the Gates of Richmond*, 97, 100, 102–03, 110–12, 118, 151–53, 158; Robert G. Tanner, *Stonewall in the Valley: Thomas J. "Stonewall" Jackson's Shenandoah Valley Campaign, Spring 1862* (Garden City, N.Y., 1976), 155–57, 160, 176, 186–88, 191, 195, 200–02, 219, 245, 247–48, 250.

19. Freeman, *R. E. Lee*, 2: 58–74; Sears, *To the Gates of Richmond*, 117–45; *OR*, I, 11, pt. 1: 933–94.

20. Freeman, *R. E. Lee*, 1: 75–80.

21. *OR*, I, 11, pt. 1: 1005–46; pt. 2: 489–94; Sears, *To the Gates of Richmond*, 204–48; Bevin Alexander, *Robert E. Lee's Civil War* (Holbrook, Mass., 1998), 12–21.

22. *OR*, I, 11, pt. 2: 494–95; Sears, *To the Gates of Richmond*, 249–307; Alexander, *Robert E. Lee's Civil War*, 21–25.

23. *OR*, I, 11, pt. 2: 495–98; Sears, *To the Gates of Richmond*, 308–36; William W. Averell, "With the Cavalry on the Peninsula," *B&L* 2: 432.

24. John J. Hennessy, *Return to Bull Run: The Campaign and Battle of Second Manassas* (New York, 1993), 21–26.

25. Ibid., 23–30; *OR*, I, 12, pt. 2: 176–86; Alexander, *Robert E. Lee's Civil War*, 41–49.

26. *OR*, I, 12, pt. 2: 551–54, 563–65, 641–45; Hennessy, *Return to Bull Run*, 54–95, 153–93.

27. *OR*, I, 12, pt. 2: 554–59, 565–68, 645–48; Hennessy, *Return to Bull Run*, 309–455.

28. *OR*, I, 19, pt. 1: 144–45; Stephen W. Sears, *Landscape Turned Red: The Battle of Antietam* (New Haven, Conn., 1983), 111–13; Silas Colgrove, "The Finding of Lee's Lost Order," *B&L* 2: 603.

29. *OR*, I, 19, pt. 1: 148–50; Sears, *Landscape Turned Red*, 180–297.

30. Alexander, *Robert E. Lee's Civil War*, 93–96, 113–14.

31. *OR*, I, 19, pt. 1: 4–24, 32–33, 67–88, 142–43, 151–53; Sears, *Landscape Turned Red*, 298–345.

32. Longstreet, "Battle of Fredericksburg," 70.

33. *OR*, I, 21: 61–73, 82–95, 545–56; Alexander, *Robert E. Lee's Civil War*, 117–20.

34. Alexander, *Robert E. Lee's Civil War*, 133; Nolan, *Lee Considered*, 76–80.

35. Freeman, *R. E. Lee*, 2: 479–80.

36. Walter H. Hebert, *Fighting Joe Hooker* (Indianapolis, 1944), 164–67.

37. Freeman, *R. E. Lee*, 2: 481–84; Thomas, *Robert E. Lee*, 279.

38. Jed Hotchkiss and William Allan, *The Battle-fields of Virginia: Chancellorsville . . .* (New York, 1866), 15–16; Edward G. Longacre, *Lee's Cavalrymen: A History of the Mounted Forces of the Army of Northern Virginia, 1861–1865* (Mechanicsburg, Pa., 2000), 167–68.

39. Freeman, *R. E. Lee*, 2: 489–91.

40. Ibid., 491–93; Longacre, *Lee's Cavalrymen*, 167–75; John Bigelow, Jr., *The Campaign of Chancellorsville: A Strategic and Tactical Study* (New Haven, Conn., 1910), 89–105.

41. Freeman, *R. E. Lee*, 2: 483–84, 493–95; Jeffry D. Wert, *General James Longstreet, the Confederacy's Most Controversial Soldier: A Biography* (New York, 1993), 228–29.

42. Herman Hattaway and Archer Jones, *How the North Won: A Military History of the Civil War* (Urbana, Ill., 1983), 311–25; Freeman, *R. E. Lee*, 2: 483; REL, *Lee's Dispatches: Unpublished Letters of General Robert E. Lee, C.S.A., to Jefferson Davis and the War Department of the Confederate States of America, 1862–65*, ed. Douglas Southall Freeman and Grady McWhiney (New York, 1957), 69.

43. Steven A. Cormier, *The Siege of Suffolk: The Forgotten Campaign, April 11–May*

4, 1863 (Lynchburg, Va., 1989), 13–15, 41–50; Freeman, *R. E. Lee*, 2: 483–84.

44. Freeman, *R. E. Lee*, 2: 482–83, 502–04; Thomas, *Robert E. Lee*, 277–79.

45. *OR*, I, 25, pt. 2: 713–14.

46. Ibid., pt. 1: 796; pt. 2: 744–45; REL, *The Wartime Papers of Robert E. Lee*, ed. Clifford Dowdey and Louis H. Manarin (Boston, 1961), 439.

Three

1. Bigelow, *Campaign of Chancellorsville*, 126–28.

2. Ibid., 128.

3. Ibid., 128–29.

4. Ibid., 128; Darius N. Couch, "Sumner's 'Right Grand Division'," *B&L* 3: 119–20.

5. Jennifer Crocker and Lora E. Park, "The Costly Pursuit of Self-Esteem," *Psychology Bulletin* 130 (2004): 392–95.

6. Ibid.; Bigelow, *Campaign of Chancellorsville*, 130.

7. Hebert, *Fighting Joe Hooker*, 183; Bigelow, *Campaign of Chancellorsville*, 130.

8. Couch, "Sumner's 'Right Grand Division'," 120; Darius N. Couch, "The Chancellorsville Campaign," *B&L* 3: 155.

9. Bigelow, *Campaign of Chancellorsville*, 130.

10. Hebert, *Fighting Joe Hooker*, 17–18; *Celebration of the Two Hundredth Anniversary of the Settlement of Hadley, Massachusetts, at Hadley, June 8, 1859 . . .* (Northampton, Mass., 1859), 11–61.

11. Hebert, *Fighting Joe Hooker*, 18–19; Alice Morehouse Walker, *Historic Hadley: A Story of the Making of a Famous Massachusetts Town* (New York, 1906), 97; Thomas Kearny, *General Philip Kearny, Battle Soldier of Five Wars . . .* (New York, 1937), 30n.

12. Hebert, *Fighting Joe Hooker*, 19.

13. Henry Villard, *Memoirs of Henry Villard, Journalist and Financier, 1835–1900* (2 vols. Boston, 1904), 1: 347–48.

14. William F. G. Shanks, *Personal Recollections of Distinguished Generals* (New York, 1866), 187–91.

15. Hebert, *Fighting Joe Hooker*, 20–21; Debbie Pogue, USMA Special Collections, to the author, Feb. 8, 2005; *Register of Officers and Cadets U.S. Military*

Academy (1834, p. 21; 1835, p. 22; 1836, p. 21; 1837, p. 22).

16. Debbie Pogue, USMA Special Collections, to the author, Feb. 8, 2005; *Register of Officers and Cadets U.S. Military Academy* (1834, p. 15; 1835, p. 13; 1836, p. 10; 1837, p. 7).

17. McWhiney and Jamieson, *Attack and Die*, 41–42; Donald, "Refighting the Civil War," 89; *Register of Officers and Cadets U.S. Military Academy* (1836, p. 10); Hebert, *Fighting Joe Hooker*, 21.

18. Hebert, *Fighting Joe Hooker*, 20.

19. Ibid., 21–22; John K. Mahon, *History of the Second Seminole War, 1835–1842* (Gainesville, Fla., 1967), 219–44; John and Mary Lou Missall, *The Seminole Wars: America's Longest Indian Conflict* (Gainesville, Fla., 2004), 23–50.

20. Mahon, *History of the Second Seminole War*, 325–26; Hebert, *Fighting Joe Hooker*, 22–23; Harrie B. Coe, ed., *Maine—Resources, Attractions, and Its People: A History* (4 vols. New York, 1928), 1: 111–13; Scott, *Memoirs of Lieut.-Gen. Winfield Scott*, 337–42.

21. Hebert, *Fighting Joe Hooker*, 23.

22. Bauer, *Mexican War*, 4–13, 66–68; Bill, *Rehearsal for Conflict*, 50–106.

23. Hebert, *Fighting Joe Hooker*, 25–28; Bauer, *Mexican War*, 81–102; Heitman, comp., *Historical Register and Dictionary*, 1: 272, 492, 902, 1061.

24. Hebert, *Fighting Joe Hooker*, 28–29.

25. Ibid., 29–33; Scott, *Memoirs of Lieut.-Gen. Scott*, 508–19; Bauer, *Mexican War*, 296–301, 313–17; Bill, *Rehearsal for Conflict*, 278–83, 293–96; Fleming, *West Point*, 122; Wert, *General James Longstreet*, 44–45.

26. Milton H. Shutes, "'Fighting Joe' Hooker," *California Historical Society Quarterly* 16 (1937): 304.

27. Bauer, *Mexican War*, 371–74; Scott, *Memoirs of Lieut.-Gen. Scott*, 415–17, 584.

28. Hebert, *Fighting Joe Hooker*, 35–36; Shutes, "'Fighting Joe' Hooker," 304–05.

29. Hebert, *Fighting Joe Hooker*, 36–38; Shutes, "'Fighting Joe' Hooker," 305; John W. Caughey, *California: A Remarkable State's Life History* (Englewood Cliffs, N.J., 1970), 266–67.

30. Alexander K. McClure, *Col. Alexander K. McClure's Recollections of Half a Century* (Salem, Mass., 1902), 348.

31. Hebert, *Fighting Joe Hooker*, 39–40; Shutes, "'Fighting Joe' Hooker," 306.

32. Hebert, *Fighting Joe Hooker*, 38; Shutes, "'Fighting Joe' Hooker," 305–06;

Caughey, *California*, 200–01; Warren A. Beck and David A. Williams, *California: A History of the Golden State* (Garden City, N.Y., 1972), 285.

33. Hebert, *Fighting Joe Hooker*, 39–42; Shutes, "'Fighting Joe' Hooker," 306–07.

34. Hebert, *Fighting Joe Hooker*, 38, 293; George Fort Milton, *Conflict: The American Civil War* (New York, 1941), 253; Thomas Lawlor to Samuel P. Bates, Oct. 23, 1880, SPB MSS, PSA.

35. Hebert, *Fighting Joe Hooker*, 41–42; Shutes, "'Fighting Joe' Hooker," 307; John F. Marszalek, *Commander of All Lincoln's Armies: A Life of General Henry W. Halleck* (Cambridge, Mass., 2004), 95; Ezra J. Warner, *Generals in Blue: Lives of the Union Commanders* (Baton Rouge, La., 1964), 195–97.

36. Marszalek, *Commander of All Lincoln's Armies*, 166; JH to SPB, May 29, June 28, 1878, SPB MSS, PSA.

37. Hebert, *Fighting Joe Hooker*, 44–45.

38. Ibid., 45–46; Shutes, "'Fighting Joe' Hooker," 307; Richard H. Orton, comp., *Records of California Men in the War of the Rebellion, 1861 to 1867* (Sacramento, Cal., 1890), 5–6.

Four

1. Davis, *Battle at Bull Run*, 239; Detzer, *Donnybrook*, 309–16, 400, 409–10.

2. Hebert, *Fighting Joe Hooker*, 47–48.

3. Ibid., 48–49; *California Alta*, Feb. 28, 1863.

4. *California Alta*, Feb. 28, 1863.

5. Hebert, *Fighting Joe Hooker*, 50.

6. Ibid., 50–52.

7. Shutes, "'Fighting Joe' Hooker," 306; Edward G. Longacre, "Damnable Dan Sickles," *CWTI* 23 (May 1984): 16–18; Gerard Patterson, "Daniel Butterfield," *CWTI* 12 (Nov. 1973): 13–16.

8. *OR*, I, 11, pt. 1: 464–70; Sears, *To the Gates of Richmond*, 68–82.

9. Hebert, *Fighting Joe Hooker*, 91, 318n–19n; Bigelow, *Campaign of Chancellorsville*, 6.

10. *OR*, I, 11, pt. 1: 21–23; JH to Ira Harris, May 12, 1862, GLC; Charles S. Wainwright, *A Diary of Battle: The Personal Journals of Col. Charles S. Wainwright, 1861–1865*, ed. Allan Nevins (New York, 1962), 60, 153.

11. *OR*, I, 11, pt. 1: 818–20; Wainwright, *Diary of Battle*, 77.

12. R. B. Marcy to Samuel P. Heintzelman, June 25, 1862, JH MSS, HEHL; Sears, *To the Gates of Richmond*, 282–83, 294, 301; Hebert, *Fighting Joe Hooker*, 110–12, 118.

13. Hebert, *Fighting Joe Hooker*, 119–21; Hennessy, *Return to Bull Run*, 118–37.

14. Hebert, *Fighting Joe Hooker*, 122–25; Hennessy, *Return to Bull Run*, 243–58.

15. *OR*, I, 19, pt. 1: 213–19; Hebert, *Fighting Joe Hooker*, 126–43; Sears, *Landscape Turned Red*, 176–215, 273–74, 296, 310; James Harrison Wilson, *Under the Old Flag: Recollections of Military Operations in the War for the Union, the Spanish War, the Boxer Rebellion, etc.* (2 vols. New York, 1912), 1: 117; Marsena R. Patrick, *Inside Lincoln's Army: The Diary of Marsena Rudolph Patrick, Provost Marshal General, Army of the Potomac*, ed. David S. Sparks (New York, 1964), 164.

16. Hebert, *Fighting Joe Hooker*, 145–48; Bruce Catton, *Glory Road: The Bloody Route from Fredericksburg to Gettysburg* (Garden City, N.Y., 1952), 3–7.

17. *OR*, I, 21: 355–57; Hebert, *Fighting Joe Hooker*, 149–59.

18. George Meade, *The Life and Letters of George Gordon Meade, Maj.-General, United States Army* (2 vols. New York, 1913), 1: 332.

19. Ibid., 346, 352; Warren W. Hassler, *Commanders of the Army of the Potomac* (Baton Rouge, La., 1962), 128; Copy of General Order #8, HQ, Army of the Potomac, Jan. 23, 1863; JH to SPB, June 29, 1878; both, SPB MSS, PSA; *OR*, I, 21: 998–99.

20. *OR*, I, 21: 1004–05.

21. Hebert, *Fighting Joe Hooker*, 164–66; Patrick, *Inside Lincoln's Army*, 208, 212.

22. Hebert, *Fighting Joe Hooker*, 165–66; Bigelow, *Campaign of Chancellorsville*, 7–10; *Joint Committee on the Conduct of the War* (3 vols. in 8. Washington, D.C., 1863–68), 4 (1865): 111.

23. Bigelow, *Campaign of Chancellorsville*, 10.

24. Ibid; Hassler, *Commanders of the Army of the Potomac*, 132.

25. *JCCW*, 4 (1865): 111–12; JH to SPB, June 29, 1878, Sept. 22, 1879, SPB MSS, PSA.

26. *JCCW*, 4 (1865): 111–12.

27. Ibid; JH to SPB, May 29, June 28, 1878, SPB MSS, PSA; *OR*, I, 25, pt. 2: 5–6.

28. Hassler, *Commanders of the Army of the Potomac*, 129; Robert McAllister, *The Civil War Letters of General Robert McAllister*, ed. James I. Robertson, Jr. (New Brunswick, N.J., 1965), 238.

29. Patrick, *Inside Lincoln's Army*, 237; William A. Allison to Stockton Bates, Jan. 31, 1863, GLC; Charles Adams, et al., *A Cycle of Adams Letters, 1861–1865*, ed. Worthington Chauncey Ford (2 vols. Boston, 1920), 1: 241; Meade, *Life and Letters*, 1: 318.

30. Daniel E. Sutherland, *Fredericksburg and Chancellorsville: The Dare Mark Campaign* (Lincoln, Neb., 1998), 95.

31. Adams, et al., *Cycle of Adams Letters*, 1: 250; Oliver O. Howard, *Autobiography of Oliver Otis Howard, Maj. Gen., United States Army* (2 vols. New York, 1907), 1: 347.

32. Patrick, *Inside Lincoln's Army*, 218, 227–28; Wainwright, *Diary of Battle*, 162; Meade, *Life and Letters*, 1: 365.

33. Wainwright, *Diary of Battle*, 161, 182; Meade, *Life and Letters*, 326; Adams, et al., *Cycle of Adams Letters*, 1: 232.

34. JH to Edwin M. Stanton, Apr. 23, 1863, SPB MSS, PSA.

35. JH to SPB, Oct. 5, 1878, July —, 1879, SPB MSS, PSA.

36. Wainwright, *Diary of Battle*, 215; Sutherland, *Fredericksburg and Chancellorsville*, 68; Patrick, *Inside Lincoln's Army*, 210, 213–14.

37. Adams, et al., *Cycle of Adams Letters*, 2: 14, 38; Charles F. Adams, *Charles Francis Adams, 1835–1915: An Autobiography* (Boston, 1916), 161.

38. Meade, *Life and Letters*, 1: 351.

39. *JCCW*, 4 (1865): 74; John J. Hennessy, "'We Shall Make Richmond Howl': The Army of the Potomac on the Eve of Chancellorsville," in Gary Gallagher, ed., *Chancellorsville: The Battle and Its Aftermath* (Chapel Hill, N.C., 1996), 9–10; Sutherland, *Fredericksburg and Chancellorsville*, 104.

40. Hennessy, "'We Shall Make Richmond Howl'," 10.

41. Ibid.; *JCCW*, 4 (1865): 73; Bigelow, *Campaign of Chancellorsville*, 36; Sutherland, *Fredericksburg and Chancellorsville*, 97.

42. Bigelow, *Campaign of Chancellorsville*, 36.

43. Ibid., 46; Sutherland, *Fredericksburg and Chancellorsville*, 98, 100.

44. Hennessy, "'We Shall Make Richmond Howl'," 10–11; *JCCW*, 4 (1865): 74.

45. Bigelow, *Campaign of Chancellorsville*, 49–50.

46. Sutherland, *Fredericksburg and Chancellorsville*, 98.

47. Copy of Circular, HQ Army of the Potomac, Mar. 21, 1863; JH to SPB, Dec. 8, 1876; both, SPB MSS, PSA; Bigelow, *Campaign of Chancellorsville*, 47–48.

48. *JCCW*, 4 (1865): 74.

49. Bigelow, *Campaign of Chancellorsville*, 47; Sutherland, *Fredericksburg and Chancellorsville*, 101; Edwin C. Fishel, *The Secret War for the Union: The Untold Story of Military Intelligence in the Civil War* (Boston, 1996), 1–6, 284–86, 348–49, 358–63, 370–411.

50. Charles M. Evans, *The War of the Aeronauts: A History of Ballooning during the Civil War* (Mechanicsburg, Pa., 2002), 276–87; Bigelow, *Campaign of Chancellorsville*, 19; Stephen W. Sears, *Chancellorsville* (Boston, 1996), 147, 150.

51. *JCCW*, 4 (1865): xlii; Hennessy, "'We Shall Make Richmond Howl'," 12; Edward G. Longacre, *Lincoln's Cavalrymen: A History of the Mounted Forces of the Army of the Potomac, 1861–1865* (Mechanicsburg, Pa., 2000), 124–27.

52. Bigelow, *Campaign of Chancellorsville*, 39–40, 44–45, 487–88; Hennessy, "'We Shall Make Richmond Howl'," 12–14; Hassler, *Commanders of the Army of the Potomac*, 133; Julia Lorrilard Butterfield, ed., *A Biographical Memoir of General Daniel Butterfield, Including Many Addresses and Military Writings* (New York, 1904), 113; Howard, *Autobiography*, 1: 381.

53. Hennessy, "'We Shall Make Richmond Howl'," 13; Edward G. Longacre, *The Man Behind the Guns: A Biography of General Henry Jackson Hunt, Chief of Artillery, Army of the Potomac* (South Brunswick, N.J., 1977), 138–41.

54. William H. Medill to "Dear Sister Kate," Mar. 15, 1863, Hanna-McCormick MSS, Library of Congress.

55. McClure, *Recollections*, 347–48.

Five

1. *JCCW*, 4 (1865): xlii.

2. Ibid., 115–16; Bigelow, *Campaign of Chancellorsville*, 9, 107–08.

3. Bigelow, *Campaign of Chancellorsville*, 139–41; Edward J. Stackpole, *Chancellorsville: Lee's Greatest Battle* (Harrisburg, Pa., 1958), 89–98; Sears, *Chancellorsville*, 101, 118–19.

4. Hassler, *Commanders of the Army of the Potomac*, 134–36; *OR*, I, 25, pt. 1:

1066–68, 1081; pt. 2: 213–14, 220–21; Stackpole, *Chancellorsville*, 107; Edward G. Longacre, "The Raid That Failed," *CWTI* 26 (Jan. 1988): 16, 18.

5. Bigelow, *Campaign of Chancellorsville*, 166–67; *JCCW*, 4 (1865): 116; *OR*, I, 25, pt. 1: 1065–67.

6. *JCCW*, 4 (1865): xliii, 75, 102–03; Sears, *Chancellorsville*, 132; Sutherland, *Fredericksburg and Chancellorsville*, 132; Couch, "Chancellorsville Campaign," 157.

7. *JCCW*, 4 (1865): xliii; Sears, *Chancellorsville*, 131–32; Sutherland, *Fredericksburg and Chancellorsville*, 132.

8. Fishel, *Secret War for the Union*, 360–62; Sears, *Chancellorsville*, 130–32.

9. Fishel, *Secret War for the Union*, 347–49; Sears, *Chancellorsville* 121–22.

10. Stackpole, *Chancellorsville*, 108–09; Sears, *Chancellorsville*, 131.

11. Stackpole, *Chancellorsville*, 92, 94–95; Couch, "Chancellorsville Campaign," 171; Catton, *Glory Road*, 4.

12. REL, *Wartime Papers*, 439.

13. Ibid.

14. Ibid., 440.

15. Ibid., 440–41.

16. Ibid., 438; Raleigh E. Colston, "Lee's Knowledge of Hooker's Movements," *B&L*, 3: 233.

17. REL, *Wartime Papers*, 441.

18. *OR*, I, 25, pt. 2: 752–53.

19. Janet Hewett, et al., comps., *Supplement to the Official Records of the Union and Confederate Armies* (3 series, 99 vols. Wilmington, N.C., 1994–2001), 4: 514.

20. Sutherland, *Fredericksburg and Chancellorsville*, 129; Stackpole, *Chancellorsville*, 162, 169–70, 363; Meade, *Life and Letters*, 1: 369.

21. Sutherland, *Fredericksburg and Chancellorsville*, 101; T. Harry Williams, *Lincoln and His Generals* (New York, 1952), 237.

22. Sears, *Chancellorsville*, 144; Williams, *Lincoln and His Generals*, 237–38; Sutherland, *Fredericksburg and Chancellorsville*, 133; *OR*, I, 25, pt. 2: 263.

23. Couch, "Chancellorsville Campaign," 157n; Sears, *Chancellorsville*, 144; A. M. Gambone, *Major General Darius Nash Couch: Enigmatic Valor* (Baltimore, 2000), 122.

24. Warner, *Generals in Blue*, 95; Gambone, *Darius Nash Couch*, 122.

25. Francis A. Walker, *History of the Second Army Corps in the Army of the Potomac* (New York, 1891), 213–14.

26. *OR*, I, 25, pt. 2: 255–56, 262–63; *JCCW*, 4 (1865): xliii, 75, 102–03, 116–17; Bigelow, *Campaign of Chancellorsville*, 173–74.

27. Bigelow, *Campaign of Chancellorsville*, 173n.

28. Sears, *Chancellorsville*, 63–65, 137–38.

29. Sears, *Chancellorsville*, 138–39; Catton, *Glory Road*, 172–73.

30. Bigelow, *Campaign of Chancellorsville*, 174–75.

31. Ibid., 173, 178; Stackpole, *Chancellorsville*, 113, 115–16.

32. Bigelow, *Campaign of Chancellorsville*, 175, 179.

Six

1. *OR*, I, 25, pt. 1: 215, 505, 627, 669.

2. Ibid., 1058.

3. Ibid.

4. Ibid., 1065; Longacre, *Lincoln's Cavalrymen*, 139–40; Sears, *Chancellorsville*, 120–21.

5. JH to SPB, Apr. 2, 1877, SPB MSS, PSA.

6. *OR*, I, 25, pt. 1: 213, 215; Bigelow, *Campaign of Chancellorsville*, 174; Sears, *Chancellorsville*, 146.

7. Bigelow, *Campaign of Chancellorsville*, 187; Patrick, *Inside Lincoln's Army*, 237; Sears, *Chancellorsville*, 143, 147, 150.

8. Longacre, *Fitz Lee*, 105–06; Freeman, *R. E. Lee*, 2: 505–06.

9. *OR*, I, 25, pt. 2: 268; Bigelow, *Campaign of Chancellorsville*, 178–79; Longacre, *Man Behind the Guns*, 144–45.

10. *OR*, I, 25, pt. 2: 268.

11. Ibid., pt. 1: 253, 557; pt. 2: 276.

12. Ibid., pt. 1: 205–14; Sears, *Chancellorsville*, 154–55.

13. *OR*, I, 25, pt. 1: 208–09, 213–14, 253, 566.

14. Bigelow, *Campaign of Chancellorsville*, 146, 187–88; *OR*, I, 25, pt. 1: 505, 627, 669.

15. Bigelow, *Campaign of Chancellorsville*, 187–88, 194.

16. *OR*, I, 25, pt. 1: 1058.

17. Ibid., 1058, 1065, 1073–77, 1081–82, 1088; Longacre, "Raid That Failed," 18–19, 21.

18. Bigelow, *Campaign of Chancellorsville*, 188; Sears, *Chancellorsville*, 134, 146, 163.

19. *OR*, I, 25, pt. 1: 796; Bigelow, *Campaign of Chancellorsville*, 193.

20. *OR*, I, 25, pt. 1: 1045; Freeman, *R. E. Lee*, 2: 509; Sears, *Chancellorsville*, 163; REL, *Wartime Papers*, 441–42; Fishel, *Secret War for the Union*, 379.

21. *OR*, I, 25, pt. 1: 1000; Charles C. Osborne, *Jubal: The Life and Times of General Jubal A. Early, C.S.A., Defender of the Lost Cause* (Chapel Hill, N.C., 1992), 143–44.

22. James Power Smith, "Stonewall Jackson's Last Battle," *B&L* 3: 203.

23. Freeman, *R. E. Lee*, 2: 508–09; *OR*, I, 25, pt. 1: 796.

24. Freeman, *R. E. Lee*, 2: 510–11; Osborne, *Jubal*, 144.

25. REL, *Wartime Papers*, 441–42; *OR*, I, 25, pt. 2: 756–57.

26. REL, *Wartime Papers*, 442.

27. *OR*, I, 25, pt. 1: 796; Freeman, *R. E. Lee*, 2: 511–13.

28. Bigelow, *Campaign of Chancellorsville*, 194–95.

29. *OR*, I, 25, pt. 1: 1046; Bigelow, *Campaign of Chancellorsville*, 197; Longacre, *Lee's Cavalrymen*, 178.

30. *OR*, I, 25, pt. 1: 1046, 1098; Sears, *Chancellorsville*, 163.

31. Bigelow, *Campaign of Chancellorsville*, 195–96; Sears, *Chancellorsville*, 163–64.

32. Alfred Pleasonton, "The Successes and Failures of Chancellorsville," *B&L* 3: 173–74; *New York Times*, May 22, 1863.

33. *OR*, I, 25, pt. 1: 627, 669; Bigelow, *Campaign of Chancellorsville*, 197–98.

34. *OR*, I, 25, pt. 2: 292–93; Bigelow, *Campaign of Chancellorsville*, 198–200.

35. *OR*, I, 25, pt. 1: 506, 525, 545–46; Bigelow, *Campaign of Chancellorsville*, 199–200.

36. *OR*, I, 25, pt. 1: 862, 870–71; Bigelow, *Campaign of Chancellorsville*, 203–04.

37. Freeman, *R. E. Lee*, 2: 511–12; *OR*, I, 51, pt. 2: 698; REL, *Wartime Papers*, 444; Bigelow, *Campaign of Chancellorsville*, 209.

38. Lafayette McLaws, *A Soldier's General: The Civil War Letters of Maj. Gen. Lafayette McLaws*, ed. John C. Oeffinger (Chapel Hill, N.C., 2002), 179.

39. *OR,* I, 25, pt. 2: 756.

40. Ibid., 757.

Seven

1. Longacre, *Man Behind the Guns,* 194.

2. Noel G. Harrison, *Chancellorsville Battlefield Sites* (Lynchburg, Va., 1990), 16–20, 52–54, 80–82, 99–102; Sears, *Chancellorsville,* 192–93; SPB, "Hooker's Comments on Chancellorsville," *B&L* 3: 218.

3. Sears, *Chancellorsville,* 193; Walker, *History of the Second Army Corps,* 220; Harrison, *Chancellorsville Battlefield Sites,* 24–25.

4. *OR,* I, 25, pt. 1: 506, 525, 627–28, 669, 728; Bigelow, *Campaign of Chancellorsville,* 213–14.

5. Freeman, *R. E. Lee,* 2: 511–12; G. Moxley Sorrel, *Recollections of a Confederate Staff Officer* (New York, 1905), 135; *OR,* I, 25, pt. 1: 849–50, 862, 865, 870–71; Bigelow, *Campaign of Chancellorsville,* 214.

6. Freeman, *R. E. Lee,* 2: 513; *OR,* I, 25, pt. 1: 809, 850.

7. Freeman, *R. E. Lee,* 2: 514; Clifford Dowdey, *Lee* (Boston, 1965), 343–44; REL, *Wartime Papers,* 446.

8. Douglas Southall Freeman, *Lee's Lieutenants: A Study in Command* (3 vols. New York, 1942–44), 2: 526–27; Long, *Memoirs of Robert E. Lee,* 251.

9. Freeman, *R. E. Lee,* 2: 514–15; Bigelow, *Campaign of Chancellorsville,* 231–32.

10. *OR,* I, 25, pt. 1: 797; REL, *Wartime Papers,* 447; Bigelow, *Campaign of Chancellorsville,* 232–33; Gary Gallagher, "East of Chancellorsville: Jubal A. Early at Second Fredericksburg and Salem Church," in Gary Gallagher, ed., *Chancellorsville: The Battle and Its Aftermath* (Chapel Hill, N.C., 1996): 40–41.

11. *OR,* I, 25, pt. 1: 305–06, 384; *JCCW,* 4 (1865): 122–23; Alexander Moore memorandum, Apr. 30, 1863, GLC; Stackpole, *Chancellorsville,* 147.

12. Bigelow, *Campaign of Chancellorsville,* 211–12; Daniel Butterfield to John Sedgwick, Apr. 30, 1863 [several messages], JH MSS, HEHL.

13. Bigelow, *Campaign of Chancellorsville,* 212; Stackpole, *Chancellorsville,* 148–49.

14. William Swinton, *Campaigns of the Army of the Potomac* (New York, 1882), 275.

15. *OR,* I, 25, pt. 2: 292, 306; John Sedgwick to Daniel Butterfield, Apr. 30, 1863 [several MSS], JH MSS, HEHL.

16. *OR*, I, 25, pt. 2: 307, 310; John Sedgwick to Daniel Butterfield, Apr. 30, 1863 [with endorsement by Butterfield], JH MSS, HEHL.

17. *OR*, I, 25, pt. 1: 301, 308, 312–13; John Gibbon to Daniel Butterfield, Apr. 30, 1863, JH MSS, HEHL; Bigelow, *Campaign of Chancellorsville*, 229–30.

18. *OR*, I, 25, pt. 1: 305, 384; pt. 2: 304–05, 314.

19. Daniel Butterfield to Henry W. Slocum, Apr. 30, 1863; Ulric Dahlgren to Joseph Hooker, Apr. 30, 1863; both, JH MSS, HEHL; Bigelow, *Campaign of Chancellorsville*, 221; Stackpole, *Chancellorsville*, 145.

20. *OR*, I, 25, pt. 1: 171.

21. Ibid., 506, 525; Sears, *Chancellorsville*, 177.

22. *OR*, I, 25, pt. 1: 215, 525.

23. Ibid., 506; Harrison, *Chancellorsville Battlefield Sites*, 17.

24. *OR*, I, 25, pt. 1: 506, 546, 669; Bigelow, *Campaign of Chancellorsville*, 218–21.

25. *OR*, I, 25, pt. 1: 506, 525, 669; Richard Meade Bache, *Life of General George Gordon Meade, Commander of the Army of the Potomac* (Philadelphia, 1897), 260.

26. Freeman Cleaves, *Meade of Gettysburg* (Norman, Okla., 1960), 105.

27. *OR*, I, 25, pt. 1: 506–07; Sears, *Chancellorsville*, 180–81; Bigelow, *Campaign of Chancellorsville*, 222.

28. *OR*, I, 25, pt. 1: 627–28, 669; Oliver Otis Howard, "The Eleventh Corps at Chancellorsville," *B&L* 3: 190–92; Bigelow, *Campaign of Chancellorsville*, 221–22.

29. Bigelow, *Campaign of Chancellorsville*, 225; Sears, *Chancellorsville*, 192.

30. Harrison, *Chancellorsville Battlefield Sites*, 17.

31. Ibid., 19.

32. Pleasonton, "Successes and Failures of Chancellorsville," 174.

33. Ibid.; Bigelow, *Campaign of Chancellorsville*, 217n–18n.

34. *OR*, I, 25, pt. 2: 309.

35. Ibid., 293, 309.

36. Ibid., 306–07.

37. Sears, *Chancellorsville*, 192; Stackpole, *Chancellorsville*, 173; Bigelow, *Campaign of Chancellorsville*, 225.

38. Patrick, *Inside Lincoln's Army*, 239.

Eight

1. *OR*, I, 25, pt. 1: 797; Bigelow, *Campaign of Chancellorsville*, 242, 253.

2. Freeman, *R. E. Lee*, 2: 516; *OR*, I, 25, pt. 1: 797.

3. *OR*, I, 25, pt. 1: 797.

4. Ezra J. Warner, *Generals in Gray: Lives of the Confederate Commanders* (Baton Rouge, La., 1959), 79–80; Sears, *Chancellorsville*, 250; Gallagher, "East of Chancellorsville," 36–41; Osborne, *Jubal*, 145–46.

5. *OR*, I, 25, pt. 1: 797; Freeman, *R. E. Lee*, 2: 516–17; Osborne, *Jubal*, 145–46.

6. *OR*, I, 25, pt. 1: 796–97, 1046–47; Longacre, *Lee's Cavalrymen*, 180–82; Freeman, *R. E. Lee*, 2: 516.

7. Freeman, *R. E. Lee*, 2: 517; Freeman, *Lee's Lieutenants*, 2: 528–29; Bigelow, *Campaign of Chancellorsville*, 242; Hewett, et al., comps., *Supplement to the Official Records*, 4: 516; Robert K. Krick, "Lee at Chancellorsville," in Gary Gallagher, ed., *Lee the Soldier* (Lincoln, Neb., 1996), 362–63.

8. Bigelow, *Campaign of Chancellorsville*, 244–45.

9. Edward Porter Alexander, *Fighting for the Confederacy: The Personal Recollections of General Edward Porter Alexander*, ed. Gary Gallagher (Chapel Hill, N.C., 1989), 196; Smith, "Stonewall Jackson's Last Battle," 204.

10. Stackpole, *Chancellorsville*, 148–51; Meade, *Life and Letters*, 1: 379; *JCCW*, 4 (1865): 65; Alexander Moore memorandum, Apr. 30, 1863; Bigelow, *Campaign of Chancellorsville*, 244; Hewett, et al., comps., *Supplement to the Official Records*, 4: 486.

11. *OR*, I, 25, pt. 2: 324; Bigelow, *Campaign of Chancellorsville*, 240–41.

12. Hebert, *Fighting Joe Hooker*, 198; Stackpole, *Chancellorsville*, 168.

13. *OR*, I, 36, pt. 2: 330–31, 336–45; 51, pt. 1: 1033–34; Bigelow, *Campaign of Chancellorsville*, 244, 248, 265; *JCCW*, 4 (1865): 128–29; Hewett, et al., comps., *Supplement to the Official Records*, 4: 640; Richard Elliott Winslow, *General John Sedgwick: The Story of a Union Corps Commander* (Novato, Calif., 1982), 67–68.

14. *OR*, I, 25, pt. 1: 507, 525; Bigelow, *Campaign of Chancellorsville*, 247, 250–51; Hewett, et al., comps., *Supplement to the Official Records*, 4: 486–87; George G. Meade to JH, May 1, 1863, JH MSS., HEHL; Meade, *Life and Letters*, 1: 372; Augustus C. Hamlin, *The Battle of Chancellorsville* . . . (Bangor, Me., 1896), 10; Richard A. Sauers, *Meade, Victor of Gettysburg* (Washington, D.C., 2003), 40;

Ethan S. Rafuse, *George Gordon Meade and the War in the East* (Abilene, Tex., 2003), 62–63.

15. Stackpole, *Chancellorsville*, 167–72; Ernest B. Furgurson, *Chancellorsville, 1863: The Souls of the Brave* (New York, 1992), 130–32.

16. Hebert, *Fighting Joe Hooker*, 199; Bigelow, *Campaign of Chancellorsville*, 478n.

17. *JCCW*, 4 (1865): 125.

18. *OR*, I, 25, pt. 2: 326, 328; Bigelow, *Campaign of Chancellorsville*, 250–51.

19. *OR*, I, 25, pt. 2: 322, 325, 327, 336–37; Bigelow, *Campaign of Chancellorsville*, 251.

20. *OR*, I, 25, pt. 1: 507, 627, 669; pt. 2: 328; Bigelow, *Campaign of Chancellorsville*, 249–50; Hebert, *Fighting Joe Hooker*, 199–200; Walker, *History of Second Army Corps*, 221.

21. Couch, "Chancellorsville Campaign," 159; Gambone, *Major General Darius Nash Couch*, 125.

22. Couch, "Chancellorsville Campaign." 159.

23. Ibid; *OR*, I, 25, pt. 1: 311–12, 525–26, 670; Walker, *History of Second Army Corps*, 221–23; David M. Jordan, *Winfield Scott Hancock: A Soldier's Life* (Bloomington, Ind., 1988), 70.

24. Walker, *History of Second Army Corps*, 224.

25. Couch, "Chancellorsville Campaign," 161.

26. Bigelow, *Campaign of Chancellorsville*, 243–47, 252–53, 256; Stackpole, *Chancellorsville*, 178–80, 184, 186–87, 189–92; Krick, "Lee at Chancellorsville," 364.

27. *OR*, I, 25, pt. 1: 865–66, 1047, 1049; Stackpole, *Chancellorsville*, 192–94; Bigelow, *Campaign of Chancellorsville*, 253.

28. Freeman, *R. E. Lee*, 2: 517–18.

29. Ibid., 518–19.

30. Thomas M. R. Talcott, "General Lee's Strategy at the Battle of Chancellorsville," *SHSP* 34 (1906): 13–17.

31. Longacre, *Fitz Lee*, 108; Freeman, *R. E. Lee*, 2: 520.

32. Talcott, "Lee's Strategy at Chancellorsville," 13, 16–17; Long, *Memoirs of Robert E. Lee*, 252, 258; Freeman, *R. E. Lee*, 2: 520–21.

33. *OR*, I, 25, pt. 2: 330.

Nine

1. Smith, "Stonewall Jackson's Last Battle," 205; Hewett, et al., comps., *Supplement to the Official Records*, 4: 517; Long, *Memoirs of Robert E. Lee*, 258; Freeman, *R. E. Lee*, 2: 521–22.

2. Freeman, *R. E. Lee*, 2: 523.

3. Bigelow, *Campaign of Chancellorsville*, 273; Dowdey, *Lee*, 347.

4. Freeman, *R. E. Lee*, 2: 523–24; Bigelow, *Campaign of Chancellorsville*, 273–74.

5. Freeman, *R. E. Lee*, 2: 524; *OR*, I, 25, pt. 1: 798; Bigelow, *Campaign of Chancellorsville*, 274.

6. *OR*, I, 25, pt. 1: 798, 825, 829, 851, 855, 867, 871.

7. Ibid., 811; Freeman, *R. E. Lee*, 2: 525.

8. *OR*, I, 25, pt. 2: 765.

9. Ibid.

10. *JCCW*, 4 (1865): xlv, 95, 105; *OR*, I, 25, pt. 2: 851–52; Hewett, et al., comps., *Supplement to the Official Records*, 4: 487–88.

11. Bigelow, *Campaign of Chancellorsville*, 271–72, 276; Stackpole, *Chancellorsville*, 219–20; Rafuse, *George Gordon Meade*, 64; Pleasonton, "Successes and Failures of Chancellorsville,"177.

12. Harrison, *Chancellorsville Battlefield Sites*, 83–86.

13. Howard, "Eleventh Corps at Chancellorsville," 195–96.

14. Sears, *Chancellorsville*, 228–29; Stackpole, *Chancellorsville*, 218–19; John D. McKenzie, *Uncertain Glory: Lee's Generalship Re-examined* (New York, 1997), 118.

15. JH to SPB, Aug. 29, 1878, SPB MSS, PSA.

16. *OR*, I, 25, pt. 1: 385; JH to SPB, June 26, 1876, Apr. 2, 1877, SPB MSS, PSA; Howard, "Eleventh Corps at Chancellorsville," 195; SPB, "Hooker's Comments on Chancellorsville," 218.

17. McAllister, *Civil War Letters*, 195; Patrick, *Inside Lincoln's Army*, 240–41.

18. HJ to SPB, Apr. 2, 1877, Dec. 24, 1878, SPB MSS, PSA.

19. JH to SPB, Dec. 24, 1878, SPB MSS, PSA.

20. SPB, *The Battle of Chancellorsville* (Meadville, Pa., 1882), 191.

21. Freeman, *R. E. Lee*, 2: 526–28; Sutherland, *Fredericksburg and Chancellorsville*, 155–56; Krick, "Lee at Chancellorsville," 369.

22. Freeman, *R. E. Lee*, 2: 528; *OR*, I, 25, pt. 1: 798, 871, 877–78.

23. Smith, "Stonewall Jackson's Last Battle," 206; Freeman, *R. E. Lee*, 2: 528–29.

24. Hamlin, *Battle of Chancellorsville*, 20, 83; C. Irvine Walker, *The Life of Lt. Gen. Richard Heron Anderson of the Confederate States Army* (Charleston, S.C., 1917), 137.

25. SPB, "Hooker's Comments on Chancellorsville," 218.

26. Sears, *Chancellorsville*, 264; Couch, "Chancellorsville Campaign," 162; *OR*, I, 25, pt. 2: 360–61.

27. *OR*, I, 27, pt. 2: 362.

28. Ibid., pt. 1: 385–86; pt. 2; 363; *JCCW*, 4 (1865): 146–47; Bigelow, *Campaign of Chancellorsville*, 279; Fishel, *Secret War for the Union*, 401.

29. *OR*, I, 25, pt. 1: 386.

30. Ibid. pt. 1: 386; pt. 2: 370; Stackpole, *Chancellorsville*, 216–17; Bigelow, *Campaign of Chancellorsville*, 280–83; Hewett, et al., comps., *Supplement to the Official Records*, 4: 593; W. A. Swanberg, *Sickles the Incredible* (New York, 1956), 181–82; Thomas Keneally, *American Scoundrel: The Life of the Notorious Civil War General Dan Sickles* (New York, 2002), 266; Sears, *Chancellorsville*, 254–56.

31. *OR*, I, 25, pt. 1: 386–87, 630, 670; Bigelow, *Campaign of Chancellorsville*, 283, 285; Howard, *Autobiography*, 1: 369.

32. Sears, *Chancellorsville*, 256; *OR*, I, 25, pt. 1: 386–87; pt. 2: 867, 871, 912, 924.

33. *OR*, I, 25, pt. 1: 387; Sears, *Chancellorsville*, 254–56.

34. *OR*, I, 25, pt. 1: 387; Daniel E. Sickles to JH, May 2, 1863, JH MSS, HEHL.

35. Hamlin, *Battle of Chancellorsville*, 12–13; Stackpole, *Chancellorsville*, 231–32; Alexander, *Fighting for the Confederacy*, 201–02.

36. Hunter McGuire, "General T. J. ('Stonewall') Jackson . . . His Career and Character," *SHSP* 25 (1897): 110.

37. Bigelow, *Campaign of Chancellorsville*, 281–82; Fitzhugh Lee, *General Lee* (New York, 1894): 247.

38. Alexander, *Fighting for the Confederacy*, 202; Smith, "Stonewall Jackson's Last Battle," 207; Longacre, *Fitz Lee*, 109; Fitzhugh Lee, "Chancellorsville," *SHSP* 7 (1879): 572.

39. Fitzhugh Lee, "Chancellorsville," 572.

40. Ibid.

41. *OR*, I, 25, pt. 1: 890, 940, 1004; Sears, *Chancellorsville*, 291–93.

42. Hamlin, *Battle of Chancellorsville*, 16.

43. *OR*, I, 25, pt. 1: 885, 941, 1004.

Ten

1. Sears, *Chancellorsville*, 264.

2. Stackpole, *Chancellorsville*, 213.

3. *OR*, I, 25, pt. 1: 652; *JCCW*, 4 (1865): 126; Bigelow, *Campaign of Chancellorsville*, 276–77, 277n; SPB, *Battle of Chancellorsville*, 177; Hamlin, *Battle of Chancellorsville*, 21; Howard, "Eleventh Corps at Chancellorsville," 196 and n; John A. Carpenter, *Sword and Olive Branch: Oliver Otis Howard* (Pittsburgh, Pa., 1964), 44–45; H. M. Kellogg to JH, July 7, 1872; JH to SPB, June 26, Aug. 8, 1876, Apr. 2, 1877, Nov. 29, 1878; all, SPB MSS, PSA.

4. Howard, "Eleventh Corps at Chancellorsville," 196; Bigelow, *Campaign of Chancellorsville*, 279–80; Stackpole, *Chancellorsville*, 224–25; *OR*, I, 25 pt. 1: 230.

5. *OR*, I, 25, pt. 1: 230, 234; Bigelow, *Campaign of Chancellorsville*, 287.

6. *OR*, I, 25, pt. 1: 628, 633–34; *JCCW*, 4 (1865): 179–80; Bigelow, *Campaign of Chancellorsville*, 287–88.

7. Bigelow, *Campaign of Chancellorsville*, 288.

8. Sears, *Chancellorsville*, 263–65.

9. Stackpole, *Chancellorsville*, 238–40; Bigelow, *Campaign of Chancellorsville*, 296–97, 302–05, 308–13; Howard, *Autobiography*, 1: 370–72; Howard, "Eleventh Corps at Chancellorsville," 197–200; Carpenter, *Sword and Olive Branch*, 46–47; Theodore A. Dodge, *The Campaign of Chancellorsville* (Boston, 1881), 92–96; *JCCW*, 4 (1865): 180; Carl Schurz to JH, May 9, 1863, JH MSS, HEHL.

10. Howard, *Autobiography*, 1: 373; Howard, "Eleventh Corps at Chancellorsville," 200–01; Stackpole, *Chancellorsville*, 241, 244.

11. Stackpole, *Chancellorsville*, 244; Sears, *Chancellorsville*, 228–29.

12. Hamlin, *Battle of Chancellorsville*, 54, 148; Bigelow, *Campaign of Chancellorsville*, 301–02.

13. Bigelow, *Campaign of Chancellorsville*, 302, 306–07, 310–11.

14. Ibid., 307, 314–15; Alexander, *Robert E. Lee's Civil War*, 158–59; McAllister, *Letters*, 300–03; Hamlin, *Battle of Chancellorsville*, 167.

15. Pleasonton, "The Successes and Failures of Chancellorsville," 179; *JCCW*, 4 (1865): 28; Hamlin, *Battle of Chancellorsville*, 90–92, 151; Bigelow, *Campaign of Chancellorsville*, 305–06, 309; Stackpole, *Chancellorsville*, 249–52; Longacre, *Lincoln's Cavalrymen*, 148.

16. Alfred Pleasonton to JH, May 2, 1863, JH MSS, HEHL; *JCCW*, 4 (1865): xlvi, 29–30; Pleasonton, "Successes and Failures of Chancellorsville," 177–80, 180n; Longacre, *Lincoln's Cavalrymen*, 148–49; Hamlin, *Battle of Chancellorsville*, 82–95, 149–51; James F. Huntington, "The Artillery at Hazel Grove," *B&L* 3: 188.

17. *OR*, I, 25, pt. 1: 387–88; Alexander, *Robert E. Lee's Civil War*, 158; Stackpole, *Chancellorsville*, 256–57; Hamlin, *Battle of Chancellorsville*, 16, 79–80; James I. Robertson, Jr., *General A. P. Hill: The Story of a Confederate Warrior* (New York, 1987), 184; McWhiney and Jamieson, *Attack and Die*, 86.

18. Robertson, *General A. P. Hill*, 184–85.

19. Ibid., 185–86.

20. Ibid., 186.

21. *OR*, I, 25, pt. 1: 389; Bigelow, *Campaign of Chancellorsville*, 313.

22. *OR*, I, 25, pt. 1: 389–90, 409, 670, 678–79; Sears, *Chancellorsville*, 300–02; Bigelow, *Campaign of Chancellorsville*, 325–28; *JCCW*, 4 (1865): xlvi, 7; Hamlin, *Battle of Chancellorsville*, 152–54; SPB, *Battle of Chancellorsville*, 173–74.

23. *OR*, I, 25, pt. 1: 389; Stackpole, *Chancellorsville*, 265–66.

24. *OR*, I, 25, pt. 1: 799, 826, 851.

25. Ibid., 799, 824, 834; Stackpole, *Chancellorsville*, 227; Freeman, *R. E. Lee*, 2: 526, 531; Alexander, *Fighting for the Confederacy*, 210.

26. Freeman, *R. E. Lee*, 2: 531–32.

27. Ibid., 532–33; Thomas, *Robert E. Lee*, 283–84; Cooke, *Life of Gen. Robert E. Lee*, 238–39; Bigelow, *Campaign of Chancellorsville*, 315–19; Stackpole, *Chancellorsville*, 255–62; Hewett, et al., comps., *Supplement to the Official Records*, 4: 519–20; James I. Robertson, Jr., *Stonewall Jackson: The Man, the Soldier, the Legend* (New York, 1997), 725–29.

28. Freeman, *R. E. Lee*, 2: 533.

29. Ibid., 533–34.

30. Ibid., 534–35; *OR*, I, 25, pt. 2: 769; REL, *Wartime Papers*, 451–52.

31. Freeman, *R. E. Lee*, 2: 535–37; *OR*, I, 25, pt. 1: 799–800, 826, 851.

32. Bigelow, *Campaign of Chancellorsville*, 342–44; Stackpole, *Chancellorsville*, 276–81.

33. Thomas Donahue to Almira Winchell, May 3, 1863, GLC.

34. *OR*, I, 25, pt. 1: 215; pt. 2: 361; *JCCW*, 4 (1865): 95, 125.

35. *OR*, I, 25, pt. 2: 363; *JCCW*, 4 (1865): 95–96, 146–47; Daniel Butterfield to John Sedgwick, May 2, 1863 [two messages], JH MSS, HEHL; JH to SPB, Apr. 2, 1877, SPB MSS, PSA; Bigelow, *Campaign of Chancellorsville*, 333–35; Winslow, *General John Sedgwick*, 69; Stackpole, *Chancellorsville*, 314–15.

36. *OR*, I, 25, pt. 2: 365–66; *JCCW*, 4 (1865): 105, 129, 147; SPB, *Battle of Chancellorsville*, 184–85; Couch, "Chancellorsville Campaign," 165; Wainwright, *Diary of Battle*, 214; Winslow, *General John Sedgwick*, 69–70.

37. *OR*, I, 25, pt. 2: 385; Bigelow, *Campaign of Chancellorsville*, 383.

38. *OR*, I, 25, pt. 1: 886–87.

39. Ibid., 887.

40. Ibid.

41. Alexander, *Robert E. Lee's Civil War*, 161.

42. Ibid., 799, 887; Nancy Scott Anderson and Dwight Anderson, *The Generals: Ulysses S. Grant & Robert E. Lee* (New York, 1988), 294; Emory M. Thomas, *Bold Dragoon: The Life of J. E. B. Stuart* (New York, 1986), 210–11.

43. *OR*, I, 25, pt. 1: 887–88.

44. Freeman, *R. E. Lee*, 2: 537–38; Justus Scheibert, *Seven Months in the Rebel States during the North American War, 1863*, ed. William Stanley Hoole (Tuscaloosa, Ala., 1958), 74–75.

45. Ibid., 75.

46. *OR*, I, 25, pt. 1: 390, 409; Sears, *Chancellorsville*, 312–13.

47. *OR*, I, 25, pt. 1: 887–88; Sears, *Chancellorsville*, 336–37; Hebert, *Fighting Joe Hooker*, 212–13.

Eleven

1. Gallagher, "East of Chancellorsville," 41, 43.

2. Ibid., 43–44; *OR*, I, 25, pt. 1: 1001; Osborne, *Jubal*, 146–47.

3. Osborne, *Jubal*, 147–48; Freeman, *R. E. Lee*, 2: 529–30; Bigelow, *Campaign of Chancellorsville*, 332–33; *OR*, I, 25, pt. 1: 800.

4. Osborne, *Jubal*, 148–50.

5. *OR*, I, 25, pt. 1: 558; Stackpole, *Chancellorsville*, 314–15.

6. *OR*, I, 25, pt. 1: 558; Stackpole, *Chancellorsville*, 315; Winslow, *General John Sedgwick*, 70; Huntington W. Jackson, "Sedgwick at Fredericksburg and Salem Heights," *B&L* 3: 225.

7. Ibid., 558–59; *JCCW*, 4 (1865): 96.

8. Winslow, *General John Sedgwick*, 71; Jackson, "Sedgwick at Fredericksburg and Salem Heights," 225, 227.

9. *OR*, I, 25, pt. 1: 215, 350, 558–59.

10. Ibid., 558–59; *JCCW*, 4 (1865): 19, 88, 96; Hewett, et al., comps., *Supplement to the Official Records*, 4: 632–33, 641.

11. *OR*, I, pt. 1: 559; JH to SPB, Apr. 2, 1877, SPB MSS, PSA; Sutherland, *Fredericksburg and Chancellorsville*, 167; Winslow, *General John Sedgwick*, 71.

12. *OR*, I, 25, pt. 1: 1001; Sutherland, *Fredericksburg and Chancellorsville*, 165; Winslow, *General John Sedgwick*, 73–74.

13. *OR*, I, 25, pt. 1: 559, 599–600, 609; pt. 2: 390–92; Stackpole, *Chancellorsville*, 324–25; *JCCW*, 4 (1865): 19, 97, 130; Hewett, et al., comps., *Supplement to the Official Records*, 4: 633–35, 641–42, 646, 649–50; John Sedgwick to JH, May 3, 1863, JH MSS, HEHL; Bates, *Battle of Chancellorsville*, 186; Winslow, *General John Sedgwick*, 74–75; Jackson, "Sedgwick at Fredericksburg and Salem Heights," 227–29.

14. *OR*, I, 25, pt. 1: 558, 1001; Edward Porter Alexander, *Military Memoirs of a Confederate: A Critical Narrative* (New York, 1907), 352.

15. Edward K. Gould, *Major-General Hiram G. Berry* . . . (Rockland, Me., 1899), 266–67; Furgurson, *Chancellorsville, 1863*, 224–25; Bigelow, *Campaign of Chancellorsville*, 350–51; Hebert, *Fighting Joe Hooker*, 211–12.

16. Bigelow, *Campaign of Chancellorsville*, 352, 354–55; Sears, *Chancellorsville*, 323, 325–26; *OR*, I, 25, pt. 1: 392, 460–63.

17. *OR*, I, 25, pt. 1: 362–63, 913, 935; Sears, *Chancellorsville*, 324–28.

18. *OR*, I, 25, pt. 1: 389–90, 671, 679–80, 826–27, 851, 894–95, 907–08, 917; Bigelow, *Campaign of Chancellorsville*, 346–50, 352–54.

19. *OR*, I, 25, pt. 1: 414–15, 803, 888, 952–53, 967–68, 984–85, 996–97, 1004–05; Sears, *Chancellorsville*, 328–36; Bigelow, *Campaign of Chancellorsville*, 352–58.

20. Sears, *Chancellorsville*, 339–43.

21. Ibid., 343–47, 359; *OR*, I, 25, pt. 1: 830, 871–72, 875, 888, 925.

22. SPB, "Hooker's Comments on Chancellorsville," 221.

23. Ibid.; *JCCW*, 4 (1865): 31; Couch, "Chancellorsville Campaign," 170.

24. Couch, "Chancellorsville Campaign," 167.

25. Ibid., 168.

26. Ibid., 169; *OR*, I, 25, pt. 1; 215.

27. Couch, "Chancellorsville Campaign," 169.

28. *JCCW*, 4 (1865): 31; Sears, *Chancellorsville*, 339.

29. Bigelow, *Campaign of Chancellorsville*, 364; Bache, *Life of General George Gordon Meade*, 272–73.

30. Couch, "Chancellorsville Campaign," 170.

31. *OR*, I, 25, pt. 2: 377; Stackpole, *Chancellorsville*, 309–11; Daniel Butterfield to JH, May 3, 1863, JH MSS, HEHL; Williams, *Lincoln and His Generals*, 240.

32. *OR*, I, 25, pt. 2: 377.

33. Ibid., 378.

34. Ibid., 379; Williams, *Lincoln and His Generals*, 240–41.

35. *OR*, I, 25, pt. 2: 378.

36. Ibid., 352; *JCCW*, 4 (1865): 139; Bigelow, *Campaign of Chancellorsville*, 322.

37. *OR*, I, 25, pt. 1: 1076, 1079; pt. 2: 356.

38. Ibid., pt. 1: 1058, 1074, 1077–78; William Averell diary, May 3, 1863, GLC.

39. *OR*, I, 25, pt. 1: 1074–75, 1078; Longacre, "Raid That Failed," 18.

40. *OR*, I, 25, pt. 1: 1076, 1078–79; Longacre, "Raid That Failed," 19; Longacre, *Lincoln's Cavalrymen*, 141–42.

41. *OR*, I, 25, pt. 1: 1080; *JCCW*, 4 (1865): 140; William Averell diary, May 4–6, 1863, GLC.

42. *OR*, I, 25, pt. 1: 1072–73.

43. Ibid., 1073.

44. Bigelow, *Campaign of Chancellorsville*, 378; Stackpole, *Chancellorsville*, 298; JH to SPB, Apr. 2, 1877, SPB MSS, PSA; Walker, *History of Second Army Corps*, 233–35.

45. *OR*, I, 25, pt. 1: 392–93, 313–14, 730–31.

46. Sears, *Chancellorsville*, 358–59; Stackpole, *Chancellorsville*, 299–304; Bigelow, *Campaign of Chancellorsville*, 364–65, 368–69; Sutherland, *Fredericksburg and Chancellorsville*, 170–71.

47. Bigelow, *Campaign of Chancellorsville*, 362; *OR*, I, 25, pt. 1: 731.

48. *OR*, I, 25, pt. 1: 731.

49. Ibid., 314, 319–20; Bigelow, *Campaign of Chancellorsville*, 369; Walker, *History of Second Army Corps*, 236–38; Jordan, *Winfield Scott Hancock*, 72–73; Carol Reardon, "The Valiant Rearguard: Hancock's Division at Chancellorsville," in Gary Gallagher, ed., *Chancellorsville: The Battle and Its Aftermath* (Chapel Hill, N.C., 1996): 159–64.

50. Reardon, "The Gallant Rearguard," 161–62; Stackpole, *Chancellorsville*, 247–48.

51. Reardon, "The Gallant Rearguard," 165.

52. Ibid., 166–69.

53. Sears, *Chancellorsville*, 364–65; Freeman, *R. E. Lee*, 2: 541–42; Thomas, *Robert E. Lee*, 285–86; Charles Marshall, *An Aide-de-Camp of Lee*, ed. Sir Frederick Maurice (New York, 1927), 173.

Twelve

1. *OR*, I, 25, pt. 2: 769; Freeman, *R. E. Lee*, 2: 542–43.

2. Freeman, *R. E. Lee*, 2: 544; *OR*, I, 25, pt. 1, 801, 826, 830, 835, 863; pt. 2: 769–70; Bigelow, *Campaign of Chancellorsville*, 379.

3. Stanley F. Horn, ed., *The Robert E. Lee Reader* (Indianapolis, 1949), 294.

4. Ibid., 294–95.

5. *OR*, I, 25, pt. 1: 855–56; Hewett, et al., comps., *Supplement to the Official Records*, 4: 677; Harrison, *Chancellorsville Battlefield Sites*, 161–63; Stackpole, *Chancellorsville*, 329–31; Furgurson, *Chancellorsville, 1863*, 274; Ralph Happel, *Salem Church Embattled* (Washington, D.C., 1980), 38–39; Osborne, *Jubal*, 158.

6. *OR*, I, 25, pt. 1: 559, 826–827, 830, 835, 856, 863; Hewett, et al., comps., *Supplement to the Official Records*, 4: 677; Bigelow, *Campaign of Chancellorsville*, 397–98; Happel, *Salem Church Embattled*, 41.

7. *OR*, I, 25, pt. 1: 559, 568, 801, 858–59; pt. 2: 394; *JCCW*, 4 (1865): 48, 97; Stackpole, *Chancellorsville*, 333, 336; Bigelow, *Campaign of Chancellorsville*, 398–99; Alexander, *Military Memoirs of a Confederate*, 352–54; Happel, *Salem*

Church Embattled, 43–45; Winslow, *General John Sedgwick*, 78; Jackson, "Sedgwick at Fredericksburg and Salem Heights," 230–31.

8. *OR*, I, 25, pt. 1: 568, 617–18, 801, 863; pt. 2: 395, 770; Hewett, et al., comps., *Supplement to the Official Records*, 4: 635–36.

9. *OR*, I, 25, pt. 1: 351, 600, 801, 1001–02; pt. 2: 401, 407; *JCCW*, 4 (1865): 20; Bigelow, *Campaign of Chancellorsville*, 407; Osborne, *Jubal*, 159.

10. *OR*, I, 25, pt. 1: 802, 851, 869, 872, 875–76, 1001–02; pt. 2: 770; REL, *Wartime Papers*, 453–54; Freeman, *R. E. Lee*, 2: 548–51; Bigelow, *Campaign of Chancellorsville*, 405.

11. Gallagher, "East of Chancellorsville," 48–49.

12. Freeman, *R. E. Lee*, 2: 551–52; Stackpole, *Chancellorsville*, 340, 342; Bigelow, *Campaign of Chancellorsville*, 407–10; Krick, "Lee at Chancellorsville," 372–73.

13. Freeman, *R. E. Lee*, 2: 552, 554; *OR*, I, 25, pt. 1: 802; Alexander, *Fighting for the Confederacy*, 213; Gallagher, "East of Chancellorsville," 49, 51; Krick, "Lee at Chancellorsville," 373.

14. *OR*, I, 25, pt. 1: 560, 600, 609–10; pt. 2: 396, 404–05; *JCCW*, 4 (1865): 20, 60, 97; Hamlin, *Battle of Chancellorsville*, 163–64; Stackpole, *Chancellorsville*, 337–38; Bigelow, *Campaign of Chancellorsville*, 407; David M. Jordan, *"Happiness Is Not My Companion": The Life of General G. K. Warren* (Bloomington, Ind., 2000), 76–77.

15. *OR*, I, 25, pt. 2: 408–10; *JCCW*, 4 (1865): 49, 97; Stackpole, *Chancellorsville*, 338–39; Bigelow, *Campaign of Chancellorsville*, 411.

16. Freeman, *R. E. Lee*, 2: 554; *OR*, I, 25, pt. 1: 560–61, 568, 600–01, 802; *JCCW*, 4 (1865): 20–21; Hewett, et al., comps., *Supplement to the Official Records*, 4: 637, 650; REL, *Wartime Papers*, 454–55; Alexander, *Military Memoirs of a Confederate*, 357; Stackpole, *Chancellorsville*, 342; Gallagher, "East of Chancellorsville," 52–53; Happel, *Salem Church Embattled*, 47–48; Jackson, "Sedgwick at Fredericksburg and Salem Heights," 232; Winslow, *General John Sedgwick*, 82.

17. *OR*, I, 25, pt. 1: 561, 601; pt. 2: 412; Bigelow, *Campaign of Chancellorsville*, 415.

18. JH to SPB, Apr. 2, 1877, SPB MSS, PSA; Wainwright, *Diary of Battle*, 197; Sutherland, *Fredericksburg and Chancellorsville*, 173.

19. *OR*, I, 25, pt. 2: 411; John Sedgwick to JH, May 4, 1863, JH MSS, HEHL; Bigelow, *Campaign of Chancellorsville*, 421.

20. *OR*, I, 25, pt. 1: 561, 569, 601; *JCCW*, 4 (1865): 77, 98, 132–33; Wainwright, *Diary of Battle*, 214; Stackpole, *Chancellorsville*, 344; Bigelow, *Campaign of Chancellorsville*, 421–22; Winslow, *General John Sedgwick*, 84; Dodge, *Campaign of Chancellorsville*, 223–24.

21. Wainwright, *Diary of Battle*, 212, 214.

22. Ibid., 212–13.

23. *JCCW*, 4 (1865): 142.

24. SPB, "Hooker's Comments on Chancellorsville," 222.

25. *OR*, I, 25, pt. 2: 381, 399–400, 404, 407; Wert, *General James Longstreet*, 238, 242; Sorrel, *Recollections of a Confederate Staff Officer*, 155; Wainwright, *Diary of Battle*, 199–200; Sears, *Chancellorsville*, 406–07.

26. Meade, *Life and Letters*, 1: 371; Sears, *Chancellorsville*, 410.

27. Bigelow, *Campaign of Chancellorsville*, 378; Walker, *History of Second Army Corps*, 233–35.

28. *OR*, I, 25, pt. 1: 250–51; Bigelow, *Campaign of Chancellorsville*, 378.

29. Wainwright, *Diary of Battle*, 192–93.

30. Ibid., 193–94; *JCCW*, 4 (1865): 91, 94; *OR*, I, 25, pt. 1: 250; Longacre, *Man Behind the Guns*, 149.

31. Hewett, et al., comps., *Supplement to the Official Records*, 4: 671; REL, *Wartime Papers*, 457; Happel, *Salem Church Embattled*, 50; Freeman, *R. E. Lee*, 2: 556.

32. Freeman, *R. E. Lee*, 2: 556; *OR*, I, 25, pt. 1: 393, 888; Bigelow, *Campaign of Chancellorsville*, 416.

33. Freeman, *R. E. Lee*, 2: 557; Hewett, et al., comps., *Supplement to the Official Records*, 4: 520–21; Bigelow, *Campaign of Chancellorsville*, 425.

34. *OR*, I, 25, pt. 1: 802; Sutherland, *Fredericksburg and Chancellorsville*, 177; Freeman, *R. E. Lee*, 2: 557.

35. *JCCW*, 4 (1865): 134–35.

36. Ibid., 13, 70, 78, 134–36, 144; Meade, *Life and Letters*, 1: 373–74, 378; Couch, "Chancellorsville Campaign," 171; Bigelow, *Campaign of Chancellorsville*, 419–20; Stackpole, *Chancellorsville*, 346–49.

37. *JCCW*, 4 (1865): 133–34; Bigelow, *Campaign of Chancellorsville*, 431; Meade, *Life and Letters*, 1: 373.

38. Hewett, et al., comps., *Supplement to the Official Records*, 4: 490; Bigelow, *Campaign of Chancellorsville*, 422–23.

39. Bigelow, *Campaign of Chancellorsville*, 427–28; Stackpole, *Chancellorsville*, 349–50; Alexander Moore memorandum, May 5, 1863, GLC.

40. Bigelow, *Campaign of Chancellorsville*, 428–29; *OR*, I, 25, pt. 1: 251; Couch, "Chancellorsville Campaign," 171; Gambone, *Darius Nash Couch*, 135; Isaac Pennypacker, *General Meade* (New York, 1901), 124–25.

41. *OR*, I, 25, pt. 1: 508, 516; Bigelow, *Campaign of Chancellorsville*, 429–30.

42. *OR*, I, 25, pt. 2: 779–80; REL, *Wartime Papers*, 456.

43. Freeman, *R. E. Lee*, 2: 557.

44. *OR*, I, 25, pt. 2: 421–22, 434.

45. Bigelow, *Campaign of Chancellorsville*, 434.

Epilogue

1. *JCCW*, 4 (1865): 142.

2. Sears, *Chancellorsville*, 492, 501; Nolan, *Lee Considered*, 81; Furgurson, *Chancellorsville, 1863*, 364–65.

3. Sutherland, *Fredericksburg and Chancellorsville*, 185.

4. William A. Allison to Stockton Bates, June 24, 1863, GLC; Sutherland, *Fredericksburg and Chancellorsville*, 190.

5. Adams, et al., *Cycle of Adams Letters*, 2: 6.

6. Sutherland, *Fredericksburg and Chancellorsville*, 185; Patrick, *Inside Lincoln's Army*, 243, 247–48; Emerson Gifford Taylor, *Gouverneur Kemble Warren: The Life and Letters of an American Soldier, 1830–1882* (Boston, 1932), 111.

7. Meade, *Life and Letters*, 1: 372–73, 379.

8. Ibid., 372, 377–78, 382; Sears, *Chancellorsville*, 422.

9. Meade, *Life and Letters*, 1: 372–73, 376, 379; Pennypacker, *General Meade*, 126; Bigelow, *Campaign of Chancellorsville*, 436–37.

10. Sears, *Chancellorsville*, 437; Patrick, *Inside Lincoln's Army*, 256; Wainwright, *Diary of Battle*, 212–13.

11. Bigelow, *Campaign of Chancellorsville*, 457–58.

12. Ibid., 441–42, 458; *OR*, I, 25, pt. 1: 1059–60, 1088–89; Ben F. Fordney, *Stoneman at Chancellorsville: The Coming of Age of Union Cavalry* (Shippensburg, Pa., 1998), 19; Longacre, "Raid That Failed," 21.

13. *OR*, I, 25, pt. 1: 1060, 1065, 1082, 1089, 1091–92; George Stoneman to JH, May 7, 1863, JH MSS, HEHL; JH to SPB, Oct. 2, 1875, SPB MSS, PSA; Stackpole, *Chancellorsville*, 112; Bigelow, *Campaign of Chancellorsville*, 442–43.

14. *OR*, I, 25, pt. 1: 1060; Bigelow, *Campaign of Chancellorsville*, 442–44.

15. *OR*, I, 25, pt. 1: 1060–61, 1083–87, 1097–98; George Stoneman to JH, May 7, 1863, JH MSS, HEHL; Longacre, "Raid That Failed," 21, 44–45; Bigelow, *Campaign of Chancellorsville*, 444–46, 448–51, 453, 455, 457.

16. *OR*, I, 25, pt. 1: 1061–62, 1071–72, 1082, 1092–95, 1098; Bigelow, *Campaign of Chancellorsville*, 445–47, 450; Longacre, "Raid That Failed," 45.

17. *OR*, I, 25, pt. 1: 1061–63; George Stoneman to JH, May 7, 1863, JH MSS, HEHL; Bigelow, *Campaign of Chancellorsville*, 447–50, 452, 454–55.

18. *OR*, I, 25, pt. 1: 1063–65; JH to SPB, Apr. 2, 1877, SPB MSS, PSA; Bigelow, *Campaign of Chancellorsville*, 454, 456–59.

19. Sutherland, *Fredericksburg and Chancellorsville*, 180–81; Sears, *Chancellorsville*, 439–40; Longacre, "Raid That Failed," 49.

20. *OR*, I, 25, pt. 1: 171; pt. 2: 438, 440; Bigelow, *Campaign of Chancellorsville*, 437, 485; *JCCW*, 4 (1865): 134.

21. *OR*, I, 25, pt. 1: 805; Bigelow, *Campaign of Chancellorsville*, 484.

22. Patrick, *Inside Lincoln's Army*, 260.

23. Michael Fellman, *The Making of Robert E. Lee* (New York, 2000), 132–33.

24. Freeman, *R. E. Lee*, 2: 559, 561.

25. Patrick, *Inside Lincoln's Army*, 243.

Bibliography

Unpublished Materials

Allison, William A. Correspondence. Gilder Lehrman Collection, New York, N.Y.

Averell, William W. Diary, 1863. Gilder Lehrman Collection.

Donahue, Thomas. Letter of May 3, 1863. Gilder Lehrman Collection.

Hooker, Joseph. Correspondence. Ferdinand Dreer and Simon Gratz Collections, Historical Society of Pennsylvania, Philadelphia, Pa.

_____. Correspondence. Gettysburg College Library, Gettysburg, Pa.

_____. Correspondence. Gilder Lehrman Collection.

_____. Correspondence. Samuel P. Bates Papers, Pennsylvania State Archives, Harrisburg.

_____. Papers. Henry E. Huntington Library, San Marino, Calif.

Lee, Robert E. Correspondence. Eleanor Brockenbrough Library, Museum of the Confederacy, Richmond, Va.

_____. Correspondence. George Bolling Lee Papers. Virginia Historical Society, Richmond.

_____. Correspondence. Lee Family Papers. Virginia Historical Society.

_____. Correspondence. Lee Headquarters Papers. Virginia Historical Society.

_____. Correspondence. U.S. Army Military History Institute, Carlisle Barracks, Pa.

Medill, William H. Letter of March 15, 1863. Hanna-McCormick Papers, Library of Congress, Washington, D.C.

Moore, Alexander. Memorandum of Operations, Second Army Corps, April 28–May 5, 1863. Gilder Lehrman Collection.

Newspapers

Alta California

Daily Richmond Examiner

New York Herald

New York Times

Richmond Daily Enquirer

Articles and Essays

Allan, William. "Memoranda of Conversations with General Robert E. Lee." In Gary Gallagher, ed., *Lee the Soldier* (Lincoln: University of Nebraska Press, 1996): 7–24.

Averell, William W. "With the Cavalry on the Peninsula." In Robert Underwood Johnson and Clarence Clough Buel, eds., *Battles and Leaders of the Civil War* (4 vols. New York: Century Co., 1887–88), 2: 429–33.

Bates, Samuel P. "Hooker's Comments on Chancellorsville." In Robert Underwood Johnson and Clarence Clough Buel, eds., *Battles and Leaders of the Civil War* (4 vols. New York: Century Co., 1887–88), 3: 215–23.

Colgrove, Silas. "The Finding of Lee's Lost Order." In Robert Underwood Johnson and Clarence Clough Buel, eds., *Battles and Leaders of the Civil War* (4 vols. New York: Century Co., 1887–88), 2: 603.

Colston, R. E. "Lee's Knowledge of Hooker's Movements." In Robert Underwood Johnson and Clarence Clough Buel, eds., *Battles and Leaders of the Civil War* (4 vols. New York: Century Co., 1887–88), 3: 233.

Couch, Darius N. "The Chancellorsville Campaign." In Robert Underwood Johnson and Clarence Clough Buel, eds., *Battles and Leaders of the Civil War* (4 vols. New York: Century Co., 1887–88), 3: 154–71.

_____. "Sumner's 'Right Grand Division'." In Robert Underwood Johnson and Clarence Clough Buel, eds., *Battles and Leaders of the Civil War* (4 vols. New York: Century Co., 1887–88), 3: 105–20.

Crocker, Jennifer, and Lora E. Park. "The Costly Pursuit of Self-Esteem." *Psychology Bulletin* 130 (2004): 392–414.

Davis, Jefferson. "Robert E. Lee." *North American Review* 40 (1890): 55–66.

Donald, David H. "Refighting the Civil War." In David H. Donald, *Lincoln Reconsidered* (New York: Alfred A. Knopf, 1956): 82–102.

Gallagher, Gary. "Another Look at the Generalship of R. E. Lee." In Gary Gallagher, ed., *Lee the Soldier* (Lincoln: University of Nebraska Press, 1996): 275–89.

_____. "East of Chancellorsville: Jubal A. Early at Second Fredericksburg and Salem Church." In Gary Gallagher, ed., *Chancellorsville: The Battle and Its Aftermath* (Chapel Hill: University of North Carolina Press, 1996): 36–64.

Guernsey, Alfred H. "The Campaigns of Robert E. Lee." *Galaxy* 11 (1871): 641–51, 818–26.

Hassler, William W. "'Fighting Joe' Hooker." *Civil War Times Illustrated* 14 (August 1975): 5–6, 8–9, 36–37, 41–46.

Hennessy, John J. "'We Shall Make Richmond Howl': The Army of the Potomac on the Eve of Chancellorsville." In Gary Gallagher, ed., *Chancellorsville: The Battle and Its Aftermath* (Chapel Hill: University of North Carolina Press, 1996): 1–35.

Howard, Oliver Otis. "The Eleventh Corps at Chancellorsville." In Robert Underwood Johnson and Clarence Clough Buel, eds., *Battles and Leaders of the Civil War* (4 vols. New York: Century Co., 1887–88), 3: 189–202.

Huey, Pennock. "The Charge of the Eighth Pennsylvania Cavalry." In Robert Underwood Johnson and Clarence Clough Buel, eds., *Battles and Leaders of the Civil War* (4 vols. New York: Century Co., 1887–88), 3: 186–87.

Huntington, James F. "The Artillery at Hazel Grove." In Robert Underwood Johnson and Clarence Clough Buel, eds., *Battles and Leaders of the Civil War* (4 vols. New York: Century Co., 1887–88): 188.

Jackson, Huntington W. "Sedgwick at Fredericksburg and Salem Heights." In Robert Underwood Johnson and Clarence Clough Buel, eds., *Battles and Leaders of the Civil War* (4 vols. New York: Century Co., 1887–88), 3: 224–32.

Krick, Robert K. "Lee at Chancellorsville." In Gary Gallagher, ed., *Lee the Soldier* (Lincoln: University of Nebraska Press, 1996): 357–80.

Lawley, Francis. "General Lee." In Gary Gallagher, ed., *Lee the Soldier* (Lincoln: University of Nebraska Press, 1996): 75–94.

Lee, Fitzhugh. "Chancellorsville." *Southern Historical Society Papers* 7 (1879): 545–85.

Longacre, Edward G. "Damnable Dan Sickles." *Civil War Times Illustrated* 23 (May 1984): 16–25.

_____. "The Raid That Failed." *Civil War Times Illustrated* 26 (January 1988): 15–21, 44–45, 49.

Longstreet, James. "The Battle of Fredericksburg." In Robert Underwood Johnson and Clarence Clough Buel, eds., *Battles and Leaders of the Civil War* (4 vols. New York: Century Co., 1887–88), 4: 70–85.

McGuire, Hunter. "General T. J. ('Stonewall') Jackson . . . His Career and Character." *Southern Historical Society Papers* 25 (1897): 91–112.

Patterson, Gerard. "Daniel Butterfield." *Civil War Times Illustrated* 12 (November 1973): 13–19.

Pendleton, W. Nelson. "Personal Recollections of General Lee: An Address Delivered at Washington and Lee University . . . Jan. 19, 1873." *Southern Magazine* 15 (1874): 603–36.

Pleasonton, Alfred. "The Successes and Failures of Chancellorsville." In Robert Underwood Johnson and Clarence Clough Buel, eds., *Battles and Leaders of the Civil War* (4 vols. New York: Century Co., 1887–88), 3: 172–82.

Randolph, William Fitzhugh. "Chancellorsville: The Flank Movement That Routed the Yankees . . ." *Southern Historical Society Papers* 29 (1901): 329–37.

Reardon, Carol. "The Valiant Rearguard: Hancock's Division at Chancellorsville." In Gary Gallagher, ed., *Chancellorsville: The Battle and Its Aftermath* (Chapel Hill: University of North Carolina Press, 1996): 143–75.

Shutes, Milton H. "'Fighting Joe' Hooker." *California Historical Society Quarterly* 16 (1937): 304–20.

Smith, James Power. "Stonewall Jackson's Last Battle." In Robert Underwood Johnson and Clarence Clough Buel, eds., *Battles and*

Leaders of the Civil War (4 vols. New York: Century Co., 1887–88), 3: 203–14.

Stiles, Robert. "Address Delivered before Washington and Lee University on January 19th, 1875, the Fifth Anniversary Celebration of the Birth of General R. E. Lee." *Transactions of the Southern Historical Society* 2 (1875): 41–52.

Swift, Eben. "The Military Education of Robert E. Lee." *Virginia Magazine of History and Biography* 35 (1927): 97–160.

Talcott, Thomas M. R. "General Lee's Strategy at the Battle of Chancellorsville." *Southern Historical Society Papers* 34 (1906): 1–27.

Williams, T. Harry. "The Military Leadership of North and South." In David H. Donald, ed., *Why the North Won the Civil War* (Baton Rouge: Louisiana State University Press, 1960): 23–47.

Books and Pamphlets

Adam, Graeme M. *The Life of General Robert E. Lee . . . with a Record of the Campaigns of the Army of Northern Virginia.* New York: A. L. Burt Co., 1905.

Adams, Charles, et al. *A Cycle of Adams Letters, 1861–1865.* Edited by Worthington Chauncey Ford. 2 vols. Boston: Houghton Mifflin Co., 1920.

Adams, Charles F. *Charles Francis Adams, 1835–1915: An Autobiography.* Boston: Houghton, Mifflin Co., 1916.

Alexander, Bevin. *Robert E. Lee's Civil War.* Holbrook, Mass.: Adams Media Corp., 1998.

Alexander, Edward Porter. *Fighting for the Confederacy: The Personal Recollections of General Edward Porter Alexander.* Edited by Gary Gallagher. Chapel Hill: University of North Carolina Press, 1989.

_____. *Military Memoirs of a Confederate: A Critical Narrative.* New York: Charles Scribner's Sons, 1907.

Alexander, Frederick Warren, comp. *Stratford Hall and the Lees Connected with Its History . . .* Oak Grove, Va.: privately published, 1912.

Anderson, Archer. *Robert Edward Lee: An Address Delivered at the Dedication of the Monument to General Robert Lee at Richmond, Virginia, May 29, 1890.* Richmond, Va.: Wm. Ellis Jones, 1890.

Anderson, Nancy Scott, and Dwight Anderson. *The Generals: Ulysses S. Grant & Robert E. Lee.* New York: Alfred A. Knopf, 1988.

Arnold, James R. *Jeff Davis's Own: Cavalry, Comanches, and the Battle for the Texas Frontier.* New York: John Wiley & Sons, Inc., 2000.

Bache, Richard Meade. *Life of General George Gordon Meade, Commander of the Army of the Potomac.* Philadelphia: Henry T. Coates & Co., 1897.

Bates, Samuel P. *The Battle of Chancellorsville.* Meadville, Pa.: Edward T. Bates, 1882.

Bauer, K. Jack. *The Mexican War, 1846–1848.* New York: Macmillan Publishing Co., Inc., 1974.

Beck, Warren A., and David A. Williams. *California: A History of the Golden State.* Garden City, N.Y.: Doubleday & Co., Inc., 1972.

Bigelow, John, Jr. *The Campaign of Chancellorsville: A Strategic and Tactical Study.* New Haven, Conn.: Yale University Press, 1910.

Bill, Alfred Hoyt. *Rehearsal for Conflict: The War with Mexico, 1846–1848.* New York: Alfred A. Knopf, 1947.

Bowen, John J. *The Strategy of Robert E. Lee.* New York: Neale Publishing Co., 1914.

Boyd, Thomas. *Light-Horse Harry Lee.* New York: Charles Scribner's Sons, 1931.

Bradford, Gamalial. *Lee, the American.* Boston: Houghton Mifflin Co., 1912.

_____. *Union Portraits.* Boston: Houghton Mifflin Co., 1916.

Brock, Robert A. *Gen. Robert Edward Lee, Soldier, Citizen and Christian Patriot . . .* Atlanta: H. C. Hudgins & Co., 1897.

Brooks, William E. *Lee of Virginia: A Biography.* Indianapolis: Bobbs-Merrill Co., 1932.

Bruce, Philip A. *Robert E. Lee.* Philadelphia: George W. Jacobs & Co., 1907.

Butterfield, Julia Lorrilard, ed. *A Biographical Memoir of General Daniel Butterfield, Including Many Addresses and Military Writings.* New York: Grafton Press, 1904.

Cameron, William E. *The Life and Character of Robert E. Lee: An Address to A. P. Hill Camp, C. V.* Petersburg, Va.: privately issued, 1901.

Carpenter, John A. *Sword and Olive Branch: Oliver Otis Howard.* Pittsburgh, Pa.: University of Pittsburgh Press, 1964.

Catton, Bruce. *Glory Road: The Bloody Route from Fredericksburg to Gettysburg.* Garden City, N.Y.: Doubleday & Co., Inc., 1952.

Caughey, John W. *California: A Remarkable State's Life History.* Englewood Cliffs, N. J.: Prentice-Hall, Inc., 1970.

Celebration of the Two Hundredth Anniversary of the Settlement of Hadley, Massachusetts, at Hadley, June 8, 1859 . . . Northampton, Mass.: Bridgman & Childs, 1859.

Cleaves, Freeman. *Meade of Gettysburg.* Norman: University of Oklahoma Press, 1960.

Coe, Harrie B., ed. *Maine—Resources, Attractions, and Its People: A History.* 4 vols. New York: Lewis Historical Publishing Co., Inc., 1928.

Comstock, Cyrus B. *The Diary of Cyrus B. Comstock.* Edited by Merlin E. Sumner. Dayton, Ohio: Morningside, 1987.

Connelly, Thomas L. *The Marble Man: Robert E. Lee and His Image in American Society.* Baton Rouge: Louisiana State University Press, 1977.

Cooke, John Esten. *A Life of Gen. Robert E. Lee.* New York: D. Appleton & Co., 1871.

Cormier, Steven A. *The Siege of Suffolk: The Forgotten Campaign, April 11–May 4, 1863.* Lynchburg, Va.: H. E. Howard, 1989.

Cullum, George Washington, comp. *Biographical Register of the Officers and Graduates of the United States Military Academy at West Point, New York.* 2 vols. Boston: Houghton, Mifflin Co., 1891.

Dabney, Robert L. *Life and Campaigns of Lieut.-Gen. Thomas J. Jackson (Stonewall Jackson).* New York: Blelock & Co., 1866.

Dalbiac, P. H. *Chancellorsville and Gettysburg.* New York: Macmillan Co., 1911.

Davis, Burke. *Gray Fox: Robert E. Lee and the Civil War.* New York: Rinehart & Co., 1956.

Davis, William C. *Battle at Bull Run: A History of the First Major Campaign of the Civil War.* Garden City, N.Y.: Doubleday & Co., Inc., 1977.

DePeyster, J. Watts. *Personal and Military History of Philip Kearny, Major-General United States Volunteers.* New York: Rice & Gage, 1869.

Detzer, David. *Donnybrook: The Battle of Bull Run, 1861.* New York: Harcourt, Brace, Inc., 2004.

Dodge, Theodore A. *The Campaign of Chancellorsville.* Boston: James R. Osgood & Co., 1881.

Doubleday, Abner. *Chancellorsville and Gettysburg.* New York: Charles Scribner's Sons, 1882.

Dowdey, Clifford. *Lee.* Boston: Little, Brown & Co., 1965.

Earle, Peter. *Robert E. Lee.* New York: Saturday Review Press, 1973.

Evans, Charles M. *The War of the Aeronauts: A History of Ballooning during the Civil War.* Mechanicsburg, Pa.: Stackpole Books, 2002.

Fellman, Michael. *The Making of Robert E. Lee.* New York: Random House, 2000.

Fishel, Edwin C. *The Secret War for the Union: The Untold Story of Military Intelligence in the Civil War.* Boston: Houghton Mifflin Co., 1996.

Fleming, Thomas J. *West Point: The Men and Times of the United States Military Academy.* New York: William Morrow & Co., Inc., 1969.

Fordney, Ben F. *Stoneman at Chancellorsville: The Coming of Age of Union Cavalry.* Shippensburg, Pa.: White Mane Books, 1998.

Freeman, Douglas Southall. *Lee's Lieutenants: A Study in Command.* 3 vols. New York: Charles Scribner's Sons, 1942–44.

———. *R. E. Lee: A Biography.* 4 vols. New York: Charles Scribner's Sons, 1934–35.

Furgurson, Ernest B. *Chancellorsville, 1863: The Souls of the Brave.* New York: Alfred A. Knopf, 1992.

Gallagher, Gary. *Stephen Dodson Ramseur, Lee's Gallant General.* Chapel Hill: University of North Carolina Press, 1985.

Gambone, A. M. *Major General Darius Nash Couch: Enigmatic Valor.* Baltimore: Butternut & Blue, 2000.

Garnett, John J., ed. *Biographical Sketch of General Robert Edward Lee, with His Reports of the Battles of Chancellorsville and Gettysburg . . .* New York: privately issued, 1890.

Gilman, Bradley. *Robert E. Lee.* New York: Macmillan Co., 1915.

Gough, J. E. *Fredericksburg and Chancellorsville: A Study of the Federal Operations.* London: Hugh Rees Ltd., 1913.

Gould, Edward K. *Major-General Hiram G. Berry . . .* Rockland, Me.: Press of the Courier-Gazette, 1899.

Hamlin, Augustus C. *The Battle of Chancellorsville* . . . Bangor, Me.: privately issued, 1896.

Handel, Michael L. *Masters of War: Sun Tzu, Clausewitz and Jomini.* Portland, Ore.: Frank Cass, 1992.

Happel, Ralph. *Salem Church Embattled.* Washington, D.C.: Eastern National Park and Monument Association, 1980.

Harrison, Noel G. *Chancellorsville Battlefield Sites.* Lynchburg, Va.: H. E. Howard, Inc., 1990.

Hassler, Warren W. *Commanders of the Army of the Potomac.* Baton Rouge: Louisiana State University Press, 1962.

Hattaway, Herman, and Archer Jones. *How the North Won: A Military History of the Civil War.* Urbana: University of Illinois Press, 1983.

Hebert, Walter H. *Fighting Joe Hooker.* Indianapolis: Bobbs-Merrill Co., 1944.

Heitman, Francis B., comp. *Historical Register and Dictionary of the United States Army* . . . 2 vols. Washington, D.C.: Government Printing Office, 1903.

Hendrick, Burton J. *The Lees of Virginia: Biography of a Family.* Boston: Little, Brown & Co., 1935.

Hennessy, John J. *Return to Bull Run: The Campaign and Battle of Second Manassas.* New York: Simon & Schuster, 1993.

Hewett, Janet, et al., comps. *Supplement to the Official Records of the Union and Confederate Armies.* 3 series, 99 vols. Wilmington, N.C.: Broadfoot Publishing Co., 1994–2001.

Horn, Stanley F., ed. *The Robert E. Lee Reader.* Indianapolis: Bobbs-Merrill Co., 1949.

Hotchkiss, Jed, and William Allan. *The Battle-fields of Virginia: Chancellorsville* . . . New York: D. Van Nostrand, 1866.

Howard, Oliver O. *Autobiography of Oliver Otis Howard, Major General, United States Army.* 2 vols. New York: Baker & Taylor Co., 1907.

Joint Committee on the Conduct of the War. 3 vols. in 8. Washington, D.C.: Government Printing Office, 1863–68.

Jomini, Antoine Henri. *Summary of the Art of War.* Translated by G. H. Mendell and W. P. Craighill. Westport, Conn.: Greenwood Press, 1977.

Jones, J. William. *Life and Letters of Robert Edward Lee, Soldier and Man.* New York: Neale Publishing Co., 1906.

_____. *Personal Reminiscences, Anecdotes, and Letters of Gen. Robert E. Lee.* New York: D. Appleton & Co., 1876.

Jordan, David M. *"Happiness Is Not My Companion": The Life of General G. K. Warren.* Bloomington: Indiana University Press, 2001.

_____. *Winfield Scott Hancock: A Soldier's Life.* Bloomington: Indiana University Press, 1988.

Kearny, Thomas. *General Philip Kearny, Battle Soldier of Five Wars . . .* New York: G. P. Putnam's Sons, 1937.

Keller, Allan. *Thunder at Harper's Ferry.* Englewood Cliffs. N.J.: Prentice-Hall, Inc., 1958.

Keneally, Thomas. *American Scoundrel: The Life of the Notorious Civil War General Dan Sickles.* New York: Doubleday & Co., Inc., 2002.

Lattimore, Ralston B., ed. *The Story of Robert E. Lee, as Told in His Own Words and Those of His Contemporaries.* Philadelphia: Eastern National Park and Monument Association, 1964.

Lee, Edmund Jennings. *Lee of Virginia, 1842–1892: Biographical and Genealogical Sketches of the Descendants of Colonel Richard Lee . . .* Philadelphia: privately published, 1895.

Lee, Fitzhugh. *General Lee.* New York: D. Appleton & Co., 1894.

Lee, Robert E. *Lee's Dispatches: Unpublished Letters of General Robert E. Lee, C.S.A., to Jefferson Davis and the War Department of the Confederate States of America, 1862–65.* Edited by Douglas Southall Freeman and Grady McWhiney. New York: G. P. Putnam's Sons, 1957.

_____. *The Wartime Papers of R. E. Lee.* Edited by Clifford Dowdey and Louis H. Manarin. Boston: Little, Brown & Co., 1961.

Lee, Robert E., Jr. *Recollections and Letters of General Robert E. Lee.* Garden City, N.Y.: Garden City Publishing Co., 1926.

Lincoln, Abraham. *The Collected Works of Abraham Lincoln.* Edited by Roy P. Basler, et al. 8 vols. New Brunswick, N.J.: Rutgers University Press, 1953.

Long, A. L. *Memoirs of Robert E. Lee: His Military and Personal History . . .* Philadelphia: J. M. Stoddart & Co., 1886.

Longacre, Edward G. *Fitz Lee: A Military Biography of Major General Fitzhugh Lee, C.S.A.* New York: Da Capo Press, 2005.

_____. *Lee's Cavalrymen: A History of the Mounted Forces of the Army of Northern Virginia, 1861–1865.* Mechanicsburg, Pa.: Stackpole Books, 2002.

_____. *Lincoln's Cavalrymen: A History of the Mounted Forces of the Army of the Potomac, 1861–1865.* Mechanicsburg, Pa.: Stackpole Books, 2000.

_____. *The Man Behind the Guns: A Biography of General Henry Jackson Hunt, Chief of Artillery, Army of the Potomac.* South Brunswick, N.J.: A. S. Barnes & Co., Inc., 1977.

Mahon, John K. *History of the Second Seminole War, 1835–1842.* Gainesville: University of Florida Press, 1967.

Marshall, Charles. *Address Delivered before the Lee Monument Association, at Richmond, Virginia, October 27th, 1887* . . . Baltimore: John Murphy & Co., 1888.

_____. *An Aide-de-Camp of Lee: Being the Papers of Colonel Charles Marshall* . . . Edited by Sir Frederick Maurice. Boston: Little, Brown & Co., 1927.

Marszalek, John F. *Commander of All Lincoln's Armies: A Life of General Henry W. Halleck.* Cambridge, Mass.: Harvard University Press, 2004.

Mason, Emily Virginia. *Popular Life of Gen. Robert Edward Lee.* Baltimore: John Murphy & Co., 1872.

McAllister, Robert. *The Civil War Letters of General Robert McAllister.* Edited by James I. Robertson, Jr. New Brunswick, N.J.: Rutgers University Press, 1965.

McCabe, James D. *Life and Campaigns of General Robert E. Lee.* New York: Blelock & Co., 1867.

McCaslin, Richard B. *Lee in the Shadow of Washington.* Baton Rouge: Louisiana State University Press, 2001.

McClure, Alexander K. *Colonel Alexander K. McClure's Recollections of Half a Century.* Salem, Mass.: Salem Press Co., 1902.

McIntosh, David G. *The Campaign of Chancellorsville.* Richmond, Va.: Wm. Ellis Jones's Sons, 1915.

McKenzie, John D. *Uncertain Glory: Lee's Generalship Re-Examined.* New York: Hippocrene Books, 1997.

McLaws, Lafayette. *A Soldier's General: The Civil War Letters of Major General Lafayette McLaws*. Edited by John C. Oeffinger. Chapel Hill: University of North Carolina Press, 2002.

McWhiney, Grady, and Perry D. Jamieson. *Attack and Die: Civil War Military Tactics and the Southern Heritage*. University, Ala.: University of Alabama Press, 1982.

Meade, George. *The Life and Letters of George Gordon Meade, Major- General, United States Army*. 2 vols. New York: Charles Scribner's Sons, 1913.

Milton, George Fort. *Conflict: The American Civil War*. New York: Coward-McCann, Inc., 1941.

Missall, John, and Mary Lou Missall. *The Seminole Wars: America's Longest Indian Conflict*. Gainesville: University of Florida Press, 2004.

Mitchell, Joseph B. *Decisive Battles of the Civil War*. New York: G. P. Putnam's Sons, 1955.

Morrison, James L., Jr. *"The Best School in the World": West Point, the Pre-Civil War Years, 1833–1865*. Kent, Ohio: Kent State University Press, 1986.

Nelligan, Murray H. *Custis-Lee Mansion: The Robert E. Lee Memorial*. Washington, D.C.: National Park Service, 1962.

Nolan, Alan T. *Lee Considered: General Robert E. Lee and Civil War History*. Chapel Hill: University of North Carolina Press, 1991.

Oates, Stephen B. *To Purge This Land with Blood: A Biography of John Brown*. New York: Harper & Row, 1970.

Orton, Richard H., comp. *Records of California Men in the War of the Rebellion, 1861 to 1867*. Sacramento, Calif.: J. D. Young, 1890.

Osborne, Charles C. *Jubal: The Life and Times of General Jubal A. Early, C.S.A., Defender of the Lost Cause*. Chapel Hill, N. C.: Algonquin Books, 1992.

Osborne, John Ball. *The Story of Arlington: A History and Description of the Estate . . .* Washington, D.C.: privately issued, 1899.

Page, Thomas Nelson. *Robert E. Lee, Man and Soldier*. New York: Charles Scribner's Sons, 1911.

_____. *Robert E. Lee, the Southerner*. New York: Charles Scribner's Sons, 1908.

Pappas, George S. *To the Point: The United States Military Academy, 1802–1902*. Westport, Conn.: Praeger, 1993.

Patrick, Marsena R. *Inside Lincoln's Army: The Diary of Marsena Rudolph Patrick, Provost Marshal General, Army of the Potomac.* Edited by David S. Sparks. New York: Thomas Yoseloff, 1964.

Pennypacker, Isaac R. *General Meade.* New York: D. Appleton & Co., 1901.

Pinchon, Edgcumb. *Dan Sickles, Hero of Gettysburg and "Yankee King of Spain."* New York: Doubleday, Doran & Co., Inc., 1945.

Powell, Mary G. *The History of Old Alexandria, Virginia, from July 13, 1749, to May 24, 1861.* Richmond, Va.: William Byrd Press, Inc., 1928.

Rafuse, Ethan S. *George Gordon Meade and the War in the East.* Abilene, Tex.: McWhiney Foundation Press, 2003.

Register of the Officers and Cadets of the U.S. Military Academy . . . West Point, N.Y.: privately published, 1825–29, 1833–37.

Richardson, Charles. *The Chancellorsville Campaign: Fredericksburg to Salem Church.* New York: Neale Publishing Co., 1907.

Robertson, James I., Jr. *General A. P. Hill: The Story of a Confederate Warrior.* New York: Random House, 1987.

_____. *Stonewall Jackson: The Man, the Soldier, the Legend.* New York: Macmillan Publishing USA, 1997.

Royster, Charles. *Light-Horse Harry Lee and the Legacy of the American Revolution.* New York: Alfred A. Knopf, 1981.

Rusling, James F. *Men and Things I Saw in the Civil War Days.* New York: Eaton & Mains, 1899.

Sanborn, Margaret. *Robert E. Lee, the Complete Man, 1861–1870.* Philadelphia: J. B. Lippincott Co., 1967.

Sauers, Richard A. *Meade, Victor of Gettysburg.* Washington, D.C.: Brassey's, Inc., 2003.

Scheibert, Justus. *A Prussian Observes the American Civil War: The Military Studies of Justus Scheibert.* Translated and edited by Frederic Trautmann. Columbia: University of Missouri Press, 2001.

_____. *Seven Months in the Rebel States during the North American War, 1863.* Edited by William Stanley Hoole. Tuscaloosa, Ala.: Confederate Publishing Co., 1958.

Scott, Winfield. *Memoirs of Lieut.-General Scott, LL. D., Written by Himself.* New York: Sheldon & Co., 1864.

Sears, Stephen W. *Chancellorsville*. Boston: Houghton Mifflin Co., 1996.

_____. *Landscape Turned Red: The Battle of Antietam*. New Haven, Conn.: Ticknor & Fields, 1983.

_____. *To the Gates of Richmond: The Peninsula Campaign*. New York: Ticknor & Fields, 1992.

Sedgwick, John. *Correspondence of John Sedgwick, Major-General*. 2 vols. New York: De Vinne Press, 1902–03.

Shanks, William F. G. *Personal Recollections of Distinguished Generals*. New York: Harper & Brothers, 1866.

Shepherd, Henry Elliott. *Life of Robert Edward Lee*. New York: Neale Publishing Co., 1906.

Somerville, Mollie. *Washington Walked Here: Alexandria on the Potomac . . .* Washington, D.C.: Acropolis Books, 1970.

Sorrel, G. Moxley. *Recollections of a Confederate Staff Officer*. New York: Neale Publishing Co., 1905.

Stackpole, Edward J. *Chancellorsville: Lee's Greatest Battle*. Harrisburg, Pa.: Stackpole Co., 1958.

Sutherland, Daniel E. *Fredericksburg and Chancellorsville: The Dare Mark Campaign*. Lincoln: University of Nebraska Press, 1998.

Swanberg, W. A. *Sickles the Incredible*. New York: Charles Scribner's Sons, 1956.

Swinton, William. *Campaigns of the Army of the Potomac*. New York: Charles Scribner's Sons, 1882.

Tanner, Robert G. *Stonewall in the Valley: Thomas J. "Stonewall" Jackson's Shenandoah Valley Campaign, Spring 1862*. Garden City, N.Y.: Doubleday & Co., Inc., 1976.

Taylor, Emerson Gifford. *Gouverneur Kemble Warren: The Life and Letters of an American Soldier, 1830–1882*. Boston: Houghton Mifflin Co., 1932.

Taylor, John M. *Duty Faithfully Performed: Robert E. Lee and His Critics*. Dulles, Va.: Brassey's, Inc., 1999.

Taylor, Walter Herron. *Four Years with General Lee: Being a Summary of the More Important Events Touching the Career of General Robert E. Lee . . .* New York: D. Appleton & Co., 1877.

_____. *General Lee: His Campaigns in Virginia, 1861–1865, with Personal Reminiscences.* Norfolk, Va.: Nusbaum Book & News Co., 1906.

Thomas, Emory M. *Bold Dragoon: The Life of J. E. B. Stuart.* New York: Harper & Row, 1986.

_____. *Robert E. Lee: A Biography.* New York: W. W. Norton & Co., 1995.

Tremain, Henry E. *In Memoriam: Major-General Joseph Hooker.* Cincinnati: Robert Clarke & Co., 1881.

Trent, William P. *Robert E. Lee.* Boston: Small, Maynard & Co., 1899.

Truett, Randle Bond. *Lee Mansion, Arlington, Virginia.* New York: Hastings House, 1943.

Villard, Henry. *Memoirs of Henry Villard, Journalist and Financier, 1835–1900.* 2 vols. Boston: Houghton Mifflin Co., 1904.

Wainwright, Charles S. *A Diary of Battle: The Personal Journals of Colonel Charles S. Wainwright, 1861–1865.* Edited by Allan Nevins. New York: Harcourt, Brace, & World, 1962.

Walker, Alice Morehouse. *Historic Hadley: A Story of the Making of a Famous Massachusetts Town.* New York: Grafton Press, 1906.

Walker, C. Irvine. *The Life of Lt. Gen. Richard Heron Anderson of the Confederate States Army.* Charleston, S.C.: Art Publishing Co., 1917.

Walker, Francis A. *History of the Second Army Corps in the Army of the Potomac.* New York: Charles Scribner's Sons, 1891.

Warner, Ezra J. *Generals in Blue: Lives of the Union Commanders.* Baton Rouge: Louisiana State University Press, 1964.

_____. *Generals in Gray: Lives of the Confederate Commanders.* Baton Rouge: Louisiana State University Press, 1959.

The War of the Rebellion: A Compilation of the Official Records of the Union and Confederate Armies. 4 series, 70 vols. in 128. Washington, D.C.: Government Printing Office, 1880–1901.

Weigley, Russell F. *The American Way of War: A History of United States Military Policy and Strategy.* New York: Macmillan Publishing Co., Inc., 1973.

_____. *A Great Civil War: A Military and Political History, 1861–1865.* Bloomington: Indiana University Press, 2000.

Wert, Jeffry D. *General James Longstreet, the Confederacy's Most Controversial Soldier:* A Biography. New York: Simon & Schuster, 1993.

White, Henry Alexander. *Robert E. Lee and the Southern Confederacy, 1807–1870.* New York: G. P. Putnam's Sons, 1897.

Williams, T. Harry. *Lincoln and His Generals.* New York: Alfred A. Knopf, 1952.

Wilson, James Harrison. *The Campaign of Chancellorsville . . . A Critical Review.* Wilmington, Del.: C. L. Stoey, 1911.

_____. *Under the Old Flag: Recollections of Military Operations in the War for the Union, the Spanish War, the Boxer Rebellion, etc.* 2 vols. New York: D. Appleton & Co., 1912.

Winslow, Richard Elliott. *General John Sedgwick: The Story of a Union Corps Commander.* Novato, Calif.: Presidio Press, 1982.

Winston, Robert W. *Robert E. Lee: A Biography.* New York: William Morrow & Co., 1934.

Woodworth, Steven E. *Davis and Lee at War.* Lawrence: University Press of Kansas, 1995.

Young, James C. *Marse Robert, Knight of the Confederacy.* New York: Rae D. Henkle Co., 1929.

Index

Numbers in italics indicate pages with illustrations or maps.
"REL" indicates Robert E. Lee, "JH" Joseph Hooker.

crosses Germanna
Ford, 146
crosses Kelly's Ford, 137
fails to reinforce
position, 274
headquarters of, 189
injury to, 189
May 2 troop positions
of, 189–91
May 3 troop
positions, 218
on JH, 100, 109
ordered to remain at
Chancellorsville,
159–61
supports Sickle's advance,
196-97
warned of Confederate
movements, 194-95,
204-7
Howe, Albion P.
at Banks's Ford, 259
at Marye's Heights,
229–31
at Salem Church, 254,
255, 256–57
Fredericksburg positions
of, 228, 252
Huey, Pennock, 151, 152,
172, 211
Humphreys, Andrew A.,
102, 146, 188
Hunt, Henry J.
covers army's retreat,
266-67
demoted by JH, 109
duties at
Chancellorsville, 237
knowledge of terrain, 223
returned to field
command, 263

Ingalls, Rufus, 241
inspection reforms, 105
Iverson, Alfred, 236

Jackson, Thomas Jonathan
"Stonewall," *153*

at Cedar Mountain,
54–55
at Falling Waters, 46
at Fredericksburg, 22,
58–59
at Gaines's Mill, 52
at Harpers Ferry
surrender, 56
at Hazel Grove, 178
at Second Bull Run, 55
attack on Eleventh
Corps, *207*, 207–12
Chancellorsville positions
of, 167, 169–70,
185–86
demeanor of during
flank march, 198, 200
flank march of, 191–94,
198–201, *201*
importance of to
REL, 280
reacts to Union
movement near
Chancellorsville,
152–54
reacts to Union
movements at Kelly's
Ford, 141–42
sacks Pope's supply
depot, 55
Shenandoah Valley
Campaign of, 50, 57
wounding and
recuperation of,
216–17, 251, 264
Johnson, Richard W., 39
Johnston, Albert S., 38, 49
Johnston, Joseph E., *29*
as Quartermaster
General, U. S. A., 41
at Fair Oaks, 92–93
at First Bull Run, 47
at Harpers Ferry, 44-46
at West Point, 28
at Yorktown, 49–51
in Mexican War, 36
on REL, 30, 51
Joint Committee on the

Conduct of the War, 96,
99, 261
Jomini, Antonio Henri
influence of on REL, 2,
30, 33, 38
military theories of, 2
*Summary of the Art of
War*, 30–33, 38
*Traite des Grands
Operations Militaires*, 38
*Vie Politique et Miliaire
de Napoleon*, 83
Jones, John R, 236

Kearny, Philip, *92*
at Fair Oaks, 93
at Williamsburg, 92
institutes corps
badges, 106
relationship with JH, 81
Keen, Charles W., Jr., 205
Keenan, Peter, 211
Kelly's Ford, 62, 113-15,
129-32, 137
Kershaw, Joseph B.
at Salem Church, 254
Chancellorsville positions
of, 167, 186
Fairview offensive of, 237
opposes Sedgwick, 251
reacts to Union
movements at Kelly's
Ford, 142
Key, Philip B., 90
Kilpatrick, H. Judson, 276
King's Schoolhouse (Oak
Grove), Battle of, 93

Lacy, R. T., 180, 183–84
Lane, James H., 213, 235
Lee, Ann Hill Carter
(mother of REL), 24, 25,
26, 33
Lee, Annie Carter (daughter
of REL), 35
Lee, Ann (sister of REL), 24
Lee, Catherine (sister of
REL), 24, 25